Lotus Notes
in the Enterprise

Bill Kreisle
Dan Schulz

M&T BOOKS

M&T Books
A Division of MIS:Press, Inc.
A Subsidiary of Henry Holt and Company, Inc.
115 West 18th Street
New York, New York 10011

ISBN 1-55851-456-2

97 98 97 96   4 3 2 1

Associate Publisher: Paul Farrell   **Managing Editor:** Cary Sullivan
Editor: Debra Williams Cauley   **Copy Editor:** Winifred Davis
Technical Editor: Charles Connor   **Production Editor:** Anthony Washington

Contents

Chapter 5: Developing a Notes Application 301

Introduction

About the Authors

Bill Kreisle is an experienced technologist with extensive experience in Notes administration and development, networking, and client/server applications development. A former IS Manager at several small companies, he was recently responsible for the installation and administration of a half-million dollar Lotus Notes network at a software company in the midwestern United States, and currently works as a technology manager for a consulting company in Minneapolis.

A short, round, bearded man with wild eyes, Bill is frequently seen roaming the halls waving his arms wildly and talking to nobody in particular about some revolutionary new idea. A former US Marine/bodyguard/roadie Bill is given a great deal of leeway in his arm waving, and occasionally saves a company a ton of money.

Dan Schulz is a veteran C, C++, and API programmer whose work has been instrumental in projects for IBM, the Mayo Clinic, and the same midwestern software company Bill worked at. After helping IBM increase its patent library a couple of times, Dan helped build Dexterity, a client/server development tool. In his spare time, Dan helped create the Integration Manager for Lotus Notes, an application that allows Lotus Notes users to move information between Notes databases and accounting software. The Integration Manager for Lotus Notes won a Lotus Partner Beacon Award for Innovation in 1995.

A tall, bearded man with wild eyes, Dan is frequently seen roaming the halls waving his arms wildly and talking to nobody in particular about some revolutionary new idea. A large and scary guy prone to break out into song (he once sang for the Pope, although its not clear whether or not he was invited to), Dan, too, is given a great deal of leeway in his arm waving, and occasionally helps his company make a ton of money.

Bill and Dan bumped into each other in the hallway one day, and, after they untangled their arms, started working together on projects that required using the Notes API to integrate Notes into the corporate network. They developed numerous applications together that facilitated process reengineering, better systems integration, and fostered a general sense that simply using their creations made users cool.

Their projects were successful because they combined two different perspectives with Notes and applications development. The first perspective was that of a person who knew Notes Administration on a low level and Notes Development at a high level, and who also had experience deploying systems on a large scale. The second perspective was that of a person who was a skilled C, C++ and API developer who understood Notes programming from a low-level perspective and had experience creating complex software applications to perform in a client/server environment.

While Bill and Dan were working together on Notes applications, Bill began writing *teach yourself... Lotus Notes* for MIS:Press. Bill's charm, talent, and willingness to take whatever money was offered to him led to the opportunity to produce a second book. Not wanting to write YAMR (yet-another manual rehash), Bill approached Dan about producing a book that combined their two perspectives. That book became this book, and both Bill and Dan would like to take this opportunity to say "Thanks for reading with us."

About This Book

This book is designed to be a useful tool for experienced API developers who are working with Notes for the first time, a foundation for beginning Notes Developers, and a bridge for developers already familiar with Notes development who want to include API development in their work.

The first half of this book (Chapters 1 through 5) gives experienced C, C++, and Visual Basic programmers who haven't worked with Notes exposure to key concepts of Notes, and hands on experience developing Notes applications. It also gives all types of developers an insight into how Notes works from an administrative standpoint. This information is included because understanding how Notes works from an administrative standpoint is crucial to successful implementation of Notes on an enterprise level—it exposes the best points to hook into Notes for your project's needs.

The second half of the book (Chapters 6 through 10) demonstrates using the Notes API's to extend Notes. It covers the structure of a Notes database, selection of the proper tool and API set, and detailed examples with source code of applications written to be useful to you immediately.

Here is a chapter-by-chapter breakdown of this book:

- Chapter 1 provides an introduction to Notes, giving you a brief look at Notes' history, and a working definition some of Notes' important elements and concepts. The chapter finishes with examples of how businesses are using Notes today, and a discussion on how Notes may be used by businesses tomorrow.

- Chapter 2 examines Notes from an administrative standpoint, discussing the components of a Notes installation and the processes Notes follows when it leverages features like Mail-Enabling and Replication. This chapter also includes information about the InterNotes family of products.

- Chapter 3 addresses what Notes means to a developer, covering the tools Lotus provides to develop applications, as well as suggesting processes for development in Notes.

- Chapter 4 examines the building blocks of Notes applications in detail, discussing Documents, Responses, Forms, Views, Fields, Navigators, and so on.

- Chapter 5 ties the first four chapters together, inviting you to build an application in Notes from scratch and to examine the development process.

- Chapter 6 introduces you to the different API tools available to extend Notes, and gives you some guiding principles for deciding which tool is best suited for the task at hand.

- Chapter 7 examines using the Notes C API and invites you to follow along as Dan builds a database-viewing utility.

- Chapter 8 illustrates the HiTest C API by creating a program to monitor and retrieve documents stored in any database at specified intervals.

- Chapter 9 details the HiTest VB API by creating a Visual Basic program to monitor and track mail usage in a Notes domain.

- Chapter 10 looks at the Internet, and discusses how Notes and the Notes API can be used to facilitate the flow of information to and from the World Wide Web using CGI.

As you look at the outline, you'll notice that between the first and second half of the book is a gray area. While the first half examines developing applications, it isn't an exhaustive reference for the function language and LotusScript. Similarly, while the second half of the book examines using C, C++, and Visual Basic, it doesn't provide extensive instructions on how to use Visual Basic or a C compiler to create Windows, OS/2, or Mac OS programs. It is expected that the documentation provided by Lotus, Microsoft, or other development tool vendors will be used to fill in these blanks.

How to Use this Book

If you are an experienced API programmer and are working with Notes for the first time, it is recommended that you read Chapters 1 through 6, followed by the chapters that pertain to the tool you will be using to develop your program. The first few chapters may show you how to do what you want without having to go to the API, or if the API is needed, where to look in Notes for the information you need to get the job done.

If you are a new Notes Developer, Chapters 1 through 6 are suggested, followed by the Lotus documentation for developing applications in Notes, Release 4. When you reach a point where you want to accomplish things in Notes that are outside of the scope of the built-in language, then the remaining chapters that pertain to the language you are most comfortable developing in outside of Notes are recommended.

If you are an experienced Notes Developer, Chapters 2, 5, and 6 should be of interest, followed by the remaining chapters as your needs require and experience allows.

What Notes Means to Its Users and Their Organization

This chapter is designed to introduce new Notes developers (and experienced applications developers who haven't worked with Notes yet) to the history, concepts, and uses of Notes. It covers a lot of information in general detail (a technique sometimes referred to as the view from 10,000 feet) relying on subsequent chapters to elaborate on key ideas and elements. The brief outline below indicates the development of the chapter.

- A brief history of Lotus Notes
- Defining Lotus Notes
- Comparing knowledge to information
- Documents, Fields, Rich Text, Forms, and Responses
- Views, Navigators, and Folders
- Notes Clients, Notes Servers, Replication, Mail Enabling
- Agents, and Workflow
- How businesses use Lotus Notes today

- Standard applications
- Integration applications
- A real life example of how Lotus Notes is being used
- How businesses can use Lotus Notes tomorrow

A Brief History of Notes

At Data General in the early 1980s, an engineer named Ray Ozzie was thinking out loud with his friends. He'd been talking about his experiences with PLATO (a combination of hardware and software that the University of Illinois used to exchange chats, games, and text-based files), and a product that a friend of his was working on at Digital Equipment Corporation called DEC Notes (a program similar to PLATO that was designed to store and retrieve documents in a mainframe/minicomputer environment).

Ozzie believed strongly that the two packages he'd been exposed to were going to have an impact on how people used computers someday. Because they focused on capturing the unstructured information that is the basis of knowledge, Ozzie knew they would be powerful tools to help people work together. But since the two products were based on client's accessing a central server, he had a difficult time reconciling their role with another technology that he felt was going to impact how people worked in the future—the linking of personal computers using a Local Area Network, and the idea that tasks and files could be shared between the PCs both as clients and servers.

Sensing opportunity, Ozzie began to envision a software application that would combine the emerging trends he was seeing. With help from friends, he mapped out a system that would leverage the power of these newly emerging personal technologies for delivering distributed information. Once he had a basic shell for an application in his head, he began to try to sell his idea to a number of software companies. It was a hard sell for Ray, as he relied more on the excitement of his vision's potential to influence investors than sales projections. A number of companies heard Ozzie's pitch and turned him down (including, ironically, Microsoft).

When Ozzie approached Mitchell Kapor (the founder of Lotus Development Corporation) with his idea, Kapor didn't say "No," outright. Impressed with Ozzie's vision, Kapor offered him a handshake deal—if Ray would work on an advanced version of Lotus 1-2-3 called Symphony, Lotus would fund a group to build his idea at the completion of the project. Ozzie agreed, and began to work on, and eventually completed Symphony in 1984. As promised by Kapor, Ozzie found funding from Lotus waiting for him to form Iris Associates and to continue his work. A new application called Lotus Notes was born.

The original specification for the work began optimistically. Using a simple interface that would allow users to share knowledge, Ozzie estimated that he would complete his Lotus Notes application in about 18 months. A short way into the project, however, Ray soon realized that making his application the truly distributed package he wanted would require more time. He needed a large infrastructure of services, including a security model, a shared directory service (to allow the security model to be distributed), internetwork and interapplication messaging to facilitate information exchange, and a method of synchronizing data.

Unfortunately for Ozzie, the LAN was still in its infancy, and no one was building any of the tools he would need—he'd have to build them on his own. This was analogous to, as Jamie Lewis said in an article for *PC Week* about the development of Lotus Notes, "wanting to build a house, but having to build a dam to generate your own electricity, dig a sewage system, find a water supply, and cut your own roads." The project estimate went from 18 months to many years, but Ozzie's enthusiasm for the project was not diminished, and Iris Associates began their work.

In many ways, it could be argued that the lack of distributed systems development tools available to Ozzie and his team was a good thing. After all, you can directly credit the challenge Ozzie and his team faced with a number of highly creative solutions that more conventional systems developers had not currently (and, in some cases might not have ever) considered if ready-made tools to solve the problems were on hand. Ideas like document-oriented data modeling, client/server mail-enabling of applications, and the use of two-way replication as a tool to synchronize not only data but also design elements, emerged as Lotus Notes was being built.

A year prior to the completion of Notes, Lotus purchased the source code for the program from Iris, and established a relationship in which Lotus was responsible for the marketing and sales of the product, providing Iris with royalties from the sale. By 1989, the first version of Lotus Notes was ready to ship. Lotus Notes was released with a price tag of $62,500.00 for the first 100 users. At those prices, it was a product in search of a client. Eventually, however, Lotus began to penetrate the corporate world. Customers evaluated, installed, and understood. Trade magazines began to talk about a concept called "groupware."

Consulting organizations, drawn to Notes' document-oriented data model and replication services, found it especially appealing, and became Lotus' primary customers in the early years. As these companies began to rely more and more on Notes to run their business, they began to request enhancements. Since the customers making these requests represented thousands of Notes seats, Iris began its work on what would become the second major release of the product.

Attracted by the interest larger organizations had in Notes, smaller companies began to experiment with it, as well. Since smaller organizations did not have the resources of their bigger customers, Lotus began to ease the 100-user minimum purchase requirement, and worked to create a third version of Notes that would make development easier and take advantage of more operating systems. It began to work.

As the smaller companies became more interested, so did Lotus' competitors. Microsoft began to promise its own version of Notes. Novell touted a version of Notes, too. So did IBM. But, what took Ozzie years to refine and build wasn't going to spring up overnight. The "Notes Killers," as they were dubbed by the press, seemed to be permanently on the horizon, never quite sailing into view.

Five years from the time Notes was first released, it had gone through three major releases and was in the hands of over a million users. The broad range of server and client platforms combined with the introduction of Notes starter kits priced at about $1,000.00 for a server and two clients made Notes accessible to many more types of businesses.

Without question Notes was a market leader in a class of applications it had created. Iris Associates, created with help from Lotus, went full circle and returned to become a wholly owned subsidiary of its benefactor, purchased for $84 million.

At an overflowing conference called *LotusSphere* held in Orlando in early 1995, Lotus CEO Jim Manzi estimated that by 1997 Lotus would reach 20 million desktops. Ray Ozzie, now the "venerable father" of Notes, was on hand to demonstrate the upcoming, greatly improved Lotus Notes, Release 4, that would be shipping in the same year. Partnerships with AT&T, Apple, HP, Oracle, and other major players in the industry, combined with the long awaited announcement that a less-expensive, run-time version of Notes was going to be introduced to the market made the 20 million desktop number believable. Articles in business magazines ran with headlines like "Why Microsoft Can't Stop Lotus Notes."

At the same time that Lotus was basking in its dominance of the groupware market, another phenomenon was emerging. Businesses were starting to use the Internet. A network that had been the province of the government and academics for years was finally going commercial. Magazines touted the Net as the future. Businesses, it would seem, agreed with the magazines, as record amounts of investment capital flowed into Internet products and services. For a while, it was speculated that the Internet would be the long touted "Notes-Killer."

But Lotus and Iris were ready for the phenomenon, with a series of tools under the *InterNotes* name that were designed to allow corporations to integrate Notes with the Internet. To hedge its bets, Lotus was also already at work on Network Notes, a joint venture between AT&T and Lotus that would allow Notes to distribute information in a way very similar to the way World Wide Web Servers did. Similar agreements with other telephone companies nationwide and internationally were under way.

It was a strategy that the press found impressive. It was a strategy that IBM found very impressive, too. In mid-1995, for a record-setting 3.3 billion dollars, IBM purchased Lotus Development Corporation. While this gave IBM a number of products, the primary reason for the purchase was to acquire Lotus Notes and the InterNotes product lines.

The press speculated that Lotus (a much more relaxed company than IBM) would not be able to survive in IBM's legendary corporate structure. Senior Lotus executives, made millionaires overnight by IBM's acquisition, were expected to leave Lotus in droves. Some did. But Ray Ozzie and the core of Iris remained, and it turns out, that was all IBM would need.

By 1996 (again, at an overflowing LotusSphere), Notes 4.0 was finally ready. As headlines like "Notes Takes Its Long Awaited Bow" heralded its arrival, conference attendees saw Notes and its clear and complete integration with the Internet in a new light. Lou Gerstner, CEO of IBM was on hand to talk about how Lotus was leveraging its IBM relationship to its full advantage. In the six months since IBM had acquired Lotus, Notes seats had increased 200%, reaching an installed base of 4.5 million. Major pricing changes that would make the Notes client competitive with offerings from NetScape and other Internet companies were announced, and tools for 1996 promised to make Notes the key to a powerful information infrastructure for all types of businesses.

Which brings us to today (which will be a distant tomorrow as you read these words). Of course, other milestones in the life of Notes may have occurred since this book was published. But, it is clear to us that where Lotus is headed in the future is up to you and others who share your desire to learn about Notes and what it can do. Both Dan and I, as representatives of those who have gone before you, wish you success in your endeavor, and we invite you to the next section to learn more about what Notes is today, and where we can take it tomorrow.

Defining Lotus Notes

To begin our journey into this section, you'll need to lend us your imagination for a moment...

Imagine, as you read these words, someone being introduced to Notes for the first time. This person may be a corporate decision maker evaluating using Notes in her company, or a new employee being given a class on Notes as part of his orientation. Regardless of the circumstances, imagine this person asking, "What is Lotus Notes?"

Now, imagine a second person, responsible for explaining what Notes is, talking to the first. Maybe he's a member of the IS department or a trainer. Quite possibly, she's a consultant, specifically hired to introduce Notes. Regardless, picture the second person drawing in a deep breath and saying "Notes is darned hard to explain."

As someone who has attended (and later, given) dozens of discussions and classes on Notes, we can tell you from experience that that's a common answer. It's also a true answer. Notes *is* hard to explain. Not because the concept of Notes is complicated—sharing information is a pretty simple premise. The problem is, that in being a tool used to share knowledge and information, there's not much that Notes isn't:

Notes is a database technology.

It's a workflow engine.

It's a compound document store.

It's client/server computing.

It's word processing.

It's electronic mail.

It's enterprise data distribution.

It's even a multi-platform integrated development environment.

Frankly, almost all the buzzwords we're accustomed to reading in the computer press every day apply to Lotus Notes in some fashion.

Consequently, distilling the essence of Notes into a couple of short sentences is a challenge even Lotus faces. As recently as 1993 (several years into the life of Notes), Lotus was criticized by the computer press for not being able to define Notes "in 25 words or less."

Now, since it is common knowledge that only propeller heads read programming books, we could probably get away with a definition something like this:

Lotus Notes is a client/server database system that utilizes a document-centric computing paradigm to encapsulate nonstructured data and objects and distribute them via replication, mail-enabling, and workflow based on an X.400 compliant directory structure.

Technically correct—yet practically impossible to explain to anyone but a fellow propeller head. Worse, the definition doesn't capture what Notes *is* at all. (If you want to be pigeon holed as a developer forever, and have the rungs above you on the corporate ladder sawed off before your eyes, feel free to spit that thing out at your next team meeting.) Let's try again with this one: "Lotus Notes is a tool to collect, organize, and share knowledge and information."

That's much better, but it goes to the opposite end of the definition scale. It's too easy. Just leave that definition hanging out at the meeting, and you'll probably hear somebody say to you, "I'm a technical person, in technical times, constantly bombarded with vague marketing crap like that. If you don't know what Notes is, just say so."

OK. We agree, it's tough to leave that definition out there by itself. However, if you'll indulge us and follow along to the next section, let's consider the definition word by word. By the time we've finished, you'll see the concepts and building blocks of Notes that make that definition work.

Comparing Knowledge to Information

Lotus Notes is a tool to collect, organize, and share KNOWLEDGE and INFORMATION.

NOTE

Knowledge, in the context of our definition of Notes, is loosely structured information that is difficult to break down into small fields. For example, take a discussion between several people at a meeting. While listening to the conversation, one meeting attendee learns something about the personality of another, and perhaps picks up an insight into that second person's profession. However, another attendee at the meeting may learn something completely different from it. You see, she already knew the part the first person picked up on and was paying attention to something someone else said. What was learned by each person participating in the meeting, taken in total, is their knowledge. It can't be collected; it must be shared. (Meaning that if any individual in the room was responsible for writing down the meeting's minutes, that person's interpretation of the meeting would be different from the person sitting next to him or her. Everyone must participate in summarizing the meeting to share their knowledge.)

This is very different from data, or information. *Information* is something that breaks easily into discrete components. Some examples of information include:

- A spreadsheet of sales figures where everything fits into a row or column.
- A database of hardware vendors which contains a collection of short text and numeric fields for names, addresses, and telephone numbers.

Of course, information is still important—you couldn't organize your knowledge without it. (Imagine a library with no card catalog, or a list of customer likes and dislikes but no customer list!) But like the card catalog in a library, information in Notes is peripheral to the goal of collecting knowledge.

Since we haven't returned your imagination from the first time you lent it to us in this section, let's use it again to help illustrate why Notes' ability to collect knowledge is important.

In this scene, picture a room full of bank executives assembled to discuss innovations in banking. The group is about to hear from a local expert on Lotus Notes. Skipping the introduction, and the obligatory joke, let's tune in to the presentation for a few minutes:

I'm told that speaking to a room full of Bank Presidents is like speaking to a group of children with Attention Deficit Disorder. If I don't have your attention in the first five minutes, I've lost you for the entire show. With that in mind, I'd like to make this simple statement, that, given your occupation, I hope will get your attention. As I haven't been a bank officer in recent history, you'll have to forgive me if it preys too much on the stereotypical banker.

Here goes:

[Next Slide] Business clip art of some shocked executive type.

If you aren't looking at Lotus Notes, or something very similar to it to enhance your communications today, you are letting money slip through your fingers. Not 2%, not 8%, but, in some cases, percentages with three digits in them and no decimal."

(Stereotypes, evolve for a reason, apparently, as the audience sits up and listens more closely.)

How well did that work? Pretty well, I'd say. Let me add some of the reasons I'm confident in that statement…

[Next Slide] 400% written in giant letters.

1. Independent studies by International Data Corporation and others show companies investing in Notes getting as much as a 400% return on their investments.

2. Based on my experiences with Notes, I know what Notes is ideally suited to contain. And that's knowledge. Why would that be important to you? Well, knowledge, the saying goes, is power. And money, another saying continues, changes everything.

But when you can combine the two…you have something that will keep you alive while your competitors are falling by the wayside. You have an advantage.

Let me give you an example.

[Next Slide] Business clip art of two people sitting at a desk

I want to buy a new house. I save, I shop, I compare. Eventually, I find a house and make an offer. I go to the bank. The mortgage officer talks to me, qualifies me, sizes me up. He decides I'm worth the paperwork, so we begin. My income. My wife's income. My potential to continue earning income. Why I was 90 days past on a $30.00 student loan payment when I was twenty one. What I spend a month on everything. Eventually, all of the information is collected. There are forms to fill out. Papers to sign. Releases, waivers, and so on.

Now, having served four years in the Marines, I'm a veteran. More papers to get, sign, and deliver. Eventually, I buy the house. Aside from meeting the financial criteria, two things were needed to complete this transaction. Information, which I supplied, and knowledge, which was what the loan officer had to have. Which forms under which circumstances? How do you make the call when the numbers say borderline? What's the best way to present this information to ensure approval?

I went through all of this about two years ago. The bank I got the mortgage from sold it almost immediately, so they made a little money, but today, none of the information they collected is worth anything to them. It just sits in their computer, for analysis and historical reasons. The lien belongs to the company that gives me the payment book, and they're the ones collecting the interest now.

But out of that transaction two years ago, what still has value to that bank, and, in fact, has most likely become even more valuable to them? The knowledge locked up in that loan officer's head. Because with that knowledge, she can continue to generate income. The better she gets at it, in fact, the more mortgages she can process, and the more likely she is to qualify the loans so that her approval rate is higher than average. Knowledge and information is worth far more than information alone.

And banks have plenty of systems for capturing information today. I know this because I can call in over my telephone and get my current balance, line of credit, and similar information. There's lots of information being stored somewhere.

But where is the knowledge being stored? What if we could store that knowledge somewhere—share it with less experienced loan officers—and not just a few officers, but all of them, in all of our branches…

(The sound of pens scribbling furiously on paper begin to fill the room as one executive after another makes a note to ask their IT Director about Notes when they get back to the office.)

"That sounds pretty good, doesn't it?"

(A dozen or so heads nod in agreement as they write.)

"Which brings me to Lotus Notes…"

And which takes us to the next section.

Utilizing Documents, Fields, Rich Text, Forms, and Responses

NOTE

Lotus Notes is a tool to *COLLECT* organize, and share knowledge and information.

Documents, Fields, Rich Text, and Forms

Notes collects knowledge by storing it in databases of Documents. These databases are in turn stored on Notes Servers or a Notes Client's local drive. They are represented to a Notes user by an icon on the Notes Client Workspace, as illustrated in Figure 1.1.

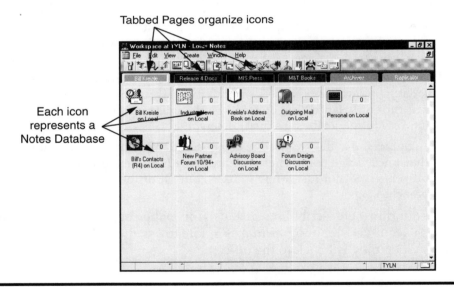

Figure 1.1 Icons on the pages of the Workspace represent databases located on the local hard drive or Notes Servers.

Each Notes Document in a Notes database is a combination of information and knowledge. Number, Date, Text, and Keywords fields contain the information (data that allows Documents to be sorted and retrieved later based on common values). A specially designed Notes field called a *Rich Text field* holds knowledge. Rich Text fields can contain text with formatting, sounds, pictures, or even other programs, making them well suited for containing loosely structured information.

The fields for each Document are displayed to the user for editing and reading using one or more Forms. Figure 1.2 illustrates a Notes Document, Notes Fields, and a Form.

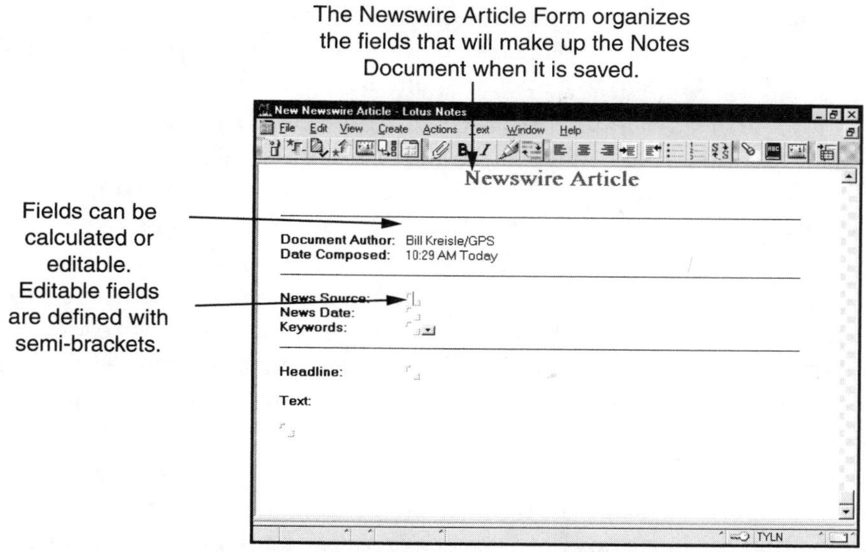
The Newswire Article Form organizes the fields that will make up the Notes Document when it is saved.
Fields can be calculated or editable. Editable fields are defined with semi-brackets.
New Newswire Article - Lotus Notes
File Edit View Create Actions Text Window Help
Newswire Article
Document Author: Bill Kreisle/GPS
Date Composed: 10:29 AM Today
News Source:
News Date:
Keywords:
Headline:
Text:
TYLN

Figure 1.2 The Fields of this Notes Documents are arranged using a Form.

Which brings us to a few questions you're probably asking:

> "How does a Document in Notes translate into a container for a discussion?"
>
> "What's the difference between a Notes Document and a word processing document?"
>
> "Doesn't it boil down to one person typing in the meeting's minutes?"

The answer to these questions is this: What turns Notes into a container for knowledge is the combination of Rich Text, the Notes Document we've just discussed, and another, special type of Notes Document, called a Response Document.

Response Documents

Response Documents (generally referred to in Notes as Responses) are similar to standard Notes Documents in that they can combine information and knowledge using different types of fields. However, Response Documents are special in that they are designed to be associated with other Notes Documents or Responses in a parent-child relationship. If you were to think of a database of Notes Documents as similar to a book and its pages, you could think of Responses as Post-It notes you might attach to a specific page in the book.

Just as you can have more than one Post-It note on a page, a Document can have more than one Response associated with it. Keeping that analogy, a Response to Response Document would be similar to one Post-It note placed on top of another.

Responses and Rich Text are the keys that allow Notes to store discussions. A conversation in a meeting may start with a main subject and follow different threads based on one or more person's response. In the same fashion, Notes databases can have a main topic stored as a Document, with one or more Response Documents associated with it and each other.

Going back to the idea that a bank could benefit from storing knowledge about how to qualify and process mortgage applications, imagine that the bank has Lotus Notes on every bank officer's PC, and that all of the loan officers have access to a Notes discussion database that uses Documents as main topics, and Responses as answers. New loan officers could ask questions in the form of Documents, and experienced loan officers could answer in the form of Responses. Over time, as questions are asked and answered, a collection of knowledge begins to amass. A year later, a new loan officer could review the database before asking a question, and probably find that it's already been answered.

Responses also allow the creation of Documents that aren't discussion-related, but should be associated with a main topic. For example, imagine a database of magazine articles. In the magazine, think of each article as a separate Document in a Notes database. After creating a magazine article, Documents containing reference information used in writing the article are associated with it through Response Documents. Articles based on a single source will have only one Response associated with them. Other articles, based on many sources will have many Responses.

Utilizing Views, Navigators, and Folders

Lotus Notes is a tool to collect, ORGANIZE and share knowledge and information.

NOTE

Views and Navigators

Which brings us to the next key word in my definition of Notes—the word *organize*. Once collected, Notes organizes knowledge by presenting it to the user in one or more Views. *Views* are developer-defined windows that help you organize the Documents stored in a database. They display selected fields for each Document in a manner similar to a list. Documents within the View can be grouped by category to help you find information. Returning to the book analogy, a View would be similar to a table of contents or an index that organized the information in the book concisely.

A database will usually have more than one View. For example, a discussion database may have a Main View where all Documents and Responses are displayed in a linear list by date, a By Author View, where all Documents and Responses are categorized under the name of the person who created them, and a By Category View, where Documents are categorized by common values in a field on the Documents and Responses.

Navigators allow users to create a more visual interface to the elements of Notes, such as Views, Documents, or Agents. A Navigator might be a map or a collection of pictures that symbolize the type of data you will see if you select them. Clicking on a picture of a state might open a View that only displays Documents that pertain to that state, for example, or run an Agent that gives the user more choices about the state.

Navigators can occupy the entire Database Window (see Figure 1.3), or Navigators and Views can be used together, with each element being displayed in a separate pane of a Database Window (see Figure 1.4).

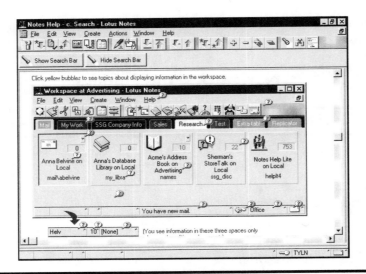

Figure 1.3 A full-screen Navigator. Clicking on different areas of the Navigator causes Notes to open Views, Folders, or other Notes databases.

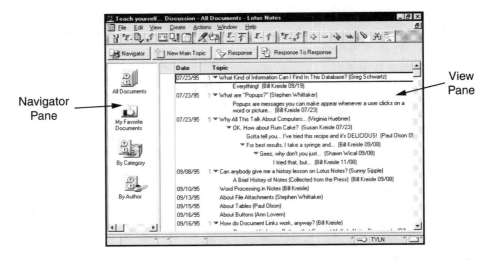

Figure 1.4 An illustration of a Database Window, a Notes Navigator, and a Notes View.

Folders

Folders are containers designed to collect Documents into a logical group. Folders differ from Views in that a Folder's only selection criteria is whether or not a Document has been moved to it. For example, a Trash Folder may contain documents from multiple Views. In our book analogy, a Folder might be thought of as a separate notepad where you make a list of page numbers you'll want to refer to in the future.

Notes Clients, Notes Servers, Replication, and Mail Enabling

Lotus Notes is a tool to collect, organize, and *SHARE* knowledge and information.

NOTE

Notes Clients and Servers

The next key word of our definition, *sharing*, refers to Notes Clients connecting to a Notes Server, or Notes Servers connecting to each other to open databases and examine their Documents. Each Notes Client and Server is made unique by an *ID file* that is installed on the computer containing the Client or Server software. In addition to establishing the identity of each Server and Client, the ID file is used for authentication, encryption, and access control. Connections between Notes Clients and Notes Servers can be made via an existing network, or through dial-up/X.25, as illustrated in Figure 1.5.

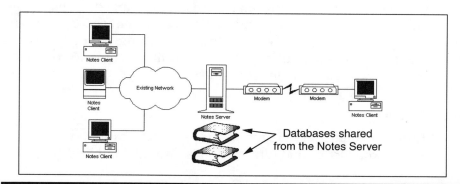

Figure 1.5 Notes distributes Documents and the actions involved in retrieving them using a client/server approach.

Replication

Besides allowing Notes Clients to open databases to examine Documents, Notes Servers also share information through Replication. *Replication* is a process used by Notes to manage Document additions, deletions, and edits between databases that share the same Replica ID, keeping their contents synchronized (see Figure 1.6). Two databases can share a Replica ID, or two hundred, and the principle of replication remains the same.

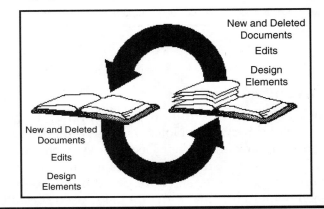

New and Deleted
Documents

Edits

Design
Elements

New and Deleted
Documents

Edits

Design
Elements

Figure 1.6 Replication is a process that synchronizes the contents of Notes Databases that share the same Replica ID.

During a Replication, only information that has changed in the Replica databases is moved across the network or modem connection between a Notes Client and Notes Server. Employees working remotely can use Notes databases "off-line" all day, and call in the evening to replicate a day's worth of work in a matter of minutes!

Mail Enabling

In addition to client/server architecture and replication, a third way Notes shares knowledge and information is through Mail Enabling.

Mail Enabling allows Notes Servers to route Documents between each other as messages. (We typically think of mail enabling as "e-mail"—a tool people use to send messages to other people. However, Notes' use of mail enabling also allows people to send information to a database instead of a person.)

To put this in context, imagine sending a Document you are working on directly from your desk to a book in the corporate library. When the Document arrives, the table of contents and the index of the book are automatically updated for the next person who checks out the book. Or, imagine telling a magazine in a library to automatically move or copy some of its pages into a book at another library whenever an article about a specific topic is printed. As you can see, this is a powerful part of Notes.

Mail Enabling also allows Notes users to have individual Notes Databases to use as their electronic mail database. Each user's mail database contains Forms for creating messages, replies, tasks, and so on. These Forms can be used as they are provided by Lotus, or customized to suit an organization's needs. Figure 1.7 illustrates the standard Lotus Notes Mail Memo Form.

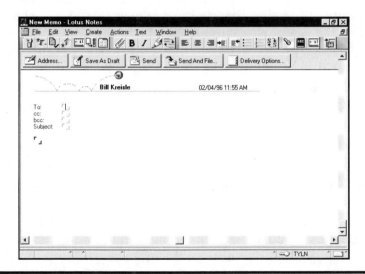

Figure 1.7 A Document in a Notes Database that uses the Lotus Notes Mail Memo Form.

Agents and Workflow

Notes is a tool or collect, organize and share knowledge and information *AUTOMATICALLY*.

NOTE

Welcome to the bonus round. In this section, we examine the addition of the word automatically to our definition.

Agents

Another powerful feature of Notes is the ability to create and run Agents. *Agents* are user/designer created programs written in LotusScript or Notes' Formula language to automate or streamline common processes. A simple Agent might be a single instruction telling Notes to save a Document whenever a button is pressed. A more complex Agent could have many instructions executing in sequence— for example, creating a new Document and automatically filling in some of the Document's fields based who the user is and on what she was doing when the Agent was started. With Notes Release 4, Agents written using Lotus Script can also include external programs written in languages such as Visual Basic or C++.

Agents can be scheduled to run at specific times on a Notes Client or a Notes Server, or they can be launched by the user on demand.

Workflow

Agents, combined with mail-enabling become the basis for *Workflow*. From Notes' perspective, a workflow is a combination of Notes' features that automate or streamline common user processes or tasks.

In other words, a workflow is anything that makes knowledge or information move more efficiently throughout your organization.

Like Agents, Notes workflows can be extremely simple or very complex.

A simple example of a workflow would be a Notes database that periodically sends a mail message to a user telling her how many

Documents have been added in the previous day that mention her name or the name of a product that she is researching. In this workflow, an Agent runs automatically on the server, checking any new Documents for her name or the name of her product. If it finds new Documents that match the search conditions, it sends the user a message using mail-enabling. This saves the user from having to open the database every day to search for new Documents that may interest her.

For a more complex workflow example, imagine that a company using Notes wants to track its employees' time-cards more effectively. Using Notes, the company creates a series of time-card databases. The first database is shared by all employees from a public Notes Server. In this database, employees can enter their time cards and save them. Once the time card is saved, the employee is no longer allowed access to it, nor can he see any other employees' time cards.

Weekly, a supervisor reviews the time-card database. If the supervisor agrees with the information an employee has entered on his time card, she marks the time card as approved. If the supervisor disagrees with the information, she runs an Agent that sends the employee an e-mail asking for more information.

Every night, an Agent runs on the Notes Server that scans the time-card database for Documents marked approved. If it finds any, it forwards them using mail-enabling to another time-card database on the accounting department's Notes Server. By moving the time cards to another server where only members of the accounting department have access, the time cards are less likely to be altered by a supervisor or employee later. Figure 1.8 illustrates this process.

The accounting department uses many different Notes Views in their time card database to analyze the information:

One View displays how many employees worked more than 40 hours per week.

Another View sorts the total hours worked from the most to the least.

A third View displays employees who haven't submitted timecards for the last pay period.

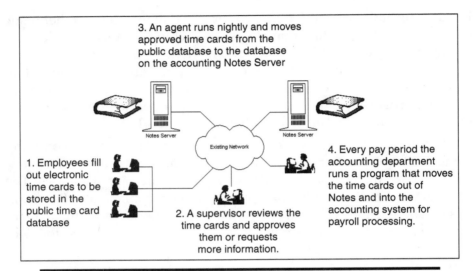

3. An agent runs nightly and moves approved time cards from the public database to the database on the accounting Notes Server

Notes Server

Existing Network

Notes Server

1. Employees fill out electronic time cards to be stored in the public time card database

2. A supervisor reviews the time cards and approves them or requests more information.

4. Every pay period the accounting department runs a program that moves the time cards out of Notes and into the accounting system for payroll processing.

Figure 1.8 Notes uses mail enabling as the basis for creating a workflow.

Finally, on payday, the accounting department runs another Agent that exports the information in the time-card database into a format that can be read by the company's accounting software and payroll checks are then generated.

How Businesses Use Notes Today

Now that we have a working definition for Lotus Notes, it's time to reinforce that definition with a discussion about how businesses are using Lotus Notes to store knowledge and information today. This discussion will introduce you to the five categories that most 'out of the box' solutions built in Notes fall under, and give us a chance to examine how Notes can be used to collect information for other applications. To finish this examination of how businesses use Notes today, we'll see how a software company uses Notes to create a powerful business solution for its partners and customers.

Standard Notes Applications

As a general rule, there are five standard application types that Notes applications fall under:

- Discussion Applications
- Broadcasting Applications
- Reference Applications
- Tracking Applications
- Workflow/Approval Applications

We refer to these application types as *out of the box* because they can be used "right out of the box"—they can be successfully implemented by an experienced Notes developer without any external tools or programming knowledge. Other possible types of applications suited to Notes are data warehousing, data reporting, or systems integration. We'll discuss these applications later in this chapter, under the heading, "How Businesses Can Use Lotus Notes Tomorrow."

Discussion Applications

Discussion Applications are one of the flagship applications of Notes showcasing a number of Notes' strengths. To understand the power of a Discussion Application, consider the following information:

Every business is the sum of the experience and knowledge contained in its people. Because of this, it is extremely important to an organization to ensure that it creates an environment where individual knowledge is collected and shared across a company or a team. In a traditional setting, this occurs through discussions in person, meetings, by way of telephone, or through electronic mail (e-mail).

Except for e-mail, most of the knowledge transferred in this fashion is rarely recorded on a computer. It's recorded on white-boards, tablets, or yellow gummed notes instead. While having a notepad or collection of papers satisfies individual or small-group needs, it makes the knowledge obtained difficult to share on a large scale. As a result, a person with specialized knowledge often answers the same question repeatedly as different people arrive at the conclusion that they need a given piece of information. Additionally, most of the traditional methods of discussion (telephone calls, person-to-person conversations, or meetings) require that people be available at the same time. Discussion Applications in Notes eliminate many of these issues.

Discussion Applications are databases that use Documents to enter main topics and Response Documents to collect individual information or opinions that should be associated with them.

It should be noted that Discussion Applications are the Notes feature most commonly imitated by competitors in the workgroup software market. However, no competitor to date has combined all the following features in their imitation:

> Because Discussion Applications are stored on a Notes Server, topics in a database are collected and shared by people throughout an organization. New members to a group can review a long-standing discussion before asking questions, reducing the number of times shared knowledge must be repeated by the discussion participants.

> Security on the server—the Access Control List, (ACL)—can limit the number of people allowed to participate in a discussion. The ACL can control the discussions a user can participate in, as well as establish the level a user can participate in a discussion. What this means is that some users can be allowed to create new topics, and edit topics posted by others, while another group of users might only be allowed to read what is being discussed but not add to it or change it.

> Rich Text allows discussion participants to more appropriately communicate their information than plain text. As an example, a user wanting to know about a particular feature of a computer program might include a screen shot of the actual button or menu command along with their question. Or, a discussion participant who responds to a question might include illustrations explaining the steps needed to solve a problem.

> Finally, replication allows the database to be distributed to many physical locations and still remain current.

All of these strengths combine to make an application that is effective because it is unconstrained by time, distance, or software incompatibilities. If a person wants to respond to a question at 3:00 AM using his Macintosh at home, then replicate his response with an OS/2 server in the morning so that a coworker using a PC can read it, he can! If someone else takes a two-week vacation, she can easily catch up on the discussion when she returns because everything has been stored in a Notes database.

Some examples of discussion applications include:

- New ideas discussion

    Marketing or product-development departments can post new ideas or brainstorming topics, and each member of the group has the opportunity to respond to the idea or provide supporting information.

- Project discussion

    Project descriptions are the main Documents, and informal discussions regarding the project's scope or status are entered as Responses.

- Executive discussion

    By using Notes' security to restrict access to executive-level employees, the database can serve as a collection of topics and Responses relating to company officers. This type of application is especially useful to companies in which the senior officers spend a great deal of time traveling.

- Sales discussion

    A database of sales-related questions or topics and Responses can be extremely powerful in companies where the sales force includes remote employees.

- Expert discussion

    Company employees post questions as Documents to a discussion database that is owned by an employee or group of employees with specialized skills. Answers to each question and supporting information are added as Responses.

Broadcast Applications

Every company has low-priority yet time-sensitive information to share with its employees (a company picnic, a luncheon seminar, or a memo about parking-lot maintenance, for example). This broadcast information is traditionally stored on paper and delivered through bulletin-board postings, internal mail, or electronic mail. Bulletin boards and internal mail require labor to print, photocopy, and post or deliver their information.

Electronic mail is effective, but forces noncritical information into the same mailbox as urgent messages and requests, often irritating mail users who receive large amounts of what they perceive as junk mail. Using Notes to create broadcast applications provides an alternative delivery method for noncritical, company-wide information. Stored in public directories and replicated throughout the company's Notes servers, these databases create an effective one-way information flow (from the sender to the recipients). Because most of the information in a broadcast application is read-only, Responses are usually not a part of the database.

Responses could be included however, to encourage people to share their ideas about a given broadcast topic. (A company picnic announcement, for example, might allow employees to compose a Response if they want to bring food items or refreshments.)

Some examples of broadcast applications include:

- Internal news

  Moving-company newsletters or departmental updates into broadcast databases can reduce internal photocopying and printing costs, allow information to be delivered faster, and allow the employees responsible for creating the materials to work in collaboration.

- External news

  Storing information obtained from a clipping service or other outside source (an Internet mailing list, for example) in a broadcast database consolidates information and reduces multiple subscriptions to an information service or list.

- Personal announcements

  A broadcast database that allows anyone to post information they want announced company-wide (Weddings, Births, Autos for Sale) and centralizes this information into a monitored, nonintrusive, medium.

Reference Applications

As businesses grow and mature, policies, procedures, and knowledge are documented. Some of this information may be printed as a book (an employee handbook, for example). Other information may be stored in a binder (telemarketing scripts or internal systems documents).

Aside from the obvious cost of maintaining the knowledge on paper (consider changes to an employee handbook after 1,000 copies just came in from the printer), costs also originate from distribution and creation.

Reference Applications are Notes databases designed to support or replace existing printed reference materials. These databases can reduce the cost of preparation and distribution dramatically (if you make a change to the employee handbook, for example, it's updated company-wide when the next replication occurs). They also allow collaborative efforts in the creation of the documents. Sharing a Document on a Notes Server lets Jon enter original content, to be embellished by Bob. After Bob finishes, Sally (who spells better than a computer) proofreads the work. Finally, Bruce (the boss), approves it to be distributed company-wide.

Some examples of Reference Applications are:

- Business policies

  A business policies database could contain travel and expense guidelines, on-line instructions for filling out company forms, or a guide to company benefits.
- Knowledge bases

  Examples of a knowledge base include a database of answers to commonly asked questions or a comprehensive collection of information about each of the company's products.

- Document library

  A document library could be a collection of white papers on technologies used by a manufacturing firm or a collection of standard contracts at a law firm.

Tracking Applications

All businesses have information that they want to track and update on a daily basis. It may be a customer base where calls and correspondence to and from the customer are recorded; a shipping manifest where shipping information is added daily; or a project tracking system where hours spent on a given project are recorded as they are worked. Generally, this kind of information requires input from multiple sources. Jack in sales may create the original Customer Document. Alice in support, however, will be the one on the phone with the Customer next week when they discover that "some assembly required" means a degree in engineering and a six-year-old assistant.

Tracking applications are a challenge to businesses, because tracking different events usually requires a variety of software packages. (Examples include a network-based contact manager, a shipping-and-receiving program, or a project-management package.) While Notes isn't suited for real-time tracking applications, its flexible development structure combined with replication and security makes it a powerful tool to apply to a variety of less rapid-transaction-oriented situations.

Tracking applications may be Documents only or a combination of Documents and Responses. In some cases, a Document may have many different types of Responses. For example, a project database where the project information is stored in a Document and Responses for entering time spent, resources required, and project notes are all associated with the main Document.

Some examples of tracking applications are:

- Employee tracking and evaluation

  In personnel, a tracking database can be used to track the interview, hiring, and ongoing performance of each employee.

- Process improvement tracking

  In this example, a tracking database is used to record the ongoing status of process improvement initiatives across the company.

- Help desk or customer support tracking

  Companies with telephone support departments or internal help desks can use Notes to track calls. Actions taken to support the customer may be stored in Responses or with the main Document.

Workflow/Approval Applications

A final, important example of how a business can use Lotus Notes is in Workflow applications. Workflow/Approval applications are Notes databases that use background tasks or Notes' built-in mail capability to route knowledge according to predefined rules. These applications can be complex, such as a "cradle-to-grave" human resources system that tracks information about each employee in the company and routes information based on calendar events or changes in performance to accounting and select supervisors. They can also be deceptively simple, such as a database that uses a background macro to send out reminders through electronic mail.

A Workflow application can be a combination of the other applications we've discussed to this point. As an example, imagine a Help Desk database (a tracking application) at a medium-size company. The help desk supervisor reviews the database weekly, and uses a specially designed View to determine the five most frequently asked questions for the week. After he reviews the questions, he forwards a sample question and answer for each of the top questions to a Help Desk Top 10 database (a broadcast application). Supervisors in the company use the Help Desk Top 10 database to look for trends in their departments and to help identify possible education needs in the company.

Some other examples of Workflow applications include:

A product-support database where problems and fixes are marked *internal use only*, or *public*. If a posted problem and fix are marked public, they are automatically routed to another database. That database, in turn, is replicated out to customer sites.

A company meeting database that allows employees to enter a meeting date and time, agenda, and a list of attendees. One day before the meeting, e-mail is sent to all attendees reminding them of the upcoming event along with the proposed agenda.

Integration Applications

After reading all the examples of standard ways that Notes can be used, it might be tempting to say that, in summary, "Businesses can (and do) use Lotus Notes for almost anything." Which, based on what we've talked about so far, would be a reasonable assumption. But, there are some applications that Notes, by its design, does not handle well.

For example, information that requires heavy numerical analysis of large numbers or records isn't well served by Notes. Nor is data that must be collected and analyzed in real time (such as a point-of-sale application that must decrement a master inventory database when a sale is made in real time). Finally, information that is heavily dependent on relational linking, joins, and record locking (accounting data, for example) isn't a strong application candidate for Notes.

However, because of Replication, Workflow, and other Notes features, it is possible that Notes is a good method for *collecting* some of the data we've just discussed, with the ultimate destination of that data being another application. An example of this might be using Notes as a front end for some modules of an accounting application, such as Payables Management. In such a scenario, expense reports could originate and move in Notes from user to user by Mail Enabling. The reports, when approved, would then be stored in an accounting package to be applied to the proper accounts in General Ledger by the accounting software.

These types of applications generally require a third-party tool and knowledge of another application development language to successfully implement, but, as you can imagine, provide excellent rewards for the work.

A Real-Life Example of How Lotus Notes Is Being Used

While the generic examples we've discussed up to this point more than illustrate the power of Notes as a tool to collect knowledge, we can't help feeling that people are bombarded with so many promises about technology today that most of them have become the show-me type. With that in mind, this section examines how a software company uses Lotus Notes every day, and ties the examples we've just reviewed to a business perspective.

Introducing Great Plains Software

Great Plains Software (GPS) is a privately owned business headquartered in Fargo, North Dakota. Since the company began in 1981, the employees who comprise GPS have worked to fulfill a mission that is focused sharply on the people and businesses they serve: To improve the life and business success of partners and customers by providing superior accounting software, services and tools. Great Plains fulfills this mission by being a leading developer of accounting and financial management software.

How Great Plains Software Is Using Lotus Notes

While Great Plains uses Notes for a number of internal applications that improve the quality of their software and streamline processes, the application we're going to discuss addresses an ongoing challenge for any company that supports a large number of geographically dispersed partners and customers—how to transfer the knowledge accumulated through the design, creation, and support of products to partners and customers in a timely and efficient manner?

The answer, in Great Plains' case, is PlainsOnline (Figure 1.9); a set of Lotus Notes databases designed by the Information Services team to allow GPS and Partners to share up-to-date information by way of CompuServe's Enterprise Connect Service and AT&T's Network Notes:

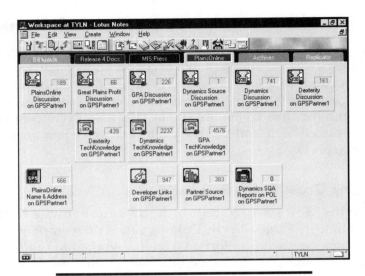

Figure 1.9 The PlainsOnline Notes databases.

When talking about PlainsOnline, there are two components we'd like to discuss.

1. The technical implementation (because it simply wouldn't be possible without Notes).

2. The types of applications that comprise the PlainsOnline solution.

The technical implementation is illustrated in Figure 1.10.

Using Figure 1.10 to map the flow of information from GPS to its Customers and Partners:

1. Information and knowledge move from GPS' internal Notes Servers to the external Notes Server via Replication and Workflow.

2. The GPS external Notes Server connects to CompuServe and AT&T periodically to update replicas maintained by each service provider.

3. Once CompuServe's and AT&T's databases are updated, customers and partners can connect and replicate the information to their own Notes Servers or Notes Clients.

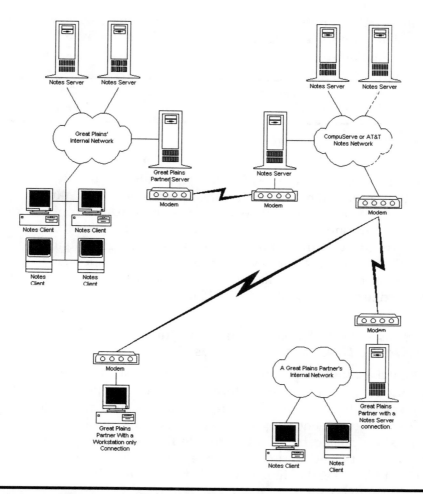

Figure 1.10 A conceptual view of how PlainsOnline connects GPS and its partners.

This arrangement allows GPS and its partners access to the knowledge and information GPS wants to share regardless of the size of their organization, 24 hours a day. The one-person consulting business can use a single Notes client to connect and replicate, while larger organizations already using Notes internally can connect their server to CompuServe or AT&T directly and replicate automatically. Along with replication, both CompuServe and AT&T allow Notes users connected to their system to transfer electronic mail via Notes to any other user or server on their networks.

NOTE

> Notes users can also send and receive electronic mail through CompuServe's and AT&T's gateways to the Internet, MCI mail, and dozens of other systems.

Another point is that since AT&T and CompuServe are providing the connection, replication, and mail transfer services, Great Plains has the advantage of thousands of local access telephone numbers to its information around the world, as well as a solution that can be scaled to thousands of customers and partners. All things considered, the CompuServe and AT&T networks represent a very powerful way to move knowledge and information. Which leads us to wonder what kind of knowledge and information Great Plains is sharing.

Dynamics, Dexterity, Great Plains Accounting, and PlainsOnline Discussion Databases

These databases allow partners to communicate with Great Plains and with each other in a discussion format. Examples of how partners and customers use them include posting a topic designed to seek out other partners with experience approaching a particular problem, responding to a question posted by GPS to provide feedback about one of Great Plains' products, and participating in a discussion thread designed to help Great Plains set the direction for PlainsOnline in the future.

These discussion databases offer many advantages:

1. Since the conversations between partners, customers, and Great Plains are saved in the database, new users can review the database to see what issues have already been discussed and resolved before they post a question.

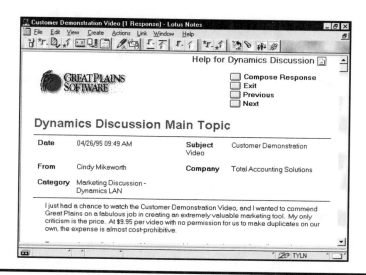

Figure 1.11 A Document from the Dynamics Discussion database.

2. Because the database is open to virtually thousands of experts on Great Plains' products, the amount of knowledge that can be applied to a problem or question posted is the sum of the participants. This means that useful Responses can be given to almost any question that can be asked.

Developer Links and PlainsOnline Address Database

The Developer Links and PlainsOnline Address databases are reference applications. Developer Links contains information about all of Great Plains' partners that can be filtered through a number of views, including views by geography, by product line, or by the types of services offered. Once a user locates a partner or customer she wishes to communicate with, she can use the physical address and telephone number in the Developer Links database to gather more information, or use the PlainsOnline Address database to look up an electronic mail address to request information electronically (see Figures 1.12 and 1.13).

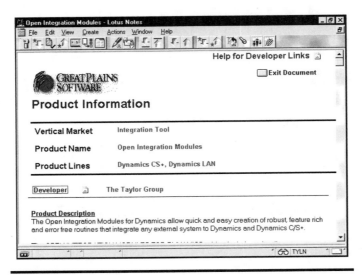

Figure 1.12 A Document from the Developer Links database.

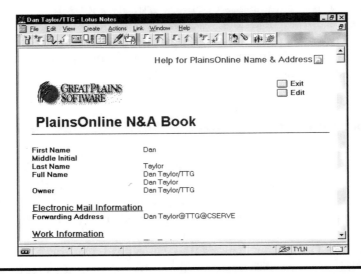

Figure 1.13 A Document from the PlainsOnline Address database.

The Developer Links and PlainsOnline Address database offer the following advantages:

1. Replication allows information to stay up-to-date throughout the community of partners. Changing an address or a telephone in one place ensures that it will, over time, be updated in all locations.

2. Views and powerful search capabilities within Notes make it easy to locate partners based on very specific criteria. For example, using Full Text Searching, a user can look for a partner located in Texas that has a point-of-sale application developed in Dexterity.

The Partner Source Database

The Partner Source is an example of a broadcast application in Notes (see Figure 1.14). It is designed to provide up-to-date information about Great Plains' products, strategy, and direction. Some examples of the information you might find in the Partner Source include class schedules for Great Plains University, competitive information, a copy of Great Plains' Schedule (a schedule for product releases over the next year), and the Strategy (a Document detailing future product directions).

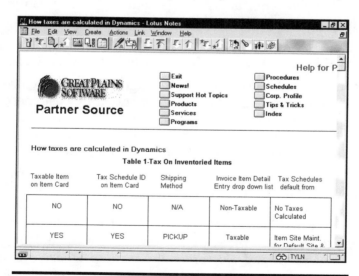

Figure 1.14 A Document from the Partner Source database.

Advantages offered by the Partner Source include:

1. Rich Text fields allow the Partner Source to include graphics and formatting, making information easier to present and read (for example, some files are distributed in Adobe Acrobat's PDF format).

2. Replication ensures that timely information is delivered throughout the partner community.

The PlainsOnline Support Database

The PlainsOnline support database is an internal tracking application, designed to collect information about partner calls to Great Plains for support. When a new support request is received, information about the partner calling is automatically filled in from the PlainsOnline Address book.

By collecting information into a single database shared from a Notes Server, support personnel can use the database as a reference for troubleshooting problems, and management can have a comprehensive view of the types of calls being placed for support.

The Dynamics and Dexterity TechKnowledge Databases

The Dynamics and Dexterity TechKnowledge databases are used by the partners as reference guides to problems reported by customers to Great Plains Support along with solutions (see Figure 1.15). We didn't include these two databases in our previous discussion of reference applications because they are also excellent examples of a Workflow/Approval application.

On Great Plains internal Notes network, support personnel compose a new problem/solution Document for the TechKnowledge database based on new calls. The Document is routed to the support person's supervisor, where it is verified for accuracy. From there, the Document travels to the Design and Documentation group where it is edited to ensure that it communicates the problem and solution effectively. Finally, the Document is moved to the External Notes Server at Great Plains to be replicated to the CompuServe and AT&T Network.

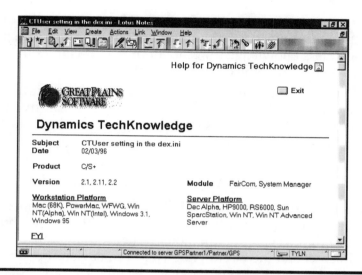

Figure 1.15 A Document from the Dynamics TechKnowledge database.

How Businesses Can Use Lotus Notes Tomorrow

Hopefully, by the time you've reached this section, you're generating your own ideas about how your company can use Lotus Notes. You've seen how Notes can collect and distribute knowledge and information enterprise-wide, and you've got "Lotus Notes is a tool to collect, organize, and share information (automatically)," memorized and ready to go at a moment's notice.

Redefining Lotus Notes

However, we first want to turn your eyes to the future, where, in embodying the definition of Notes we've just discussed (that is, in using it to collect, organize, and share knowledge) something fundamental happens to our definition. It changes.

It may change to something like, "Notes is the information infrastructure that unites our disparate hardware and software platforms to allow seamless knowledge transfer." Or it may become simply, "Notes is where we live." But it will change, regardless.

Why? Well, imagine that your business is already using Lotus Notes to achieve our first definition using variations of the five standard application types we've discussed. Now let's examine the factors that will lead to the second definition.

Intra-, Inter-, and Extra-Enterprise Networks

One of the biggest factors in redefining Notes in the context of your company is the emergence of the Internet as a tool to connect businesses. Being able to disseminate information on-demand at relatively low cost using the Internet and the World Wide Web is an obvious opportunity that businesses are taking advantage of today, both internally and externally.

However, as with any other medium to transfer knowledge, even though the delivery mechanism is inexpensive and relatively easy to implement, steps must be taken to ensure that the content of what is being delivered is collected often and accurately. And those steps have to involve the entire organization if they're going to succeed. Just as it defeats the purpose of collecting the knowledge of a meeting by having a single person be responsible for writing the meeting's minutes, it is impractical for a single person (a Webmaster, if you will) to be responsible for the collection and dissemination of a company's knowledge.

Ideally, you want an environment where the knowledge and information is collected interactively, and in an ongoing fashion. You want to have active discussions, knowledge databases, and information databases that can be incorporated into your existing processes.

Additionally, as you are exposing your company's information to outside sources, there are times when you are going to want to restrict the information that is "published" to the world, but not interfere with the process that collects it all.

Which is where Lotus Notes fits in. You already know that Lotus Notes is an effective tool for coordinating information and knowledge resources internally. We'll call Lotus Notes in that internal mechanism for distributing information an intra-enterprise network (see Figure 1.16).

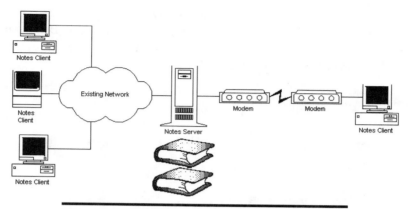

Figure 1.16 Notes in the intra-enterprise network.

Looking at the previous example of how Great Plains Software uses Lotus Notes, you can also see how Notes can be used to transfer that internally gathered information to other businesses. Looking at Notes in that context, let's call the result an inter-enterprise network (see Figure 1.17).

By that logic, adding the World Wide Web to the equation creates the extra-enterprise network—a network that incorporates direct internal, business-to-business, and business-to-customer connections.

Lotus Notes has the potential to be the glue that binds these networks together. Notes client/server architecture, replication, security, and mail-enabling make it an ideal tool to build knowledge collection/dissemination platforms on.

Connecting the Notes Servers in your network to other Notes Servers at other businesses—using direct connections or a service like Worldcom or CompuServe—allows subsets of that knowledge to be transferred to other businesses using the same security and architecture.

Adding the InterNotes Web Publisher technology that is included with every Notes 4.0 server, companies can take Notes databases and convert them into World Wide Web Documents often, easily, and accurately, making more specific subsets of information available to an even broader audience. Besides, InterNotes Web Publisher allows the World Wide Web to be used as a collection point to move information into a Notes database.

Notes users can also connect directly to World Wide Web servers from their Notes Client Software using the InterNotes Web Browser and InterNotes Web Retriever technology that is a part of every Notes Release 4.0 Server (see Figure 1.18).

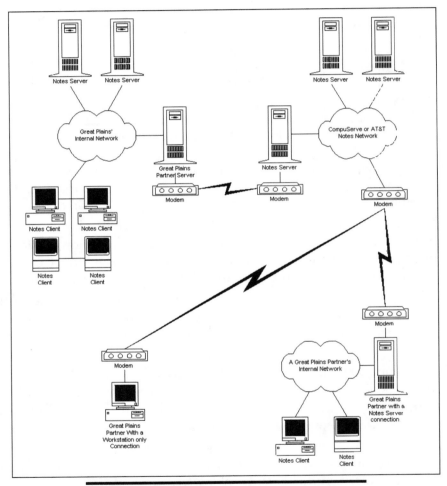

Figure 1.17 Notes in an inter-enterprise network.

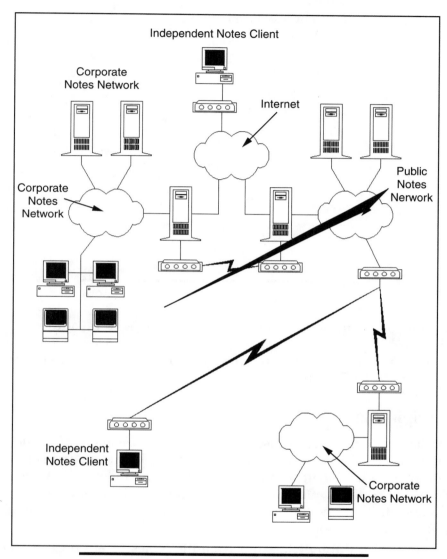

Figure 1.18 Notes in the extra-enterprise network.

Or, to look at it a different way (see Figure 1.19):

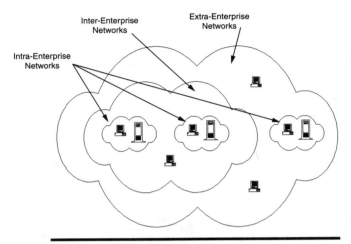

Figure 1.19 Notes in the extra-enterprise network.

Continued integration of the Internet and Notes to be addressed in subsequent releases of Notes make the addition of the extra-enterprise to the network even easier as support for Java, HTTP, and HTML are added directly to Notes Servers.

Multiple Platforms

Another major factor in the use of Notes as an information infrastructure is the fact that Notes runs on a wide array of hardware and software platforms. Notes Clients can run on Windows, Windows 95, Windows NT, Mac OS, OS/2, Sun Solaris, and other UNIX platforms. Notes Servers can run on Windows 95/NT, OS/2, Novell NetWare, and multiple UNIX platforms, as well.

Figures 1.20 through 1.23 illustrate the Notes Client on Windows, Windows 95, OS/2 Warp, and the Mac OS.

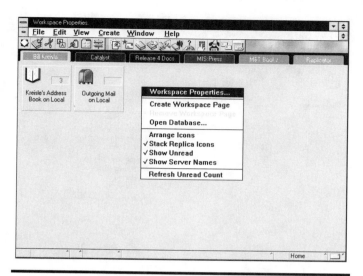

Figure 1.20 The Notes Client on Windows/Workgroups/NT.

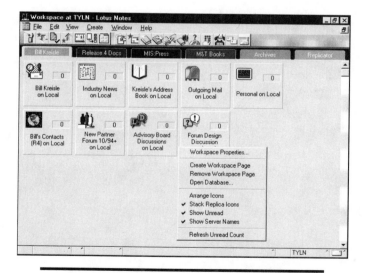

Figure 1.21 The Notes Client on Windows 95/NT.

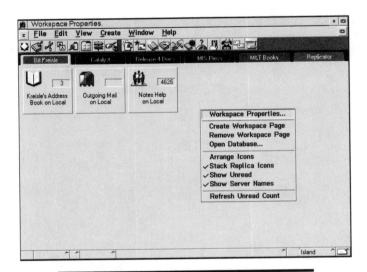

Figure 1.22 The Notes Client on OS/2 Warp.

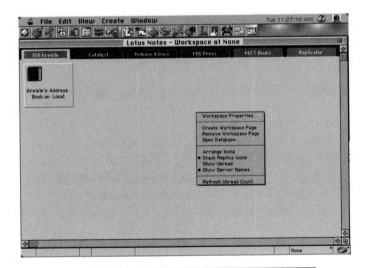

Figure 1.23 The Notes Client on the Mac OS.

In fact, no other client/server applications environment runs on as many platforms as Lotus Notes. That advantage allows applications developers to concentrate on the information and processes needed to develop an application instead of the implementation details of how to make the solution work for all users in the company.

Scheduling and Electronic Mail

A clearly emerging trend for electronic communications is the migration to client/server architecture, a model that Lotus Notes Mail has followed since its creation. Already strong in this area, Lotus' decision to give its 12 million cc:Mail users the opportunity to connect their newest cc:Mail client to a cc:Mail post office or a Lotus Notes database will only continue to improve Notes.

An additional trend is the integration of scheduling and task management features into electronic mail systems to allow greater flexibility in group collaboration. While not available at the time of this writing, demonstrations at LotusSphere 1996 already show a clean integration between Lotus Notes and the features of Lotus Organizer.

In addition, the Notes Server's support of MAPI as a mail transport protocol allows Microsoft Exchange, Microsoft Schedule+, and other MAPI based applications to use Notes as a messaging transport mechanism.

Third-Party Tools, Lotus Components, and the Notes APIs

A final factor that will influence your company's definition of Notes is the availability of a number of significant third-party tools that help integrate Notes with corporate data and existing information distribution mechanisms.

NotesPump

NotesPump, for example, allows the bi-directional exchange of information between Notes and SQL databases. This opens up the possibility of using Notes as a data warehouse or executive information system.

For example, imagine being able to tell your sales force that they can get up-to-the-minutes sales information by sending an electronic mail message to the mail address "Sales Update." When the mail message arrives at the Sales Update database, Notes uses NotesPump to query the sales tracking system and to mail a summary of the query back to the sender of the message. Or, imagine extracting a subset of the sales database to a Notes Database with multiple views that sort and display the information based on region, salesperson, product, and so on.

NotesPump also allows you to use Notes as a front end for SQL databases when real-time exchange of information isn't needed. For example, a group of travel expense forms could be entered into the accounting system as a "batch" using NotesPump after Notes' workflow and mail enabling are used to generate the forms and solicit the proper approvals.

The Lotus Fax Server

The Lotus Fax Server (LFS) integrates inbound and outbound faxing into your existing Notes network, and therefore the existing workflow. For example, if you had NotesPump and the Lotus Fax Server installed, when your SQL inventory database determines that an item needs to be re-ordered, a trigger in the SQL table could send an electronic mail message to a Notes database. That Notes database, could in turn, generate a purchase order and route it for approval. Once approval is secured, the Notes database could then send a fax to the vendor with the order!

Besides allowing faxes to be sent and received by Notes, the Lotus Fax Server also allows other Windows 95/NT/3.11 applications to send faxes using a print-to-fax driver that interfaces the application with the LFS.

LN:DI, Phone Notes, and Video Notes

Lotus Notes:Document Imaging (LN:DI) integrates a document imaging server into the Notes network, allowing documents to be retrieved on demand from within Notes.

Phone Notes integrates telephony and Notes, giving users a Notes front end for programming interactive voice response applications and creating Notes applications where information can be accessed by telephone.

Video Notes integrates video conferencing technology into Notes Documents, as well as on-screen collaboration tools. Some example applications of Video Notes might be on-demand training or company information, or real-time teleconferencing among geographically dispersed sites.

And the list goes on. In fact, we've only covered the third-party solutions that Lotus itself offers...hundreds of other tools to make Notes more effective in the enterprise are offered by thousands of Lotus' business partners.

Lotus Components

Not available at the time of this writing, but a clearly important factor in Notes application development, Lotus Components are OCX's (OLE automation enabled applications) that will allow applets to be plugged into Notes Documents. These applets will use the Rich Text capabilities of Notes as a container for spreadsheet, charting, and scheduling information. Some applets are already in Alpha testing, and by the time this book is published, will likely be available.

The Notes APIs

Finally, if there isn't a third party application or Lotus Component that integrates Notes and your data or processes, three versions of the Notes API allow you the flexibility to create one. The Notes C API, the HiTest C API, and the HiTest Tools for Visual Basic are all designed to allow developers to access the key components of a Notes Network and integrate them with outside applications, data, or processes.

We'll discuss these APIs starting in Chapter 6 of this book.

Summary

- Lotus Notes is a tool to collect, organize, and share knowledge.
- Knowledge is not the same as information, or data, in that knowledge is loosely structured and difficult to break into consistent components for storage and retrieval. Because

knowledge is loosely structured, it depends on information to organize it (similar to a card catalog at a library).

- Notes collects knowledge into databases of Documents.

- Documents are containers designed to combine information and knowledge through the use of text, number, and date fields combined with a special Notes field called a Rich Text field.

- A Rich Text field can contain formatted text, graphics, sound, video, or even other programs.

- Response Documents are a special type of Notes Document designed to be related to other Documents or Responses in the same way a Post-It note is related to the sheet of paper it is attached to.

- Once Notes collects a database of Documents, it organizes and presents its Documents to users through Navigators, Views, and Folders.

- Notes shares information by allowing Notes Clients to share the same database on a Notes Server. The Notes Clients use Navigators, Views, and Folders to locate and work with Documents.

- Notes also shares information through Replication, Mail Enabling, and Workflow.

  1. Replication allows multiple *replicas* of a database existing in a number of physical locations to synchronize their contents on command.

  2. Mail enabling allows Notes users to exchange electronic mail and Documents with each other, or with Notes databases. It also allows Notes databases to exchange mail and Documents with users or other databases.

  3. Mail Enabling, combined with Agents, creates the basis for Workflow in Notes.

- *Workflow* is defined for this book as any system that helps to move information and knowledge throughout an organization by automating or streamlining user processes or tasks.

- While Notes isn't the ideal development environment for every application a business may use to solve problems, it is uniquely suited to five distinct classes of applications:

  1. *Discussion Applications*: Applications that take advantage of Response Documents to create links between main ideas and supporting information.

  2. *Broadcast Applications*: Applications that take advantage of Rich Text and replication to ensure that timely, easy-to-read information is distributed.

  3. *Reference Applications*: Applications that take advantage of Rich Text, Views, and Notes' powerful search capabilities to make knowledge accessible.

  4. *Tracking Applications*: Applications that are generally combined with Workflow to create automatic solutions to common business problems.

  5. *Workflow/Approval*: Any combination of the first four applications that automate the flow of information or knowledge throughout an organization.

- In cases where Notes isn't the proper tool to store information, its Replication and Mail Enabling features may still make it an innovative way to collect information to be passed to another application.

- Businesses that recognize Notes' strengths can create powerful tools in Notes that improve processes, streamline information, and increase the overall level of knowledge within an organization. Using Notes as an Intranet and InterNotes to reach the Internet, those benefits can extend beyond the organization to an entire industry.

- Once Notes becomes a part of an organization, the definition of Notes will change to reflect its use as an information infrastructure.

What Notes Means to an Administrator

In Chapter 1, we looked at Notes from 10,000 feet and learned what it is and how businesses use it. In this chapter, we're going to look beneath the surface of Notes to examine how it works from an administrative perspective.

We're approaching Notes from this angle because we believe that developers armed with an understanding of Notes' administrative processes create more powerful solutions for their customers. If you're waiting for us to quote an IDC study to show why we feel that way, we're going to disappoint you. But, before you skip this chapter thinking its too arcane, too esoteric, or simply not applicable to a developer, indulge us and consider the following story.

Imagine being a skilled surgeon who can cut, suture, and repair the human body better than anyone. After a dozen years of being a highly renowned lifesaver, you decide to take a vacation. Maybe a drive across country. While you're driving through New Mexico, you notice a jeep coming up behind you at high speed with a siren flashing. It turns out that they want to get your attention. After you pull over, an Army officer climbs out of the jeep and approaches your window.

"Are you a surgeon?" he asks.

"Why, yes I am," you answer, "how did you. . . ?"

"Please come with me. We have a medical emergency," he interrupts.

You get in the jeep with the officer and ride onto an Air Force base. You're escorted to a building. When you enter it, you see what looks like an operating room. On a table in the operating room, is some sort of alien.

"We've been keeping him alive by feeding him Twinkies for the past 20 years," the officer begins, "but he just fell over about an hour ago, and our regular physician for him is. . . well . . . let's just say he's out of town. The alien says that his pilionester is damaged. According to him, it's like our appendix. He has to have it removed immediately. You're our only hope."

You're dazed, stunned, and outraged that the government has kept this a secret. You're also more than a little curious how these guys knew you were a surgeon as you drove by. But you took an oath that transcends your personal feelings. No time for questions, now. You're needed—so you get into surgical scrubs. You walk to the table, scalpel in hand.

Then, reality smacks you in the face with an aluminum skillet. How are you going to do this? You have no idea what to administer for an anesthetic. . . if you operate without one, what level of stress can the patient tolerate before you do more damage than good? Where do you make the incision? If you cut here, what's the relationship of that green thing to the yellow thing? Can you remove it? Can you bypass it?

The irony of it all: You're an expert in surgery, and yet you have to operate blindly!

Fortunately, Notes doesn't have a pilionester. But you get the idea. If you're new to Notes but an experienced API developer, you already know a lot about the job at hand. You know how to use your tools, how to develop quality software, and how to turn questions into answers. But to be your most effective, you also need to know where to begin your work, and what the actions you take on one component of Notes will mean to rest of the installation.

Which is where we hope this chapter can help by examining the following topics:

- Notes' Security Model
- Notes Clients and Notes Servers
- Mail Enabling concepts
- Replication concepts
- InterNotes concepts

The Notes Security Model

We'll begin our examination of Notes by looking at its most fundamental building blocks, identity and security. In other words, how Notes Clients and Notes Servers identify and connect with each other, and how access to databases and Documents is controlled. We'll start by examining ID Files, and then move on to Notes Server, database, Document, and field security. We'll wrap up the section by discussing what Notes' security means to an applications developer.

ID Files

Establishing Identity

As you recall from Chapter 1, computers running the Notes Client software connect to computers running Notes Server software to share databases through both network and modem connections (see Figure 2.1).

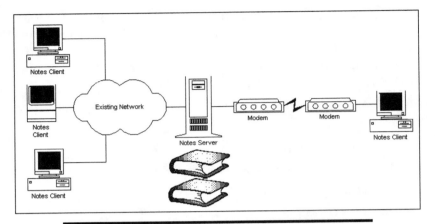

Figure 2.1 Notes Clients connecting to a Notes Server.

The identity of each Notes Client and Notes Server installation is determined through the use of an ID file. This encrypted file contains:

- A name (John Smith or Notes Server One, for example)
- One or more passwords
- A set of certificates that establish the ID file's relationship to other Notes Clients and Notes Servers in a network
- A collection of keys used for encryption and authentication
- An internal ID number used by Notes

A Notes Client or Notes Server can change its identity on a network by switching ID files. (See Figure 2.3.)

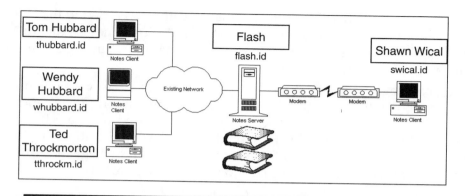

Figure 2.2 Notes ID files give each element of a Notes network its identity.

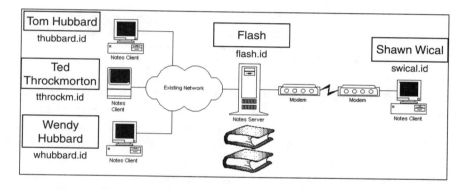

Figure 2.3 Changing ID files changes the identity of the Notes Client.

Container for Certificates

Notes Client and Notes Server ID files are generated using Notes and a binary file called a *Certifier ID*. The Certifier ID contains a certificate (a string of digits uniquely created by the installation process) which is issued in turn to each Notes Client and Server ID file it is asked to certify. There can be more than one Certifier ID in a Notes Network, meaning that there may be multiple certificates in a Notes Client's or Notes Server's ID file. A Certifier ID can also be used to generate other Certifier IDs that are related to it.

The use of Certifier IDs to create other Certifier IDs is tied to the X.400 standard of user identification. In this standard, a user may be identified by a common name, one or more organizational units, an organization, and an optional country code.

Looking at Figure 2.4, Vegas Ventures is an *Organization* Certifier, used in turn to create the Entertainment and Administration *Organizational Unit* Certifiers. The Entertainment Certifier was used to create ID files for Tom Jones and Englebert Humperdink. The Administration Certifier was used to create ID files for another employee of Vegas Ventures named Tom Jones, and also for Jack Johnson (see Figure 2.4).

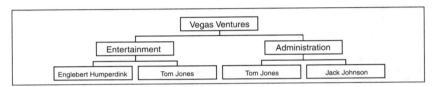

Figure 2.4 A sample X.400 identification tree.

Notes' reason for this naming convention is to reduce the occurrence of duplicate user names within a large network. You can see in Figure 2.4 that two Tom Joneses are in the Vegas Ventures organization. If both user's IDs were created using generally common names and only the Organization Certifier ID , both IDs would be Tom Jones/Vegas Ventures. This would be very confusing to a mail program, or a database that was designed to be accessed by one Tom Jones/Vegas Ventures, but not the other.

It isn't until you create the two Tom Jones IDs using the Entertainment and Administration Certifier IDs, respectively, that you arrive at Tom Jones/Entertainment/Vegas Ventures and Tom Jones/Administration/-Vegas Ventures, giving you unique user names.

Organizational units can be a double-edged sword. Too many organizational units (you can have up to five) result in extremely long user names that make addressing mail and adding users to the access lists of a database difficult. Too few organizational units (you don't have to have any) may result in duplicate user names in an organization.

Certifier IDs share their certificates with their ancestors. This means that an ID file generated by a Certifier ID automatically contains the certificates of the generating ID and its parents, as illustrated in Figure 2.5.

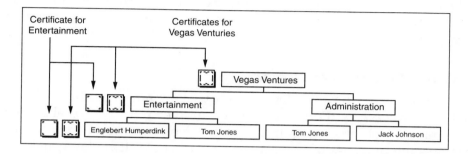

Figure 2.5 ID files contain certificates from each of its ancestors.

NOTE   Some organizations that have had Notes installed for a long time may not use hierarchically Certified IDs (meaning a series of IDs generated by an Organizational Certifier ID and Organizational Unit Certifier IDs). Instead, all Server and Client IDs are generated using a single "flat" Certifier. In "flat" organizations, only the common name of the Client and Server is shown in the ID as the user's name, and all ID's share the "flat" Certifier's certificate.

This common certificate between Notes Clients and Notes Servers is important. Unless told to do otherwise, a Notes Server will not allow any Notes Client to connect to it that isn't using an ID file with a common certificate. (Meaning the ID file of the Client or Server attempting to connect was generated using the same Certifier ID as the Notes Server's ID, or the two ID's share a common ancestor.) This is designed to prevent anyone who does not have a Certifier ID from generating a false identity to obtain access to information on a Notes Server.

Container for Keys

In addition to containing certificates that allow Notes Servers to establish a user's identity, Notes Client and Notes Server ID files also contain security and encryption keys. There are at least two security keys in every Notes ID file. One is public, and can be exported and shared with other users. The other key is private, and cannot be seen or removed from the ID file. These keys are used during the connection of a Notes Client to a Notes Server or two Notes Servers to each other to perform authentication. Additional keys stored in the ID are for private encryption.

Baseline for Software Licensing

Besides establishing the identity of a user or server within a Notes network, the Notes ID file also serves another purpose—establishing how many licenses are required within a Notes network. Each ID file requires the purchase of one license for the type of ID being generated (Notes Client or Notes Server).

Two types of Servers and three types of Clients can be generated in Notes, each with a different licensing cost. Notes Server IDs are the most expensive Notes License, followed by the license for a full Notes Client ID. Both ID types offer unrestricted access to Notes' features. Less expensive IDs can be generated for the Notes Client, exchanging some features of Notes for a lower licensing price.

An ID file that is stamped for *Notes Desktop* functionality will give the user access to any Notes database. It will not, however, allow the user to modify the design elements of a database except to create private Agents and Folders. This is often referred to as a read-only Notes Client.

An ID file that is stamped for *Lotus Notes Mail* functionality will give the user access to Notes' Mail features. It will also allow the user to open databases created using one of several predefined templates preapproved for Lotus Notes Mail users. A Lotus Notes Mail client cannot, however, open databases that do not inherit their design from one of these preapproved database templates. The Lotus Notes Mail Client is the least expensive, and the least flexible type of Notes Client.

Server Access Restrictions

Establishing a session between a Notes Client and a Notes Server requires that the Client undergo authentication by the Server. In Notes, this process is similar to one you might follow when writing a check to pay for merchandise at one of those "members only" discount stores. You present a check to the cashier, who in turn, must verify that you are the proper person to be writing the check you just presented. He asks to examine your driver's license, and looks at it to see if he trusts the issuing authority. (For example, if it is a New York driver's license, does it have the proper formatting and seals that a New York license usually has?)

Once the cashier determines that he can trust the issuing authority, he then checks the picture in the license to see if it matches the face of the person presenting the check. If the pictures match, he then verifies that the information on your license matches the information on the check you presented. Once satisfied that you are who you claim to be on the check, the cashier asks you to show your membership card. He then keys in your social security or membership number to see if there is a reason that the central computer thinks you shouldn't use a check with this store. If the computer can't think of any reason to deny you access to the store's merchandise, it tells the cashier to accept your check as legal tender and you leave with the merchandise you wanted.

Transferring this process to a Notes Clients connection to a Notes Server, the Notes Client seeks out the Notes Server on the network or through a dial-up connection. Once it reaches the server, it presents a copy of its certificates to the Notes Server for inspection. The Notes Server examines the certificates to see if there are any that it and the Client trying to connect to it have in common (that is, both IDs come from the same issuing authority).

If the Notes Server finds a common certificate, the Notes Server then sends an encrypted message to the Notes Client using its private key. If the Notes Client does share the same ancestry as the Notes Server, it will be able to use its keys to decrypt the message and return the correct answer to the Notes Server. If the Client returns this correct message, the Notes Server then checks to see if you're a member of the club allowed to access it. If found in the first list, it then checks a second list to see if a Notes Administrator has requested that the name the Notes Client is using be denied access for any reason.

If the certificate checks out, the encryption test is passed, the membership list is current, and nobody has requested that the Notes Client be denied access, the Notes Server opens a connection between the Notes Client and Server called a *session*. This allows the Notes Client to look for merchandise (in this case, database Documents) and leave with its selection.

Occasionally, a user will want to use their ID file to access a Notes Server that does not share a certificate with them. When this happens, a process known as cross-certification must be performed. In *cross certification*, both parties who want to connect (a Notes Client and Notes Server, or two Notes Servers) follow an administrative process to build a trust relationship between the Client and Server IDs. This allows an authentication to take place whenever the one party (Client or Server) attempts to access information held by the other (a Notes Server). The process differs depending on whether the Client and Server are both from hierarchical organizations, "flat" organizations, or a combination of the two.

Database Access Restrictions

Once a Notes Client and a Notes Server have established a session, the Notes Client can open databases on the Notes Server and examine Documents contained in those databases using designer-specified Forms and Views.

However, it should not be assumed that a Notes Client can open all databases on the Notes Server. The Client will only be allowed to open databases where the identity of the Client is explicitly included in the database's Access Control List (ACL).

The ACL is an element of every Notes database used to relate user identities with a set of privileges within it. These privileges include:

- The ability to add Documents without seeing the contents of the database (Depositor privilege);
- The ability to read Documents in a database but not add new ones (Reader privilege);
- The ability to read Documents as well as create new Documents and edit Documents that were previously created using the same ID file (Author privilege);
- The ability to read, create, and edit documents that have been created previously using the same ID file, as well as Documents created using other IDs (Editor privilege);
- The ability to read, create, and edit Documents, as well as the ability to add design elements to the database such as Forms, Views, Agents, Folders, and Navigators (Designer privilege);

- The ability to employ all privileges, including the ability to make changes to the Access Control List or delete the database from a server (Manager privilege).

A user can also be explicitly denied access to a database in the ACL by associating their name with the No Access privilege.

These privileges can be further refined within the ACL. For example, a user with Editor privileges may be able to create documents and edit the documents of others, but not delete documents. Another user with Editor privileges may only be allowed to edit existing documents, but not create or delete Documents.

An Access Control List in effect on a Notes Server can also be used by a Notes Client. This means that the same access restrictions a server applies to a user can be enforced by that user's Notes Client software when it is accessing a local replica of the database. This is accomplished using an optional setting (called Local Security) in the Access Control dialog.

Figure 2.6 illustrates the Access Control dialog box (started by selecting **File, Database, Access Control. . .** from the **Notes Client** menu or by right clicking a database and choosing **Access Control. . .**)

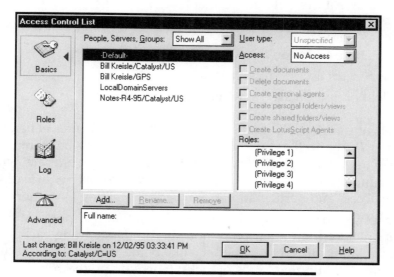

Figure 2.6 The Access Control dialog box.

View, Folder, Form, and Document Restrictions

It is possible for Documents, Forms, Folders, and Views to be hidden from, or made visible to, only specified users. This is accomplished by combining explicit names or groups of users in the ACL, called Roles, with special Field types within Notes. In addition to being able to restrict users from seeing Documents, it is also possible to restrict users from copying or printing Documents. Since many graphical operating systems provide a key that will capture the current screen to a printer or file, this shouldn't be considered a true security feature.

Field and Section Restrictions

Besides being able to restrict a user's access to a Document, it is possible to restrict access only to portions of a Document, using encryption and Access-Controlled sections.

Looking at Notes' Security Model from a Developer's Perspective

As a developer, you can draw on an extensive security feature set within Notes. These features fall into distinct levels:

1. Server access.
2. Database access on a server.
3. Document access within a database.
4. Field or Section access within a Document

All levels of security rely on the certificate stored in ID files generated by a Certifier ID, as well as any encryption keys that may be stored within the ID. The levels of security in Notes provide developers with an excellent foundation on which to build applications that require different levels of access and participation from users in creating Documents.

However, security is so extensive in Notes, that it is possible to leave inadvertent "holes" in security by not fully understanding each security feature's relationship to the other. It's like being given all the pieces you need to make a hundred kinds of locks. How you put each lock together using the pieces, and where you choose to install the locks, will determine how effective they are.

The simpler you can make the security model during the planning phase (provided you still satisfy the user's requirement), the more likely you will be to have a 'bulletproof' application from a security standpoint.

The elements available to a developer for security will usually fall within the second and third levels of access (access to the database and access to the Documents in the database). The Access Control List will be the most-used feature. The use of Roles (groups of people in the Access Control List) combined with Reader Names Fields, Author Names Fields, and Document and View Properties will be the second most-used features. The reason that these features will be most often used is that they are centrally administered. Changing a user's privileges in an Access Control List need only be done once; the change can then be replicated to other databases.

Less-often used security features available to the developer are in the third and fourth level of access—Document security, Encrypted fields, and Access-Controlled Sections. There are a couple of reasons that these levels of security might be your last choice in implementing security in Notes.

1. An organization using hierarchical naming may present a challenge to a development process that relies on Document level security. If names change constantly as users move to different departments (changing the Organizational Unit in their name), the designing of databases that rely extensively on individual names creates a maintenance issue for developers. It is also an issue for Notes administrative staff.

   Third-party administrative tools and new features in Notes, Release 4.0 make changing a name in an ACL easier. However, changing names in each Document can still be troublesome. Whenever possible, assign names in the ACL to Roles, and use the Roles in the Document security model. That way, when the name changes in the ACL, the Role reflects the correct name for the Documents, as well.

2. When using encrypted fields, you must remember that each user who will access a Document containing them must have the

proper key to decrypt the field stored in their ID file. If you have a process where application users are constantly changing, this causes administrative overhead in ensuring that keys are added and removed from a user's ID file. In addition, if a user's ID file becomes corrupted, they will lose the ability to open fields encrypted using the key you provided them. This means you must keep a backup copy of every key you create, which in itself may compromise security depending on the purpose of the application.

3. An Access-Controlled Section blocks off access to a specific portion of a Document instead of the entire Document. These sections are only a casual security measure—Lotus does not call them a security feature at all, in fact. A number of workarounds exist for skilled users to defeat them.

Notes Clients and Notes Servers

In this section, we'll examine the Notes Client and Notes Server software, highlighting what files are critical to their operation, and discussing how a developer can use them.

The Notes Client

The Notes Client software can be installed on a local hard drive to be used by a single user, or on a file server to be shared by multiple users. When the software is shared from a file server, a subset of files that allow each user to have a unique configuration is moved to the user's local hard drive.

Versions of the Notes 4 Client for 16 and 32 bit Windows, 32 bit OS/2, the Mac OS, and some flavors of UNIX are available.

As you would expect with any platform version of the Notes Client, a number of executable and dynamic-link library files are a part of the installation. Besides these standard file types, the Notes also relies on the following files to remember user preferences and configuration information:

NOTES.INI

One of the primary uses for the **NOTES.INI** file is to point the Notes program to the Notes Data Directory. The Notes Data Directory is a relative path used by the Notes Client as its root. It is where the program will look for additional Notes databases (.NSF files) that control configuration, and is the default location it will provide to users when they select File, Database, Open from the Notes Client menu.

Another setting in the **NOTES.INI** file governs what types of connections the Notes Client will use to reach Notes Servers (SPX, TCP/IP, NetBEUI, COM1, COM2, etc). These connection types are referred to by the Notes as **Ports**.

The **NOTES.INI** file also contains the location of the currently active ID file. As you read earlier, this ID file establishes the Client's Identity within a Notes Network. In addition, the ID file also tells the Notes Client what functionality should be made available to the current user.

Additional settings in the **NOTES.INI** file are controlled from the User Preferences dialog box in the Notes Client (made active by selecting File, Tools, User Preferences... from the Notes Client menu—see Figure 2.7).

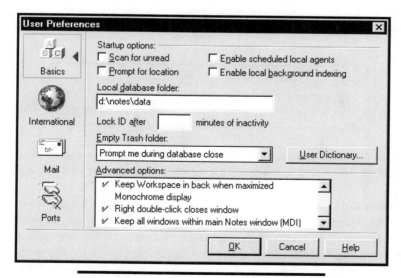

Figure 2.7 The User Preferences dialog box.

NOTE

On the Mac OS, the Notes Preferences file serves the same purpose as the NOTES.INI file on Windows/NT/95 and OS/2.

NAMES.NSF

This file is a Notes database that the Notes Client uses to refer to Person, Group, Server Connection, and Location Documents. The Location and Server Connection Documents allow the Notes Client to establish connections with Notes Servers by providing information about the Server's Names, what ports to use to connect, and what schedule to follow in making connections (see Figure 2.8 and 2.9).

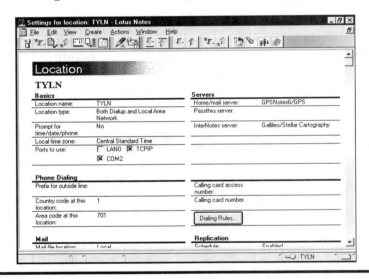

Figure 2.8 A Location Document in NAMES.NSF on the Notes Client.

The Person and Group Documents are for the Notes Client's use when creating mail messages or enforcing access control. A user who regularly communicates with electronic mail users whose names are not stored in the company's shared Name and Address book can store those names in their local **NAMES.NSF** file to prevent retyping the entire address each time they wish to send a message (see Figures 2.10 and 2.11).

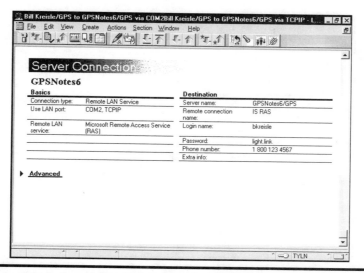

Figure 2.9 A Connection Document in NAMES.NSF on the Notes Client.

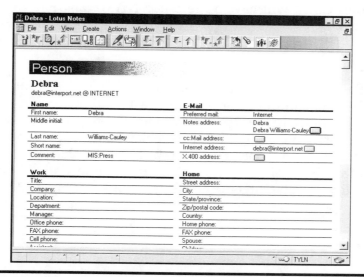

Figure 2.10 A Person Document in the **NAMES.NSF** file on the Notes Client.

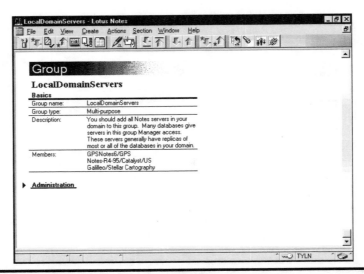

Figure 2.11 A Group Document in the **NAMES.NSF** file on the Notes Client.

Every Notes Client will have a file called **NAMES.NSF** in their Notes Data Directory.

LOG.NSF

LOG.NSF is used by the Notes Client to track events that occur while the Notes Client is running. For example, a Location Document in the **NAMES.NSF** file may specify that the Notes Client should call a specific server and perform a replication. This replication event will be noted in the LOG.NSF file using one or more of the Log's Pre-Defined Documents (Event, Mail Event, Replication, Activity, Phone Call, Phone Call-Incoming, Phone Call-Outgoing, Session, or Size—see Figure 2.12).

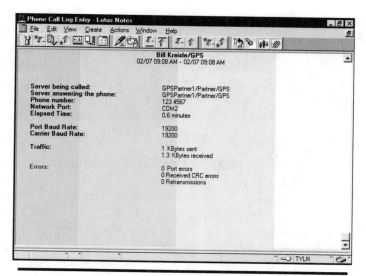

Figure 2.12 A Phone Call Document in the **LOG.NSF** file.

MAIL.BOX

The **MAIL.BOX** file is a Notes database that is used to hold mail messages for Notes Clients while they are working remotely (Mobile Notes). When a Notes Client connects to a Notes Server after working remotely, the contents of the Notes Client's **MAIL.BOX** can be transferred to the Notes Server's **MAIL.BOX** file for processing and delivery.

The Notes Server

The Notes Server software must be installed on the local drive of the machine that will function as the Server. Besides the Notes Server software, a copy of the Notes Client software must also be installed on platforms that support a graphical interface for administration purposes.

Platforms such as Novell NetWare that do not support graphical interfaces at the Server must have a copy of the Notes Client installed on a workstation. The workstation is used to connect to the file server and map the directory containing the Server software as a local drive.

The Notes Server uses the same shared file types as the Notes Client for configuration/operation—**NOTES.INI**, **NAMES.NSF**, **LOG.NSF** and **MAIL.BOX**. However, subtle differences exist between how the Notes Server and Notes Client will use these files. Other files that a Notes Server may use are **MAILOBJ.NSF**, **STATREP.NSF**, and **CERTLOG.NSF**.

NOTES.INI

As with the Notes Client's **NOTES.INI** file, this file contains information about where the Notes Data Directory is located. It also contains entries that specify what types of connections should be used to reach other Notes Servers (SPX, TCP/IP, NetBEUI, COM1, COM2, etc). The NOTES.INI file also contains the location of the currently active ID file for the Server and the Notes Client software that is installed to control the Server. These two applications share the same **NOTES.INI** file.

In addition the **NOTES.INI** file on the server is where Notes third-party tools can be registered to load automatically. Also, processes such as database compaction, view updates, index updates, and database design refreshing can be scheduled to occur.

NAMES.NSF

As with the Notes Client, the **NAMES.NSF** database on a Notes Server contains Person, Group, Server, Location, and Connection Documents. Some of the Documents have additional fields for the server's use (for example, a copy of a user's public key can be stored in the Person Document on a Notes Server). Additional Documents in the **NAMES.NSF** file control event monitoring and reporting (see Figure 2.13).

The People and Group Documents are for the Notes Server's use when creating and routing mail messages, and for enforcing access control.

Every Notes Server will have a file called **NAMES.NSF** in their Notes Data Directory. The difference between a Notes Server and a Notes Client, however, is that some servers may contain exact replicas of the **NAMES.NSF** on another Notes Server. Servers that share a common Name and Address Book are defined in Notes as sharing the same Domain. A Domain is an identity for collection of Notes Servers, used for mail routing. The reason Notes Servers in the same Domain share the same Name and Address book are: to allow common connection settings within the Domain; and to ensure that each Server knows the names of all Notes Clients and Servers in the Domain.

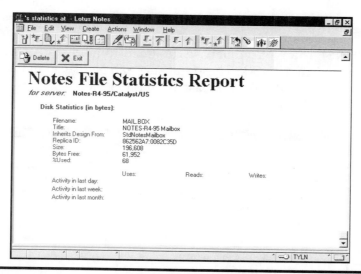

Figure 2.13 A Person Document in the **NAMES.NSF** file of a Notes Server.

LOG.NSF

LOG.NSF is used by the Notes Server to track events that occur while the Notes Server is running. Phone connections, replications, users accessing the server, and scheduled events are all tracked by a Notes Server, as well as database size and usage statistics and server statistics.

MAIL.BOX and MAILOBJ.NSF

The **MAIL.BOX** file is a Notes database file that is used by Notes Servers to relay and deliver mail messages. **MAILOBJ.NSF** is used by the Notes Mail system to centralize large attachments that are sent to multiple users.

CERTLOG.NSF

CERTLOG.NSF is used by Notes Servers to track ID files created by Certified IDs. This is a useful centralized reference database for determining how many licenses of Notes are required in a Notes network.

STATREP.NSF

STATREP.NSF is a Notes database designed to hold statistics about the Notes Servers in a network. These statistics can be placed in the database directly, or mailed into the database from other Notes Servers. This is an optional feature of Notes (see Figure 2.14).

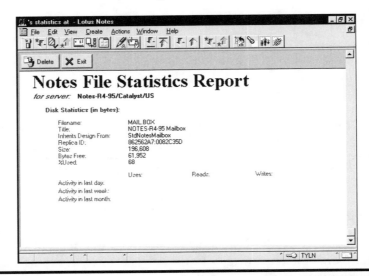

Figure 2.14 A Statistics Reporting Document from the **STATREP.NSF** database.

Notes Servers and Notes Clients from a Developer's Perspective

NOTES.INI

There are functions in the Notes Development language that allow users to write information to the **NOTES.INI** file. It is usually intended that these variables be written to the Notes Client's INI file for later reference. It is possible—under some circumstances, however—to have a Notes Server write values to the Server's **NOTES.INI** file. This may cause unexpected results the next time the Agent is run, or when a Notes Client tries to run the Agent, so be sure to test Scripts and Formulas that use .INI file settings thoroughly.

If you plan to write an add-in task for Notes, or a third-party application, the INI file is a rich source of information about how Notes is installed on the user's computer. Details about the settings in the **NOTES.INI** file are available in the Lotus Notes Knowledgebase and the Server Administration Guide.

NAMES.NSF

When creating third-party applications or applications that need to refer to the names of every user within a domain, the Server's Name and Address book provides a centralized resource. Groups created in the Server's Name and Address book may also be used in Access Control Lists. In addition, the Server's Name and Address book may be replicated to a Notes Client using a new filename and cascaded with the **NAMES.NSF** using the Location Document in the Notes Client's **NAMES.NSF** file.

Since the Server's Name and Address book is a critical feature of a running Notes network, caution should be exercised in writing information directly to the Name and Address book from third-party applications. Since the Name and Address book replicates throughout an organization, a corrupt Document or design element could shut down the entire network!

WARNING

The Name and Address book is always open whenever a Notes Server is running. As such, it is possible that it isn't being backed up on a regular basis. Always use caution when developing applications that interface directly with the Notes Name and Address book. Be sure there is a backup copy of **NAMES.NSF** that is recent and available to restore from before you begin.

LOG.NSF

New functions in Notes, Release 4.0, and the addition of LotusScript make is possible to generate log entries when tasks are performed in applications you develop. If you are building a workflow application, or an application that requires tracking, **LOG.NSF** might suit your needs.

However, since **LOG.NSF** is open and in use whenever the Notes Client or Notes Server is in use, don't overload the file with erroneous entries. You could slow the performance of Notes as it runs through its regular administrative functions.

Mail Enabling Concepts

Now that we know what makes up a Notes network, it's time to begin looking at how Notes Clients and Notes Servers transfer information. As you read earlier, we know Notes shares data using file sharing, mail enabling, and replication. File sharing concepts were included in earlier sections; next on the list is mail-enabling, or how Notes allows person-to-person, database-to-database, and database-to-person (or vice-versa) Document transfer.

Person-to-Person-Document Transfer via Mail Enabling

Lotus Notes Mail

In this section, we're going to examine how mail enabling works in Lotus Notes by looking at it in networked and remote settings. We'll begin by examining the user electronic mail system, Lotus Notes Mail. Lotus Notes Mail operates in Notes by combining server Client and Server elements such as:

- A network of Notes Clients and Servers.
- Notes databases that share a common design (Lotus Notes Mail).
- A Document in these common databases with the fields necessary for Notes to deliver it as a Mail Message.
- The **NAMES.NSF** file on the Notes Client and/or the Notes Server.
- The **MAIL.BOX** file on the Notes Client and/or the Notes Server.

Since all databases are inherently mail-enabled in Notes, Mail databases are simply Notes databases that are designed to collect messages. What makes a mail database different from other databases is that it is associated with a personal record in the Notes Name and Address Book (**NAMES.NSF** file) on one or more servers. This makes each database listed in the Name and Address Book in a Person record a Document repository for a specific user.

The **MAIL.BOX** file, as we discussed earlier, is a "holding cell" for Notes Documents. It may be on the Notes Client's hard drive and on a Notes Server, depending on whether or not the Client uses a dedicated or on-demand network connection.

To help understand how these components work together, we're going to trace the life of a Notes Mail message as it is being sent from one Notes Client on the Network to another. The players involved in this narration will be Tom, Wendy (Notes Clients), and Flash (a Notes Server) (see Figure 2.15).

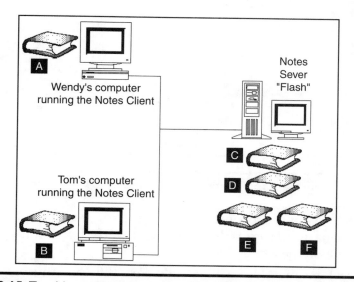

Figure 2.15 Two Notes Clients and a Notes Server. The Notes Clients are using Server -Based Mail.

Since both Tom and Wendy have a dedicated connection to the Notes Server, they will be using what is referred to as *server-based mail*. Server-based mail is mail that is automatically routed to a Notes Server the moment it is sent.

Using Figure 2.15 as our reference, let's examine the steps Tom takes to send a message to Wendy, and the steps Notes Clients and Notes Servers take to deliver the message.

1. The first step Tom needs to take to send a message to Wendy is tocreate a new Document in his Lotus Notes Mail database (E) (see Figure 2.16). This Document has a number of fields associated with it. The two most important fields (the ones required by Notes to send a Document as a message) are the From field and the SendTo field. A number of optional fields, make the message more useful.

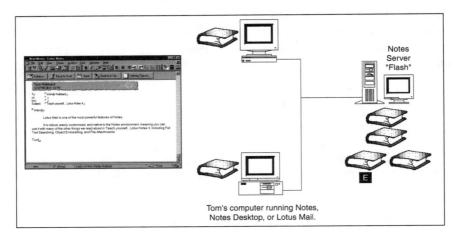

Figure 2.16 Creating a new Lotus Notes Mail memo.

2. Once the new Document is created, addressed, and filled with information, Tom will send it to Wendy by clicking the **Send** button on the Action Bar.

3. A task on the Notes Client called MAILER is activated when the Send button is clicked. MAILER checks the **SendTo** field (a field designed to allow the user to specify an address) on the Document. It looks through the Notes Client's Personal Name and Address Book (B) to see if there is anything special about the addresses the SendTo field contains (Wendy). Special actions MAILER on a name in the SendTo field might include:

Converting the Name to a forwarding address listed in a Person Record for Wendy;

Translating the Name to the proper delivery syntax to transmit the Document to a Notes Server in another network

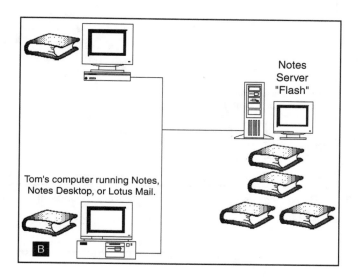

Figure 2.17 Checking the Personal Name and Address Book for Wendy's address.

4. There is no entry for Wendy in Tom's local Name and Address book. The Notes Client converts the names in all of the addressee (SendTo and, optionally, CopyTo and BlindCopyTo) fields into a Recipients field (a field used internally by Notes to contain fully qualified mail addresses). It then contacts Tom's home server, Flash, over the network. Once a session between Tom's Client and Flash is established, the Client deposits Tom's message in Flash's MAIL.BOX file (C).

5. The Notes Server Flash has a task running called ROUTER that checks the MAIL.BOX (C) and discovers the new message. The Recipients field says is addressed to Wendy. Flash looks up the address for Wendy by checking the Server's **NAMES.NSF** file (D) to see if there is a Person Document for her. Flash finds the entry, and it says that Wendy's mail file is located on the Notes Server, Flash (F).

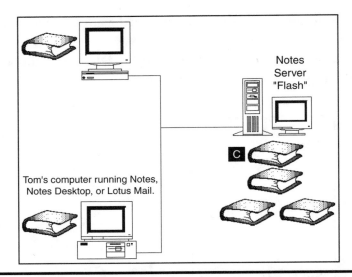

Figure 2.18 Delivering the message to the temporary mailbox file on the Notes Server,"Flash".

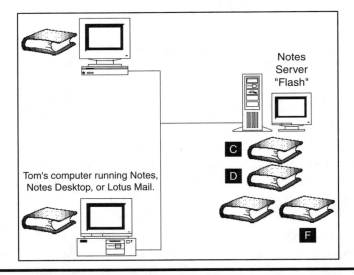

Figure 2.19 The Notes Server, Flash, looks up Wendy's address to find out what it should do next.

6. Flash deposits Tom's message into Wendy's mail file (F). The next time Wendy opens her mail file using her Notes Client, she will see Tom's message.

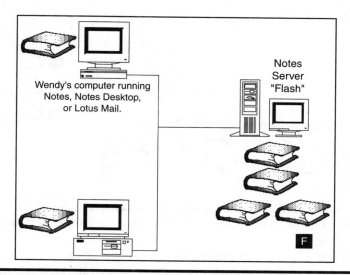

Figure 2.20 When Wendy opens her Lotus Notes Mail database, she will see the new message.

What happens if there is more than one Notes Server in your network? The same principle is followed. If the addressee has a mail database on another Notes Server, the Server processing the message contacts the next Server and deposits a copy of the message in its temporary mailbox file. That Server in turn looks up the address and processes it, based on whether or not it contains the addressees mail file or that file is on another Notes Server.

Mobile Lotus Notes Mail

In cases where a user has an on-demand (modem) connection to the Notes network, mail is routed a little differently. Let's add another user, Ted, to the network we created in Figure 2.15, and make Ted a Mobile Notes user who connects to the Notes Server Flash using a modem. Figure 2.21 illustrates our new addition:

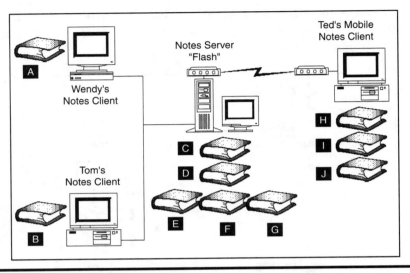

Figure 2.21 The Network in Figure 2.16 with the addition of a remote user.

Using Figure 2.21 as our reference, we're going to trace mail in two directions this time—from Wendy to Ted and from Ted to Tom. Before we start tracing steps however, let's compare Figure 2.15 and 2.21 to see what's been added. The modems and a PC for the new Notes Client are obvious enough. But why do you suppose Ted's machine has more databases locally than Tom or Wendy's (H, I, J), and one more database is added to Flash's drive (G)?

The answer is that Ted's connection to the network is intermittent. He doesn't stay connected constantly; he only dials in when he needs to exchange information or he wants to check for new mail. That means that in addition to his Personal Name and Address Book (I), he needs to duplicate the resources that the Notes Server has to work off-line. These resources include a **MAIL.BOX** file (H), and a Replica of the Server's mail database for Ted on his local hard drive (J).

So what's the file that was added to the Notes Server, Flash (G)? It is a replica of Ted's Lotus Notes Mail database. Why does he need to have two mail files?

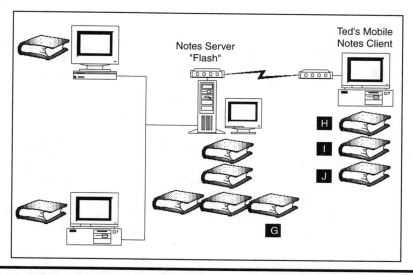

Figure 2.22 The additional files needed to add a Mobile Lotus Notes Mail user.

The answer is related to the fact that Ted is only occasionally connected to the Notes network while Tom, Wendy, and other Notes Clients are connected constantly. When a mail message is sent by Tom or Wendy to Ted, Notes Server Flash's ROUTER task doesn't want to have to wait for Ted to call in to clear the message out of its MAIL.BOX file—it wants to put it away and get busy looking for the next incoming message. To do this, Flash uses a replica of Ted's Lotus Notes Mail file to deposit messages whenever one is addressed to Ted.

How these new files affect mail routing is displayed as we trace the steps for Wendy to send a message to Ted, and then for Ted to send a message to Tom.

1. Wendy composes, addresses, and then mails her message to Ted.

2. Wendy's Notes Client's MAILER task checks its Personal Name & Address Book (A) for an entry for Ted. It doesn't find one, so it creates a Recipients field using the addresses Wendy provided and delivers the Document to Wendy's mail server, Flash. (It places the message in Flash's MAIL.BOX file (C).)

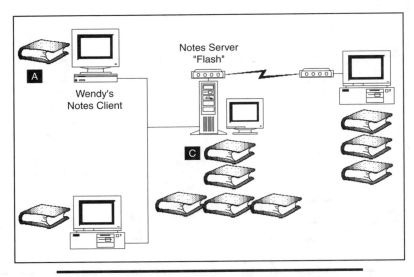

Figure 2.23 Wendy's message to Ted begins its journey.

3. Flash checks the **MAIL.BOX** file, and finds a message addressed to Ted. After searching through the Server's Name & Address Book (D), Flash discovers that it has a replica of Ted's mail file (G).

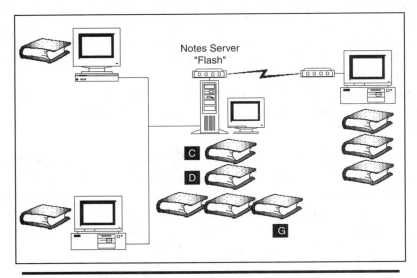

Figure 2.24 Flash looks for Ted's address to decide what to do next.

4. Flash deposits the message into Ted's mail file (G).

5. Ted establishes a connection with Flash by modem. Once connected, Ted initiates a replication event between his local mail database (J) and his mail database on Flash. Ted's Notes Client pulls the message that Flash delivered.

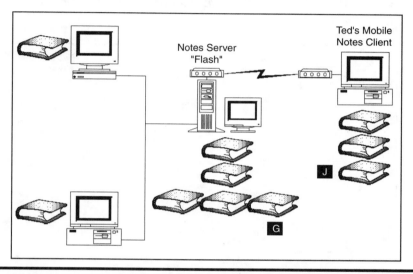

Notes Server "Flash"

Ted's Mobile Notes Client

J

G

Figure 2.25 Ted connects to Flash and replicates his Lotus Notes Mail database.

6. Ted disconnects his Notes Client from Flash, and reads his mail.

7. As Ted reads Wendy's message, it makes him think of a question he wants to ask Tom. So Ted composes a message for Tom using his local replica of his mail database and sends it.

8. The MAILER task on Ted's Notes Client checks Ted's currently active location record, and determines that Ted is set up for Workstation based mail. It then checks Ted's Personal Name & Address Book (I) for to see if it has an address for Tom. There's no information about Tom in Ted's Personal Name & Address Book. So, the Notes Client converts the addressee into a Recipients field that is added to the Documents as it is deposited in Ted's local **MAIL.BOX** file (H).

9. A few minutes later, Ted finishes answering his mail, and he calls the Server Flash again. He initiates a replication between Flash and his Notes Client, and this time, he also transfers outgoing mail using the Replicator Page. The message to Tom, along with any other messages Ted composed or replied to, are moved from the **MAIL.BOX** file on Ted's Notes Client to the MAIL.BOX file on the Notes Server, Flash (C).

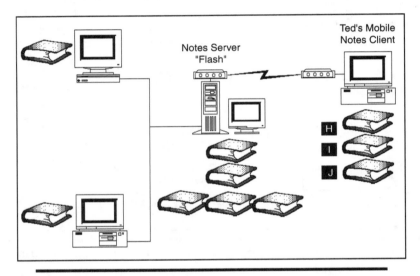

Figure 2.26 Ted's Notes Client prepares a message for delivery.

10. The Notes Server Flash's ROUTER task checks the **MAIL.BOX** file (C), and discovers a message addressed to Tom. Flash checks the Server's Name and Address Book and determines that Tom has a mail file on Flash (E), so it deposits the mail message in Tom's mail database.

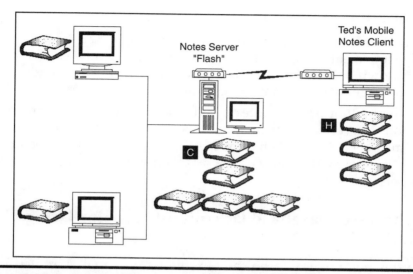

Figure 2.27 Ted's Notes Client uses the modem connection to move mail from its temporary mailbox file to Flash's temporary mailbox file.

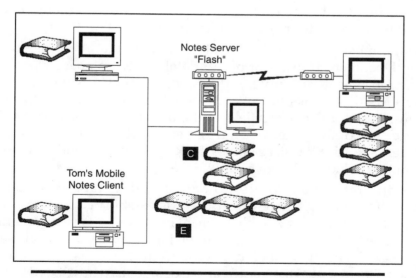

Figure 2.28 Flash delivers Ted's message to Tom's mail database.

Whew!

As you can see, how Notes delivers mail isn't rocket science, but it isn't exactly simple either. Of course, if you were to break any electronic mail system down and follow a message from one point to another, you'd find it was a little more complex than you would have guessed.

But the bottom line is, Notes delivers mail based on two modes of operation—server-based mail and workstation based mail. Workstation-based mail clients have their own MAIL.BOX file, and they maintain a replica of their mail database to work with while not connected to a Notes Server.

Database-to-Database Document Transfer Using Mail Enabling

Up to this point, we've technically examined how mail is routed from point A to point B in a Notes Network using Lotus Notes Mail as an example. However, as we implied in earlier sections, mail enabling in Notes is not limited to person-to-person communication. Databases can send Documents to each other via Agents or user-triggered events without using the Lotus Notes Mail database.

For the most part, the same underpinnings that allow person-to-person Document transfer apply to database-to-database Document transfer. Documents are created, addressed, and sent. A Notes Client's or Server's MAILER looks for a SendTo field, examines the addresses it contains, creates a Recipients field, and moves the Document to a Client or Server **MAIL.BOX** file. When a Server **MAIL.BOX** file receives the message, its ROUTER task examines the Recipients field and processes is according to values in the **NAMES.NSF** file.

One difference that applies to database-to-database Document transfer, however is where the address is established and resolved. Instead of being associated with a person by way of a Person Document in the Name and Address book, the receiving database in a Database-to-Database transfer is associated with an address, using a Mail-In Database Document. This allows any Documents whose SendTo field contains a specific string (such as "Problem Reports Database" or "Product Suggestions") can be mailed to a database associated with the listed address.

Another difference that emerges when using Database-to-Database Document transfer is the fields that are involved. A Notes database typically stores one copy of a Form and uses that copy to present all Documents that are created using it. Figure 2.30 illustrates this concept.

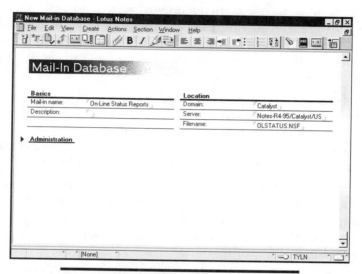

Figure 2.29 A Mail-In Database Document

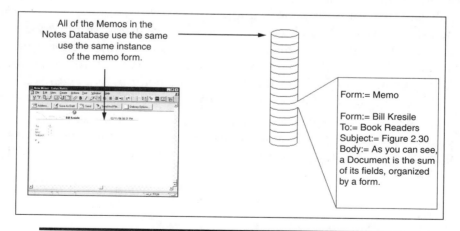

Figure 2.30 Multiple Documents will use a single instance of a Form.

Since all the Lotus Notes Mail Databases in a Notes network share the same original design, they also share a common Memo Form. This makes transferring a Document from one Lotus Notes Mail database to another very easy.

In database-to-database transfer however, it is possible that the two databases that are transferring Documents don't share a common Form, or share a Form with the same name but different fields. To gain a better understanding of this process, let's follow a Document from one database to another in a workflow environment.

In this example, we will be using two databases—the first database will be a technical support database that is used by telephone support personnel to log calls. The second database will be a question-and-answer database that is used by the telephone support staff as a reference when handling calls. Both databases will have a Form called Incident.

The call-tracking database's Incident Form has several fields on it. Some of the fields will be for the customer's name, address, telephone number, support contract number, and so on. Two of the fields we want to remember in particular are fields called Problem Description and Problem Resolution.

The reference database's Incident Form also has several fields on it. However, since the database is primarily focused on Problems and Solutions, they are not necessarily the same fields in the call tracking database's Incident form. For example, instead of knowing the customer who called in with the problem, it would be more useful simply to know who logged the Incident internally, and the date and time the Document was added to the database. Of course, the two fields Problem Description and Problem Resolution would be helpful, too. Figures 2.31a and 2.31b illustrate our two Incident Forms.

For our example, we'll assume that the call-tracking and reference databases are both on the same Notes Server, Flash. Tom and Wendy's Notes Clients will also be on hand to help us again, as illustrated in figure 2.32.

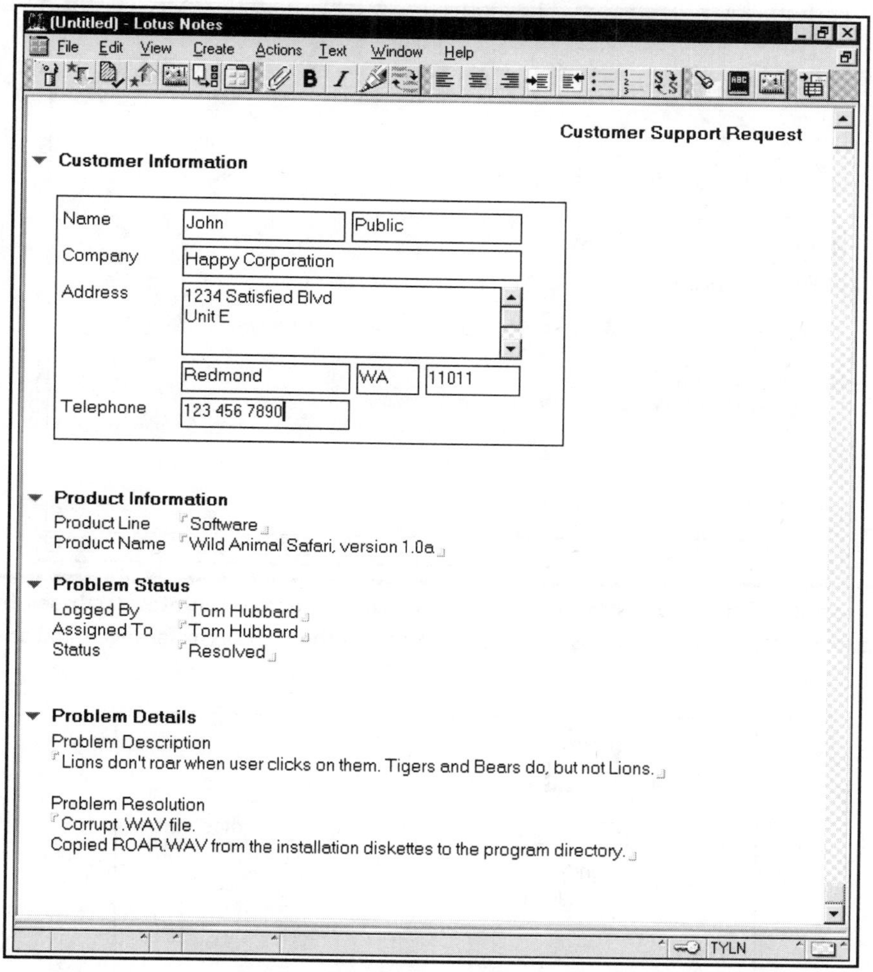

Figure 2.31a Two Forms can share the same name in different Notes databases, but contain different fields. This is the Incident Form in the call tracking database.

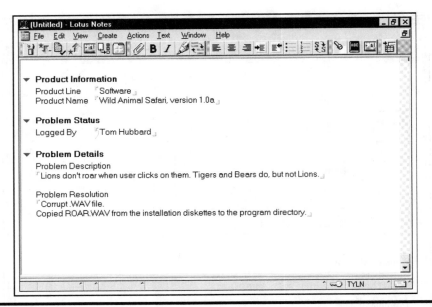

Figure 2.31b Two Forms can share the same name in different Notes databases, but contain different fields. This is the Incident Form in the support-reference database.

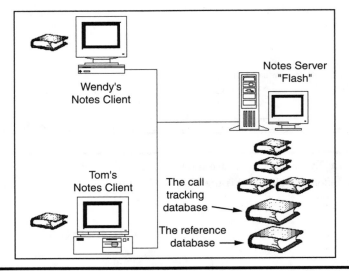

Figure 2.32 Setting the stage for a database-to-database Document transfer.

Now that we have the basics—we need to add a little more background and a process to finish out the section.

Imagine that Tom works in product support, and that Wendy is his supervisor. Tom receives a call about a problem with the Wild Animal Safari software that his company manufactures. He creates an Incident Form in the contact-tracking database to record the call. After he fills in the customer's name and support information, he enters the customer's problem in the Problem Description field of the Incident Form. It's a problem that Tom hasn't seen before, so Tom checks the reference database to see if there are any problems already recorded that are similar to the customer's problem.

He doesn't find an existing Document that will help him. So, after a few minutes of troubleshooting, Tom locates and fixes the problem for the customer. He enters what he did to solve the problem in the Problem Resolution field of Incident Form.

Some time later, Wendy opens the call-tracking database to a View that is designed to display newly created Incident Forms. She finds Tom's Document, reviews the problem and solution, and decides that it may be a problem that other support people will encounter. She launches an Agent labeled "Submit to Reference Database" that mails the Document to the reference database.

Here's the code for the Agent:

```
FIELD SendTo := "Product Support Reference Database";
@MailSend;
```

That code is all it takes to Mail Enable the application. What it does translates as follows:

A **SendTo** field—which, as we discussed earlier, is a required field for mailing Documents using Notes—is created for this Document and filled with an address. The address in this case is the address of the reference database as detailed in the Mail In Database Document in Notes Server Flash's Public Name and Address Book. The **@MailSend** function is called to trigger the MAILER task on the Notes Client.

The MAILER task converts the SendTo field into a Recipients field. It then deposits the Document in the Notes Client's **MAIL.BOX** file if the user is remote, or the Notes Server's **MAIL.BOX** file if the user is networked.

ROUTER examines the **Recipients** field, and, just as it did for person to person mail transfer, it looks up the location of the database where it should deposit the Document. If the database is on the Server where the ROUTER task is running, it deposits the Document. If the database is on another Server in the network, ROUTER locates the other Server or a route to it, and passes the Document to another Server's **MAIL.BOX** for processing.

The Document, once delivered to the reference database, is then viewed using the reference database's version of the Incident Form. To be more specific, we're going to oversimplify for a moment. For the purpose of our illustration, think of the Notes Document that was just transmitted in our example as having a format similar to the following while it was in transit:

```
Form: "Incident Form"
SendTo: "Product Support Reference Database"
CustFirstName: "John"
CustLastName: "Public"
CustCompany: "Happy Company"
CustAddress: "1234 Satisfaction Avenue, Unit E"
CustCity: "Redmond"
CustState: "WA"
CustZip: "12345"
CustTele: "123 456 7890"
ProductLine: "Software"
ProcuctName: "Wild Animal Safari, version 1.0a"
LoggedBy: "Tom Hubbard"
AssignedTo: "Tom Hubbard"
Status: "Resolved"
ProblemDescription: "Lions don't roar when you click on them. Bears
and tigers do, but Lions don't."
ProblemResolution: "Corrupt .WAV File. Copied ROAR.WAV from the
install disk to solve problem."
```

Basically, the field names and their contents are being transmitted. Notice, however, that nothing is being transmitted that indicates where the fields should be on a Form, or what labels should be next to the fields. What Notes relies on in this case is the value stored in the Form field of the Document. In our sample Document's case, the value is "Incident Form."

When this Document is inserted in the reference database, Notes will try to display it using a Form by that name. Since the reference database contains a form by that name, everything is great. If the reference database didn't have a form by that name, however, Notes would try to display it using the database's default Form, or display an error.

As we found earlier, the Incident Form in the reference database doesn't contain as many fields as the Incident Form in the call tracking database. Does that mean that the fields that aren't in the reference database's Incident will be deleted when a Document sent from the call tracking database arrives? No. The fields will still be in the Document, but they won't appear on the Form since they aren't a part of it. In fact a savvy Notes user could examine the fields by selecting the Document in a view, and opening the Properties for Document dialog.

Since the fields aren't needed, however, a special type of agent in a Notes database called a Mail/Paste Agent could be used to delete the unnecessary fields using the following code:

```
FIELD CustFirstName := @DeleteField;

FIELD CustLastName := @DeleteField;

FIELD CustCompany := @DeleteField;

FIELD CustAddress := @DeleteField;

FIELD CustCity := @DeleteField;

FIELD CustState := @DeleteField;

FIELD CustZip := @DeleteField;

FIELD CustTele := @DeleteField;
```

Mail/Paste Agents can also be used to alter the value of Fields as they are mailed into a database, or to change the type of form that should be used to display a Document by changing the value of the Form field.

Person-to-Database (or vice versa) Document Transfer Using Mail Enabling

Of course, it isn't difficult to imagine that if Notes can be used to transfer Documents from person to person and from database to database, that it can also be used to transfer Documents from person to database (and vice versa). Technically, there is nothing new to add to the process of this transfer—he same elements that were used in our previous examples are required.

However, database-to-person Document transfer is a good logical point to talk about another option of mail enabling in Notes called Forms Routing. In our previous examples, the Document being transferred between mail and other databases depended on the receiving database to have a copy of the Form it needed to display it.

When you begin to build solutions in Notes designed to use mail enabling, however, it becomes apparent that this could be a serious limitation to the types of applications you could design. Say, for example, you decide to use Notes to automate common paper processes in a business. How practical would it be to require a mail database to have a copy of every form a company might use?

When you changed the design on a Form in one database to include a new field, how would you get that design change transferred to all of the other databases that have a copy of that Form?

Notes solves this problem by allowing Documents to store a copy of the Form used to create them as a series of fields in the Document. This makes the Document "portable" in that it can be opened by any Notes database and displayed using the correct Form.

When a Form is stored in a document, its name is stored in an internal field called $Title. Additional information is stored in the $Info, $WindowTitle, and $Body fields. If you later want to remove the form's association with a document, you can create an agent that removes the stored form information and designates another form to display the document.

If you wish to remove a stored Form from a Document, you can use an Agent with code similar to the following snippet to do so:

```
FIELD $Title := @DeleteField;
FIELD $Info := @DeleteField;
FIELD $WindowTitle := @DeleteField;
FIELD $Body := @DeleteField;
FIELD Form := "Memo"
```

This removes the stored form and adds a **Form** field to the Document.

Mail Enabling from a Developer's Perspective

As you can see, Mail Enabling opens up a powerful range of applications for use in Notes. The idea of creating Documents that can be routed seamlessly between people and databases is a rich one, allowing you a great deal of flexibility in automating processes. Besides, since Notes Mail is just as effective for Mobile users as it is for networked ones, solutions can be deployed remotely.

Some of the key things to understand when developing Mail Enabled applications have been covered in the preceding sections:

- Mail Enabling is accomplished using the MAILER and ROUTER task on Notes Clients and Notes Servers in conjunction with the **NAMES.NSF** file and the **MAIL.BOX** file. In essence, Mail Enabling in Notes is the automatic transfer of a Document from one database to another.

- Documents are transferred as a collection of fields and values. They generally depend on a Form stored in the receiving database when displayed.

- The Form field on a Document allows you to have different Forms using the same name in different databases depending on your process requirements.

- Forms can be stored as a series of fields with the Document to allow them to be opened by any Notes database, even if it doesn't contain the form originally used to create it.

- Agents can automatically act on a Document the moment it is mailed or pasted into a database.

Some other things worth mentioning about Mail Enabling:

- Additional Agents can be run on databases or Documents to trigger automatic mailings dependent on circumstance. For example, a database could automatically notify a person whenever a new document is added to it, or whenever the value of a specific Document is changed.

- These Agents will use the **@MailSend** or **@Command([MailSend])** function in the Notes function language, or the Send method in LotusScript.
- When creating third-party applications that want to use Notes as a mail mechanism, it is possible to deposit Documents directly into the **MAIL.BOX** file of a Notes Client or Notes Server. This provides that a Recipients field is a part of the Document and the Recipients field contains a valid address for a person or database in it.

Replication

In this section, we're going to cover another cornerstone in the foundation of Notes--Replication. We'll begin our discussion by defining Replication and discussing what it means to an organization. Next, we'll discuss some important Replication concepts and what the process of Replication means in general both to a Notes Administrator and a Notes Applications Developer.

What Is Replication?

Replication is a process that moves changed Documents (meaning a Document that has been added, deleted, or edited) bi-directionally between two databases. It does this by first comparing Documents based on a unique ID assigned to each Document and a time and date stamp, and then merging the most recent actions into each copy.

What Does Replication Mean to Lotus Notes?

Replication allows information to be distributed across an enterprise without regard for geographical or time boundaries. Information can be updated in a Notes database at 3:00 AM in California and replicated to the home office minutes or days later. Regardless of the time of the Replication, the changes will be reviews and added to the database.

Since Replication is a process that moves only changed information, Replication is also a process that allows Notes Clients and Notes Servers to connect intermittently for short periods of time using modems or the Internet. This allows a single Notes Server to be used by many remote employees.

Important Replication Concepts

To better understand Replication and its implications to an organization, we first need to examine a few underlying Replication concepts.

Replication IDs

One of the first things to understand about Replication is that it cannot be performed arbitrarily between Notes databases. It can only occur between databases that share the same Replication ID.

The reason for this is simple—what would happen if a user tried to initiate a replication between his mail database and another database containing completely different information (say, a database of recipes)? Documents would be added to the recipe database that required a Memo Form to display properly, while other Documents would be added to the mail database that needed a Recipe Form. Chocolate chip cookies would be mixed in with directives forbidding wearing chicken suits during office hours. In other words, a real mess would occur.

By definition, a Replication ID is a very long number that is randomly generated whenever a new Notes database is created by a designer. The number is a part of the database that cannot be removed or changed. Whenever a new Replica of a database is created, the Replication ID generated for the first database is stamped on the new Replica, as well.

This unique stamping mechanism, combined with the fact that Notes will *not* allow replication to occur between databases that do not share the same Replica ID, prevents accidents like the ones we described above from happening.

To see a Notes database's Replica ID, select it on the Workspace and choose, **File**, **Database**, **Properties...** from the Notes Client menu. You can also right-click on the database's icon on the Workspace and choose **Properties...** from the pop-up menu that appears. Once the Properties for Database dialog box is opened, click the Information tab (the tab with the lowercase i on it).

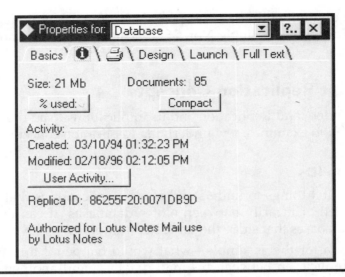

Figure 2.33 The Properties for Database dialog box's Information tab will show you a database's Replica ID.

Document IDs

Once Notes has established that two databases share the same Replica ID, it needs a mechanism to compare Documents. This mechanism is presented in the form of a Document ID, a unique number that is assigned to every Document in a Notes database. While, in theory, two databases that aren't replicas may contain Documents that have the same Document ID, the programming of Notes is such that only one instance of a Document ID will exist among replicas. (or, in other words, once assigned, a Document ID will not be duplicated in a database or any of its Replicas again).

Deletion Stubs

Since Replication is not a time-dependent process, it is possible that a change made to a database may not be moved to all Replicas of that database for days, weeks, or even months. This poses a challenge to handling Document deletions, in that some remnant of the Document must be kept for a specified period of time to allow the deletion to be successfully moved between all replicas. This remnant is known as a *Deletion Stub*. The Deletion Stub contains the Document ID and the time and date of its deletion.

Over a period of time that can be specified by a Notes Developer or Administrator, the Deletion Stub can be "purged" from a Notes database in order to free up space. By default, this interval is 90 days. The assumption is that all Replicas will have received the deletion within that time.

Replication Histories

A replication history is a special index Notes keeps that contains a unique signature for each Document in a database along with the time the Document was added, deleted, or edited. Notes compares Document IDs, the date the last action was performed on a Document, then the number of changes made to a Document to determine whether a change is needed in one of the replicas. In our example, after reading both databases and comparing their replication histories, Notes was able to determine that both of the Documents we added to the database on the Server were new. Then, using the replication settings of the local replica, it decided that of the two new Documents, only one met the selection criteria.

Replication Histories are used as a time-saving mechanism for the Replication process. Once a Replication History is established between two Notes Servers, the next Replication will only compare Documents that have been changed since the last time the two Servers Replicated.

Replication Histories can be cleared from a Notes database to force two replicas compare every Document by ID and date and time.

Replication Security

If two replicas of a database exists on two separate Notes Servers, it's possible to have different privileges for each server stored in the database's Access Control List. By way of example, a Notes Server that replicates a database with another Notes Server can be restricted to Reader Access in order to force it to accept anything added to the other Server's database, but not to send anything that has been added at its home location.

Why would you want to do that? Well, let's say you maintain a database of technical notes that you want to share with your customers. You want customers to get any up-to-date information you add to the database, and you want to encourage them to add to the database themselves.

However, you don't want Documents that customer A adds to his database to replicate back to your Server, because then those changes would be moved to Customers B, C, D, and so on. By giving the customer's Notes Server reader access, you could enforce this restriction.

Selective Replication

Selective replication allows you to replicate only certain Forms, Folders, or Documents with specific values in their fields. As an example of how you might use selective replication, let's imagine we have a Notes database that contains current events. The database is maintained by the research department. Because the research department's specialty is research, they keep every Document they add to the database in case they need to refer to it again. Other departments, however, would like a replica of the database that only has the most recent events. To solve this, the other department's servers use replication formula to only replicate Documents that were added in the last 15 days. This accomplishes two things:

(1) It reduces the size of the current events database on all the other servers in the company; and (2) it gives the customers a small, easy to navigate database that won't overwhelm anyone dropping into it to catch up on the industry.

Field-Level Replication

A new and important feature in Notes Release 4.0 is called *Field Level Replication*. Field level replication allows a Notes Server or Workstation to compare Documents down to the field level, and only to move changes in a field instead of an entire Document. This is useful for a number or reasons, not the least of which is that it allows users who connect by way of modem to Replicate faster.

As an example of how Field Level Replication works, imagine that you download a piece of shareware from the Internet, and after evaluating it, you want to share it with other people at your company. You create a Document in a Notes database and enter a description of the shareware in a text field, along with an attachment (the actual shareware program) in a Rich Text field.

A couple of days pass. During that time, some people with whom you work that happen to be on the road call in and download the new Notes Document containing the shareware program. Later, you realize that you forgot to include a piece of important licensing information about the shareware. You open the Document in the Notes database and make a change to the text field that contains the description.

With versions of Notes before Release 4.0, that action would have caused the entire Document you changed to re-replicate to the remote users the next time they called in an initiated a replication. Assuming that the shareware files took up a little over a megabyte, that would mean that in addition to the 15 minutes they spent replicating the Document the first time, they'd have to spend an another 15 minutes downloading the Document again. All that time, just to get one sentence that was added to the text field of the Document.

Of course, even with Notes, Release 4.0 the user would still spend the first 15 minutes downloading the Document for the first time. However, the *second* time, only the text field that changed would be replicated to the user, taking about 15 seconds. That saved the remote user over 14 minutes! Imagine, if you replicate a database that has several small changes made to it regularly how much time you'll save!

Field-level replication is especially important for sites that distribute a single Notes database to several thousand sites (as some public Notes networks do).

Replication Conflicts

Occasionally, circumstances occur which will cause Notes to believe that a change should be made to the same Document in both databases. (The same Document was edited at both locations by someone before a replication occurs, for example.) In these cases, Notes decides—based on the time stamp in each Document and the number of changes made to the Document—which Document is a *winner* and which Document is a *loser*. The winner is displayed as a normal Document in the database. The loser is . . .

Did you say deleted? No, Notes would never do that. The loser is displayed as a Response Document with the winner as its parent. This flags the Document for human intervention. These cases are called *replication or save conflicts*. Depending on the size of your Notes database and the number of times Documents are changed, replication or save conflicts may occur frequently or never at all. In circumstances where replication conflicts occur frequently, it's possible to reduce conflicts through creative administration.

Replication from an Administrator's Perspective

As you might imagine, Replication is one of the most challenging things for a Notes Administrator to manage effectively. Making sure that Notes Servers aren't overloaded by being in a constant state of Replication, minimizing Replication conflicts, and ensuring that users have timely information becomes quite a juggling act. One of the first steps Administrators take in managing Replication is setting up a replication topology and schedule.

Replication Topology and Schedules

The Replication Topology is a diagram of how Notes Servers will interconnect with each other for Replication. As a developer, your first instinct may be "just let everybody replicate with everybody," (which, from the standpoint of wanting to use Notes as an application to distribute data makes perfect sense). But let's take a few minutes to examine the impact of various topologies on an organization's ability to distribute data.

To do this, let's set up a network of five Notes Servers, as illustrated in figure 2.34.

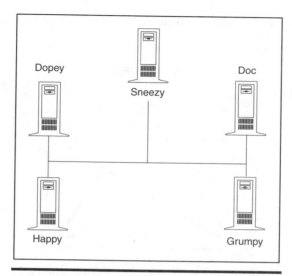

Figure 2.34 A sample network of Notes Servers

Let's assume that there is a database that you want to distribute company wide, and that a Replica of the database should reside on all five of the Notes Servers in our network. The Servers Replicate automatically based on a schedule established in their copy of the company's Name and Address Book (**NAMES.NSF**). Letting each Server Replicate with another Notes Server would mean creating the following connections from an administrative standpoint:

1. Sneezy to Dopey / Dopey to Sneezy
2. Sneezy to Doc / Doc to Sneezy
3. Sneezy to Grumpy / Grumpy to Sneezy
4. Sneezy to Happy / Happy to Sneezy
5. Doc to Dopey / Dopey to Doc
6. Doc to Grumpy / Grumpy to Doc
7. Doc to Happy / Happy to Doc
8. Dopey to Grumpy / Grumpy to Dopey
9. Dopey to Happy / Happy to Dopey
10. Grumpy to Happy / Happy to Grumpy

When all is said and done, it would look something like Figure 2.35.

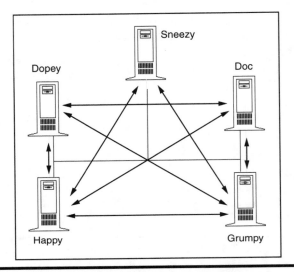

Figure 2.35 A Mesh network topology for Replication.

This topology is what Notes refers to as a Mesh topology. And, to be honest, it doesn't look too bad, does it? Ah, but now comes the fun part. Replication needs to happen on a schedule. Ideally, the schedule should be such that the time slots keep a server from having to Replicate with multiple servers at the same time. This scheduling frees up some of the Server's processing for user activities, and helps minimize Replication conflicts. So, stepping into the Administrator's shoes for a moment, plug in some times.

This year your company's going to grow. Add two more servers. How about five more? As you can see, a Mesh topology can get very complicated for an organization with more than a few servers. But, depending on how urgent the data is you are replicating, a Mesh topology can be the fastest way to get information synchronized on all servers.

In "real life," we only know of one organization that has more than three Notes Servers and uses a Mesh topology. Why? Because other ways to approach distributing Replicated information are available that are not only more easy to control, but adapt to growth.

One of them is called an End-to-End topology by Lotus, as illustrated in Figure 2.36.

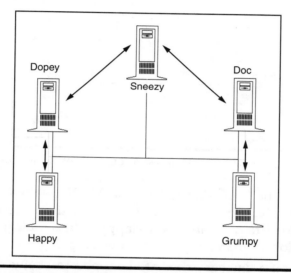

Figure 2.36 An End-to-End network topology for Replication.

In this kind of topology, Happy connects to Dopey and Replicates. Dopey connects to Sneezy and Replicates. Sneezy connects to Doc and Replicates. And Doc connect to Grumpy and Replicates. The Replication path then goes back the other way. Eventually, information is replicated up and down the line.

A second approach to the End-to-End topology is to move the data in a single direction, and connect each server to the next in line, creating a circular pattern. This is referred to as a Ring topology, as illustrated in Figure 2.37.

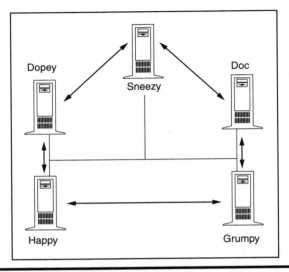

Figure 2.37 A Ring network topology for Replication

As you can see, both the End-to-End and Mesh topology make it easier to create a Replication schedule. However, the time it takes for a document added to a database on Happy to reach Grumpy is will be considerably longer than if you used a Mesh topology.

In addition, if a database needs to be replicated between Happy and Grumpy, it must also be on all of the connecting Servers. A last point to consider about End-to-End and Ring Topologies is the question "What happens if a Notes Server goes down in the middle of the chain?"

A fourth method of connecting Notes Servers for Replication is known as a Hub-and-Spoke topology. In a typical Hub-and-Spoke network, a single server becomes the Replication engine for the other Notes Servers it is connected to, as illustrated in Figure 2.38.

Like the End-to-End and Ring topologies, the Hub-and-Spoke topology is to create a Replication Schedule for than the Mesh topology. Besides, it is more flexible when new Notes Servers are added, in that one Hub-and-Spoke network can be interconnected with other Hub-and-Spoke networks, as illustrated in Figure 2.39.

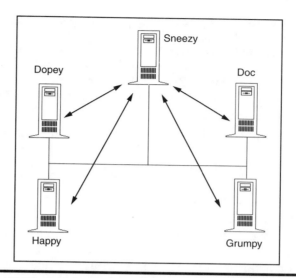

Figure 2.38 A Hub-and-Spoke network topology for Replication

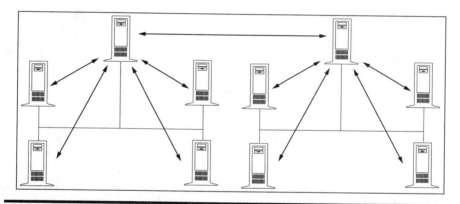

Figure 2.39 Hub-and-Spoke topologies can be combined with End-To-End or Ring Topologies to form a hybrid network topology.

The Hub-and-Spoke connection is the most commonly used method for creating a Replication topology because of its flexibility, scalability, and relative speed versus complexity.

Replication from a Developer's Perspective

As you might guess from the number of Replication ideas we've discussed up to this point, Replication is a powerful tool for distributing information. Like Mail Enabling, it offers developers the opportunity to create applications that distribute information without regard for geographic or time constraints.

However, as they say in the Spiderman comic book, "With great power comes great responsibility." The complexity of Replication stems in part from its flexibility. Selective Replication formulas combined with different privileges in the Access Control List of different Replicas create an almost limitless combination of situations you can be faced with when Replicating.

Whenever we work with a new Notes developer, to a person their first stumbling block has been caused by an unexpected behavior during Replication, or a failure to appreciate what Replication means before rolling out an application. There are a couple of obvious reasons for this:

- Notes has the ability to Replicate design elements as well as Documents. This often "trips up" new developers who forget the fact that Notes Replicates both and make changes to one that they don't intend to be put into production while working on the other.

- Replication in Notes is so robust that the number of possible combinations for more complex applications during Replication are difficult to anticipate.

Here are some examples of common developer mistakes when first working with Replication:

1. To perform maintenance on a database, a developer will replicate a database from a Notes Server to their local drive. While they work, the will delete and add Documents for testing. When they finally finish their work, the Replicate with the Notes Server, sending not only their design changes but their "testing" Documents and deletion stubs for valid Documents that should not be removed.

2. While creating an application that uses Selective Replication as a filter, the Developer codes in the name of two Servers that she

knows will Replicate with the Server where she intends to deploy her application. Because she doesn't realize that a third server is a part of the Replication Schedule for that Server, the formula allows information that was supposed to be filtered out to Replicate freely to a location she doesn't even know existed!

3. Another common mistake in this area is to create a Selective Replication formula that anticipates Server replication, but not Clients performing Replication.

Obviously, intra-, enter-, or extra-enterprise applications that rely on Selective Replication as a filter should thoroughly test before a roll-out begins. Pay particular attention to applications that plan to use Selective Replication as a security mechanism. Just one mistake in a formula or one unanticipated combination in "real-world" Replication is enough to cause your organization more headaches than they need.

Does this mean that Notes Developers should avoid using Replication as a mechanism for distributing information? Absolutely not! The power of Replication is what makes Notes unique, and it frees developers to think outside the boundaries of the corporate network while examining knowledge distribution applications. The point should be however, that when more than your "run of the mill" Replication is involved, rigorous testing should be performed.

In addition to the programmatic aspects of Replication, you must also regard it from the Administrative perspective. Knowing about the Replication Topology at your organization will help you to develop applications that take advantage of the architecture your administrator has selected.

InterNotes

The last thing we're going to discuss about Notes Administration before moving on to the development chapters is how a collection of tools developed by Lotus Development and Iris Associates under the InterNotes product name integrate Notes with the Internet.

We'll look at InterNotes from the perspective of how it delivers information to the end-user, and followed by how it allows Developers to easily move information from Notes to the World Wide Web.

The Internet and the InterNotes Web Navigator

If you've been in a cave for the last few years and haven't heard about the *Internet*, here's a quick definition—a collection of computers that share a common set of networking protocols to exchange files, electronic mail messages, and other information. If you're thinking that sounds a lot like just a plain old network, you're right. In fact, Internet is a shorter name for Internetwork. What makes the Internet distinctive from other networks however, is its size and diversity. Over 20 million machines are estimated to be connected to it. Those machines are in people's homes, at universities and colleges, at government institutions, and are part of businesses world-wide.

Much of the Internet's recent popularity is owed to the implementation of a protocol for exchanging information called the Hyper Text Transfer Protocol (HTTP). This protocol allows software to use a special language called Hyper Text Markup Language (HTML) to display information that is contained on remote machines using a local computer.

The software that uses HTML and HTTP to read information is referred to as a World Wide Web (WWW) Browser. Software that uses HTML and HTTP to disseminate information is called a World Wide Web (WWW) Server. Figure 2.40 illustrates what we've just discussed.

Looking at Figure 2.40, you might wonder, how do the World Wide Web Browsers find anything on those thousands of World Wide Web Servers? Just as the Notes Client uses information about a Notes Server, a directory, and a database name to locate information, the World Wide Web Browser use a similar system. The server name, a directory, and information about which document in the directory to retrieve are converted into what is called a Uniform Resource Locator (URL).

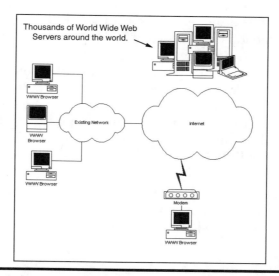

Figure 2.40 How WWW Browsers connect to WWW Servers.

As you might imagine, the Internet makes a tremendous diversity of information available to people. With 20 million-odd machines in the network (many of them belonging to computer geeks and college kids), a wide variety of topics can be found using a WWW Browser. And of course, the Internet is international. In one sitting, you can visit an Irish pub, an English leather shop, and a special site set up by the *New York Times* to broadcast some of its daily news to Internet users. It is a tool to allow the transfer of knowledge.

Hmmmm. . . so far, this doesn't look or sound very different in concept to Notes—specialized clients get their information from specialized servers. That's the first of many similarities.

Another similarity is the presentation of information. HTML documents work a lot like Documents with Rich Text Fields do in Notes—they can contain formatted text, colors, pictures, file attachments, and even run other programs. This allows information to be presented in a knowledge-oriented context, as opposed to as simply data. And, like Document Links in a Notes Rich Text Field, HTML documents can contain links to other HTML documents located on other World Wide Web Servers on the Internet.

HTML documents designed for World Wide Web Browsers and Notes Rich Text Field capabilities are so similar that, with very little effort, the entire Internet can be accessed through the Notes Client and a cooperative Notes Server using what Lotus calls its InterNotes technology. Lotus InterNotes represents an entire suite of applications designed to help Notes integrate the advantages of the Internet's diverse information base into its system without compromising the security or workflow capabilities that are contained within the Notes system. The two InterNotes applications we're going to discuss are the InterNotes Web Navigator and the InterNotes Web Retriever.

The InterNotes Web Navigator is built-in to every Notes, Release 4, Client. The InterNotes Web Retriever is included with every Notes, Release 4, Server. The two programs work together to bring information from the World Wide Web to Notes users, as illustrated in Figure 2.41.

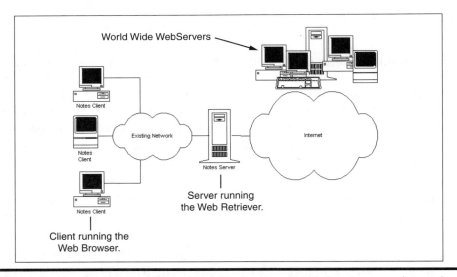

Figure 2.41 How the InterNotes Web Navigator and Web Retriever work together to bring Notes users World Wide Web documents.

What happens is this:

1. A Notes user requests information about a World Wide Web page using a Uniform Resource Locator (URL) as an address.
2. The Notes client asks the InterNotes Web Retriever to use the HTTP protocol to retrieve the HTML document and copy it into a Notes Database on the Server.

3. The Notes Client then opens the Document on the Server from the database where it is stored.

You might notice, after comparing Figure 2.40 and 2.41 and reading the three steps above, that the Notes Client never directly connects to the World Wide Web. That is something unique to the InterNotes technology. You can have all of the security of Notes, and you can minimize the interaction with the larger, less secure Internet by having only a single point of access from your internal network.

Once a Notes Server in a network is set up as an InterNotes Web Retriever, activating the InterNotes Web Navigator in the Notes Client is simple. Add the name of the InterNotes Server to the current Location Document in the Client's Name and Address Book, and Select File, Tools, User Preferences . . . from the Notes Client menu. On the Basics page of the User Preferences dialog box, ensure that Make Internet URLs (http:/...) into Hotspots is selected in the Advanced options list.

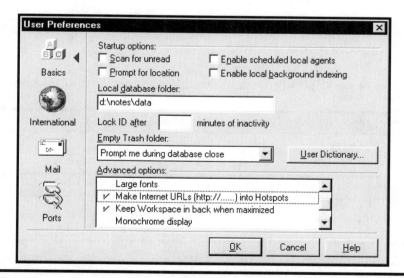

Figure 2.42 Ensuring that the Make Internet URLs (http:/...) into Hotspots setting is selected in the Advanced options list.

Once this is done, the InterNotes software at the Client translates any strings in a Rich Text Field that follow URL syntax into dynamic links. Double-clicking those links (**http://www.lotus.com** in Figure 2.43 for example), starts the process.

Internet Web Pages Related to Notes (No Responses) - Lotus Notes
File Edit View Create Actions Window Help
Close
Response
Internet Web Pages Related to Notes
Virginia Huebner on 12/16/95 at 05:30 PM
Category: Internet
Some Lotus Notes related Web Pages:
http://www.lotus.com
Lotus Development Corporation.
http://www.notes.net/home.html
Iris Associates.
http://www.worldcom.com/
WorldCom
Island

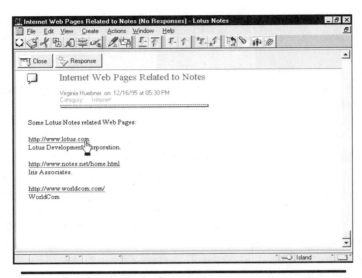

Figure 2.43 Locating an Internet URL... in the Document.

Several messages in the Notes Client Status Bar will indicate activity by the Notes Client and the Notes Server.

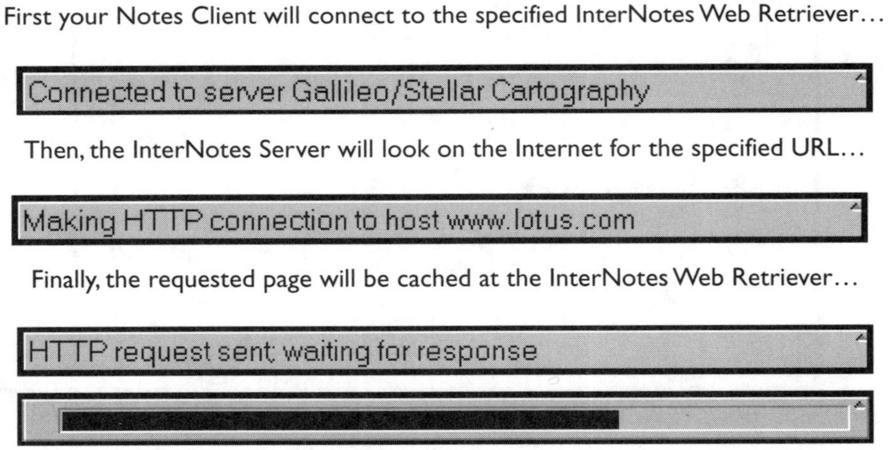

First your Notes Client will connect to the specified InterNotes Web Retriever...
Connected to server Gallileo/Stellar Cartography
Then, the InterNotes Server will look on the Internet for the specified URL...
Making HTTP connection to host www.lotus.com
Finally, the requested page will be cached at the InterNotes Web Retriever...
HTTP request sent; waiting for response

Figure 2.44 Messages that will appear in the Notes Status bar during an InterNotes session between a Notes Client and a Notes Server.

Ultimately, the URL that was activated in the Rich Text Field of a Notes Document translates into another Notes Document, as illustrated in Figure 2.45.

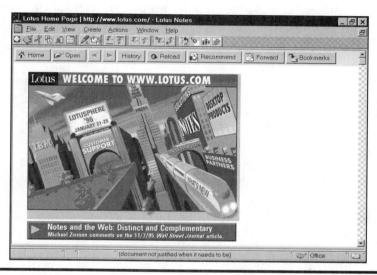

Figure 2.45 Lotus Development Corporation's World Wide Web home page.

As you can see, the InterNotes Web Navigator integrates the World Wide Web with Notes seamlessly and efficiently from the perspective of a Notes Client.

The InterNotes Web Publisher

To address World Wide Web and Notes integration from the perspective of a World Wide Web Browser client is the InterNotes Web Publisher. The InterNotes Web Publisher represents Lotus' strategy for making Notes Servers accessible to Web Browsers. Currently, the strategy is a two-pronged, with some features being available today to make a solution possible, and more seamless solutions planned for future releases of Notes. We'll discuss both solutions in this section, starting with the features available today.

Like the InterNotes Web Retriever, the InterNotes Web Publisher is a task that runs on a Notes Server. Its purpose is to make data in Notes databases accessible to World Wide Web Browsers by exporting the Documents in a Notes database to a series of files that follow the HTML format. Figure 2.46 illustrates this.

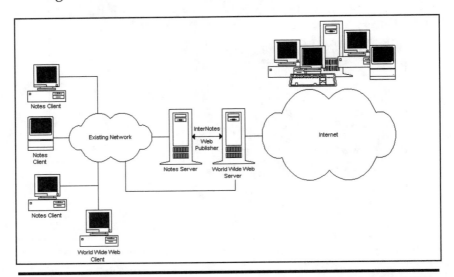

Figure 2.46 Lotus' current implementation of the InterNotes Web Publisher

A World Wide Web Server can then use the exported HTML documents to display the information that is contained in a Notes database to users who do not have a Notes Client, but do have a World Wide Web Browser. Besides making information available for display to World Wide Web Browsers, the InterNotes Web Publisher package also provides software to allow users to put data into Notes databases using HTML forms.

With future releases of Notes, the Notes Server will support the HTTP protocol directly, meaning Web Browsers can gain direct access to a Notes Server, as illustrated in Figure 2.47.

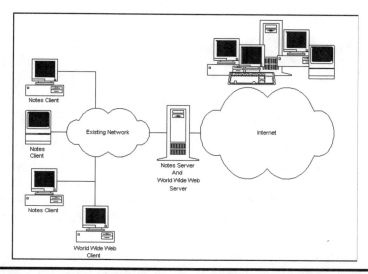

Figure 2.47 Lotus' future implementation of World Wide Web/Notes integration at the Notes Server

What Does InterNotes Mean to a Notes Developer?

The tight integration of Lotus Notes and the World Wide Web mean that Notes is well suited to manage information that can be disseminated through the Internet. Based on the Chapter 1 survey of intra-, inter-, and extra-enterprise networks, it is easy to see how Lotus Notes can allow you to develop applications that can be distributed internally; from business to business; and between businesses and customers.

At present, programmatic control of the InterNotes feature within Notes is limited—InterNotes is primarily controlled by administrative personnel as opposed to development. However, it is expected that more robust programmatic access to the features of InterNotes will be included in subsequent releases of the Notes Client and Notes Server software.

NOTE

As you move to the API section of this book, you will discover that using the examples Dan provides you have a good basis for "rolling" your own basic Web Publisher.

Summary

An understanding of the administration of a Notes Network is a powerful tool—it allows you to tailor your application to the environment in which it will run for a better fit, and it helps you to maximize the requirements planning stages of an application.

A Lotus Notes Network is a collection of computers running Notes Client and Notes Server software, interconnected through use of one or more network protocols or serial communications links. The Clients and Servers get their configuration information from a collection of files ranging from an **.INI/preferences** file to Notes databases designed specifically to administer each machine. Each Client and Server in a Notes Network has an identity, established by the ID file currently in use at each machine.

ID files that share common certificates have a trust relationship with each other. A Notes Server will only allow machines using IDs that it trusts to access it. An ID on a Notes Client or Notes Server that does not share the same certificate as another Notes Server will not, by default, allow a connection between the two machines.

An administrative processes known as cross certification can allow machines whose IDs do not share a common certificate to connect.

NOTE

Once Notes Clients and Servers are connected, they share information using client/server database access, mail enabling, and replication. Database access is controlled on a per database basis using an Access Control List (ACL). Users or groups of users must have their names associated with a specific set of privileges in the ACL in order to gain access.

Security can also be implemented at the Document level of a database, restricting certain IDs from viewing complete Documents, or portions of any Documents. The combination of Server security, database security, Document security, and partial Document security results in a very robust platform for deploying information across an organization.

However, the security model in Notes is so robust that it is sometimes possible to leave gaps in security simply because the number of security levels in combination can produce too many scenarios to adequately predict and test. Applications that use simple security methods effectively are the easiest to deploy and maintain.

As mentioned previously, in addition to direct client/server access, information in Notes databases can also be shared using Replication and Mail Enabling.

Replication is a process that allows the bi-directional exchange information between to Replica databases.

NOTE

Every Notes database is stamped with a unique identification number known as a *Replica ID* when it is created. Additional copies of a database already created can be created with a new Replica ID, or with the same Replica ID. Databases that share the same Replica ID are known as *Replicas*.

Replication occurs between two Notes Servers, or a Notes Client and a Notes Server. Notes Servers generally replicate automatically using a Replication Schedule. Notes Clients can use a Replication Schedule, but often initiate the process of Replication manually.

Replication is important to Notes because it allows remote Notes Servers or Notes Clients to have access to updated information using occasional connections instead of a dedicated connection. Information can be updated in either Replica, and only the changes made in each Replica will be moved to the other database. This minimizes connection times, and makes Replication an efficient method for distributing information across an enterprise.

In addition to replicating Documents and changes to Documents, Notes can also replicate design changes. This means that changes in programs can be distributed by updating the design of one database and allowing it to move throughout the network over time.

A Notes database contains a number of components designed to influence Replication:

- Selective Replication settings allow Notes databases to replicate subsets of the information each database contains. This allows a single large database to replicate information to several smaller databases. It also allows remote users to conserve disk space by replicating only the parts of a database in which they are interested.

- Replication Histories give Notes a point of reference when initiating the Replication process by storing the date and time of the last Replication between the two Servers or the Client and Server. This speeds Replication time considerably.

- Field Level Replication allows two Documents that have been changed to consolidate their changes, provided that each Document has changed different fields. It also allows changes made in only one Document to replicate faster because only the changed field is replicated instead of the entire Document.

- Replication Conflicts are created whenever two Notes databases have Documents that have been changed at both locations and Notes cannot resolve the conflict without human assistance.

By its nature, Replication is a process suited to applications that do not require constant updates to be spread throughout multiple locations on a real-time basis. Rather, Replication is well suited to information that changes but can be moved throughout an enterprise over time.

Information can be moved more quickly using Mail Enabling. Mail Enabling in Notes allows any Notes Database to exchange information with any other Notes Database using Notes' built-in mailing services. Like Replication, Mail Enabling is effective for both networked and occasionally connected users.

The primary uses of Mail Enabling in Lotus Notes are:

- Lotus Notes Mail—a Notes database designed to present an easy to use mail interface for exchanging information between users.

- Workflow—a combination of Agents and Mail Enabling that allows forms routing (moving information from databases to people and vice versa), and document exchange (moving information between databases automatically without human intervention).

Mail Enabling generally relies on the presence of a specific Form in the databases that will be sending and receiving Documents. However, it is possible to programmatically change the name of the Form that should be used to display a document as it moves from one database to another. This is accomplished by using Agents that are triggered whenever a document is placed in them by way of mail. It is also possible to store the Form being used in a Document to make the Document more portable (so that it can be displayed by any Notes user).

What Notes Means to a Developer

The ability to quickly develop applications that incorporate security, workflow, object containers, and replication is a powerful part of the Notes experience. As our coworkers and clients will quickly attest, we are fond of saying that "Understanding Notes development is like adding a Philips-head-screwdriver-blade to your Swiss Army Knife. You won't use it all the time, but when you need it, there's not another tool on the knife that can do its job as well."

Armed with a solid understanding of Notes development, you can be the MacGyver of information at the next business process reengineering meetings. Here's an example.

> *They:* "To better understand this process, we need to be able to track loosely structured information more effectively. The IT department says we can have a system that is client/server, remotely accessible, secure, multiplatform, and mail-enabled

in about eight to ten weeks. As soon as the system is in place, we can pick up our discussions where we're leaving off today."

You: "Before you commit to that timeline, give me a pack of chewing gum, a couple of cans of Coke, and some time with Lotus Notes. I'll have a prototype by this afternoon."

Sound too good to be true? Are we talking about a code cowboy?

It's understandable for you to feel that way. Before you make a final ruling on the subject, however, let's cover the following topics:

- The Notes development environment
- Speaking the languages of Notes
- The reusability of Notes code
- Notes' impact on the applications development process
- Extending Notes

The Notes Development Environment

Everything you need to design an application in Notes is provided in the Notes Client Software. Tools for coding, debugging, Form and View design, field definition, and even Icon design are included. The only part of a Notes database you may have to go outside Notes to create is an image you'd like to use as the basis of a Navigator.

NOTE With Notes, Release 4, it is possible to buy versions of the Notes Client software called *Lotus Notes Desktop* and *Lotus Notes Mail* that do not allow the user to access software design features except to create private Agents, Folders, and Views. What makes the design elements private is that they are not stored in the shared Notes database, but in the user's **Desktop.dsk** file on their local drive.

Creating New Elements

Using the standard Notes Client, you can access the design elements of Notes in a number of ways. To create new Agents, Forms, Folders, Navigators, Shared Fields, SubForms, or Views in a Notes database, you can use the **Create**, **Design** command on the **Notes Client** menu.

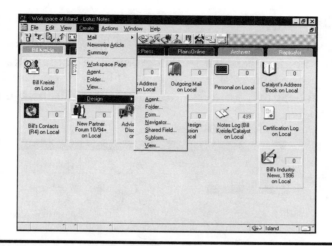

Figure 3.1 The Create Design command on the **Notes Client** menu.

When you are inside one of the newly created design elements, you can use the **Create** menu to add additional design items specific to the element you are working on. Comparing Figures 3.1 and 3.2, you can see that the changes to the **Create** menu while a new Form is being made reflect the types of design elements appropriate for a Form.

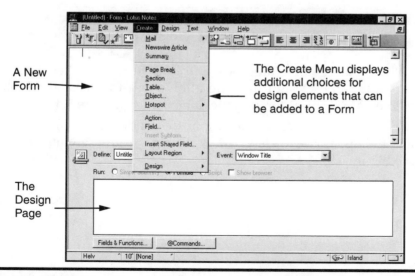

Figure 3.2 Additional items will appear on the **Create** menu relative to the current design context.

Editing Existing Elements

To make modifications to existing design elements, you use the Design section of the Folders Navigator dialog box. The Folders Navigator is a default navigator that is a part of every Notes database, selected by choosing **View, Show, Folders** from the **Notes Client** Menu while a database is open (Figure 3.3).

Figure 3.3 Opening the Folders Navigator dialog box.

In the Folders Navigator dialog box will be a heading called Design. When expanded, the Design heading allows you to access the Notes design elements currently stored in the database (see Figure 3.4).

If you do not see the Design header in the Folders Navigator dialog box while it is open, select **View, Show, Design** from the **Notes Client** menu (see Figure 3.5).

Figure 3.4 The Design heading of the Folders Navigator dialog box.

Figure 3.5 The View, Show, Design command on the Notes Client menu.

If after selecting **View, Show, Design** from the **Notes Client** menu you
still do not see the Design header in the Folders Navigator dialog box, it

is possible that you are using Lotus Notes Desktop or Lotus Notes Mail instead of a full Notes Client, or that the Design of the current database is hidden. You do not have the ability to make Design changes in these cases. You will need a full Notes Client and a database in which the design is not hidden to work with the examples in the rest of this book.

SHORTCUT

You can also open the Design header of the Folders Navigator dialog box by right-clicking on a database icon on the Workspace and choosing **Go To Design...** from the pop-up menu (see Figure 3.6).

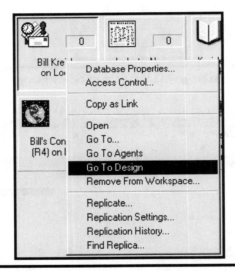

Figure 3.6 Using the right-hand mouse button to open the pop-up menu and launch the **Go To Design** command.

Once the Design header in the Folders Navigator dialog box is expanded, selecting an element from the Navigator will open a View displaying all current elements of that type (see Figure 3.7).

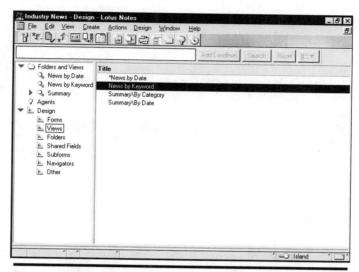

Figure 3.7 The existing Views that are stored in the database

Double-clicking on an existing element in the list opens it for editing (see Figure 3.8).

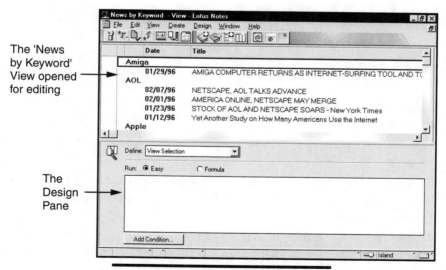

The 'News by Keyword' View opened for editing

The Design Pane

Figure 3.8 Editing a View in a database.

The Design Pane and the Properties dialog box

Whether you are creating a new design element or editing an existing one, you will add code to it using the Design Pane. The Design Pane is an area at the bottom of the Design Window (see Figures 3.2, 3.8, and 3.9 for examples).

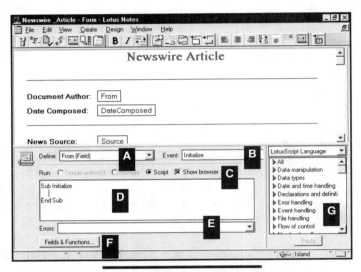

Figure 3.9 The Design Pane.

Using Figure 3.9 as our reference:

A. Use the **Define** box to associate your code with a Notes object in the current design element, such as a button, field, or action.

B. Use the **Event** box to select an event to trigger execution of your code.

C. Select the type of code—**Simple Actions**, **Formula**, or **LotusScript**—you will use with the object previously selected in the Define box.

D. Use the script editor to write, edit, and view a script, and to check script syntax. The script editor becomes active when you enter the script window (the large box in the design pane).

E. Use the **Errors** box to view messages describing syntax and other errors that occur during code entry and compilation. Selecting an error will position you on the line containing that error in the code.

F. Click **Fields & Functions** to obtain lists of currently defined fields in the database and @functions.

G. If you are using LotusScript to write code for the object, you can click the **Show browser** check box (C) which appears as an additional pane to the right of the Design Pane. The browser box provides a quick reference tool for more information about the LotusScript language, classes, constants, and variables. Drag the vertical bar separating the two panes to adjust their sizes. Click the **Show browser** box again to hide the browser.

Another place where you may need to add code for a design element is in its **Properties** dialog box. This dialog box can be activated by right-clicking on an item, and selecting the item's name from the pop-up menu (see Figure 3.10). It can also be activated by:

Selecting a design element and pressing **ALT + ENTER**;

Selecting an element and clicking the Properties SmartIcon ◈ ;

Selecting an element and choosing the appropriate **Properties...** command from the **Design** or **File** menu of the Notes Client.

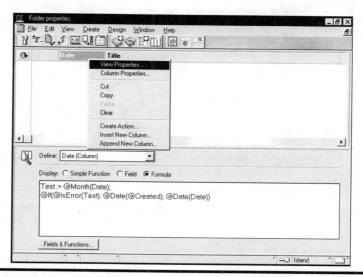

Figure 3.10 Accessing an item's properties using the right-hand mouse pop-up menu.

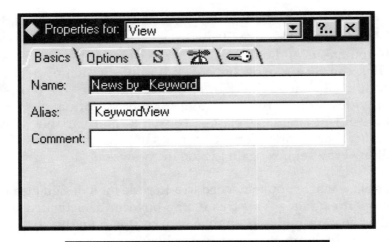

Figure 3.11 The Properties for View dialog box.

Clicking on the different tabbed pages will show you if there is any place in the Properties settings where formulas can be entered (see Figure 3.12).

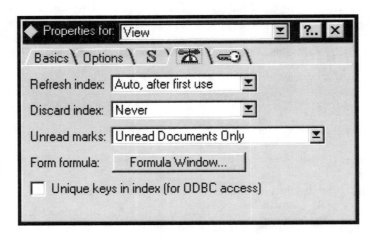

Figure 3.12 Using the Properties for View dialog box, Propeller Head page, to gain access to the View's Form Formula.

Speaking the Languages of Notes

Now that you know where to locate the design elements that are stored in a Notes database and how to associate code with the elements, it's time to discuss the three languages that Notes provides out of the box for you—the Function Language, LotusScript, and Simple Actions.

Before we begin this section, we want to point out that our discussion is not intended to be a comprehensive guide to any of the three languages. The manuals from Lotus and the on-line Help system provide a wealth of information in that regard. Instead, this section is designed to introduce you to the languages, explain their purpose, and offer suggestions at to when it would be appropriate to use them. We'll use all three languages later in this book when we build a contact management database from scratch in Chapter 5.

Notes' Function Language

Overview

The Function Language in Notes is the original Notes development language, available since the first release of the product. It was intended to provide a macro-like programming environment to allow basic programming for users without letting them "hurt themselves" by having too much power. (For example, there are no looping or branching statements in the Notes Function Language… no While/Wend, Select Case/End Case, For/Next, or even a Goto, for that matter.)

While each major release of Notes offered a greater range of functions, programming in the Function Language alone often caused developers to have a pet phrase something like "Notes giveth, and Notes taketh away." By way of example, here's the code required to save the current document and close the window after saving the changes:

```
@Command([FileSave]);
@Command([FileCloseWindow]);
```

Simple and straightforward, right? Now compare that to a code snippet posted on the Notes Business Partners Forum that, in Notes Release 3, was the only way to get a sum of the fields on a set of documents using the Function Language:

```
REM "Setup values field for sum formula.";
REM;
values := @DbLookup("" : ""; dbname; "Lookup"; Main_ID; 2);
REM;
REM "Execute sum formula.";
REM;
f := @Power(2; @Integer(@Log(@Elements(values)) / @Log(2)));
adjust := @Elements(values) - f;
list := @If(adjust = 0; values; (@Subset(values; adjust) +
@Subset(values; -adjust)) : @Subset(@Subset(values; f); adjust -
f));
@If(f > 1; @Set("f"; f / 2) + @Set("list"; @Subset(list; f) +
@Subset(list; -f)) ; "" );
@If(f > 1; @Set("f"; f / 2) + @Set("list"; @Subset(list; f) +
@Subset(list; -f)) ; "" );
@If(f > 1; @Set("f"; f / 2) + @Set("list"; @Subset(list; f) +
@Subset(list; -f)) ; "" );
@If(f > 1; @Set("f"; f / 2) + @Set("list"; @Subset(list; f) +
@Subset(list; -f)) ; "" );
@If(f > 1; @Set("f"; f / 2) + @Set("list"; @Subset(list; f) +
@Subset(list; -f)) ; "" );
@If(f > 1; @Set("f"; f / 2) + @Set("list"; @Subset(list; f) +
@Subset(list; -f)) ; "" );
@If(f > 1; @Set("f"; f / 2) + @Set("list"; @Subset(list; f) +
@Subset(list; -f)) ; "" );
@If(f > 1; @Set("f"; f / 2) + @Set("list"; @Subset(list; f) +     @S
ubset(list; -f)) ; "" );
@If(f > 1; @Set("f"; f / 2) + @Set("list"; @Subset(list; f) +
@Subset(list; -f)) ; "" );
@If(f > 1; @Set("f"; f / 2) + @Set("list"; @Subset(list; f) +
@Subset(list; -f)) ; "" );
@If(f > 1; @Set("f"; f / 2) + @Set("list"; @Subset(list; f) +
@Subset(list; -f)) ; "" );
@If(f > 1; @Set("f"; f / 2) + @Set("list"; @Subset(list; f) +
@Subset(list; -f)) ; "" );
```

```
REM;
REM "Set Tally field to sum result.";
REM;
FIELD Tally :=list;
""
```

With Release 4, there is an actual @Sum function, but you get the idea. For certain objectives, the Notes Function language is a blessing. For others—well, we'll just say it's an opportunity to take creative coding to a new level, as Wilfredo Lorenzo demonstrates with the sum function above (the formula is the intellectual property of MFJ International by the way).

The Function Language is probably one of the biggest stumbling blocks Notes has had in getting widespread use in an enterprise. This is not to imply that the Notes Function Language isn't robust and powerful in its own right. Developers who have been building solutions since Notes Release 1 have built programs that run entire organizations without the benefit of anything more than this language. However, to a new developer, the language seems esoteric, to say the least. And, since it is a language native to Notes and Notes only, it is perceived as a "single-purpose learning investment" in terms of time and resources.

That said, here's the counterpoint...

Any Notes developer that aspires to be worth his or her salt will still want to know the Function Language. Why? Because, as said before, when used as it is designed, there isn't a shorter path to developing the functionality you want in an application. (Also, as of Release 4, there are still some design elements where LotusScript isn't supported, so you will have to have a passing knowledge of the Function Language in order to develop code for those areas.)

Additionally, the LotusScript Language's **Evaluate()** Function helps to keep your time invested in the Function Language from being single-purpose learning by allowing you to combine LotusScript and the Function Language to get the results you want more quickly. Think of the Function Language as a ready-made library of routines that you can use alone or combined with LotusScript to give you the solution you need.

Syntax

General

Formulas are entered as a series of statements, which can span multiple lines and include whitespace. A statement is delimited by a semicolon. Case is not significant except within text constants (Notes will save Keywords and Functions following its own case conventions if you enter them differently).

Variables and Fields

Variables in Notes are temporary values stored in memory for the scope of the currently running script or formula. *Fields* are permanent values that are stored on Documents. A variable or field name must begin with a letter. Remaining characters can include letters, numbers, and the symbols _ and $. Spaces are not allowed. The name may contain up to 32 bytes (if you're using multibyte characters, 32 bytes is different from 32 characters).

The variable and field types supported by Notes for the Function Language are:

- *Text*—contains alphanumeric values that will not be used mathematically.
- *Rich Text* (fields only)—contains pictures, graphs, hotspots, attachments, or embedded objects and text styles such as bold, italics, underlining, different fonts, or color.
- *Keywords*—contains predefined text choices that make data entry convenient and consistent. Keyword fields can be programmed to contain all allowable selections, or to allow values to be added dynamically.
- *Number*—contains information that can be used mathematically using the characters 0 1 2 3 4 5 6 7 8 9 - + . E e
- *Time*—contains time and date information. Comprised of letters and numbers separated by punctuation.
- *Authors*—contains a text list of names (user names, group names, and access roles). An Authors field can be used in conjunction with the Author Access privilege in the Access Control List (ACL) to give people the right to edit documents without expanding their database access to include Editor Access privileges.

- *Readers*—contains a text list of names that allow you to restrict who can read documents created with a form regardless of the user's privileges in the ACL.
- *Names*—contains a list of user or server names as they appear on Notes IDs. Useful for displaying names when you don't need to assign any type of access rights to documents.

A temporary variable is created using the following syntax:

```
variableName := value;
```

The variable takes the type of the value to the right of the assignment operator. This value can be any of the field types discussed above or Boolean (a number field where zero = @False).

Some examples:

```
TimeStarted := @Today;
```

This statement sets the temporary variable TimeStarted to the value returned by the function @Today. Since the value returned by @Today is a time value, the TimeStarted variable will be of the same time type.

```
Input := @Prompt([OKCANCELEDIT];"Time Tracking"; "Enter the project
name you will be billing these hours against"; "");
```

This statement sets the Input temporary variable to the value entered by the user at the following prompt:

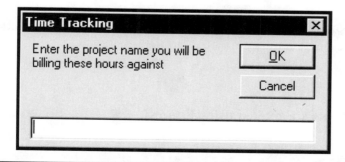

Figure 3.13 Using the @Prompt function to assign user input to a temporary variable.

The `@Prompt` function returns text values, so the value of the Input variable will be a string.

Fields are assigned values that match their predefined types. Fields can be distinguished from temporary variables by using the **FIELD** Keyword or the `@SetField` Function. For example, if a Document contains a number field called **DollarAmount**, the following statements could be used to assign it a value:

Example 1

```
FIELD DollarAmount := 1.00;
```

Example 2

```
theCost := quantity * price;
@SetField(DollarAmount; theCost);
```

Example 3

```
FIELD DollarAmount := @TextToNumber("1.00");
```

Static Values

Constants in the Notes Function Language are entered using the following conventions:

String constants are enclosed in quotation marks. Any string without quotes is assumed to be a variable or field.

```
NewVariable := "This is a string";
NewVariable := ThisIsAnotherVariable;
```

Numeric constants entered as values without quotes. (A series of numbers in quotes is considered a string.) Scientific notation may be used to enter numbers with a high decimal precision.

```
TheValue := 110.2;
```

Time constants are entered using [braces].

```
TheTime := [10:00 PM];
```

Lists are entered using a colon. List sizes are dynamic, and can be altered using math, permutation, or list operators.

```
ThreePlaces := "New York":"London":"Tokyo";
FourPlaces := ThreePlaces : "Brazil";
```

Operators

Operators and their order of precedence are shown in Table 3.1.

Table 3.1 Operators in the Function Language and their precedence.

Operator		Precedence
:=	Assignment	not applicable
:	List concatenation	1
+	Positive	2
-	Negative	
*	Multiplication	3
**	Permuted multiplication	
/	Division	
*/	Permuted division	
+	Addition, concatenation	4
*+	Permuted addition	
-	Subtraction	
*-	Permuted subtraction	
=	Equal	5
*=	Permuted equal	
<>	Not equal	
!=	Not equal	
=!	Not equal	
><	Not equal	
*<>	Permuted not equal	
<	Less than	

Table 3.1 Operators in the Function Language and their precedence. (cont.)

Operator		Precedence
*<	Permuted less than	
>*	Permuted greater than	
>	Greater than	
<=	Less than or equal	
*<=	Permuted less than or equal	
>=	Greater than or equal	
*>=	Permuted greater than or equal	
!	Logical NOT	6
&	Logical AND	
|	Logical OR	

Functions

The general format of a function in the Notes Function Language is the @ sign followed by the name of the function followed by arguments (if any) enclosed in parentheses, with multiple arguments delimited by a semicolon.

```
@function-name(argument1; argument2; ... argumentn);
```

Functions without arguments do not require parentheses.

Some functions, such as @Abstract, @Command, @PostedCommand, @DocMark, @GetPortsList, @PickList, @MailSend, @Name, and @Prompt require keyword parameters, which are static values enclosed in [braces].

For example:

```
@Name([CN]; @UserName)
```

returns the common name of the value returned by the @UserName function.

Arguments must be of the type specified by the function's description (i.e., a function that requires a text argument must use a value that is either a string constant, a variable/field that is of type text, or an @function that returns text as a value). Functions to convert data types exist in the @Function language such as @Text and @TextToNumber.

@Command and @PostedCommand are special functions in the Notes Function Language, designed to execute a Notes command. The first argument to @Command or @PostedCommand is a keyword argument that specifies the Notes command. Depending on the Notes command, other arguments may be required.

@Command and @PostedCommand are essentially the same function. The primary difference is that you must use @PostedCommand in applications that will run on a Notes R4 Server with Notes R3 Clients to ensure the same results as an R3 Client connected to an R3 Server.

Because of their large number and special status, the @Command and @PostedCommand function almost represent a fourth language in Notes.

@Functions and @Commands in Notes are saved in *proper case* (meaning the first letter of each word is captialized). You can enter them in any case you'd like. When you save the formula, they are converted.

Keywords

The Notes Formula Language includes five keywords designed to perform special functions in Notes, as shown in Table 3.2.

Table 3.2 Keywords in the Notes Function Language

Keyword syntax	Description
`FIELD fieldname := value;`	Assigns value to fieldName in the current Notes document. If the fieldName does not exist, it is created; if it already exists, the contents are replaced by value.
`DEFAULT fieldName := possiblevalue;`	If the fieldName exists in the Document being processed, associates fieldName with its current value. If the field does not already exist on the Document, the possiblevalue assigned in the DEFAULT statement is used.
	Similar to using the following conditional statement:
	FIELD fieldName := @If(fieldName = ""; value; fieldName);

Table 3.2 Keywords in the Notes Function Language (continued)

Keyword syntax	Description
`ENVIRONMENT variable := value;`	Assigns value to an environment variable in the user's **NOTES.INI** file (or **Notes Preferences** file if the software is running on the Mac OS).
	The variable specified is written to the **.INI/Preferences** file with a $ symbol prepended to it. This symbol is used to differentiate user defined values in the .INI/Preferences file from variables created by the Notes Client or Notes Server software.
	Since the scope of a variable in the Notes Function Language is the formula it is currently executing in, environment variables are sometimes used to create global values.
`SELECT logicalValue;`	In Agents, focuses the Agent to perform its task on only Documents that meet the logicalValue specified using the **SELECT** statement.
	For example:
	`SELECT @All`
	is used to run an Agent against all Documents.
`REM "comments";`	Inserts "comments" into the Notes Function formula.

Keywords must be the first entry in a statement. For example:

```
FIELD CreatedBy := @If(CreatedBy = ""; @UserName; "")
```

is a valid statement.

```
@If(CreatedBy = ""; FIELD CreatedBy := @UserName; "")
```

is invalid because the FIELD keyword is not the first word in the statement.

Keywords are displayed in Notes in uppercase. If you enter them in lowercase, Notes converts them to uppercase when saving a formula.

When to use the Notes Function language

There are two primary reasons to use the Notes Function Language:

1. When you are manipulating data within the scope of a single Document or a View, the Notes Formula Language can be an efficient tool. Examples include validation routines for fields on a Document, or fields that will be calculated for display in columns of a View.

2. When the object you are trying to attach code to only allows you to use the Formula Language. Table 3.3 lists the objects in Notes that only allow Function code to be attached to them.

Table 3.3 Objects in Notes that can only be programmed using the Notes Function Language.

Scope	Notes Object
Workspace	SmartIcons
Database	Replication formula
View design	Form formula
	Selection formula
	Column formula
	Hide action formula
Form design	Window title formula
	Section title formula
	Section access formula
	Insert subform formula
	Hide paragraph formula
	Hide action formula
Field design	Default value formula for editable field
	Input translation formula for editable field
	Input validation formula for editable field
	Value formula for computed field
	Keyword field formula
Rich Text field	Section title formula
	Hide paragraph

As you can see, there are a large number of objects in Notes, Release 4.0 that still don't support LotusScript. (Translated: If you're a new Notes developer and you just skimmed the part of the Programmer's Guide that dealt with the Function Language thinking you'd do all of your coding in LotusScript, take the manual back off the shelf and review the Function Language a little more.)

Examples of the Notes Function language

The following code uses the @If Function to check and see if the field **TotalHours** has a value of less than one. If the condition TotalHours < 1 evaluates as true, then the @Failure Function is used to interrupt the current statement and display the text constant. If TotalHours < 1 evaluates as false, then the @Success Function is used to tell the input validation routine that everything is OK.

```
@If(TotalHours < 1; @Failure("The minimum amount you can enter is 1
hour."); @Success);
```

The following formula prompts the user for a *yes* or *no* answer. If the user answers *yes*, then the @MailSend Function is used to send a mail message.

```
YesNo := @Prompt([YESNO];"More Information";
        "Would you like to request more information?");
Answer := @If(YesNo; "Yes"; "No");
@If(    Answer = "Yes";
    @MailSend(@UserName;"";"";"I'd Like More Information";
            "";"";"");
    @Return("")
    );
```

NOTE

In the Notes Function Language, two double quotes as an argument signify an empty string (NULL). This can be used to specify the default value for an argument.

LotusScript

Overview

LotusScript is a version of BASIC that was first introduced as a language in Lotus' ViP development tool and Ami Pro/WordPro word processing software. It was designed to extend an application to the point that it could manipulate its creations as objects. Before Lotus' acquisition by IBM, the company's stated intention for LotusScript was its inclusion in all desktop applications in support of better cross-application integration and "team computing" (process automation). At the time of this writing, it is unclear whether Lotus will continue its porting of LotusScript to all of its applications or whether a different language currently under development by IBM will be used, instead.

Regardless of whether LotusScript is included in all Lotus applications, the addition of the LotusScript language to Notes is considered by many analysts to be the single most significant improvement to Notes in Release 4.0. The reason for such an appraisal is that LotusScript brings a powerful tool to the Notes Development community for automating processes and moving information into and out of Notes databases. While LotusScript requires some investment in learning about object-oriented programming, Notes' classes, and the methods and properties that can be used to manipulate each object, the return on investment is a robust programming language with looping, branching, and event-driven scripting.

Another key feature of LotusScript is the ability to connect to external data using object-oriented references and the ability to include OCX's (programs written to the OLE2 specification) as part of the script.

Syntax

General
Scripts are entered as a series of statements, which can span multiple lines and include whitespace. A statement is delimited by a newline, unless the line continuation character, an underscore (_) preceded by a space or tab is used at the end of a line. Line continuation within a literal string or a comment is accomplished by enclosing the string in braces { } or vertical bars | |.

Multiple statements on a single line must be separated by a colon (:).

Looping or conditional statements must be paired with the proper end-of-loop or condition statement (i.e. `If…End If`, `For…Next`, etc.)

Variables and Fields

Variables in LotusScript are values stored in memory with a scope relative to their declaration and the point where they are declared. *Fields* are permanent values that are stored on Documents. A variable or field name must begin with a letter. Remaining characters can include letters, numbers, and the symbols _ and $. Spaces are not allowed. The name may contain up to 32 bytes (if you're using multibyte characters, 32 bytes is different from 32 characters).

Variable declarations begin with one of the words `Dim`, `Static`, `Private`, or `Public`.

- `Dim` indicates that a variable is nonstatic and private by default.
- `Static` indicates that the variable's value is saved between calls to the procedure where the variable is declared.
- `Public` indicates that the variable is visible outside the scope (module or class) where the variable is defined, for as long as this module remains loaded.
- `Private` indicates that the variable is visible only within the current scope.

Variables can be declared using any of the data types listed in Table 3.4.

Table 3.4 LotusScript variable data types

Data type	Suffix	Value range	Size
Integer	%	-32,768 to 32,767 Initial value: 0	2 bytes
Long	&	-2,147,483,648 to 2,147,483,647 Initial value: 0	4 bytes
Single	!	-3.402823E+38 to 3.402823E+38 Initial value: 0	4 bytes
Double	#	-1.7976931348623158+308 to 1.7976931348623158+308 Initial value: 0	8 bytes
Currency	@	-922,337,203,685,477.5807 to 922,337,203,685,477.5807 Initial value: 0	8 bytes

Table 3.4 LotusScript variable data types (continued)

Data type	Suffix	Value range	Size
String	$	(String length ranges from 0 to 32K characters) Initial value: "" (empty string)	(2 bytes/character)
Array		An set of elements using the same data type. An array can comprise up to 8 dimensions whose subscript bounds can range from -32768 to 32767. Initial value: Each element in a fixed array has an initial value appropriate to its data type.	Up to 64K bytes
List		A one-dimensional array of elements using the same data type. Elements in a list are referred to by name rather than by subscript.	Up to 64K bytes
Variant		Designed to contain any value, array, list, or object reference. Initial value: EMPTY	16 bytes
User-defined data type		A set of elements of possibly disparate data types, similar to a struct in the C programming language. Initial value: Member variables have initial values appropriate to their data types.	Up to 64K bytes
Class		A set of elements of possibly disparate data types together with procedures that operate on them. Initial value: When you create an instance of a class, LotusScript initializes its member variables to values appropriate to their data types, and generates an object reference to it.	
Object reference		A pointer to an OLE Automation object or an instance of a product class or user-defined class. Initial value: NOTHING.	4 bytes

After it is declared, a temporary variable is assigned a value using the Set statement if it an object, or the assignment operator (=):

```
Dim myItem as New NotesItem
Set myItem =
variableName = value
```

Unless the variableName is declared as a Variant, the value to the right of the assignment operator must match the declared type of variableName.

Some examples:

```
Dim arrayOfIntegers(5) As Integer
Dim singleInteger As Integer
Dim singleInteger%
```

In the final statement of the previous example, the % sign is used to declare the variable as an integer type.

Fields are referred to as a part of the object they belong to, using a decimal separator. Field types are the same types defined in our discussion of the Function Language. Variables declared using certain data types in LotusScript require conversion before they can be assigned to Fields. Some examples:

```
subj = doc.Subject
subj = doc.GetItemValue("Subject")
doc.Subject = | Now is the time for all good
               individuals to learn LotusScript |
```

Static Values

String constants are enclosed in quotation marks, vertical bars, or curly braces. Strings without delimiters are considered to be a variable or field.

```
NewVariable = "This is a string"
NewVariable = { This is a string that spans multiple
        lines }
NewVariable = ThisIsAnotherVariable
```

Numeric constants are entered as values without quotes. (A series of numbers in quotes is considered a *string*.) Scientific notation may be used to enter numbers with a high decimal precision.

```
TheValue = 110.2
```

Constants
Constants are static values associated with a label that you can use in your scripts. They can reference user-defined values or values built into the language. The built-in constants are defined in Table 3.5.

Table 3.5 LotusScript's built-in Constants.

Constant	Description
NULL	Used only with Variant variables to represent unknown or missing data. Many built-in functions return NULL when they are passed a NULL value.
NOTHING	The initial value of an object reference variable. As soon as you assign an object to the variable, the variable no longer contains NOTHING.
True	The numeric value -1. (In an If, Do, or While statement, which tests for TRUE or FALSE, any nonzero value is considered TRUE.)
False	The numeric value 0.
PI	The ratio of the circumference of a circle to its diameter.

NOTE

LotusScript predefines other constants in the file **LSCONST.LSS**. To include this in your scripts, use the %Include directive.

Operators

Table 3.6 lists the LotusScript operators in order of precedence.

Table 3.6 LotusScript operators in order of precedence.

Operator		Precedence
^	Exponentiation	1
- (unary)	Negation	2
*	Multiplication	3
/	Division	
\	Integer division	4
Mod	Modulo division	5
+	Positive	6
-	Negative	
&	String concatenation	7
=	Equal	8
<> or ><	Not equal	

Table 3.6 LotusScript operators in order of precedence. (continued)

Operator		Precedence
<	Less than	
<= or =<	Less than or equal	
>	Greater than	
>= or =>	Greater than or equal	
Like	Pattern matching	
Not (unary)	Logical negation	9
And	Logical and	10
Or	Logical or	11
Xor	Logical exclusive or	12
Eqv	Logical equivalence	13
Imp	Logical implication	14
Is	Object reference comparison	15

Operators with higher precedence are evaluated before operators with lower precedence. Operators with the same precedence are evaluated from left to right. To override the normal order of evaluation in an expression, use parentheses.

Subroutines and Functions
Functions in LotusScript can be predefined, user declared, or declared external to Notes. Once declared, functions are called using the following convention:

```
function-name(argument1, argument2, ... argumentn)
```

Functions that return values can be used as arguments within another function, or in conjunction with the assignment operators to store the return value in a variable or field.

If there is more than one argument for a function, it is separated from other arguments using a comma. Arguments must be of the type specified by the function's description (i.e., a function that requires a string argument must use a value that is either a string constant, a variable/field that is of type text, or a function that uses a string as its return value). Arguments can be passed by value, using `ByVal`.

Keywords

Keywords in LotusScript differ from Keywords in the Function Language in that they name LotusScript statements, built-in functions, built-in constants, and data types. Table 3.7 lists the LotusScript keywords.

Table 3.7 LotusScript Keywords

Abs	CCur	Currency	Else
Access	CDat	CVar	ElseIf
ACos	CDbl	DataType	End
ActivateApp	ChDir	Date	Environ
Alias	ChDrive	Date$	Environ$
And	Chr	DateNumber	EOF
Any	Chr$	DateValue	Eqv
Append	CInt	Day	Erase
As	Class	Declare	Erl
Asc	CLng	DefCur	Err
ASin	Close	DefDbl	Error
Atn	Command	DefInt	Error$
Atn2	Command$	DefLng	Evaluate
Base	Compare	DefSng	Event
Beep	Const	DefStr	Execute
Bin	Cos	DefVar	Exit
Bin$	CSng	Delete	Exp
Binary	CStr	Dim	FALSE
Bind	CurDir	Dir	FileAttr
ByVal	CurDir$	Dir$	FileCopy
Call	CurDrive	Do	FileDateTime
Case	CurDrive$	Double	FileLen

Table 3.7 LotusScript Keywords (continued)

Fix	Integer	LMBCS	Oct$
For	Is	Loc	On
ForAll	IsArray	Lock	Open
Format	IsDate	LOF	Option
Format$	IsElement	Log	Or
Fraction	IsEmpty	Long	Output
FreeFile	IsList	Loop	PI
From	IsNull	LSet	Preserve
Function	IsNumeric	LTrim	Print
Get	IsObject	LTrim$	Private
GetFileAttr	IsScalar	Me	Property
GoSub	IsUnknown	MessageBox	Public
GoTo	Kill	Mid	Put
Hex	LBound	Mid$	Random
Hex$	LCase	MidB	Randomize
Hour	LCase$	MidB$	Read
If	Left	Minute	ReDim
IMEStatus	Left$	MkDir	Rem
Imp	LeftB	Mod	Remove
In	LeftB$	Month	Reset
Input	Len	Name	Resume
Input$	LenB	New	Return
InputB	LenBP	Next	Right
InputB$	Let	NoCase	Right$
InputBox	Lib	Not	RightB
InputBox$	Like	NOTHING	RightB$
InStr	Line	Now	RmDir
InStrB	List	NULL	Rnd
Int	ListTag	Oct	Round

Table 3.7 LotusScript Keywords (continued)

RSet	Sqr	TimeValue	Use
RTrim	Static	To	UseLSX
RTrim$	Step	Today	UString
Second	Stop	Trim	UString$
Seek	Str	Trim$	Val
Select	Str$	TRUE	Variant
SendKeys	StrCompare	Type	Weekday
Set	String	TypeName	Wend
SetFileAttr	String$	UBound	While
Sgn	Sub	UCase	Width
Shared	Tab	UCase$	With
Shell	Tan	UChr	Write
Sin	Then	UChr$	Xor
Single	Time	Uni	Year
Space	Time$	Unicode	Yield
Space$	TimeNumber	Unlock	
Spc	Timer	Until	

When to Use LotusScript.

LotusScript can be used with any Notes Object that supports it. General rules of thumb for when to use LotusScript include whenever you are manipulating data external to the current Document you are working on, whenever the logic needed to arrive at a value requires branching or looping constructs, or whenever Formulas or Simple Actions are sufficient to accomplish a task. Obviously, you would also use LotusScript whenever you require functionality that is only available through the language, such as declaring functions from external programs, or manipulating OCXs. Table 3.8 lists all of the Notes Objects that can use LotusScript.

Table 3.8 Objects in Notes that can only be programmed using the Notes Function Language.

Scope	Notes Object
Database	Agent
View design	Action
Form design	Action
	Event
	Button
	Hotspot
Navigator design	Navigator
Layout Region design	Fields
Field design	Event
Rich text field	Button
	Hotspot

LotusScript Examples

The following example shows a script that could be attached to a **Form** button to create a new Document, copy the Subject and Body fields from the current Document into the new Document, then mail the new Document to a person called "Joe Smith."

```
Sub Click(Source As Button)
    Dim session As New NotesSession
    Dim workspace As New NotesUIWorkspace
    Dim db As NotesDatabase
    Dim uidoc As NotesUIDocument
    Dim doc1 As NotesDocument, doc2 As NotesDocument
    Dim item As NotesItem
    Set uidoc = workspace.CurrentDocument
    Set doc1 = uidoc.Document
    Set db = session.CurrentDatabase
    Set doc2 = New NotesDocument(db)
```

```
        Set item = doc1.GetFirstItem("Subject")
        Call item.CopyItemToDocument(doc2, "Subject")
        Set item = doc1.GetFirstItem("Body")
        Call item.CopyItemToDocument(doc2, "Body")
        Call doc2.Send(True, "Joe Smith")
    End Sub
```

The following example uses the `RemoveItem` method of the NotesDocument class to copy all of the **Headline** items in a database to a **Subject** item, then removes the **Headline** item.

```
    Sub Initialize
        Dim session As New NotesSession
            Dim db As NotesDatabase
            Dim dc As NotesDocumentCollection
        Dim doc As NotesDocument
        Set db = session.CurrentDatabase
        Set dc = db.AllDocuments
        For j = 1 To dc.Count
            Set doc = dc.GetNthDocument(j)
            While doc.HasItem("Headline")
                Call doc.ReplaceItemValue("Subject",
doc.GetItemValue("Headline"))
                Call doc.RemoveItem("Headline")
                Call doc.Save(True, False)
            Wend
        Next
    End Sub
```

Simple Actions

Simple actions are not an actual language in Notes—rather, they are an alternative interface to the LotusScript and Notes Function Language. We include them in this chapter because their inherent simplicity makes them a viable alternative to using the Function Language or LotusScript when you want to programmatically accomplish some goals.

Simple Actions can be a part of Forms, Views, or Agents, and are accessed by opening the Design Pane and clicking the Simple action(s) radio button (illustrated in Figure 3.14).

Once the Simple action(s) radio button is selected, the Add Action button will appear at the bottom of the formula window.

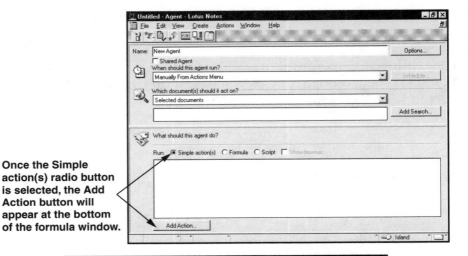

Figure 3.14 Selecting **Simple Actions** in the Design Pane.

Once the **Simple action**(s) radio button is selected, clicking the **Add Actions** button at the bottom of the formula window allows you to select from a list of predefined actions (see Figure 3.14).

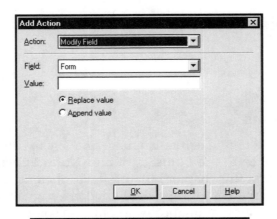

Figure 3.15 The Add Action dialog box.

Depending on the item selected in the **Action**: drop-down list, the values beneath the list change to reflect the information needed to perform the selected action. In Figure 3.15, the Modify Field action is selected, so the values beneath are the Field to be modified, the value to use, and whether or not the modification should replace any existing value in the field with the new value or append the new value to an existing value.

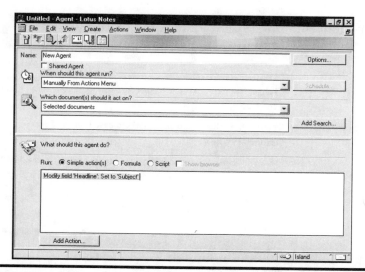

Figure 3.16 The simple action is represented as an icon in the formula window of the Design Pane.

Once an action has been selected from the **Add Action** dialog box and the user clicks OK, an icon appears in the formula window of the design pane.

Double-clicking the icon opens the action for editing. You can continue to add simple actions until you have the desired functionality for your Agent or formula.

Table 3.9 lists the simple actions available with Notes, Release 4.0.

CHAPTER THREE

Table 3.9 Simple Actions in Notes, Release 4.0

Action name	Description
Copy to Database	Copies the current Document to the database specified in the Add Action dialog.
Copy to Folder	Copes the current Document to the Folder selected in the Add Action dialog.
Delete from Database	Deletes the current Document from the database.
Mark Document Read	Toggles the read/unread indicator on the selected Document
Mark Document Unread	
Modify Field	Changes the value of the field specified to the value entered in the Add Action dialog.
Modify Fields by Form	Changes the value of the field specified based on the Form used by the Document.
Move to Folder	Moves the current Document to the Folder specified in the Add Action dialog.
Remove from Folder	Removes the current Document from the Folder specified in the add Action dialog.
Reply to Sender	Generates a mail message based on the parameters specified in the Add Action dialog when the current Document is processed.
Run Agent	Runs another Agent
Send Document	Sends the current Document to the user specified in the Document's SendTo field.
Send Mail Message	Sends a mail message based on the parameters specified in the Add Action dialog when the current Document is processed.
Send Newsletter Summary	Sends a document link along with headline information to the users specified in the Add Action dialog.
@Function Formula	Runs a formula expressed in the Notes Function language.

Reusability of Notes Code

Introducing Database Templates

While replication does, in a sense, make code reusable by allowing a single change to be distributed throughout replicas, the primary mechanism for code re-use in Notes is the Database Template.

A *Database Template* is a special class of Notes Database that other Notes databases can use to inherit design elements. (Templates are designated by an **.NTF** extension.) All elements in a Database Template can be inherited by a subscribing database, or selected elements can be inherited from multiple Database Templates on a granular level.

In Figure 3.17, the subscribing database inherits its entire design from a single Database Template. In Figure 3.18, the subscribing database inherits components of its design from multiple Database Templates.

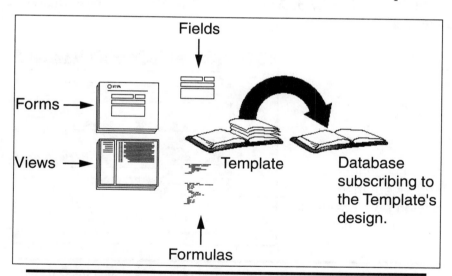

Figure 3.17 A database inheriting its entire design from a single template.

Figure 3.18 A database inheriting its design from multiple templates.

Database Templates can be stored on the database designer's local drive, or in the default directory of a Notes Server. If a Database Template is stored on a Notes Server, users with sufficient access can share the template to create new databases using the New Database dialog (see Figure 3.19).

New Databases can inherit their design from pre-made Database Templates.

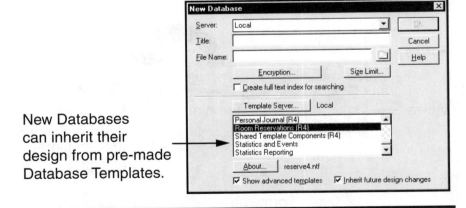

Figure 3.19 The New Database dialog box is opened using the **File, Database, New** command on the Notes Client menu.

Clicking the **Inherit future design changes** check box on the New Database dialog box causes information about the template to be stored in the newly created database. This information is used by the Notes Server to automatically update the subscribing database whenever a change is made to the template it is based on. To see if a Notes database's design is based on a template, use the **Properties for Database** dialog box shown in Figure 3.20 (opened by right-clicking on the database and choosing **Database Properties...** from the menu or by selecting **File**, **Database**, **Properties** from the Notes Client menu).

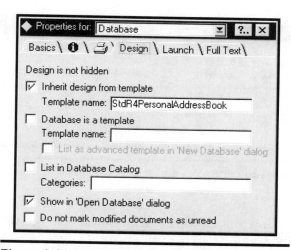

Figure 3.20 The Properties for Database dialog box.

Notice in Figure 3.20 that you can also use the **Properties for Database** dialog box to specify whether or not a database should be treated as a template by the Notes Server by clicking the **Database is a template** checkbox and entering a template name.

Using Templates to Keep Database Designs Up To Date

Once a database subscribes to a Database Template for its design elements, the subscribing database is automatically updated by a task that runs on the Notes Server called DESIGN. By default, this task is scheduled to run in the early AM on a Notes Server.

NOTE

Another good example of how understanding Notes Administration can make you a more effective developer: The DESIGN task can be disabled—check with your administrator to see if this is the case in your organization before you depend on this mechanism for updating your databases.

Additionally, you can manually force a design update by selecting a database on the Workspace and choosing **File**, **Database**, **Refresh Design** from the **Notes Client** menu. You will be prompted to select the location of the Template to use to perform the **Design Refresh**, and then prompted to continue (see Figure 3.21).

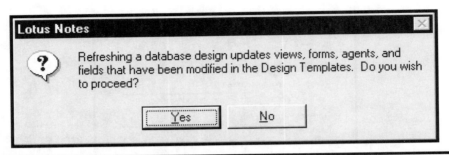

Figure 3.21 When you refresh the design of a Notes Database, you will receive this prompt.

In addition to being able to refresh a database's design from a template, you can also manually replace the entire design of a database using another template using the **File**, **Database**, **Replace Design** command on the **Notes Client** menu. This command updates the **Properties for Database** dialog box with information about the new template for future updates, and replaces all of the design elements currently in a database with the elements in the newly selected template.

The **Replace Design** command does not automatically convert a database's contents to the fields in the new design (meaning, if your new design has fields that weren't in the previous database, they will not have a value).

WARNING

Inheriting Designs from Multiple Database Templates

To have a database subscribe to design elements from multiple templates, open the Template containing the element you wish to include in your database, and copy it to the clipboard. When pasting the element into your database, you will receive the prompt illustrated in Figure 3.22.

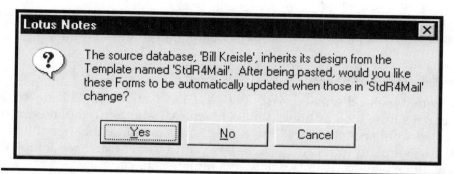

Figure 3.22 Allowing a new design element to continue to inherit its design from a Database Template.

Once the design element is pasted into the new database, you can confirm that it is inheriting its design or disable its inheritance by opening the **Folders Navigator**, selecting **Design** and the appropriate element, then right-clicking on the element to open the **Properties for Design Document** dialog box (see Figure 3.23).

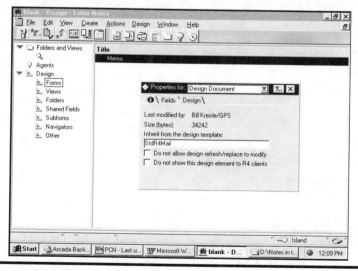

Figure 3.23 Examining the Design Document dialog box's properties.

Changing or removing the template name from the **Inherit from the design template** text box will cause the element to inherit its design from a different template or disable inheritance. Of course, you can also re-use Notes design elements by copying and pasting them from one database to another without specifying any type of inheritance.

Creating a Database Template

Now that we've discussed what Database Templates are and how to use them, it's time look at how to make them. A Database Template can be created from scratch by creating a new Notes database that is not based on any template, or it can, itself, be based on another Database Template. One quick way to create a database template is to copy the design of an existing database to another database, and then use the **Properties for Database** dialog box to name the new database as a template.

To copy a database's design into a new database, use the **File**, **Database**, **New Copy** command to open the **Copy Database** dialog box. After you have entered the new database's title and file name (using an **.NTF** extension), select the **Database design only** radio button in the Copy group (see Figure 3.24).

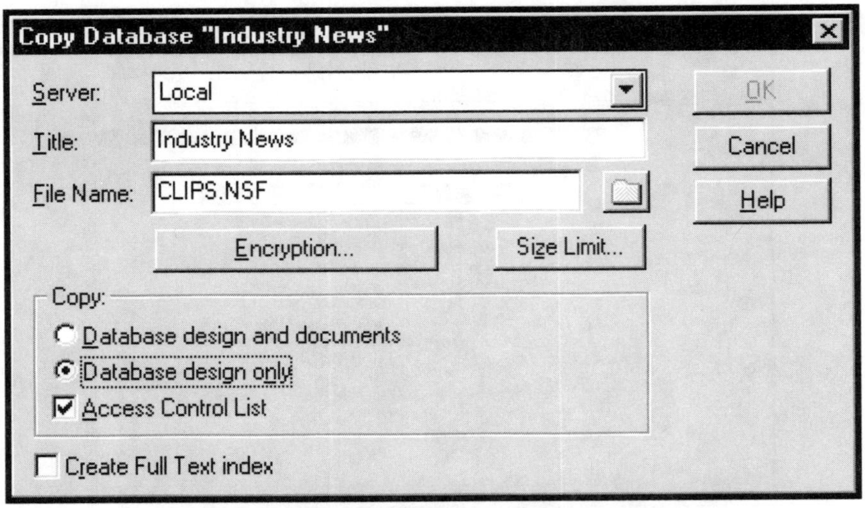

Figure 3.24 The **Copy Database** dialog box.

Once the new database copy is generated, you can make whatever changes are required by your application, then make the new database into a Template using the **Properties for Database** dialog box (see Figure 3.25).

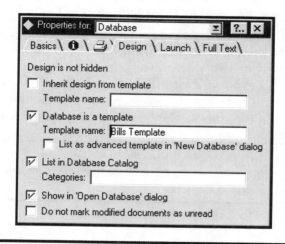

Figure 3.25 The **Properties for Database** dialog box.

This will cause the Template to appear whenever a new database is being created (see Figure 3.26).

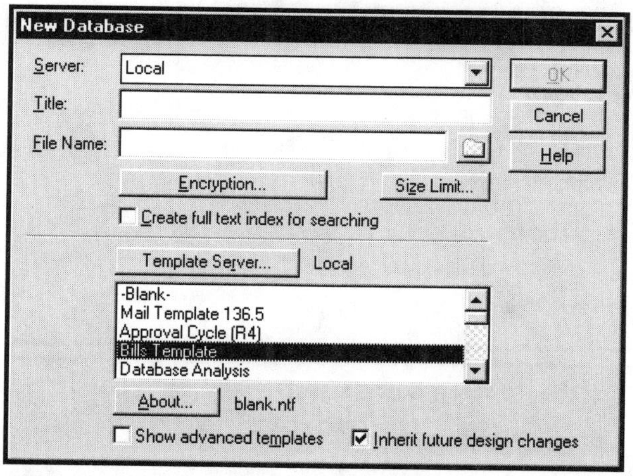

Figure 3.26 The newly created Template in the **New Database** dialog box.

Hiding Designs

After discussing all of the ways to make the code behind designs reusable, it might be good to point out that code can, by the choice of the database designer, be hidden from the users. Currently, there are two ways to accomplish this:

The first is to create a Master Template, then use that template to replace the design of a database. Check the Hide formulas and LotusScript box before clicking Replace. This allows you to have a Master Template where the design is readily available, but hides the design elements in the "production" version of the database.

WARNING

> Once you have hidden the design of a database, there is no way to unhide it. Make sure you have a backup copy of the Master Template in the event you inadvertently hide more than you meant to.

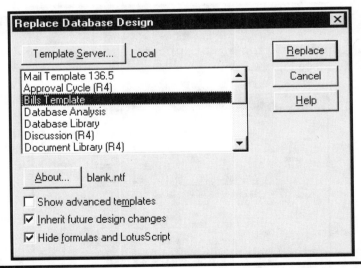

Figure 3.27 Using the **Replace Database Design** dialog box to hide the design of a subscribing database.

The second way to hide the design of a database is using a third-party tool called LNHIDE, provided by Iris Associates. This utility is available from the Iris World Wide Web server as well as the Lotus Notes Network's Knowledgebase. The purpose of LNHIDE is to scramble all design elements of a database so that they cannot be viewed by anyone, *including* the original party who scrambled the database.

Notes' Impact on the Applications Development Process

The integration of the Design Pane within the Notes Client combined with the ability to inherit, copy, and replicate design elements make Notes a Rapid Applications Development (RAD) tool. As such, the impact Notes can have on the Applications Development Process can be considerable.

Using Templates to create basic designs that embody a theme (such as a discussion database, a document store, or a contact management database), Lotus provides you with any number of applications that you can customize to your business needs within hours or even minutes. Additionally, the availability of thousands of off-the-shelf applications written in Lotus Notes by Lotus Business Partners gives users a tremendous head start in developing quality applications in Lotus Notes for their organization.

But, as Spiderman's Uncle Ben taught us when we were little, so we must teach you—"With great power comes great responsibility." The ability to quickly develop an application in Notes may lead to overpromising—a character trait guaranteed to hurt you if you're an applications developer. You want to underpromise and overdeliver, not the other way around.

Overpromising happens most frequently when a new developer working with Notes starts to look for the Grand Slam Home Run application the first time they step up to the plate. You can already see just from our discussion to this point that this is an understandable impulse. Here's a document-centric, multi-platform, mail-enabled, client/server development environment that incorporates security through Access Control and scalability through replication. Given the power of Notes, this urge to build the "Mother of all Enterprise" applications is a strong one.

And the IS Manager who stuck his or her neck out to get Notes into the company in the first place isn't going to say "Whoa. Too much, too soon," either. He's got a lot invested in seeing something big come out of Notes someday. In his mind, sooner would be preferable to later.

However, the best path to success in developing in Notes is to aim at a smaller target than an entire Air Traffic Control System your first time out. By building small applications that you can fully debug and use to work out the kinks, you accomplish two things.

1. You become a better Notes developer, learning what Notes is and is not capable of doing.
2. You give the users time to acclimate themselves to Notes and to learn how to use its features to their fullest advantage.

You definitely don't want to have a situation where you are introducing users to Notes for the first time and teaching them about your killer application that's going to replace the way they run their department all at once. There are a lot of concepts behind Notes for users to grasp. A day's training won't do it. Only time and active participation will. If you're so busy trying to get the company's entire past financial performance into a Notes View, you aren't going to have the time needed to do the handholding users want and need at the outset.

Of course, these statements are relative to your situation. If you're an API developer who's been asked to extend a Notes application to included information from the corporate mainframe and Notes is already an established technology in your business, you're going to approach Notes development differently than if you're just introducing Notes at your business and you've got this book and five others on your desk in an effort to learn as much about Notes as you can as quickly as possible.

If you're developing using third-party tools or the API, you probably have your own established methodologies to draw from, so we won't discuss them here. However, if you're learning Notes Development in an organization new to Notes, we'd like to talk a little longer.

A number of books exist that discuss the development process in Notes and its impact more robustly than we will here—Robert Larson-Hughes' and Hans Skalle's *Lotus Notes Application Development* and Mike

Falkner's *How to Plan, Develop, and Implement Lotus Notes in your Organization* both come to mind. In addition, Lotus' Accelerated Value Method (AVM) describes a development methodology that businesses can use to gain maximum productivity from Lotus Notes. You can find out more about Lotus' AVM on Lotus' World Wide Web page.

To add our two cents to the development process, we offer you these ten guidelines:

1. Remember that you are solving a problem. That problem has a flow that can be documented. Do so. Notes' RAD capabilities tends to push developers into a "code first, ask questions later" mentality. Don't do it! Capture the design on paper (or in a Notes Database) as thoroughly as possible before you begin to code.

2. Start small (common wisdom with any type of client/server development these days). Target a pilot that can scale over time to give you the ability to assess your work and Notes as a platform, and time to adapt it if necessary.

3. Use a timebox mentality. A Notes application can be developed so quickly that it may seem to appear overnight. Under those circumstances, ensure that the team of users and developers who are creating the database meet frequently throughout the development process to discuss progress and to assess the development cycle. If that means a one-hour meeting in the morning, a lunch update, and another meeting at the end of the day, that's what it means. Keep the entire team involved (including the Notes administration staff, if possible).

4. Establish interface and design standards as early as possible. Once Notes databases begin to proliferate at an organization, having guidelines in place for field-naming conventions, user interface elements, and the use LotusScript rather than the Formula Language will be significant not only for you as a developer, but also for your users.

5. Design Notes elements for reuse.

   a. Always work from a Database Template. This allows you to have a safe copy of the database's design. Resist the temptation to go directly into a production database and tweak a View or re-word the labels on a Form.

   b. When creating a button on a Form, try to write the code behind the button in such a way that it can be copied and pasted into another Form and be usable with as little reworking as possible. Add a comment at the top that explains how it could be used again.

   c. When coding elements that rely on user's names for security or workflow, try to use Roles and Groups instead of individual names. This eases administrative issues down the line for the eventual owners of the databases you are delivering.

6. Remember the International market. Even if you don't have a single customer in another country today, remember that you will tomorrow. Use Synonyms in Form and View Design. Leave adequate space on Forms for international date and time formats. (Synonyms are discussed thoroughly in the development manuals provided by Lotus.)

7. Empower individual departments to do their own development, but don't allow any database to be placed into production without a formal review of the database by your development staff to ensure that it meets standards. Help streamline the database (if necessary). Once Notes goes "production," you will be swamped with requests to have new databases put into production. Try to set aside time to provide department "power users" with formal development training in Notes, and encourage them to begin developing their own databases, drawing on your expertise when needed.

8. Take a personal responsibility to be an expert at Notes Development. Use every opportunity available to you to learn how other companies develop in Notes. Here are some suggestions:

   a. Follow the Lotus Business Partner (BP) Forum. The BP Forum is a Notes discussion database hosted on the Lotus Notes Network. It is open to all Lotus Business Partners to share ideas and experiences related to Notes.

b. Subscribe to at least one publication devoted to Notes Development.

c. Participate in Usenet discussion groups about Lotus Notes.

9. Don't substitute quantity for quality. New companies using Notes tend to have far too many databases to use effectively. Try to keep departments focused on a small subset of databases at the outset. This guideline appears to be in direct contradiction with the idea of letting departments develop their own Notes databases. But the key to remember is that you want to have departments developing databases that can capture their unique experience and knowledge, not generic discussion databases for all occasions.

10. Take time to understand your business. This is so fundamental, it seems condescending to put it here, but don't forget you're working with a tool that has literally transformed the ways companies do business! Introduced with skill, and leveraged to its strengths, Notes has provided some companies with 100—400% return on investment in a very short period of time. Conversely, implemented haphazardly, and used to crank out 100 databases a day that nobody even asked for, Notes begins to resemble the human brain. Tremendous potential, but only 10% of it is in use.

Extending Notes

Notes includes several APIs designed to allow it to be extended in an enterprise environment, as well as built-in tools such as NotesFlow, Notes F/X, OLE, and ODBC support. As the APIs are a topic we'll discuss in detail later in this book, and the built-in tools (NotesFlow, ODBC, and OLE) are covered fairly well in the Lotus Manuals, this section is dedicated to discussing ways to extend Notes using either undocumented or less described methods.

Dynamic Data Exchange (DDE)

Microsoft's original interapplication communications mechanism, DDE represents a way to access the commands and a limited number of design elements of another application. For example, a group of values from a spreadsheet can be pasted into a word processing document, and, through DDE, these values can be updated by connecting back to the original spreadsheet and getting up-to-date information.

In theory, a great tool. In practice, DDE suffered from limited architectural support, the learning curve of new Windows developers in implementing DDE-enabled applications, and Microsoft's habit of making its "standards" a moving target.

Notes' support of DDE is officially limited to the role of a DDE Client (meaning that Notes can send DDE commands to other applications, but does not accept any commands itself). This might be useful for using a button on Notes to dial a fax number in another Windows application's fax software. But, overall, the inherent instability of DDE combined with the fact that you'd have to ensure that the exact same application was installed on all clients that wanted to be a DDE client makes DDE a limited tool for extending Notes.

Now, if a Notes Client could be a DDE Server (meaning that Notes would accept DDE commands from other applications), that might be a different story. Then, you could write specific applications designed to extend Notes where it makes sense to do so. Unfortunately, if you examine the manuals that comes with Notes, you won't find any reference to Notes' use as a DDE Server.

Undocumented Notes DDE

Fortunately, if you examine other sources of information, you'll find that Notes does indeed, have an undocumented process that allows you to use Notes as a DDE Server. It turns out that you can use the link topic "Action" to send @Commands (a subset of the Notes Function Language) to the Notes Client.

What kind of application would you use this for? How about a pop-up calendar that allows you to select a date and push it back into a Notes field (see Figure 3.28)?

The project file for this calendar is included on the CD ROM in the **\DDE\SOURCE** Folder. It was written in Visual Basic 4.0, Professional Edition as a 32-bit application. You can install the application by going to the **\DDE\INSTALL** folder and running **SETUP.EXE.** I recommend you install the program in the same directory as NOTES.EXE.

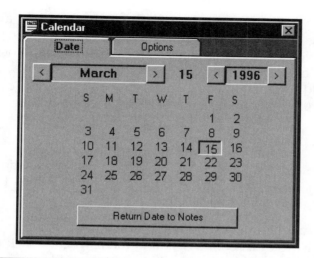

Figure 3.28 A pop-up calendar that can use DDE to push values into Notes.

The only portion of the code we need to discuss here is the portion that executes when a user clicks on the **Return Date to Notes** button:

```
Public Sub Return_Click()
    Clipboard.Clear
    If Form1.Option1(0) = True Then
        TheDate$ = Str$(CDate(Form1.MonthString.Caption
            & ", " & Form1.DayString.Caption
            & " " & Form1.YearString.Caption))
    Else
        TheDate$ = Format$(CDate(Form1.MonthString.Caption
            & ", " & Form1.DayString.Caption
            & " " & Form1.YearString.Caption),
            Form1.CustomFormatText.Text)
    End If
    Clipboard.SetText TheDate$
    Form1.CustomFormatText.LinkTopic = "Notes|Action"
    Form1.CustomFormatText.LinkMode = 2      'Manual
    Form1.CustomFormatText.LinkExecute "@Command([EditPaste])"
    Form1.CustomFormatText.LinkMode = 0      'None
    End
End Sub
```

This code basically (no pun intended) clears the clipboard, places a string on the clipboard based on the format the user chooses to return the date to Notes, and then opens a DDE session with Notes using the Action topic. Once a session is established, the program issues **@Command([EditPaste])** which pastes the contents of the clipboard into the current cursor location. Finally, the DDE session is closed.

Exciting, yet Terrifying

While the idea of using a simple interface to push information in and out of Notes like DDE has its appeal, there are some things to remember when dealing with Notes and DDE:

1. Applications aren't modal. If a user opens the pop-up calendar provided on this book's disk and then switches back to the Notes program before clicking the **Return to Notes** button, it is possible that they can reposition the cursor to a place where pasting in a date string is not helpful.

2. DDE limits you to Windows and OS/2.

3. Notes as a DDE Server is an undocumented feature. Undocumented features sometimes have a habit of disappearing with the next point release. Solutions you build today may not be around with the next release. (This particular feature has been available since Release 3, and the jump to a major point release didn't kill it, but you still need to be careful. Neither author would write a commercial product that uses the DDE Server capabilities for Notes, for example.)

Declaring Functions from other API's or DLL's

With the addition of LotusScript to Notes, the ability to use Windows API functions as well as those included in other DLL's is possible, using LotusScript's Declare Function statement. For example, adding the following lines to the Declarations section of a button in LotusScript:

```
Declare Function GetPrivateProfileString Lib "kernel32" Alias
"GetPrivateProfileStringA" (Byval lpApplicationName As String, Byval
lpKeyName As String, Byval lpDefault As String, Byval
```

```
lpReturnedString As String, Byval nSize As Long, Byval lpFileName As
String) As Long

Declare Function WritePrivateProfileString Lib "kernel32" Alias
"WritePrivateProfileStringA" (Byval lpApplicationName As String,
Byval lpKeyName As String, Byval lpString As String, Byval
lpFileName As String) As Long
```

will allow you to use the **GetPrivateProfileString** and
WritePrivateProfileString functions in the code for that button (in 32-bit
Windows). This might be useful for saving user preferences for a Notes
application in an .INI file other than **NOTES.INI**, or for checking the
value of an .INI setting in another Windows application.

The ability to use the Declare statement to reach external .**DLL** and
API functions extends Notes considerably, and allows experienced .**DLL**
developers to create re-usable routines. Some things to consider when
using API functions or DLL's are:

1. You must successfully translate between LotusScript data types
   and the data types used for the function being called. Care must
   be taken when working with parameters that expect a pointer or a
   null-terminated string. Some data types in LotusScript (such as a
   List) have no equivalent translation in C-language functions.

2. Like DDE, the use of API or .**DLL** routines restricts you to the
   operating systems that support Dynamic Link Libraries (OS/2 and
   Windows, for example). In addition, 16- and 32-bit windows
   presents problems to API declarations in that you have to test for
   your platform and call the appropriate API function. You can use
   the %If, %ElseIf, %Else, %End If directives in LotusScript to
   conditionally compile and execute code. For example:

```
%If Win32
    Declare Function ...
%ElseIf Win16
    Declare Function ...
%End If
```

Summary

- Notes provides users on all platforms with an integrated development environment. The full Notes client allows developers to create and modify all design elements. The Notes Desktop and Lotus Notes Mail Client will only allow users to create private Folders, Agents, and Views.

- The Design Pane is generally where Formulas or Scripts are associated with objects or events in Notes design elements. Some design elements will also allow code to be entered in different pages of their Properties dialog box.

- Notes offers developers three languages:

  1. The Notes Function Language is the original Notes language. It provides a collection of macro-like commands that users can execute sequentially to perform common tasks. Used to its strengths, the Function Language creates rapid applications. Used for tasks outside its design scope, the Function Language can frustrate developers with the number of steps needed to perform what would be simple tasks in other languages.

  2. The LotusScript Language is an object-oriented BASIC language that allows developers to create more robust programs, including conditional branching and event triggers. While the addition of LotusScript is a major advance in the languages of Notes, LotusScript is still not available with every design element. The Notes Function Language must still be used with these elements.

  3. Simple Actions are not a language but an interface to the Notes Function Language. Relatively powerful formulas can be created using an intuitive interface using Simple Actions.

- Notes design elements are made reusable through the creation of templates. Databases can subscribe to the design elements in a template, and the subscribing database's design will be updated automatically whenever the template(s) they subscribe to change. Another re-use feature is that design elements can be copied and pasted from one Notes database to another.

- Design elements in Notes replicate along with information. This means that a change made to the design of a database on one server can be propagated to any replicas of the database without further developer intervention.

- Notes' integrated development environment and ability to base a new design on the design of several other databases makes Notes a rapid application development tool.

The Building Blocks of Notes

This chapter fleshes out the components that make up a Notes application While we've already examined the majority of these elements on a conceptual level, the intent of this chapter is to provide specific information about the properties of each item and suggest guidelines for working with them.

A listing follows of the Notes items we'll examine in this chapter.

- Documents
- Forms
- Subforms
- Layout Regions
- Fields
- Labels
- Links, Hotspots, Pop-ups, Buttons, and Actions
- Sections
- Views
- Columns

- Folders
- Navigators
- Agents

Documents

Defining Documents

As we've seen in previous chapters, Documents are the basic level of storage in a Notes database. They provide a variable-length object container for fields, design elements, attachments, embedded objects, and pictures. This use of a single object container is the reason Notes can replicate the design as well as the information of a database.

Documents store information in Fields. One or more Forms work with the Document to provide the user with an interface to its Fields.

Fields can be added to Documents in three ways:

1. When a Form is associated with a Document using the **Create** or **View, Switch Form** command on the Notes Client Menu.

2. When an Agent or API program assigns a value to a field that does not already exist on the Document using LotusScript, Formula, Simple Actions, or the Notes API(s).

3. When the Notes Client or Notes Server software creates a special purpose or reserved field in response to an action performed by the user, an Agent, or a program. For example, opening a Document for editing may cause the $ModifiedBy field (a special purpose Notes field name) to be automatically added to it or updated by the Client or Server software.

The properties of Documents are available to developers through both the standard Notes Client and the Notes API(s). Since using an API to access individual Notes elements is covered in the second half of this book, this chapter will focus primarily on the properties of Documents that can be modified via the Notes Client. This moves the realm of our discussion to Documents that are used to store information instead of design elements.

Document Properties

You can access the properties of a Document by selecting it in a view or the Database Window and right-clicking the mouse on it to open the Properties for Document dialog box (see Figure 4.1).

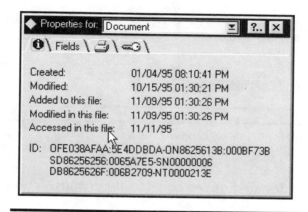

Figure 4.1 The Properties for Document dialog box.

From this dialog box, you can select the Information, Fields, Print, or Security tabs to view specific information.

Displaying Document and Field Information

The Information page of the Properties for Document dialog box (see Figure 4.1) provides you with time and document identification information for the selected Document. Some of this information, such as when the Document was last created or modified can be pulled into fields or View columns using formulas or LotusScript. Other elements, such as segments of that extremely long ID at the bottom of the Information Page (see Figure 4.1), can only be accessed through the Notes API.

The Fields page of the Properties for Document dialog box (see Figure 4.2) provides you with information about the current Document's fields and their properties.

To use the Fields page, select a field in the scrolling list on the left of the page, and examine a Field's properties in the text box on the right of the page.

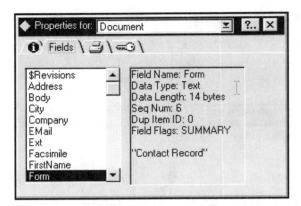

Figure 4.2 The Fields page of the Properties for Document dialog box.

Adding a Header or Footer to the Document When It Is Printed

The Print page of the Properties for Document dialog box (see Figure 4.3) provides you with an area to store header and footer information that can be used whenever that Document is printed. These settings will override the settings in the Print page Properties for Form dialog box, Properties for View dialog box, and the Properties for Database dialog box (all of which we'll examine later in this chapter).

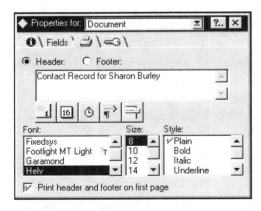

Figure 4.3 The Print page of the Properties for Document dialog box.

Restricting Access to a Document or Its Fields

The Security page of the Properties for Document dialog box allows you to restrict access to a Document on a per-name or per-group/role basis. This is equivalent to creating a Reader Names field on the Document called $Readers and assigning the field values. This option can work in conjunction with other Reader Names fields on a Document.

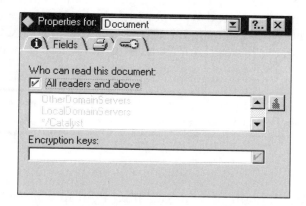

Figure 4.4 The Security page of the Properties for Document dialog box.

NOTE A common mistake most new developers make with a Reader Names field or the Security page is failing to include the names of all of the Notes Servers that should be allowed to replicate the Document among themselves. This causes a Document to be added to one Server but not to database replicas anywhere else in the organization.

If you have sufficient access, you can use the Encryption keys portion of the Security page to encrypt one or more Documents using the available encryption keys.

Forms

Defining Forms

Forms organize the fields and objects in a Document that users need to move information into and out of databases. New Forms are created using the **Create, Design, Form** command on the Notes Client menu. Existing Forms are edited by opening the Folders Navigator of a database or selecting **View, Design** from the Notes Client menu, opening the Forms header, and selecting the desired Form from the Forms View.

SHORTCUT

You can also open the Folders Navigator in a Notes database by right clicking the database's icon and selecting **Go To Design** from the pop-up menu.

A Form can be thought of as a Rich-Text item in a Design Document where text, fields, pictures, objects, buttons, hotspots, links, subforms, layout regions, sections, and colors can be combined into paragraphs creating a desired appearance and functionality. Figure 4.5 illustrates a Form being modified in the Design Pane. Figure 4.6 shows the same Form from the end user's perspective.

In the Notes development process, Forms are usually the first design elements that are created.

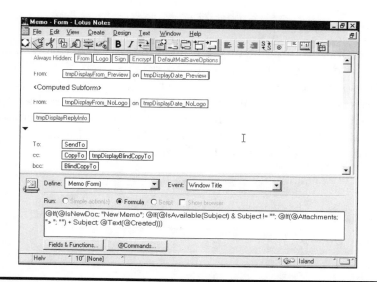

Figure 4.5 The Memo Form from the Lotus Notes Mail template as seen by an applications developer.

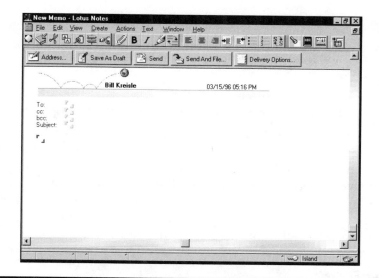

Figure 4.6 The Memo Form in a Lotus Notes Mail database as seen by the end user.

Form Properties

As Form Properties are one of the critical elements of a Notes Database, there are a number of properties to discuss when looking at the Properties for Form dialog box (see Figure 4.7). The dialog box is opened by right-clicking on the Form in the Design Pane and selecting Form Properties from the pop-up menu. These properties are presented to the applications developer using the Basics, Defaults, Launch, Print, and Security pages of the Properties for Form dialog box.

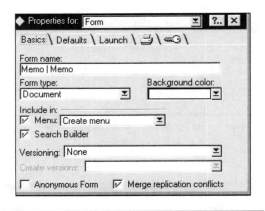

Figure 4.7 The Properties for Form dialog box.

The Basics Page of the Properties for Form Dialog Box

The Basics page of the Properties for Form dialog box allows you to specify the Form's name, type, and color; where users should have access to the Form when working with the database; what level of Document versioning the Form should allow; whether or not the Form should allow users to create Anonymous Documents; and whether or not a Notes Server should merge Replication Conflicts between Documents created with this Form automatically.

Naming Forms

To provide your Form with a Name, you can use the Form name text box at the top of the Basics page. If you look at Figure 4.7, you'll notice that the name given to the Form in the illustration is Memo | Memo. The two names separated by a vertical bar represent the use of a synonym. When a synonym is used to name a Form, the value entered on the left side of the vertical bar is used by Notes to display the Form to the user via the Create menu or the Search Builder dialog box (see Figure 4.8). The value entered to the right of the vertical bar is the name used by Notes internally when the form will be referenced programmatically.

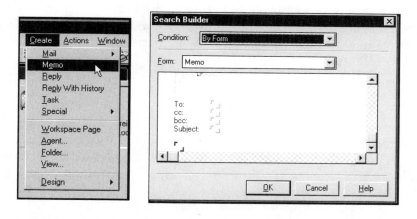

Figure 4.8 The Form's name appears in the Create menu and the Search Builder dialog box.

For Windows, OS/2, and Unix Clients, you can include a keyboard accelerator in the Form by placing an underscore (_) before the letter you wish to be the accelerator. If you do not "hard code" an accelerator key into a Form name, Lotus automatically chooses one.

If a database has more than one form, Notes sorts the names of the Forms in the **Create** menu alphabetically. If you wish to change the order in which forms will sort, you can prefix the Form's name with a number or letter. For example, using these two names for two separate forms would cause them to appear in the order listed:

1. Measurements | Measure
2. Analysis | Analyze

NOTE Notes sorts Form names as *strings*. This means a choice on the Create menu that begins with 10 will fall between the choices that start with 1 and 2. Since Notes sorts spaces prior to digits, if you are going to have more than nine numbered Forms in a menu, consider using a space prior to the single digit numbers to force them to stay together, and moving the double-digit numbers to the position after 9.

You can create cascading menus by including a backslash in the Form Name. Cascading menus allow you to group Forms by using a common prefix, a backslash, then a submenu choice. For example, create a group of Forms in a database with the following names:

```
Special\Bookmark
Special\Phone Message
Special\Serial Route Memo
Special\Memo to Database Manager
```

They would appear on the Create menu of the Notes Client as illustrated in Figure 4.9.

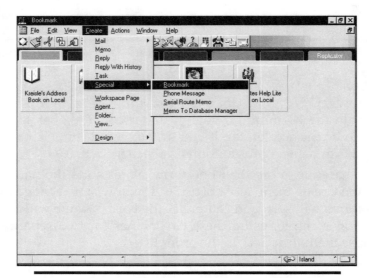

Figure 4.9 Cascading Form names on the Create Menu.

While not illustrated above, you can also use synonyms with Forms that have cascading names (i.e., `Special \ Bookmark | Bookmark` would be a valid Form name). The practice of using synonyms when naming Forms gives the designer flexibility in making modifications to the database later. It is also a good practice to use whenever you expect your database to be in service in more than one language, since the value in the left of the synonym can be changed without affecting the performance of any scripts or formulas in the database. With that in mind, it is a good idea to always use the synonym convention, even if you want both names to be the same.

Specifying the types of Documents Created by a Form

The `Form type` list box on the Basics page of the Properties for Form dialog allows you to select whether Documents that use this Form are to be Documents, Responses, or Responses to Responses. As you recall from earlier discussion, Response Documents are similar in function to yellow gummed notes on the pages of a book. Response Documents are related to the Document they are attached to, but they can be associated with another Document if desired by moving them to the next page. Response to Response Documents are analogous to gummed notes on top of earlier Post-it Notes. While Response Documents must be associated with a Document only, a Response to Response Document may be associated with a Document or another Response, up to dozens of levels.

Changing the Background Color of a Form

The Color list on the Basics page of the Properties for Form dialog allows you to specify a color to be used in the Form's background. Being able to select colors offers a great deal of flexibility in designing interface elements. However, colors should be used with restraint. Some combinations of colors are fatiguing to the human eye. Since most people are used to seeing Document-oriented information as a black-on-white document, it is our suggestion that you standardize on white as the background color, and have predefined combinations of colors that can used for the labels and fields that are added to the Form.

Specifying Where a Form Should Be Seen by the User

The "Include in" section on the Basics page of the Properties for Form dialog allows you to select whether or not a Form should be displayed in the Create menu of the Notes Client and the Search Builder dialog.

If you de-select either option, the Form will not appear in these places. The Form can still be accessed programmatically, however. The drop-down list next to the Create menu checkbox also allows you to specify whether or not the user should see the Form's name directly on the Create menu of the Notes Client, or in a dialog box that appears when the user selects **Create, Other...** from the Notes Client menu. This allows you to make less commonly used Forms in a database accessible without cluttering up the Create menu for the user.

There are a number of reasons for hiding Forms from users. Notes' robust use of a Form Formula, Print Using Form setting, and the View, Switch Forms command, combined with the logistics of an effective Workflow make it possible to have a number of different Forms for a given Document that only need to be displayed when certain conditions are met. These extra Forms may have additional fields, or fewer fields, but if every variation of the Forms isn't necessary to the user, hiding the Forms and using Notes to access them programmatically makes good sense.

NOTE

You can also hide a Form by enclosing its name in parentheses. By way of example, the name (User Preferences) | UPref might be used to create a Form that can only be opened when the users selects an Agent from the Actions menu.

Using Forms for Document Versioning

You can use the versioning properties of a Form to allow uses to exercise version control over documents that are created and edited using that form. These properties are set on the Basics page of the Properties for Form dialog box. Use the following selections in the Versioning drop-down list:

1. New versions become responses. This option saves any edits made to a Document using this Form and property as a Response

Document. The Response will be associated with the original version of the Document.

2. Prior versions become responses. This option saves any edits made to a Document using this Form and property as a main Document, and saves the previous version of the Document as an associated Response.

3. New versions become siblings. This option saves any edits made to a Document using this Form and property as a new Document, at the same level of the original version.

4. None. This option disables versioning. Any changes made are saved to the original Document are saved within it.

Once you have made a selection in the Versioning drop-down list, you can use the drop-down list below it to select whether versioning will be manual or automatic. *Automatic versioning* means that when the user elects to save changes, the version property specified will be exercised. Manual versioning allows users more flexibility in versioning, in that they must select File, Save As New Version from the Notes Client menu to create a new version—otherwise, changes are saved as part of the original Document.

NOTE

Versioning only occurs on Documents that are using a Form with a versioning property specified. If a user edits a Document using more than one Form, he can bypass the versioning feature.

You can use versioning whenever you want to have a revision history for a type of Document, or you want to have a process that captures the prior version for review before changes are accepted.

Allowing Form-based Documents to Be Anonymous

Clicking on Anonymous Form on the Basics page adds a field to the Document called $Anonymous, and assigns it a value of 1. When the $Anonymous field is present on a Document, it disables the automatic tracking by Notes of Document authors and editors.

NOTE

To ensure anonymity, you must also ensure that none of the fields you add to the Form contain references to the author or editor programmatically.

Anonymous forms are useful for allowing users to participate in suggestion databases or discussion databases where knowing the author's name might have an adverse impact.

Merging Replication Conflicts Automatically

Documents created using this form and property will allow Notes to automatically resolve replications conflicts using field-level replication. When this property is enabled and a replication conflict occurs, Notes handles it as follows:

1. If the changes are made in two separate fields on the Document, Notes creates a single Document with each field that is changed incorporated into it.

2. If changes are made in the same field on a Document, Notes creates a main document (a winner) and a response document (a loser) based on the time of edit and the number of changes made. It will be up to a human being to resolve the conflicts.

NOTE

Obviously, if a Document only has two fields, the likelihood that users will change the same field is greater than if a Document has thirty fields. If you are building a solution where you want merges resolved automatically, but are using a small number of fields, you might have to consider writing an API program or LotusScript Agent that resolves conflicts where the same field is changed in both versions of a Document.

The Defaults Page of the Properties for Form Dialog Box

Using the Defaults page of the Properties for Form dialog (see Figure 4.10), you can specify a number of automatic behaviors for a Form.

These properties include specifying a default database Form, enabling or disabling support for Notes F/X, Form storage, Form recalculation, default values for fields created based on the Form, and automatic opening and closing actions when Documents based on the Form are used.

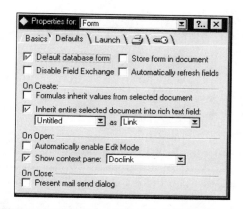

Figure 4.10 The Defaults page of the Properties for Form dialog box.

Making a Form the Default for a Database

The first option, `Default database form` specifies a Form to be used whenever Documents are mailed or pasted into a database using a Form that is not contained in the database. (Say, for example, you make the Form "Main" the default form in a database. A user pastes in a Document into your database that was created using a Form called *Widget*. Since the database the Document was pasted into does not contain a "Widget" Form, the database will automatically assign the "Main" Form to the incoming Document to allow it to be displayed.)

Only one Form in a Database can be made the Default Form. It will appear in the Forms View marked with an asterisk (see Figure 4.11). While a Default Form is not required for a database, it is recommended that you specify one Form as the Default to anticipate the possibility that a user may inadvertently paste Documents into your database that don't belong there.

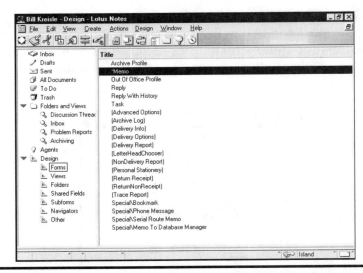

Figure 4.11 The Default Form for a Database is marked with an asterisk.

Storing the Form in the Document

As we discussed in Chapter 2, mail enabling in Notes allows users to route Documents from person to person, database to person (and vice versa), and from database to database. As the Documents move between databases, it is necessary to do one of the following to ensure that the Document can be processed effectively:

- Have a Form with the same name and similar fields in each database that the Document will travel to;
- Have a Default Form in each database that contains similar fields as the Document;
- Store the Form within the Document so that a database can open it with the correct Form regardless of what type of Forms it contains.

To use the third option, click on the Store form in Document checkbox on the Defaults page of the Properties for Form dialog box (Figure 4.10). While the most flexible option in terms of recreating a Document from database to database, this option dramatically increases the storage used by a Document. If you intend to have thousands of Documents in a database, you should consider solutions that do not rely on stored forms.

If you have a number of remote users, you should weigh the decision on stored forms, as well. In an application where hundreds of users with databases you cannot modify want to share documents remotely (such as an application on CompuServe or WorldCom), a stored form may save your life. In an application where local users go home at night and work remotely, using stored forms may cause users unnecessary delays as they must move a copy of the Form along with every Document via modem.

Disabling Field Exchange for Documents Using a Form

Clicking on `Disable Field Exchange` on the Defaults page prevents OLE and LSX objects stored on a Form from using Notes F/X to exchange information between the object's properties and Notes fields. This may be a consideration if you intend to deploy an application across multiple platforms.

Causing Fields on a Document Using This Form to Refresh Automatically

Selecting `Automatically Refresh Fields` from the Defaults page of the Properties for Form dialog box causes calculated fields on a Document to be updated whenever an editable field is changed. This option will cause Notes' performance to slow as recalculation occurs, but may be necessary if you are having users enter values that you wish to have a running total for.

You may also want to set this option if your application depends on another Notes database in a relational fashion (i.e., entering the customer id number causes fields containing customer information to be filled in from another database).

Automatically Filling in the Value of Some Fields Based on Another Document

Selecting `Formulas inherit value from selected document` on the Defaults page allows you to create fields on the Form that can automatically inherit the value of fields on the Document that was selected when the new Document is created.

For example, in a discussion database, you may wish to inherit the Subject field of the main topic whenever a response is composed. To do this, you would enable this property for the Form used to create a Response, and add a field (let's call it `OriginalSubject`) to the Response Document with the following default value formula:

```
Subject;
```

This single argument causes the OriginalSubject field to inherit the value in the field Subject. It is equivalent to the statement:

```
FIELD OriginalSubject := Subject;
```

Storing an Entire Document in the Rich Text Field of Another Document

As stated earlier, a Form is a Design Document in a Database. All of the design elements that are stored on a Form are essentially stored in a Rich Text field. Because of this, it is easy to copy an entire form and paste its contents into a Rich Text field.

Using the `Inherit entire selected document into rich text field` option on the Defaults page, it is also possible to automatically copy a selected Document and its values into a Rich Text field whenever a new Document is created using this Form and property.

NOTE This option inherits everything, including buttons, pop-ups, and links. Since buttons most likely were written to act on discrete elements of the original Form that are now merged into one field on the new Form, it is possible that the user can initiate Agents or actions that will fail.

Using the drop-down list below this option, you can also specify to inherit an entire Document as a Document Link instead of the field's contents.

Performing Tasks Automatically When a Document Based on a Form Is Opened

The On Open section of the Defaults page allows you to perform actions automatically for the user whenever they open a Document based on this Form.

Clicking on Automatically enable Edit Mode causes Notes to automatically place in Edit Mode any Document opened using this form. This action saves the user a step if the process in support of the application you are designing requires frequent editing of Documents, or if you want to create a class of Document similar in purpose to a Draft Document.

Clicking on Show Context Pane on the Defaults page allows you to open a Preview Pane of either a Parent Document or the first Document Link in the database whenever it is opened. Figure 4.12 illustrates a Response Document in a database with its parent Document in a Preview Pane.

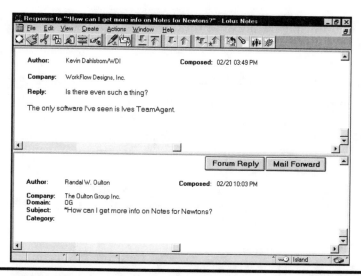

Figure 4.12 A Response Document with its parent in the Preview Pane.

Performing Tasks Automatically When a Document Based on a Form Is Closed

The `On Close` section of the Defaults page allows you to specify actions that should be performed whenever a Document based on the current Form and property are closed.

Selecting `Present mail send dialog` allows you to automate workflow processes by presenting users with a Close Window dialog box (see Figure 4.13) whenever a Document created with the current Form is closed.

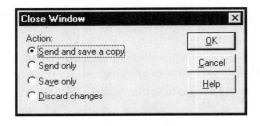

Figure 4.13 The Close Window dialog box

The Launch Page of the Properties for Form Dialog Box

The Launch page (see Figure 4.14) allows you to specify whether or not a Document Link, attachment, or OLE object should be launched automatically whenever a Document is created or opened using the Form.

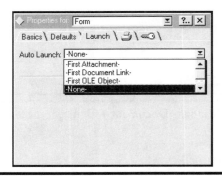

Figure 4.14 The Launch page of the Properties for Form dialog box.

Automatically Launching the First Attachment in a Form When a Document Is Created or Opened

Selecting First Attachment from the Auto Launch drop-down list will cause Notes to try to launch the first file attachment it finds in a Form, from top to bottom, left to right. If the file has an .EXE, .COM, .BAT, or other extension recognized as executable by the operating system, the program will be run automatically. If the file has any other extension, Notes will try to find the program associated with the extension and launch the program and the file.

Obviously, this action requires special considerations when you are designing an application to run on multiple platforms.

Automatically Launching the First Link in a Form When a Document Is Created or Opened

Selecting First Document Link from the Auto Launch drop-down list will cause the first Link in the Document to be launched whenever a Document is created or opened using the Form. This option might be useful for delivering disclaimer information or special instructions (even advertisements) whenever a user opens or creates a Document.

Automatically Launching an OLE Object When a Specified Action Is Performed on a Document

Selecting First OLE Object from the Auto Launch drop-down list will cause Notes to launch the first embedded object in the Form whenever it is used to perform specified actions on a Document. When this option is selected, a number of additional properties for the Form are displayed in the Launch page (see Figure 4.15).

These additional properties are provided to make Notes a robust object container. However, their dependence on common versions of software implementing OLE in a common manner, combined with the fact that Notes is designed to run on multiple platforms make them an option that should be thoroughly tested before rolling out a production application. For our part, we're going to point out that these options are covered in detail in the Notes Help database and the documentation provided by Lotus.

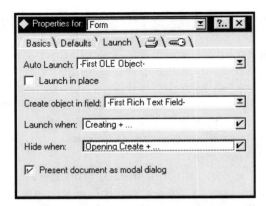

Figure 4.15 The additional properties available when First OLE Object is selected from the Auto Launch drop-down list.

The Print Page of the Properties for Form Dialog Box

The Print page of the Properties for Form dialog allows you to specify header and footer information to be printed whenever a Document using this Form is sent to a printer. The values entered here can be overridden if the Print page of the Properties for Document dialog box has information entered to print as part of the header and footer.

The Security Page of the Properties for Form Dialog Box

The Security page of the Properties for Form dialog box (see Figure 4.16) allows you to specify which users should be allowed to read and create Documents using the Form and its properties.

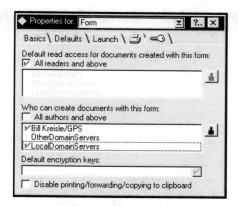

Figure 4.16 The Security page of the Properties for Form dialog box.

Specifying Who Can Read Documents Created Using a Form

Use the Default read access for documents created with this form section of the Security page to determine who should be allowed to read Documents created using the Form and its properties.

Selecting All readers and above allows any user with Reader privileges or greater in the Access Control List (ACL) of a database to read Documents created using the Form.

De-selecting All readers and above enables the list beneath the check box. Using the list, select one or more users, servers, or groups that are allowed to read Documents created using the Form. Clicking the people button to the left of the list box opens the Names dialog box (see Figure 4.17), allowing you to add more users or groups to the list.

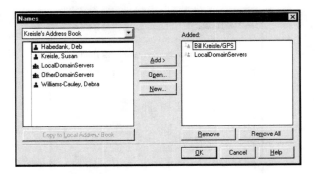

Figure 4.17 The Names dialog box.

Specifying Who Can Use a Form to Create Documents

Use the "Who can create documents with this form" section of the Security page (Figure 4.16) to determine who should be allowed to create new Documents using the Form and its properties.

Selecting "All authors and above" allows any user with Author privileges or greater in the Access Control List (ACL) of a database to create Documents using the Form.

De-selecting "All authors and above" enables the list beneath the check box. Using the list, select one or more users, servers, or groups that are allowed to create Documents using the Form. Clicking the people button to the left of the list box opens the Names dialog box (see Figure 4.17), allowing you to add more users or groups to the list.

Disabling Printing, Copying, or Forwarding a Form Through Mail

A final Form property can be enabled or disabled by selecting "Disable printing/forwarding/copying to clipboard" on the Security page of the Properties for Form dialog. When this option is enabled, Documents created using the Form cannot be printed, nor can their contents be copied to the clipboard or inherited into a Rich Text field.

NOTE

This should not be considered a hard and fast security feature as it is still possible to use the operating system (for example, the PrintScreen command in Windows) to print a portion of a Document. In addition, if the user has sufficient access, they can use the same Properties for Form dialog box to disable this feature as you used to enable it.

Automating a Form by Attaching Scripts to a Form Event

In addition to the automatic events available to a developer using the Properties for Form dialog box, it is possible to attach Scripts to other events for a Form using the Design Pane (we discussed Design Pane in Chapter 2). The events for which you can write Form event scripts are:

- *Initialize*—Precedes all other events. Occurs before a new or existing Document is displayed to the user.
- *QueryOpen*—Occurs after the Initialize event, but before a Document is displayed to the user, allowing the user to cancel opening the Document.
- *Postopen*—Occurs after a document is displayed to the user.
- *Postrecalc*—Triggered after all fields in a document are recalculated.
- *Querysave*—Occurs just before a document is saved, allowing the user to cancel saving the document.
- *Querymodechange*—Occurs before a Document is changed to read or edit mode.
- *Postmodechange*—Occurs after a Document is changed to read or edit mode.
- *Queryclose*—Occurs before a Document is closed, allowing the user to cancel closing the document.
- *Terminate*—Occurs after the document is closed.

An example of using an event script with a Form might be to record the number of times a Document is read in a newsletter database. When the Postopen event for a Form is triggered, you could write the time, user name, and subject of the Form's Document to another database. Later, when the user finished reading the Document, you could use the Terminate event to determine how long the user left the Document in read mode and write that information to the other database's Document, as well.

Subforms

Defining Subforms

Subforms are designed to be a building block for Forms. They allow a developer to group commonly used fields together and include them on multiple other Forms, as illustrated in Figure 4.18.

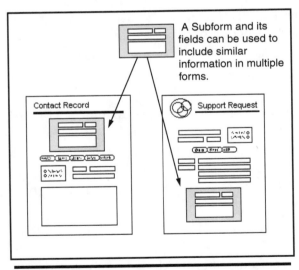

Figure 4.18 A conceptual illustration of Subforms.

Subforms are created by selecting **Create, Design, Subform** from the Notes Client menu, and they are edited using the Folders Navigator to open the Subform View. They are inserted into a Form using the **Create, Insert Subform** command on the Notes Client menu and the Insert Subform dialog box (see Figure 4.19)

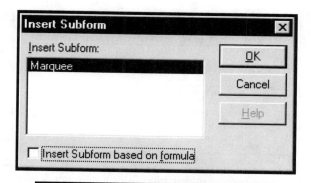

Figure 4.19 The Insert Subform dialog box.

Selecting a Subform from the list and clicking on **OK** inserts it at the current cursor location of the Form you are designing.

A simple example of a Subform might be a group of calculated fields designed to display a group of customer fields like a business card. This Subform could be placed in any Form that used these customer fields, and could be used when the Document is being read or previewed (compare Figures 4.20a and 4.20b).

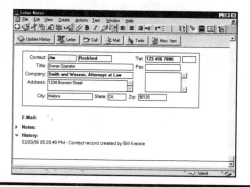

Figure 4.20a Contact information displayed using one Subform while editing.

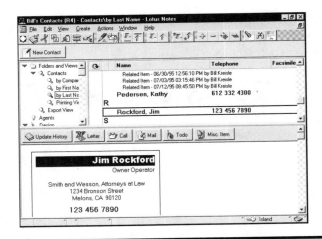

Figure 4.20b The same contact information using a different Subform while reading.

Defining Computed Subforms

Clicking 'Insert Subform based on formula on the Insert Subform dialog box (Figure 4.19) prior to clicking **OK** will cause Notes to insert a placeholder for a Computed Subform in the Form you are designing (see Figure 4.21). Use the formula window of the Design Pane to enter a Formula or Script that evaluates to the name of an existing Subform.

A Computed Subform uses a formula to determine which Subform to insert in the Form's placeholder under what circumstances

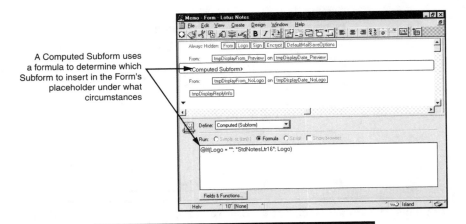

Figure 4.21 A Computed Subform and its formula.

A simple example of a Computed Subform might be a footer that you want to include at the bottom of all Documents, created by using a Form that changes based on a value the user enters into the Document to define its type.

A more complex example of how Computed Subforms are used can be found by running the **Actions, Mail Tools, Choose Letterhead** Agent. When this Agent is run the user sees a Document with a list box and an illustration of the currently selected Letterhead (see Figure 4.22).

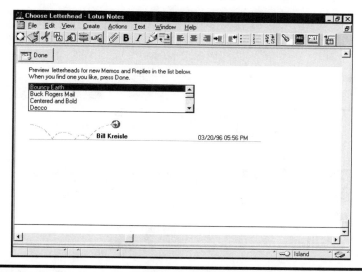

Figure 4.22 Running the Actions, Mail Tools, Choose Letterhead Agent.

When a different Letterhead style is selected from the keywords list, a new Letterhead is displayed on the Document (Figure 4.23).

The different pictures presented at the bottom of the Document are Subforms, stored in the Lotus Notes Mail database. The keywords field that is the list box on the Form has its properties set to cause Notes to recalculate the current Document whenever the selection is changed. The Postrecalc event script on the Form then uses LotusScript to close the current Document and open a new Document, causing a new Subform to be displayed based on the user's choice.

When the user closed the Document, the user set a preference that is then incorporated into the Lotus Notes Mail Memo Form (see Figure 4.24).

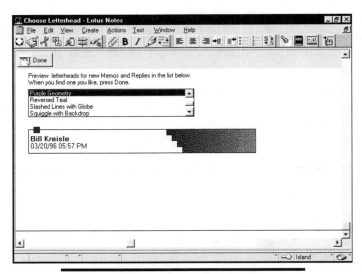

Figure 4.23 Selecting a different Letterhead.

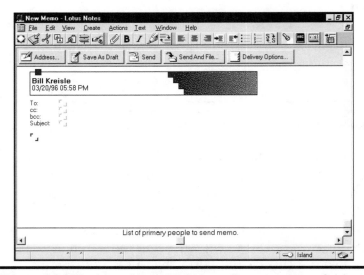

Figure 4.24 The Lotus Notes Mail Memo Form contains a Subform.

Of course, environment variables, hidden fields, and reserved fields also play a part in our second example's functionality, but the point is that—based on the user's preferences on a number of Forms—Subforms can be used to display the same information differently.

Subform Properties

The Properties for Subform dialog box (see Figure 4.25) allows the developer to give the Subform a name, as well as to set options that control whether or not a Subform can be used by other applications developers or Notes Release 3 users.

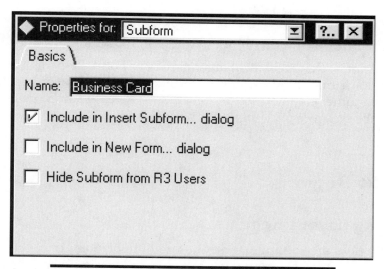

Figure 4.25 The Properties for Subform dialog box.

Naming a Subform

Like Forms, Subforms support the use of synonyms in their name. Unlike standard Forms, however, the value on the left of the synonym is not intended to appear in the Create menu or the Search Builder dialog. Rather, it is used in the Insert Subform dialog box (Figure 4.19).

Restricting the Use of a Subform

If you do not want developers to use a Subform as a part of their new Forms, de-selecting "Include in Insert Subform… dialog" will cause the Subform to be omitted from the list of available Subforms in the Insert Subform dialog box (Figure 4.19).

Promoting the Use of a Subform

If you want to encourage developers to use a Subform as a part of their new Forms, selecting "Include in New Form… dialog" will cause the Insert Subform dialog (Figure 4.19) to appear whenever a user creates a new Form in the current database.

Hiding a Subform from Notes Release 3 Users

Because Notes, Release 4, contains many new Form elements (including Subforms), it may be desirable to hide Subforms that contain Layout Regions or other elements not recognized by Release 3 from users. Select "Hide Subform from R3 Users" to accomplish this.

Layout Regions

Defining Layout Regions

Layout Regions are rectangular areas stored on a Notes Form or Subform that allow a Notes Developer place fields and design elements using a coordinate system instead of tabs and spaces. They are used to present information to the user through a more concise interface. In addition, Layout Regions can be used in conjunction with the @DialogBox function and Workspace Object's DialogBox method to give the user a dialog box interface (see Figures 4.26a and 4.26b).

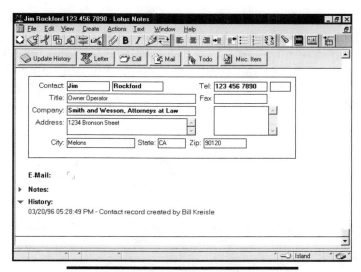

Figure 4.26a A Layout Region on a Form.

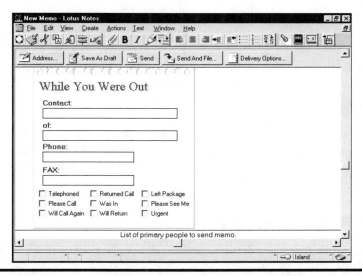

Figure 4.26b The same Layout Region presented using the @DialogBox function.

Using the @DialogBox function or DialogBox method and Agents or Actions, Layout Regions can be used to populate fields that are optional to a Form and don't need to be displayed unless the user wants to exercise them. Many examples of a Layout Region being used as a standard part of a Form or to set optional information on a Form through @DialogBox can be found in the Lotus Notes Mail Database's design.

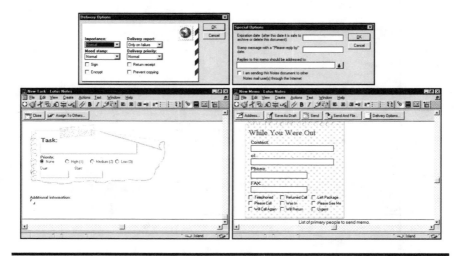

Figure 4.27 Some of the Layout Regions used in the Lotus Notes Mail database.

New Layout Regions are created by selecting **Create, Layout Region, New Layout Region** from the Notes Client menu while you are designing a Form or Subform. They are edited by opening the Form or Subform they are stored on.

Layout Region Properties

Layout Region properties include the Layout's position on a Form, its style, design time options, and settings to conditionally display a Layout Region based on the user's current context. These properties are defined using the Basics and Hide/Unhide pages of Properties for Layout dialog box (see Figure 4.28).

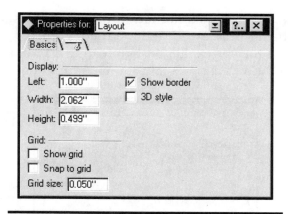

Figure 4.28 The Properties for Layout dialog box.

The Basics Page of the Properties for Layout dialog

In the Display section of Figure 4.28, use the Left, Height, and Width text boxes to control (in inches) the Layout Region's height, width, and position relative to the left margin of the Document. Clicking on the "Show Border" check box causes a lined border to appear around the Layout. Clicking on "3D Style" gives the Layout Region a solid background and can be used to give fields a beveled appearance.

The "Grid" section of this Basics page allows you to create a template for aligning design elements on a Layout Region and ensuring the elements have consistent heights and widths. Clicking on "Show grid" causes an array of pixels to be displayed on the Layout Region during design. The vertical and horizontal spacing of the grid elements is defined by the value entered in the "Grid size" text box (in inches or decimal fractions thereof).

Clicking on "Snap to grid" causes the boundaries of design elements placed on a Layout Region to align with the specified grid intervals.

Hiding Layout Regions

The Hide/Unhide page of the Properties for Layout dialog box (see Figure 4.29) allows you to define conditions under which the Layout Region and its contents should be hidden from the user. These conditions can include a combination of contexts—such as when a Document is being previewed, read, edited, copied, or printed. The condition can be further expanded by creating a custom formula that will evaluate to true or false.

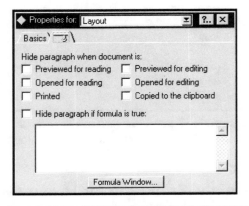

Figure 4.29 The Hide/Unhide page of the Properties for Layout dialog box.

Fields

Defining Fields

Fields are the discrete containers for information and knowledge that make up a Document. They are used to display information to, or request information from, a user via Forms. In addition to being a container for a value, fields can also contain automation, validation, or process flow Scripts or Formulas, and properties. These scripts and properties can be associated with a single-use of a field in a database, or shared on multiple forms in a database. Fields that fit the latter description are called *Shared Fields*.

Creating a Single-Use Field

New fields are created using the **Create, Field** command while you are editing a Form (see Figure 4.30). We call fields created using the **Create,**

Field command *single-use fields* (meaning their associated Formulas, Scripts, and properties are limited to that instance of the field on that particular form).

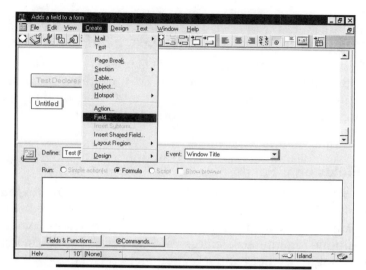

Figure 4.30 Using the Create, Field command.

Creating a Shared Field

Shared Fields are created by selecting **Create, Design, Shared Field** command on the Notes Client menu. They are then placed on Forms and Subforms using the **Design, Insert Shared Field** command. Developers who are experienced with other development languages may be tempted to assume that a Shared Field is one of two things that it isn't:

1. The first mistake is to think of a Shared Field as a global value. It is important to note that Shared Fields do not share a common value, but rather a common set of Scripts or Formulas. Each Document created with a Form that uses a Shared Field in a database will be affected when the Formulas, Script, or properties associated with that field changes. The Documents will not be affected, however, when the *value* of that field changes.

2. The second mistake is to think of a Shared Field as a Field Type in a Data Dictionary. The scope of a Shared Field in Notes is the

database it is a part of. While it is possible to use a Notes Template to create a Data Dictionary, the fields used to populate this template do not have to be Shared Fields.

Converting Shared Fields to Single-Use Fields, and Vice Versa

Shared Fields can be converted to single-use fields by selecting them on a Form, and using **Edit, Cut** followed by **Edit, Paste** on the Notes Client menu. Single-use fields can be converted to shared fields by selecting them and choosing **Design, Share this Field** from the Notes Client menu.

Placing Fields on a Form

Fields can be placed on Forms, Subforms, and Layout Regions. How fields are placed in these area depends on the what they are being placed on. On Forms and Subforms, fields are treated like text—they are pasted in, and positioned using tabs, spaces, and paragraph settings. Figure 4.31 illustrates a single-use field and a Shared Field on a Form.

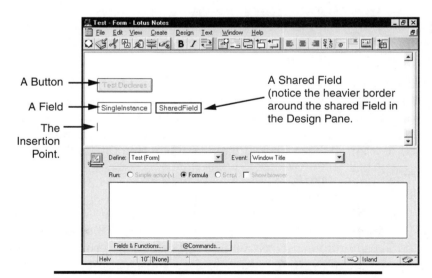

Figure 4.31 A single-use field and a Shared Field on a Form.

On Layout Regions, single-use fields can be moved using the mouse to click and drag them to different locations (see Figure 4.32). A Shared Field cannot be inserted into a Layout Region.

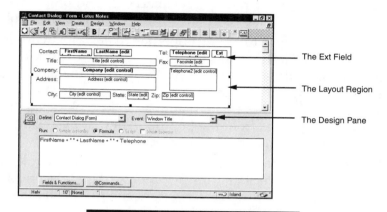

Figure 4.32 Fields on a Layout Region.

Fields can be copied, pasted, and deleted in the same manner as text—by selecting the field(s) and using accelerator keys, or by using Notes Client menu commands such as **Edit, Copy**; **Edit, Paste**; and **Edit, Cut** or **Edit, Clear**.

Associating Code with Fields

Formulas or Scripts are assigned to Fields using the Design Pane (previously discussed in Chapter 2—see Figure 4.32 for a reminder), using the Define, Event, and Run sections. The field's name is selected in the Define list, followed by the event the Formula or Script will be entered for. Finally, the Run group allows you to specify whether the code will be entered using Formulas, LotusScript, or Simple Actions.

Field Properties on Forms and Subforms

Because Notes allows different properties for fields depending on whether they are on a Form/Subform or Layout Region, we're going to break our discussion of field properties into two sections. The first section will deal with the properties that fields and Shared Fields have when they are located on Forms and Subforms. The section following will deal with the properties fields have when they are located on Layout Regions. To reduce having to qualify the two different types of properties repeatedly, the remaining references to field properties in this section refer to the properties of a field when it is on a Form or Subform.

Further, there are two different properties dialogs for working with fields and Shared Fields—the Properties for Field dialog and the Properties for Shared Field dialog. The Properties for Field dialog is opened by selecting a field on a Form and choosing **Design, Field Properties...** from the Notes Client menu, by right clicking the field and choosing **Field Properties** from the pop-up menu, or by clicking on the Properties SmartIcon while the field is selected.

The Properties for Shared Field dialog is opened by double-clicking on a shared field to open its Formula Window, then selecting **Design, Field Properties...** from the Notes Client menu or clicking on the Properties SmartIcon (see Figure 4.33).

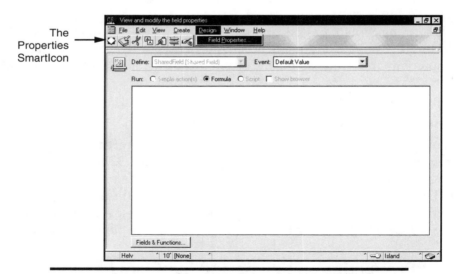

Figure 4.33 Accessing the Properties for Shared Field dialog box.

Since both dialog boxes contain the same properties (the intent of the extra hoop to get to the Properties for Shared Field dialog is to prevent users from unintentionally changing a Shared Field's properties while working on a Form), they will be referred to in the rest of this section as the Properties for (Shared) Field dialog.

Field properties include values that are general to all fields, and values specific to the type of field being placed. General properties include the field's name, type, behavior, and actions performed by the field when various conditions (y = z, or y <> z) or Document states (editing, reading) are in effect. Additional field properties specific to the field's type include font, paragraph, multi-value, decimal, percentage, and pagination settings.

The Basics Page of the Properties for (Shared) Field dialog

The Basics Page of the Properties for (Shared) Field dialog (see Figure 4.34) allows you to specify a field's name and type. Depending on the type of field selected, more information specific to the field type may appear on the Basics page. Comparing Figure 4.34 (the Basics page for a Text field) and Figure 4.35 (the Basics page for a Number field) illustrates this.

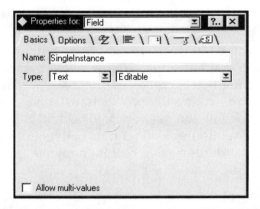

Figure 4.34 The Basics Page of the Properties for (Shared) Field dialog box (Text field).

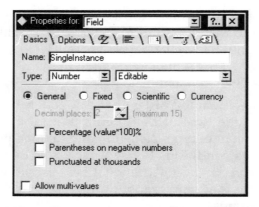

Figure 4.35 The Basics Page of the Properties for (Shared) Field dialog box (Number field).

Naming Fields

A field's name is used by Notes in Forms, Views, Scripts and Formulas to work with its value. It is set using the Name text box on the Basics page. Field names must begin with a letter and can include letters, numbers, and the symbols _ and $. Spaces are not allowed. The name can be up to 32 bytes in length.

If you intend to interface a Notes database with an API program or external data, it is a good idea to establish a field naming convention for standard Notes fields that includes the field's type. This assists you in ensuring the you are making the proper translation of field types when you are moving information between a field and a LotusScript or API program variable. We discuss field naming conventions in the Suggested Database Design Standards section of this chapter.

Setting a Field's Type

The Type values on the Basics page of the Properties for (Shared) Field dialog (see Figure 4.34) allow you to specify the type of information a field should contain. Notes provides the following field types.

- Text
- Rich Text
- Keywords
- Number
- Authors
- Readers
- Names

Each field type is examined in detail in this section. The other property that governs the field's type is whether or not it is editable, or computed. If a field is *editable,* users can change the values in a field while a Document is opened for editing. If a field is *computed*, its value is derived from a Formula or Script—users can't change the values in the field.

There are three types of computed fields in Notes:

1. *Computed*—Fields that are recalculated each time a document is created or saved, or when users choose **View - Refresh Fields** or press **F9**. The value of a Computed field is set using Formulas or Scripts.

2. *Computed when composed*—Fields whose values are calculated when the Document is first created (and never recalculated). A Computed when composed field might be used to record the date and time a Document was created, or a unique ID number that should be assigned to all Documents.

3. *Computed for display*—Fields that are recalculated each time a Document is opened for editing or reading. Computed for display fields might be used for providing running totals of a Document's values. Since the value is recalculated only when a Document is opened, Computed for display fields cannot be used in a View.

Text Fields and Their Properties

Text fields are designed to contain letters, punctuation, space, and numbers. To use numbers in a text field mathematically, you must convert the field's contents into a number using a Formula or Script command. There are no predefined formats designed to be applied to text fields (for example, #####–#### for a postal code). Any formatting of text must be done by Formulas or Script.

Text fields are used to store information, or to supplement Rich Text fields (which cannot be used in a View). For example, in a Discussion Topic or Mail Memo Form, the text field Subject is designed to be a short description of the contents of a larger Rich Text field. This short description appears in Views to help users determine the contents of a Document based on these Forms.

Text fields can be formatted to appear on a Form in a number of typefaces during design, but the characteristics of a text field cannot be changed by the user when the Form is being used to edit a Document.

Text fields can become lists by selecting "Allow multi-values" at the bottom of the Basics page of the Properties for (Shared) Field dialog box (Figure 4.35). A text list is a collection of strings, separated by a designer specified delimiter (using the Options page).

Rich Text Fields and Their Properties

The Rich Text field is one of the cornerstones of Notes. It allow users to insert pictures or graphs, hotspots, attachments, or embedded objects. It also allows the user to employ text styles such as bold, italics, underlining, different fonts, or color. A Rich Text field's flexible object storage properties is well suited to capturing loosely structured information. Further, its text formatting capabilities make it suited to the Document-oriented development model.

A Rich Text field's only serious drawback for application development is the fact that the wide variety of objects that a Rich Text field can hold makes it impossible to display it in a View. Further, the values in a Rich Text field cannot be returned in most Formulas (an exception being @DBLookup).

In LotusScript, however, methods exist to manipulate Rich Text fields using Scripts.

Keywords Fields and Their Properties

Keywords fields are designed to make data entry more convenient or reliable by offering a list of predefined values for a field to a user during editing. Keywords can be presented as a text prompt, a group of check boxes, or a group of radio buttons (as illustrated in Figure 4.36).

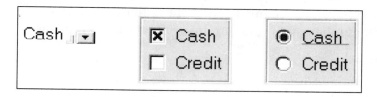

Figure 4.36 Presenting keywords as a text list, check boxes, or radio buttons.

When keywords are displayed as a text prompt, the user can open a dialog box with all available choices by clicking on the small down arrow next to the field or by placing the cursor in the field and pressing **Enter**. Users can also begin typing a keyword in a text keyword prompt and have the closest matching value appear in the list.

A programmer can predefine the values in a keywords field manually or programmatically. To enter choices manually, select "Enter choices (one per line)" from the Choices drop-down list that appears when Keywords is the selected Type on the Basics page (see Figure 4.37).

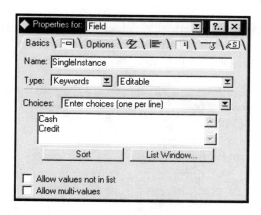

Figure 4.37 Creating a list of keywords manually.

A special behavior of a keyword list that is entered manually is support for synonyms in the list. Like synonyms for Formulas or Views, this feature allows you to change the value of the keyword itself without affecting how existing Formulas or Scripts handle the choices. For example, if you were creating a survey where you wanted users to rate something on a scale of one to five, but didn't want the users to have to deal with numbers, you could create a keywords list like this:

```
Excellent | 1
Above Average | 2
Average | 3
Below Average | 4
Poor | 5
```

When referring to the value of the keywords list, Formulas and Scripts would be looking for 1 through 5. The user, however, would see the range of text values from Excellent to Poor.

NOTE

As mentioned before when we discussed synonyms and Forms, using synonyms in keywords fields helps applications designed in Notes port to other languages.

To enter choices programmatically, select "Use formula for choices" from the Choices drop-down list, and enter a formula designed to return a list in the window below it (see Figure 4.38).

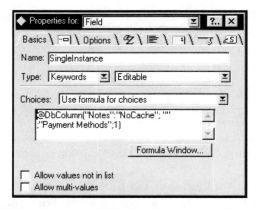

Figure 4.38 Populating a keywords field programmatically.

The most common way to produce an automatic list of keywords is to use the Notes Function Language command **@DBColumn**. @DBColumn typically is used to open a specified Notes database on a specified server and to return the value of a column in a specified View as a list. This is a useful feature for allowing keyword lists that expand as a database is used (such as a list of contributing authors, or a list of topic categories).

@DBColumn also supports connections to other data sources via ODBC or Lotus' DataLens to return a value list to a Notes database from another file type.

NOTE

If you want to connect to a column in a Notes view for your list of choices, a more convenient way to specify which view, database, and column to use than the @DBColumn function is selecting "Use view dialog for choices" from the Choices drop-down list on the basics page. This provides you with a quick interface into the databases and views currently installed on your Workspace (see Figure 4.39).

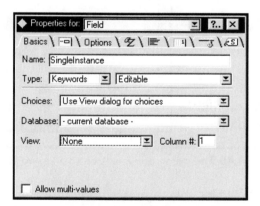

Figure 4.39 The Use view dialog for choices keyword option on the Basics page of the Properties for (Shared) Field dialog box.

Two other keyword options in the Choices drop-down list designed to allow you quick development access to commonly used values are "Use address dialog for choices" and "Use access control list for choices."

These choices populate the keywords list with values from the Public Name and Address Book or the current database's Access Control List, respectively.

If you wish to allow users to add values to a field that is controlled by a keyword list that aren't in the original list of keywords, click on "Allow values not in list" at the bottom of the Basics page. If this option does not appear with a specific keyword option, it means that this functionality is not supported by that selection. When "Allow values not in list" is checked, users selecting keywords presented using the text list interface option will be able to type in keywords that aren't in the current list, or add them using the dialog interface. The dialog interface (see Figure 4.40) is accessed by clicking the small down arrow next to the keyword list or by placing the cursor in the keyword list and pressing **Enter**.

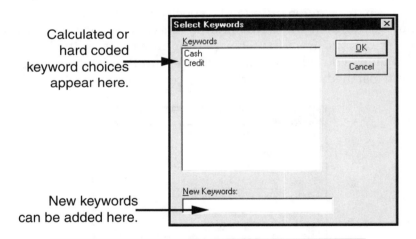

Calculated or hard coded keyword choices appear here.

New keywords can be added here.

Figure 4.40 The dialog box interface to a keywords field.

If you want the user to be able to select more than one keyword from the list, click on "Allow-multi values" at the bottom of the Basics page. When this option is enabled, the user can key in choices separated by using the specified delimiter(s), or use the dialog interface to the keywords list to select multiple values (see Figure 4.41).

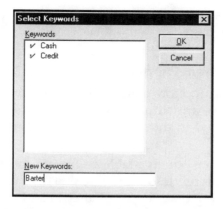

Figure 4.41 Allowing multiple values to be selected in a keywords field.

Number Fields and Their Properties

Number fields are used for information that will be used mathematically, or transferred to a numeric field in another program from Notes using the API or LotusScript. A numbers field can include the characters 0 1 2 3 4 5 6 7 8 9 - + . E e. A number of formatting options are available for number fields when the numbers type is selected on the Basics page (see Figure 4.42).

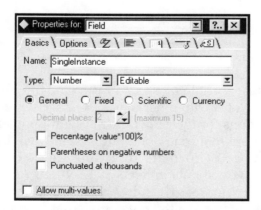

Figure 4.42 Formatting options for numbers fields on the Basics page of the Properties for (Shared) Fields dialog.

To make a numbers field into a list, select "Allow multi-values" at the bottom of the Basics page.

Time Fields and Their Properties

Time fields are used to store time and date information. They can be comprised of letters and numbers, or numbers only, separated by punctuation as defined in the time and date settings of your operating system.

A number of options are available to format how the time and date will appear when entered into a time field. These options are visible on the Basics page of the Properties for (Shared) Field dialog when the Time is selected in the Type drop-down list (see Figure 4.43).

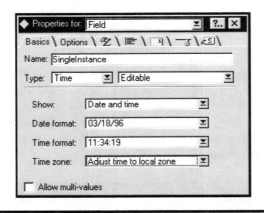

Figure 4.43 Options for the display of time fields.

Time fields present a challenge to API developers who intend to use values entered in Notes with other data systems. Users who change their date and time settings for their operating system (or even users who use the defaults on more than one operating system) will cause dates to be stored in a number of formats in a time field. For example, one Document may have the date entered as 12/10/91 (meaning December 10, 1991) using the Windows default. Another Document, entered by an international user, may have the date entered as 12/10/91 (meaning 12 October, 1991). A third user may have entered a date on OS/2 using its default formatting: 12-10-91. As you can see, keying dates for the month and day using another program becomes a challenge under these circumstances.

If you are writing API programs that will rely heavily on date values, in addition to using the date routines provided to you via the API(s), consider adding a collection of hidden numeric fields—on a Form—that are designed to contain the Day, Month, and Year as integer values as they are entered by the user. A validation Formula or Script associated with the Exiting event on a field could be used to populate these fields without user intervention.

Authors Fields and Their Properties

Authors fields are used to store a text list of names (user names, group names, and/or access roles) and are used primarily for giving people with Author privileges in the Access Control List (ACL) the right to edit documents they didn't create. This keeps such users from requiring expanded privileges in the ACL (such as Editor).

Authors fields can be set programmatically using Formulas or Scripts associated with other fields or events on the Form, or they can be user-defined. If you wish to make an Authors field user-defined, you can give the user three ready-made locations to look for names to add to the field by using the Basics page of the Properties for (Shared) Field dialog box (Figures 4.44 and 4.45).

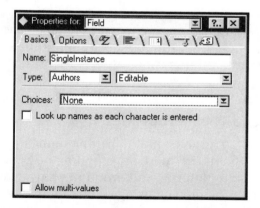

Figure 4.44 Properties for an Authors field on the Basics page of the Properties for (Shared) Field dialog box.

```
None
Use Address dialog for choices
Use Access Control List for choices
Use View dialog for choices
```

Figure 4.45 In the Options drop-down list for an Authors field.

These choices function as described earlier in the "Keywords Fields and Their Properties" section.

Readers Fields and Their Properties

Readers fields allow you to restrict who can read documents created with a Form, even if users have Reader (or higher) access in the access control list. These fields are used as a security measure (Document level security). Like an Authors field, the values in a Readers field are stored as text or a text list if "Allow multi-values" is selected. The same programming considerations and properties exist for a Readers field as for an Authors field, with the following exception:

WARNING

With the implementation of Local Security in a Notes database, you can use a Reader names field to restrict access to a Document both on the Notes Server and the Notes Client. If you are setting Reader names fields programmatically using an Agent, Formula, or Script, it is possible through a typo to deny everyone access to a field. If Local Security is enabled on the Server and the Client, *the Document may never be opened again.* As a precaution, consider making a password-protected Client ID called Readers Override, or something similar. Including this user name in all Readers fields set by a Formula or Script could be a lifesaver down the road.

Names Fields and Their Properties

Names fields display user or Notes Server names as they appear on Notes IDs. Names fields are the field type for the SendTo, cc:, and bcc: fields of the standard Notes Memo, because they treat names entered canonically as names instead of strings. For example, in a text field, you might enter the value:

```
"CN=Bill Kreisle/O=Compuware"
```

This would be nothing more than a string. However, in a Names field, entering that same value could be translated to `"Bill Kreisle/Compuware"` for mail routing.

The optional properties for a Names field are the same as an Authors or Readers field.

The Options Page of the Properties for (Shared) Field Dialog Box

The Options page of the Properties for (Shared) Field dialog box (see Figure 4.46) allows the developer to associate a help prompt for a field, determine if this field will be the focus when a Document is created or edited, control multi-value field internal and user delimiters, and set field-level security options.

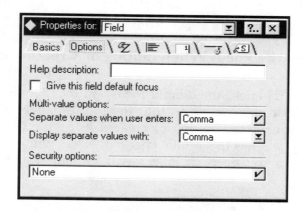

Figure 4.46 The Options page of the Properties for (Shared) Field dialog box.

Adding an Optional Help Prompt to Fields

Entering a string in the Help text box of the Options page will store that string with the Form the field is placed on. It can be seen by the user by selecting View, Show, Field Help from the Notes Client menu while editing a Document (see Figure 4.47).

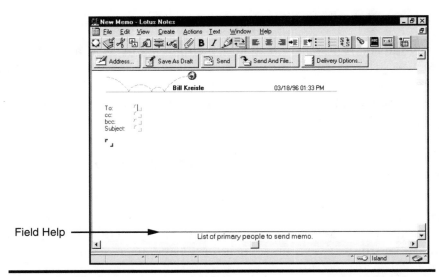

Figure 4.47 The optional Field Help display area on a Document being edited.

Giving a Field the Focus When Editing or Creating a Document

Selecting "Give this field the default focus" on the Options page causes Notes to position the cursor on that field automatically whenever a Document is opened for editing or created using the current Form. If more than one field has this option checked, Notes will give the focus to the first field with this property it arrives at, moving from top to bottom, left to right.

Specifying the Delimiters for Multi-Value Fields

The "Multi-value options" section of the Options page allows you to specify what delimiters a user can enter into a multi-value field to create separate entries, and what delimiter Notes should translate the delimiters a user enters into when the form is recalculated or saved.

The values you can use for a delimiter when entering information are one or more of those shown in Figure 4.48.

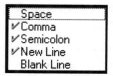

Figure 4.48 Specifying multiple delimiters for a multi-value field.

The values entered can then be translated into either spaces, commas, semicolons, new-line characters, or blank lines.

Establishing Field Level Security

Using the "Security options" section of the Options page, you can add digital signatures, encryption, or ACL-based security to a field. These options can be used individually or in combination (see Figure 4.49).

> ✔ Sign if mailed or saved in section
> Enable encryption for this field
> Must have at least Editor access to use

Figure 4.49 Field-level security options.

Selecting "Sign if mailed or saved in section" causes a digital signature created from the user's ID file to be stored with the field if it is being mailed or saved in an access controlled section. This creates a tracking mechanism for an application by authenticating the user who signed an action using the Public Name and Address book's Public Key value for that user. If the values match, Notes displays a message similar to Figure 4.50 whenever the section containing the signed field or mailed Document is opened:

> Signed by William Kreisle/NorthAmerica/Pillsbury/GrandMet on 05/0{

Figure 4.50 Using a digital signature.

Allowing the Contents of a Field to Be Encrypted

Selecting "Enable encryption for this field" on the Options page allows the user to use an encryption key to scramble a field so that the contents can only be viewed by Clients whose ID files contain the key used to encrypt it. If no private encryption keys are available, Notes encrypts the field using the public key stored in the Name and Address book for the user encrypting the field.

WARNING

Fields encrypted using a key stored in a user's ID file can be *lost forever* if the only copy of the key is in one ID and that ID becomes corrupt. Encourage users performing encryption to make a backup copy of their ID files. Further, ID files that are not password-protected, but used to generate encryption, aren't encrypted keys at all, since any user with the ID can open the field.

Adding Editor Privileges or Greater Security to a Field

Selecting "Must have at least Editor access to use" on the Options page allows you to create a field whose contents cannot be changed by users with Author privileges and below in the Access Control List.

An example of when this field might be used is in an application where users are encouraged to enter solutions to problems with a product in a database. Depending on the nature of the problem entered, a value in a field called txScope determines whether new Documents should be added to a database that InterNotes uses to publish common problems and solutions on the World Wide Web. All users except marketing communications users have Author access.

Setting the property of the txScope field such that only users with Editor privileges or greater can change it, combined with assigning txScope default value of "Private" using a Script or Formula, puts a mechanism in place where only marketing communications personnel can mark a document to be moved to the World Wide Web Server via InterNotes.

Changing the Font, Style, or Color of a Field

The Font page of the Properties for (Shared) Field dialog box (see Figure 4.51) allows you to change the appearance of a Field.

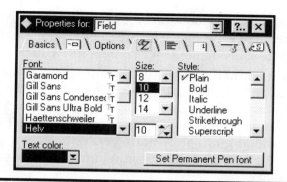

Figure 4.51 The Font page of the Properties for (Shared) Field dialog box.

Given the common nature of the properties of this page, discussion about these properties will be limited to pointing out that on applications designed to run on multiple platforms, selecting a font other than Helv, TmsRmn, or Courier ties the appearance of a field to the platform on which the Notes Client is installed.

Adjusting the Paragraph Settings of a Field

Since fields are placed on Forms in a manner similar to text, it is possible an applications developer may want to adjust the paragraph settings of a field to make a Form more usable. These options are set using the Paragraph page of the Properties for (Shared) Field dialog box (see Figure 4.52).

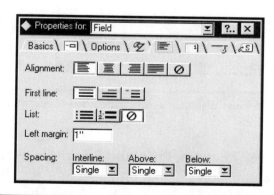

Figure 4.52 The Paragraph page of the Properties for (Shared) Field dialog box.

As with the Font page, the common nature of these properties means little discussion about them is necessary here. The only additional thing to point out about this page is the option to set a paragraph with no alignment.

As Notes is designed to run using multiple sizable windows to display information, it is inevitable that different monitor sizes and user preferences will cause your Forms to be displayed in windows smaller or larger than your original development environment. This means that depending on the alignment options you've selected, your text will either wrap to the left or right of the window unless you set the No Alignment property.

You probably would want values in a field to wrap to the confines of the window's size if the field is by itself on a line. If you have two fields on a line, however, it may be desirable to set the alignment of the paragraph the field is in to None to prevent it from breaking up the contents of the field, as illustrated in Figure 4.53.

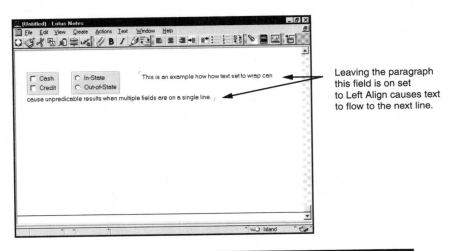

Figure 4.53 How alignment settings affect the appearance of fields.

Adjusting Printer Margins, Tabs, and Pagination for a Field

Use the Page Settings page of the Properties for (Shared) Field to set default printing behavior for fields or the paragraphs they are a part of. The tab settings apply to Rich Text fields only.

Hiding Fields

The Hide/Unhide page of the Properties for (Shared) Field dialog box (see Figure 4.54) allows you to define conditions under which the field and current paragraph should be hidden from the user. These conditions can include a combination of contexts—such as when a Document is being previewed, read, edited, copied, and/or printed. The condition can be further expanded by creating a custom formula that will evaluate to true or false.

This is a useful feature in that it allows you to display information according to the user's context, reducing visual clutter and guiding user options through their selections. It also allows you to create fields that are always hidden, to be used for calculations or in Views only.

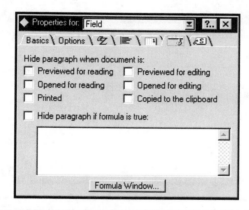

Figure 4.54 The Hide/Unhide page of the Properties for (Shared) Field dialog box.

For example, you might have a keywords field called ShippingOptions that includes the following:

```
Federal Express | 1
UPS Red | 2
USPS Priority Overnight | 3
```

Because different carriers require different information, you might display the fields that need to be filled to complete an airbill for each service based on the value of the ShippingOptions field.

Another example would be a field where you want the user to enter information in one format, but display the information entered in a different manner. Creating calculated fields that draw on the values of the editable fields, and having only editable fields appear when a Document is being edited provides you with this functionality.

Applying Styles to a Field

The Styles page of the Properties for (Shared) Field dialog box (see Figure 4.55) allows you to assign a predefined combination of paragraph, font, and spacing attributes to a field and its paragraph. Styles can be applied, created, redefined, or deleted using this page.

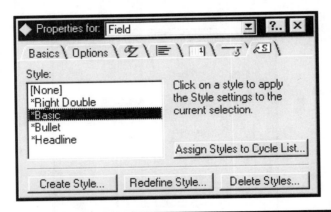

Figure 4.55 The Styles page of the Properties for (Shared) Field dialog box.

Field Properties on Layout Regions

The Interface Options Page of the Properties for Field Dialog Box

As mentioned previously, additional properties are available for fields that are used in a Layout Region as opposed to a Form or Subform. The majority of these additional properties are accessed using the Interface Options page of the Properties for Field dialog box (see Figure 4.56).

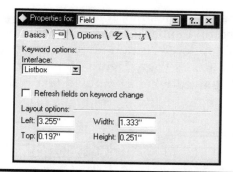

Figure 4.56 The Interface Options page of the Properties for Field dialog box.

Setting a Field's Height, Width, and Position

The "Layout options" section of the Interface Options page allows you to specify the exact coordinates (in inches or fractions thereof) for the upper-left corner of a field along with its height and width. This section is common to all field types on a Layout Region.

Field Specific Interface Options

The upper section on the Interface Options page of the Properties for Field dialog changes based on the type of field selected on the Basics page. In Figure 4.56, for example, are the keywords field's additional interface properties. Figure 4.57 illustrates the additional properties for an editable text field.

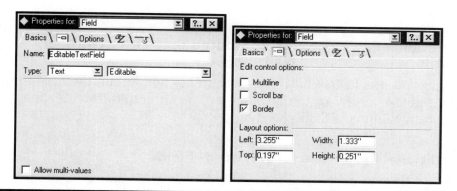

Figure 4.57 The "Edit Control options" section of the Properties for Field dialog box, enabled when editable text is the selected Type on the Basics page.

These properties may be different yet again, depending on whether the type of field selected on the Basics page is editable or computed. Figure 4.57's "Edit Control Options" section appears when editable text is the selected Type on the Basics Page. Figure 4.58 illustrates the "Static Text" section, which is displayed when computed text is the selected Type on the Basics page.

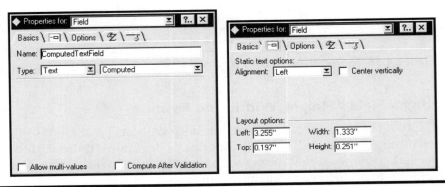

Figure 4.58 The "Static Text options" of the Properties for Field dialog box, enabled when computed text is the selected Type on the Basics page.

Additional Properties for Editable Text, Time, Number, Authors, Readers, and Names Fields

Editable text fields provide you with options to display a border, allow multiple lines to be entered in a field, and toggle whether or not the text field should use a scroll bar.

Additional Properties for Computed Text, Time, Number, Authors, Readers, and Names Fields

Computed text fields allow you to align the text within the field to the left, right, or center of the field, as well as an option to center the text vertically within the field's height.

Additional Properties for Keywords Fields

The additional properties for both editable and computed keywords fields includes the ability to display keywords as check boxes, radio buttons, a list box, or a combo box. If radio buttons or check boxes are used, additional properties specify the frame style and number of columns to use to display choices.

Additional Font properties for Computed fields on a Layout Region

Finally, all computed fields on a Layout Region share additional properties on the Fonts page of the Properties for Field dialog (see Figure 4.59).

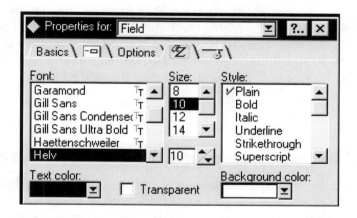

Figure 4.59 The Properties for Field dialog with additional options for computed fields on a Layout Region

These additional options at the bottom of the Fonts page allow you to specify a background color for a computed field's area, or whether the computed field's value should be displayed with a transparent background.

Labels

Defining Labels

Labels are text prompts or pictures inserted into a Form, Subform, or Layout Region to help the user understand how a form should be used.

They are created and edited on Forms and Subforms by placing the cursor at the desired location using spaces, tabs, or carriage returns and typing the desired text. They are created on Layout Regions by selecting **Create, Layout Region, Text**. They are edited on Layout Regions using the Properties for Control dialog. You can change the appearance of labels by selecting the text, paragraph, or control you wish to adjust, and using the Font page of the respective Properties dialog box.

While a relatively simple component of a Form, Subform, or Layout Region, labels are extremely important to the effective use of a Notes application. The ability to display information based on context, combined with the rich formatting capabilities labels have on Forms and Subforms means that some consideration should be given to using labels as effectively as possible to communicate needed information. This issue is examined further in this chapter in the "Suggested Database Design Standards" section.

Links, Hotspots, Pop-ups, Buttons, and Actions

Links, Hotspots, Pop-ups, Buttons and Actions are the tools that allow a developer to place process and workflow automation code in a Notes application. They provide the user with information or tools to convert complex processes into simpler ones. This section defines each of these elements and discusses their properties.

Defining Links

Links are connections between Notes Documents, Views, and Databases that a user can insert in a Rich Text field or a developer can insert in a Form. They are created by selecting the Document, View, or Database you wish to create a link from and choosing **Edit, Copy as Link,** and the name of the element you wish to link on the Copy as Link submenu (see Figure 4.60).

After issuing the **Edit, Copy as Link** command, the selected element is copied to the clipboard and can be pasted into a Form, Subform, or Rich Text field using Edit, Paste. Figure 4.61 illustrates a Rich Text field containing several Document Links.

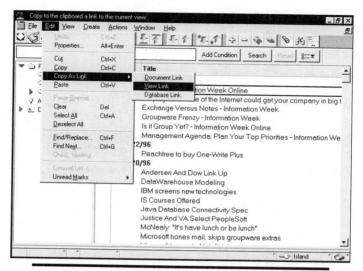

Figure 4.60 Using the **Edit, Copy as Link** command.

Double checking
any of these links
would cause the linked
Document to be opened
in a new window.

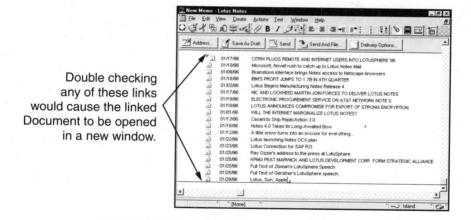

Figure 4.61 Document Links in a Rich Text field.

Links are commonly used to associate elements in an application that depend on each other, or to provide a user a quick way to reach additional information. For example, a Response Document created in a discussion database may contain a Document Link to the topic it was created in response to.

Link Properties

The only Link properties that we have not previously discussed are found on the Basics page of the Properties for Link dialog. The "Link description" field allows you to enter a description of where the user will be taken when they activate the link by double-clicking on it. The description can be seen by pressing on the Link with the primary mouse button.

Other, read-only properties on the Basics page provide information about the database, View, and Document this Link was created from.

Defining Hotspots

Hotspots allow a developer to associate an action with labels and images on a Form, Subform, or Navigator. As with Document Links, to perform the associated action, the user must double-click on the hotspot. Hotspots are created by selecting the text or paragraph you wish to associate them with, and choosing **Create, Hotspot, Link Hotspot** or **Create, Hotspot, Action Hotspot** from the Notes Client menu. An additional step prior to creating Link Hotspots is to copy a Document, Database, or View Link to the clipboard using the **Edit, Copy as Link** command.

Action Hotspots are useful when creating applications that require a more intuitive interface. Link Hotspots allow a user to simulate a hypertext link in a Hypercard or Windows Help File, as well as to mimic a Uniform Resource Locator (URL) in a Web Browser. Figure 4.62 illustrates an Action Hotspot and a Link Hotspot.

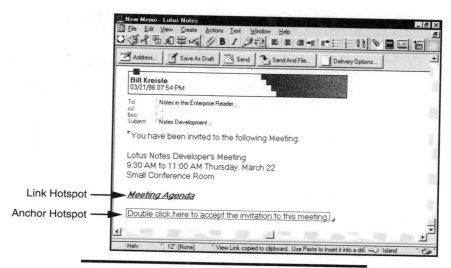

Link Hotspot ——————

Anchor Hotspot ——————

Figure 4.62 A Link Hotspot and an Action Hotspot.

Hotspot Properties

For Link Hotspots, the only properties we have not already discussed are on the Display Options page of the Properties for Hotspot Link dialog—"Link description" and "Show border around hotspot." The text entered in the field under "Link description" is the same as previously described for other Links. It is the text that will appear when the user clicks on the Link Hotspot with the primary mouse button.

For both Link and Action Hotspots, when "Show border around hotspot" is selected, a green box surrounds the hotspot area. There is currently no provision to make the border any other color.

Defining Pop-ups

Pop-ups allow a developer to provide additional information using text or a formula when a user clicks on either of them. Unlike Hotspots or Document Links, a pop-up can be activated with a single mouse click. Pop-ups are generally used to convey additional information to a user on a Form or in a Rich Text field. They are created by selecting **Create,**

Hotspot, Text Pop-up or **Create, Hotspot, Formula Pop-up** from the Notes Client menu. Figure 4.63 illustrates a Text Pop-up.

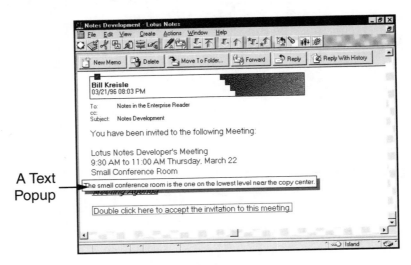

A Text Popup

Figure 4.63 A Text Pop-up.

Pop-up Properties

As with Link Hotspots, the only information we haven't discussed previously is contained on the Display Options page of the Properties for Hotspot Pop-up dialog—"Pop-up text" and "Show border around hotspot." The "Pop-up text" field is only available with Text Pop-ups, and allows you to enter the text you want displayed whenever a user clicks on a pop-up region with the primary mouse button.

The "Show border around hotspot" property is available to both pop-up types, and serves the same purpose discussed for Link Hotspots.

Defining Buttons

Buttons are areas on a Form, Subform, Layout Region, Navigator, or Rich Text field that the user can click to perform a specified action. They are created by selecting Create, Hotspot, Button from the Notes Client menu. Figure 4.64 illustrates a Document that contains buttons.

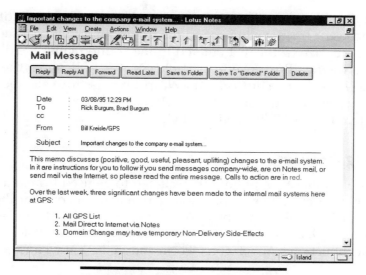

Figure 4.64 Buttons on a Document.

Button Properties

The additional properties available to a button not discussed previously are found on the Display Options page of the Properties for Button dialog box (see Figure 4.65). The "Button label" field is where the text that will appear on a button is entered. The button will adjust its size to the text entered.

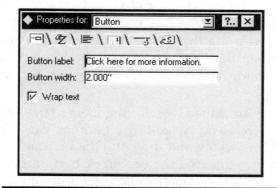

Figure 4.65 The Properties for Button dialog box.

If "Wrap Text" is selected, the value entered in the "Button width" field (using inches or fractions thereof) is the upper limit to which the button will adjust its size (if the text entered in the "Button label" field exceeds the value of the "Button width" field, Notes will wrap the text to multiple lines on the button). If "Wrap text" is not selected, Notes continues to expand the size of the button to the text, regardless of the value entered in the "Button width" field.

Defining Actions

Actions are another type of button, designed to be used from a toolbar at the top of a Form or View. This toolbar remains anchored at the top of the Form or View, allowing them to be accessed easily when users scroll through long Documents or the View Pane of the Database Window. Figure 4.66 illustrates Actions on a Form and in the View Pane.

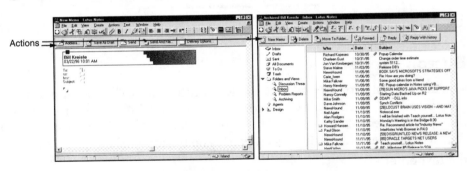

Figure 4.66 Actions.

Actions are created using the **Create, Action...** command on the Notes Client menu. When this command is selected, the Actions list in the Design Pane is made visible and the Properties for Action dialog is opened (see Figure 4.67).

Existing Actions are edited by selecting them in the Action Pane of the Design Window while you are editing a Form or View. The Action Pane can be accessed by clicking and dragging the vertical bar at the right of the Design Window towards the center, or by selecting **View, Action Pane** from the Notes Client menu while you are editing a Form or View.

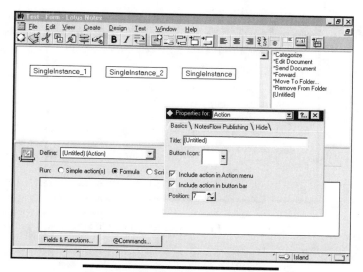

Figure 4.67 Creating a new Action.

Action buttons are a significant tool in Notes Release 4 in that they allow you to associate a collection of Agents with a specific Form or View, creating automation of tasks based on the user's context. Additionally, Actions allow you to make routines you create accessible to other applications via OLE automation.

Action Properties

The Properties for Action dialog box (see Figure 4.68) allows you to name an Action, determine how and where it will be displayed to the user, and in what contexts the Action should be visible to the user. It also allows you to set options for NotesFlow Publishing.

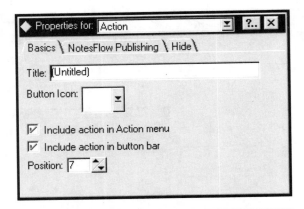

Figure 4.68 The Properties for Action dialog box.

The Basics Page of the Properties for Action Dialog Box.

Use the Title and "Button Icon" portion of the Basics page to enter the text the user will see on the Action and specify an image to display on the surface of the Action button. Lotus provides you with 132 different images, illustrated in Figure 4.69.

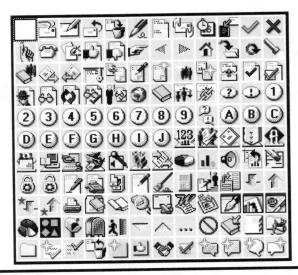

Figure 4.69 Different images that can be associated with Action buttons.

Selecting "Include in Action menu" on the Basics page causes the text entered in the Title field to appear on the Notes Client menu under the **Actions** command. Selecting "Include Action in button bar" causes the text entered in the Title field along with the button selected in the "Button Icon" section to appear on the Action bar.

The Position field is used to determine the position, from left to right, the Action should occupy on the Action bar. Notes provides six Actions automatically, all of which are set to appear in the Actions menu, but not on the Action bar. Newly created Actions will have a default position of seven.

The NotesFlow Publishing Page of the Properties for Action Dialog Box.

The NotesFlow Publishing page (see Figure 4.70) allows you to make Actions you create accessible to OLE applications that support Notes F/X, such as WordPro 96 and Freelance Graphics 96. For example, you may create a Form in Notes that launches an embedded Freelance Graphics presentation. You want to allow a user creating the presentation the ability to send a message whenever they create or edit a presentation asking for a review of the presentation by the marketing communications editor. By creating an Action called "Notify Editor for Review" and using NotesFlow Publishing, you could allow the user to issue the command directly from the Actions menu within Freelance 96.

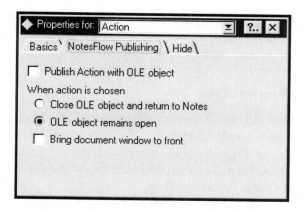

Figure 4.70 The NotesFlow Publishing page of the Properties for Action dialog box.

This functionality is controlled by selecting or de-selecting "Publish Action with OLE object" on the NotesFlow Publishing page. Its operation can also be affected by the current setting of the Form property "Disable Notes F/X" on the Defaults page of the Properties for Form dialog.

The "When action is chosen" section of the NotesFlow Publishing page determines what occurs once an Action using NotesFlow is executed. If "Close OLE object and return to Notes" is selected, the application closes (saving changes), and returns focus to Notes. If "OLE object remains open" is selected, the focus remain with the OLE object after the Action is performed.

Checking "Bring document window to front" causes the focus to return to Notes without closing the OLE object. This allows the user the opportunity to make additional input in Notes. However, it should be mentioned that unless the Action executed performs the task, the OLE object now in the background has not been saved.

The "Bring document window to front" option only applies when the document window in Notes has not been hidden.

NOTE

Hiding Actions

Like labels, buttons, or paragraphs on a Form or Subform, Actions can be hidden, depending on the user's context by using the Hide page of the Properties for Action dialog.

Action Bar Properties

If you application will use Actions, it is possible to adjust the properties of the bar the Actions will be displayed using the Properties for Action bar dialog box (see Figure 4.71). This dialog box can be opened by selecting **Design, Action Bar Properties...** from the Notes Client menu while you are editing a Form or View.

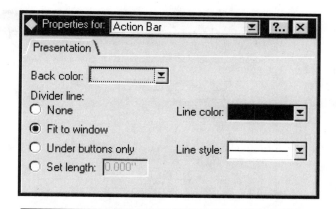

Figure 4.71 The Properties for Action bar dialog box.

Sections

Defining Sections

Sections are used to group elements on a Form or in a Rich Text field together for user convenience or security. They allow information to be collapsed or expanded based on the user's preference or their need to access the data contained within the section. Sections that group elements for convenience are called Standard Sections. Sections that are used to enforce security are called Access Controlled Sections. Access Controlled Sections are useful for workflow/approval applications that requires signatures or endorsement by select individuals. Both types of Sections have the same user interface, illustrated in Figure 4.72.

Sections are created on a Form by selecting the design elements you want to include in them, then selecting **Create, Section, Standard** or **Create, Section, Access Controlled** from the Notes Client menu. Sections are created in Rich Text fields by selecting the text you wish to include in them and selecting **Create, Section** from the Notes Client menu (only Standard Sections can be created in Rich Text fields).

The Contact Information Section expanded on a Form →

The Contact Information Section collapsed on a Form →

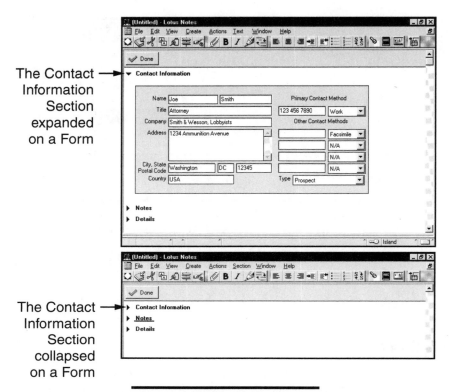

Figure 4.72 A Section on a Form.

Once created, sections are edited or removed by selecting them and using the **Section** menu that appears on the Notes Client.

Standard Section Properties

The Properties for Section dialog (Figure 4.73) allows you to define a section's behavior, access lists, and appearance. Using the Title page, you can define the text that appears when the section is collapsed, place a border around the section, and set the section indicator color.

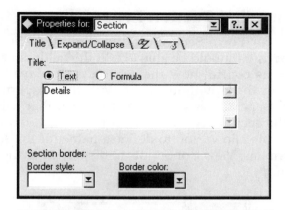

Figure 4.73 The Properties for Section dialog.

Using the Expand/Collapse page (Figure 4.74) you can set the sections default state (expanded or collapsed) in different contexts. Selecting **Hide title when expanded** causes the text entered on the Title page to be hidden when the section is expanded. Selecting **Preview Only** causes the text selected in the section to appear as a section only when the user is previewing the Document. (When accessing the Document by reading or editing, the text will not appear to be in a section.)

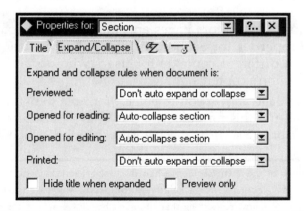

Figure 4.74 The Expand/Collapse page of the Properties for Section dialog.

Access Controlled Section Properties

The Properties for Form Section dialog (Figure 4.75) allows you to determine what users should be able to edit the fields contained within a section, as well as control how the section is displayed to those with editor access and those without it. As with the Properties for Section dialog, the Title page allows you to enter the text that will be displayed at the top of the section. An additional field on the Title page called Section Field Name allows you to define a name for the section that can be used by Formulas, Views, or Scripts to display or change access levels within a section.

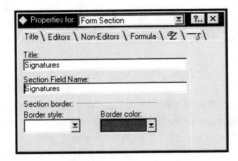

Figure 4.75 The Properties for Form Section dialog.

The Editors and Non-Editors pages are similar to the Expand/Collapse page of the Properties for Section dialog... They control the section's default state in different contexts for users who do and do not have access to the section's contents.

The Formula page allows you to enter a formula to define the section's editors. You can use this formula as a convenience to users if the Section will be editable, or as a security mechanism when the Section is computed.

WARNING

The use of the term security when discussing Sections should be thought of as "process" security (i.e., a relatively foolproof way to ensure a user doesn't accidentally allow something that shouldn't be allowed). Sections do not represent data security. Access Controlled Sections are not enforced on a Local database, meaning a Document replicated locally has not access control on the section. Additionally, a user with sufficient access can create Forms designed to display the fields in an Access Controlled Section even if a database is on a Server.

Views

Defining Views

Now that we have discussed using Forms, Subforms, Layout Regions, Fields, and a number of the automation tools that developers can use to gather information and knowledge onto Documents, the next order of business is discussing how to display those Documents to the user. The primary mechanism for the interface between a user and the Documents in a database is the View.

A *View* is a list of Documents that collects the values of fields into columns for a user. These columns can represent categories within the View, or a Document and its data. Views are presented to the user in the View Pane of the Database Window (illustrated in Figure 4.76).

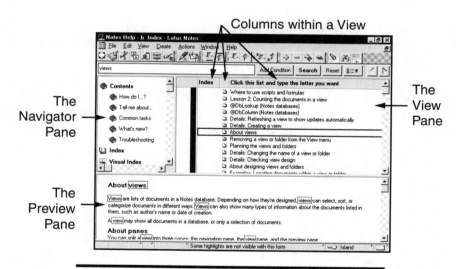

Figure 4.76 The Database Window and its components.

How Views Display Documents

In Figure 4.76, each row of information in the View Pane represents a Document (however, do not think that one line equals one Document—Documents can span multiple lines in a View, as we'll discuss later).

Since Views rely on rows and columns, it might be tempting to think of the View interface into Notes as a table interface in most windowed DBMS/RDBMS packages. However, categories, the ability to include images, Response hierarchies (which we'll examine in a few paragraphs), and the ability to adjust the color and fonts of rows and columns make it more appropriate to call a View a cross between a Rich Text field and a standard database table (a "Rich Table," if you wish).

How Views Display Categories

Categories allow the developer to break a list of Documents in a View into groups that share a common value. Typically, categories use a field that is common to all Documents to accomplish this. (The field most commonly so used is a field called *Categories*. It is used because of Notes' built in support of the Categories field from the Action Bar and the Notes Client menu. See the on-line Help or Lotus Documentation for more information about this feature.) However, Categories can also be created using a formula or a script that returns a value based on what is contained in many fields.

Categories can be collapsed and expanded by the user, allowing such users to find information more quickly than having to scroll through a View with several hundred Documents. Figure 4.77 Illustrates a View in a database that uses categories.

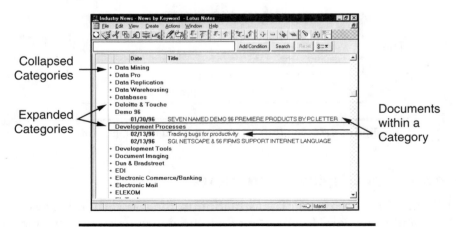

Figure 4.77 A View in a database that uses categories.

Categories can be nested to create subcategories, which can be expanded or collapsed to any level.

How Views Sort Categories and Columns

Categories are automatically sorted in ascending or descending order. It is possible to sort additional columns that are not categories to make the display of information more uniform. Further, columns that are sorted can be "hard coded" for their sort order, or the sort order can be made an option for the user. Sorting works from left to right (i.e., the sort order of the column to the left takes precedence).

How Views Display Response Documents

In addition to providing a hierarchy for Documents based on Categories, Views can also create a hierarchy of Documents based on whether or not a Document is based on a Document, Response, or Response to Response type. Notes accomplishes this by optionally indenting Response and Response to Response Documents beneath the Document they are associated with, as illustrated in Figure 4.78.

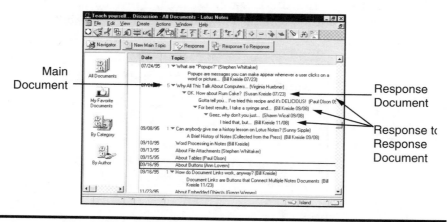

Figure 4.78 A View that displays Document, Response, and Response to Response Document types in a hierarchy.

Like categories and subcategories, Response hierarchies can be collapsed at any level (compare Figure 4.79 to Figure 4.78).

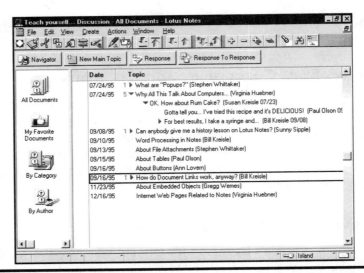

Figure 4.79 A View that displays Response hierarchies collapsed to various levels

Creating New Views

A View is created using the **Create, Design, View** command on the Notes Client menu and the Create View dialog (see Figure 4.80).

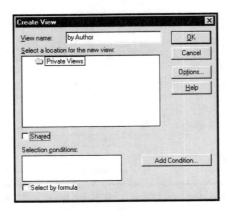

Figure 4.80 The Create View dialog box.

This dialog gives the developer the ability to create a new Shared or Private View. A Private View is a View that is not stored in the Notes database but as a part of a Notes Client's **DESKTOP.DSK** file. This allows developers or users to create views that are highly personalized to a user even if the user does not have Designer privileges in the Access Control List of a database.

While at first glance Private Views seem attractive because of the ability to customize them to each user, they can increase the size of a user's **DESKTOP.DSK** file considerably if they are created for databases with large numbers of Documents. In addition, Private Views are associated with the databases Icon on the Workspace page. If the Icon for a database is removed from a Workspace's page, all private views associated with that database are removed as well.

Besides setting a View's name and whether or not it is Private or Shared in the Create View dialog, you can also employ code re-use by basing your new View on a previously created View within the current database by clicking on the Options button.

Finally, Views can be designed to display all Documents within a database, or only a subset of them. The filter you wish to create for a View can be inserted into the Create View dialog using the Add Conditions... button or by checking "Select by formula" on the Create View dialog and entering a filter formula in the window above the checkbox.

View Properties

Once a View has been created, its properties are accessible through the Properties for View dialog box (see Figure 4.81). From this dialog, you can change a View's name, add a synonym to the View, set optional behaviors for the View, define the View's appearance, and establish access control for a View.

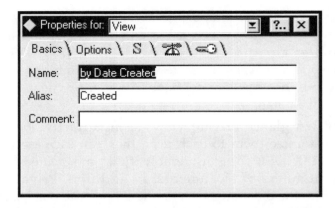

Figure 4.81 The Basics page of the Properties for View dialog box.

Naming a View

The Basics page of the Properties for View dialog box (Figure 4.81) allows you to change a View's name, add a synonym to a View, and to enter additional comments about a View's purpose. Like Forms and Subforms, synonyms used with Views establish an internal name for the View in Formulas and Scripts.

Setting Optional View Behaviors

The Options page of the Properties for View dialog box (Figure 4.82) allows you to specify how a View displays Documents and which Document types a View should include.

Selecting "Default when database is first opened" on the Options page causes Notes to open this View by default the first time the user adds to their desktop the database that it is a part of and opens the Database Window.

Selecting "Default design for new folders and views" causes this View to be selected as the basis for all new Views created by using the Create View dialog. Clicking on the Options... button on the Create View dialog allows the user or developer to override this setting.

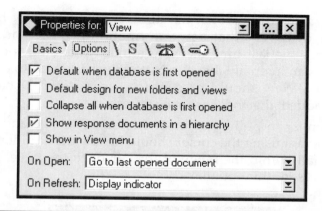

Figure 4.82 The Options page of the Properties for View dialog box.

Selecting "Collapse all when database is first opened" causes Notes to collapse all categories and response hierarchies in this View when the user opens it for the first time.

Selecting "Show response documents in a hierarchy" causes Response Documents to appear indented beneath their parent Documents. Deselecting this option allows you to treat all Documents within a View as main Documents.

Selecting "Show in View menu" causes the View's name to appear in the View menu of the Notes Client. If this option is not selected, the user must use the Folders Navigator or the **View, Go To...** command on the Notes Client to open the View.

The "On open" drop-down list allows you to specify the where the focus of the View should be placed when the View is opened by a user. Figure 4.83 illustrates the choices for this option.

Figure 4.83 View behavior options specified using the "On open" list on the Options page of the Properties for View dialog box.

The "On refresh" drop-down list allows you to specify how Notes handles the discovery that new information has been added to the database since the last time the View's index was built for display. A View index is an internal table in a Notes database used to calculate the information a View should present to a user. When Documents are changed or added, this index must be refreshed.

This is similar to pulling a cursor from a SQL table and specifying how the program using the cursor should handle the addition of records that would fall within the range of the cursor to the table. Figure 4.84 lists the choices for this option.

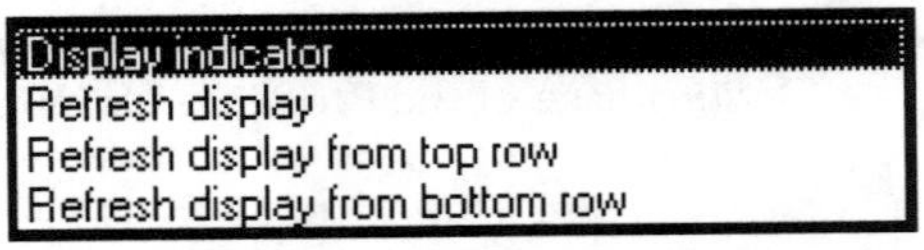

Figure 4.84 View behavior options specified using the "On refresh" list on the Options page of the Properties for View dialog box.

Selecting "Display indicator" causes Notes to put a small symbol in the upper-left corner of the View window designed to inform the user that they can click there to get more up-to-date View information (see Figure 4.85).

Selecting any other "On refresh" option causes Notes to automatically update the View with new information. Because Views can sometimes grow very large (containing thousands of Documents), use the option that refreshes a View closer to the user's most frequent location to increase their perception of performance. Translated: If the View sorts Documents such that new Documents are added to the top, refresh from the top. If the View sorts new Documents to the bottom, refresh from the bottom. If the View adds new Documents anywhere within the View, use the generic automatic refresh option.

The Refresh Icon in a view

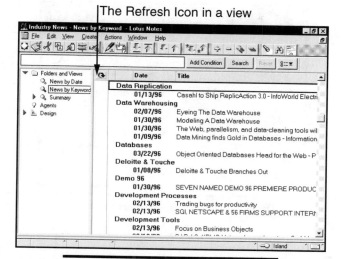

Figure 4.85 The refresh icon in a View.

The Style Page of the Properties for View Dialog Box

The Style page (Figure 4.86) allows the developer to customize the appearance of a View's rows and columns. These options include colors, number of lines per row, row spacing, and column headings.

Setting Basic View Colors

The Color section of the Style page allows you to specify a View's background color, the color that should be used on columns within a View that are totals, and the color Notes should use to display Documents that are marked as unread. As with Forms, you should consider your platforms and lowest common denominator when making color selections for Views, and bear in mind that colored backgrounds can be fatiguing on the user's eyes. Even more so than for Forms, it is important that you establish standards for Views and their color properties to help users get the most consistent look and feel from the applications they use.

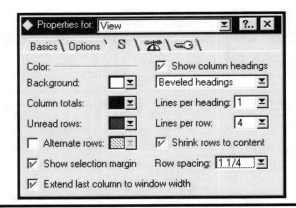

Figure 4.86 The Style page of the Properties for View dialog box.

Setting a Background Color for Every Other Row in a View

If the Alternate Rows checkbox is selected, you can also specify a color for Notes to use to display every other row within a View. This is a useful option if the information in a View's columns will be designed to span a variable number of lines. For Views that are designed Documents that will be displayed in a single line in a row, however, the reminder that colors are fatiguing to the eye is submitted for your consideration again.

Setting Column Heading Options

De-selecting "Show column headings" causes Notes to display without column headers. If this option is selected, the drop-down list beneath the check box allows you to determine the style that should be used to display the column headers as well as the number of lines Notes should allow columns headers to use to display their values.

Displaying Multiple Lines of Information in a Row

If a value greater than 1 is selected in the "Lines per row" drop-down list, Notes will wrap text within a column up to the number of lines specified. Selecting "Shrink rows to content" causes Notes to display the number of lines needed to display the available information. De-selecting this option causes Notes to use whatever value is entered in the "Lines per row" drop-down list, regardless of the amount of information that needs to be displayed within the column for each row.

Setting Row Spacing

The "Row spacing" drop-down list allows you to build in a minimum display distance between rows in a View. This option is useful when you are displaying variable line information and you do not wish to use alternate row colors to differentiate the rows.

Other View Display Options

De-selecting "Show selection margin" on the Style page causes Notes to suppress the leftmost column of a View it uses to display a deletion indicator or a selection mark. Figure 4.83 illustrates the selection margin.

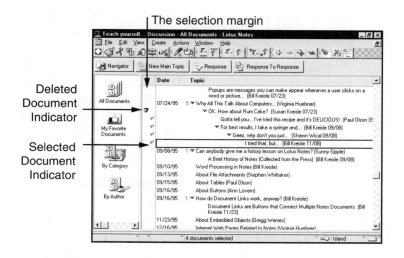

Figure 4.87 The selection margin in a View.

Selecting "Extend last column to window width" allows causes Notes to automatically adjust the last column's width to the size of the current display. This is a useful option for applications that have long text descriptions in that, combined with multiple line settings, a mechanism is created to display the information regardless of the display size available to each user.

Fine-tuning a View Based on Its Purpose

The Propeller-Head page (Figure 4.88) in the Properties for View dialog box gives you a number of options to fine-tune a Views behavior and performance. These options range from the amount of time spent recalculating View indexes and unread indicators to how a View's contents will be accessed by other programs via ODBC.

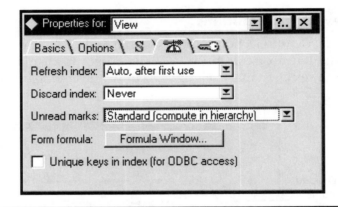

Figure 4.88 The Propeller-Head page of the Properties for View dialog box.

Tuning the Amount of Calculation Time Spent in a View

When Notes databases are shared from a Notes Server, the Notes Server dedicates a portion of its processing time to keeping the View indexes for each database up-to-date. On Notes Servers where several databases are shared simultaneously, or on Notes Servers where databases that contain thousands of documents are shared, this processing time can consume a significant chunk of the Notes Server's available resources. This resource consumption leads to slower performance for users, as they must wait for the Server to respond to their request for an up-to-date index for a database.

To help reduce the amount of processing time spent by a Notes Server, a Notes administrator has several options available to her. These options, however, are global (i.e., they affect all databases on the server). Using the Propeller-Head page of the Properties for View dialog box, a Notes applications developer has more individualized and granular options to help users gain better performance from a specific database.

One of the ways a developer has to alter a database's performance is to alter the amount of computational time Notes Servers spend recalculating a View and its unread indicators using the "Refresh index" drop-down list. The choices available to the developer in this list are:

- **Auto, after first use.** This is the default for newly created Views. It causes Notes to update the View index the first time a View is opened by the user, and then to incrementally add updates to the index each successive time the View is opened. It allows users to see up-to-date information within a View each time it is opened, and asks for server processing power only when a user opens a View.

- **Automatic.** This option tells the Server to automatically update the View index of a database regardless of whether or not the View is currently in use. Since the Server may have updated the View before a user opens it, Views can appear to display more quickly. The trade-off here is that the Server is devoting processing time to keep up-to-date a database View that may not even be opened in the next week.

- **Manual.** This option places the responsibility for updating a View on the user. The user must select View, Refresh from the Notes client menu or click the area that is used to display the refresh icon to cause Notes to update the View. While it may not seem an attractive option, it is very useful to use this update method when there are extremely large reference databases that are updated very seldom (such as a manual or guide-book). Because Notes does not spend any time refreshing the View index, the View opens very quickly.

- **Automatic, at most every.** Selecting this option allows you to enter a value in hours that Notes will use as the minimum interval it will use for automatic updates. This gives you the up-to-date content advantage of an automatically refreshed View, but limits the processing time Notes will spend on the View's index to n hour intervals.

Which option a developer uses should be based on a database's size, the importance of timely information display to the applications successful use, and the purpose of the View within the context of formulas or scripts. (If a View is going to be used with @DBColumn, @DBLookup, or @PickList, for example, having the View's index refresh set to Manual could cause information added to a database not to appear among the results of these functions.)

A second option for altering a View's performance is to reduce the amount of calculation spent displaying unread indicators. This can be done using the "Unread marks" drop-down list on the Propeller-Head page. Since Notes can display information that is collapsed under categories or parent Documents, unread documents beneath that category or collapsed hierarchy may exist that are not currently visible within the View. When that happens, an unread indicator can be displayed next to a collapsed category or hierarchy to indicate that a Document within the collapsed section is unread, or Notes can only display the unread indicator when the physical row representing the Document that is unread is visible. A third option is to turn off unread indicators altogether.

Again, the use of these options should be balanced against the needs of the user and the impact a change in their use would make on the processes users have available to them to make the information usable.

Associating One or More Specific Forms for Use with a View

Clicking on the Formula Window... button on the Propeller-Head page allows you to enter a Form Formula for the current view. A *Form Formula* is an expression that evaluates to the name of a Form synonym. Form Formulas are useful for displaying information based differently on the current View being used. For example, let's say you have a database of book titles where you have information about a book and its author stored as a collection of fields a single document. From time to time, you like to pull up an author's profile information for a promotional event or an article. To do this, you have an Author Profile View that sorts Documents based on the name entered into each document. As part of Author Profile View's properties, you have a Form Formula that evaluates to the expression "Profile." What this means to the user, is that whenever they use the Author Profile View to open a Document, the Profile Form will be used to display information. The Profile Form is a scaled-down version of a full New Title Form, allowing the users to see only the information they need.

NOTE

If a Document is saved while a Form Formula is in effect, the Form in use when the Document was saved becomes the Form that will be used in any Views that do not have a Form Formula.

Determining Who Can Use a View

The Security page of the Properties for View dialog box allows you to specify individuals, groups, or access roles that can use the View you are currently designing. If the "All readers and above" check box is de-selected on this page (see Figure 4.89), only the individuals, groups, or roles specified will be allowed to open this View.

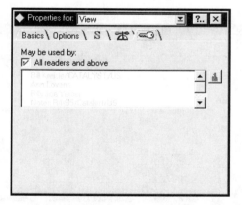

Figure 4.89 The Security page of the Properties for View dialog box.

WARNING

This should not be considered a security measure, but rather a process convenience. Users can create a Private View that allows them to see Documents not currently visible in other Views.

Columns

Defining Columns

Having discussed Views and their properties, the next major element to examine is the View's building block—one or more columns. Columns, as mentioned earlier, are placed on a View from left to right. Each *Column* is designed to hold a category or specific information about a Document.

Columns are created within a View using the **Create, Insert New Column...** or **Create, Append New Column...** command on the Notes Client menu. Once created, Columns are edited by selecting the Column in the View and using the Design Pane or Properties for Column dialog.

Determining What Is Displayed in a Column

Columns can either return the contents of a field or the result of a formula or Simple Function. This selection is made in the Design Pane using the Display radio buttons (see Figure 4.90).

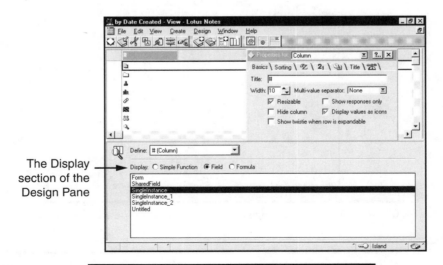

Figure 4.90 The Display section of the Design Pane.

Selecting Simple Functions is similar to using Simple Actions (an alternative interface to the Notes Function Language).

Selecting Field displays a list of available fields with the database. The value of whatever field is selected from the list is returned to the column.

Selecting Formula allows you to enter statements in the Notes Function Language in the window beneath the display section. The value returned by the last statement in the formula is displayed by the column.

Column Properties

Column properties include display, sorting, font, formatting, and programmatic access options. These options are selected through the Properties for Column dialog box (see Figure 4.91).

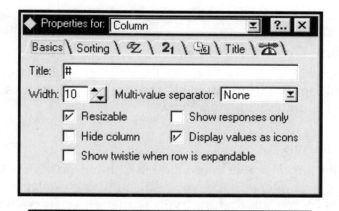

Figure 4.91 The Properties for Column dialog box.

Entering a Column's Header Information

You can specify the information that should be displayed in a Column's heading using the Title field on the Basics page of the Properties for Column dialog (Figure 4.91). Use the Title page of the dialog to determine additional attributes of the Column heading's display.

Setting a Column's Width

Use the Width field on the Basics page to set the width of a column in characters. The width will be based on a monospaced font in the point size specified on the Fonts page of the Properties for Column dialog.

Determining How Columns Handle the Display of List Fields

When a formula or field value that is a list is returned to a column, you can use the "Multi-value Separator" drop-down list on the Basics page to select what character is used for a separator in the column.

NOTE

Using New Line as a separator in conjunction with the "Lines per row" drop-down list on the Style page of the Properties for View dialog is an effective way of spreading lists out over multiple lines in a View.

Making View Columns Resizable

When Resizable is checked on the Basics page of the Properties for Column dialog, the user can click and drag the Column's header to change the Column's width in a View.

Hiding Columns

Occasionally, it is desirable to use hidden Columns in a View to affect its display. For example, let's say you want to make a database that sorts Documents by month, starting with January. Considerate of the UI, however, you want the Column that the user sees the month in to display the Month's name instead of a number. If you try to sort the Column where the Month's Name is used, it will start with April instead of January because the values are a string. To get the desired results, you could create a hidden Column to the left of the "Month String" Column, designed to return a number. You then sort the hidden column of numbers instead of the string.

NOTE

Using hidden columns for sorting prevents you from allowing the user to change the sort order of a View "on the fly."

Using Twisties

Twisties (also call·d "Hinky-Dinks" and "Hinky-Minks," according to Lotus legend), ar· small triangles that can be used to indicate that there is information in a View that can be collapsed or expanded (see Figure 4.92).

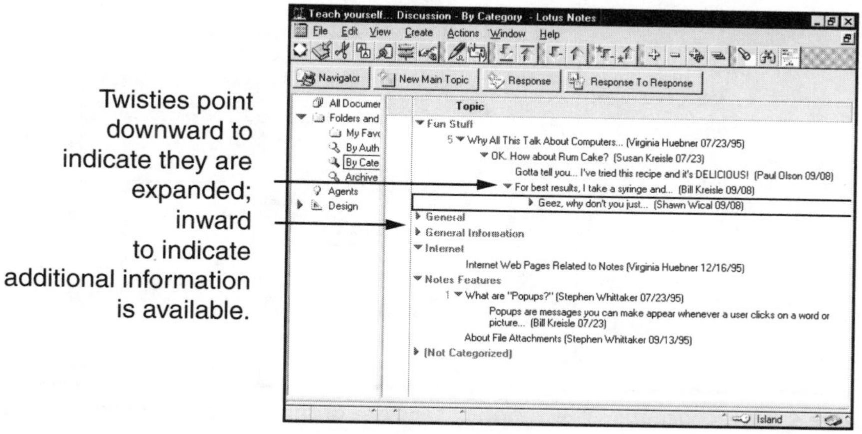

Twisties point downward to indicate they are expanded; inward to indicate additional information is available.

Figure 4.92 Twisties.

Twisties serve as both a visual indicator and an interface mechanism—clicking on a Twistie causes it to expand or collapse its contents. To include Twisties in a column that will be used as a Category or that will have Response Documents associated with it, select "Show twistie when row is expandable" on the Basics page of the Properties for Column dialog box (Figure 4.91).

Including Responses in a View

Use the "Show responses only" checkbox to use a Column to display Response Documents. While we discussed how Views display Responses earlier, some additional discussion is required to explain how the Columns that allow convention we discussed are created. Up to this point, we've thought of Views as Columns and Rows, where the contents of each Column directly correlates to a single field's value or the result of a formula. Figure 4.93 illustrates this concept.

A Document is translated into a Row in a View. It's Fields become Columns.

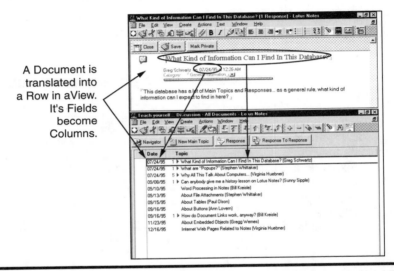

Figure 4.93 A conceptual illustration of the relationship of Documents and Fields to Columns and Rows in a View.

This image works fine when dealing with Documents only. However, it needs to be fine-tuned somewhat to include the idea of Response Documents. As you recall (see Figure 4.78), Views display Response Documents by indenting them beneath their Parent Document. To accomplish this, one Column in the View must have the "Show responses only" checkbox marked. Further, that Column must be located to the *Left* of a Column displaying information from its parent Document. Figure 4.94 illustrates this concept.

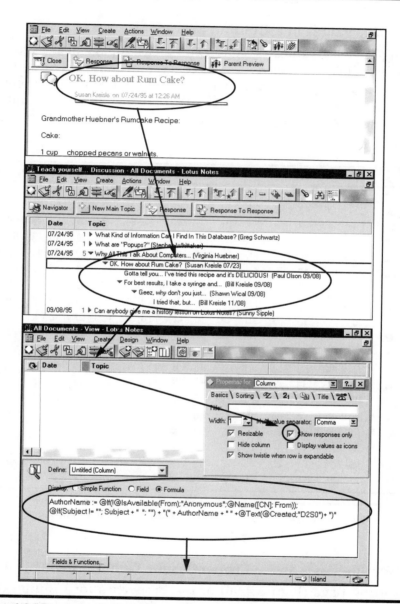

Figure 4.94 Because a Response is stored and displayed in a single column, all of the Fields in a Response that you wish to display must be concatenated into a single value, using a Formula.

Converting Values in a Column into Icons

Selecting "Display values as icons" on the Basics page of the Properties for Column dialog box allows you to convert the numbers 1 through 172 into images in a View. These images are useful for providing users with a clue about a Document's contents or purpose. Figure 4.95 illustrates the icons available and the number a field or formula must return to display them.

1	21	41	61	81	101	121	141	161
2	22	42	62	82	102	122	142	162
3	23	43	63	83	103	123	143	163
4	24	44	64	84	104	124	144	164
5	25	45	65	85	105	125	145	165
6	26	46	66	86	106	126	146	166
7	27	47	67	87	107	127	147	167
8	28	48	68	88	108	128	148	168
9	29	49	69	89	109	129	149	169
10	30	50	70	90	110	130	150	170
11	31	51	71	91	111	131	151	171
12	32	52	72	92	112	132	152	172
13	33	53	73	93	113	133	153	
14	34	54	74	94	114	134	154	
15	35	55	75	95	115	135	155	
16	36	56	76	96	116	136	156	
17	37	57	77	97	117	137	157	
18	38	58	78	98	118	138	158	
19	39	59	79	99	119	139	159	
20	40	60	80	100	120	140	160	

Figure 4.95 Using the "Display values as icons" Column property.

The Sorting Page of the Properties for Column dialog

The Sorting page (Figure 4.96) of the Properties for Column dialog allows you to create categorized or sorted columns, and give you the option to extend some sort features to the end user.

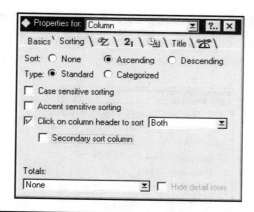

Figure 4.96 The Sorting page of the Properties for Column dialog box.

Use the Sort radio buttons to sort a column in ascending or descending order. Notes sorts columns that return text, Author Names, Reader Names, and Names fields in the following order:

- Leading Spaces
- Numbers
- Letters (case insensitive)
- Accented Letters
- Punctuation/Special Characters
- Empty Values (NULLS)

Notes sorts numeric fields based on their values.

Use the Type radio buttons to determine if the column being sorted should also be used to categorize the Documents in a View.

Select "Case sensitive sorting" if you want Notes to consider case when sorting text values.

Select "Accent sensitive sorting" if you want Notes not to consider accents when sorting text values.

Allowing Users to Change the Sort Order of a Column

Selecting "Click on column header to sort" to enable additional options on the Sorting page of the Properties for Column dialog (see Figure 4.97).

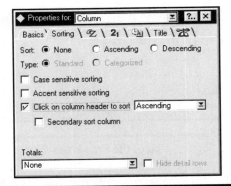

Figure 4.97 Additional options appear when you select "Click on column header to sort."

These additional choices allow you to give the user the ability to toggle between no sorting and ascending or descending sorting, or all three sort options. Selecting Change to View form the drop-down list gives you the ability to associate a View that is sorted differently with a Column in the current View.

When the user has the option to click on a column header to change its sorting order, small arrows that indicate the directions the user can toggle between appear in the Column's header, as illustrated in Figure 4.98.

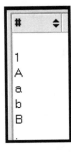

Figure 4.98 Notes uses arrows in the Column's header to indicate to the user that they can change a Column's sort order.

Using a Secondary Sort Column

If you choose to allow users to change the sort order of a Column, you can also designate a secondary sorting column to refine the sorting primary column. This secondary column sorts without action by the user, and no sorting triangle appears on it.

Totaling/Subtotaling Columns

Columns that are designed to display numeric values can use the Totals drop-down list.

Folders

Defining Folders

Closely related to Views are folders—they differ only in how Documents are collected in them for display. Where Views rely on a selection formula to determine what Documents they should display, Folders rely on user input. In other words, Folders let you store and manage related documents without putting them into a category. Folders are also convenient because they support a drag-and-drop interface.

Like Views, a Folder may be shared, or private. A difference between Private Folders and Private Views, however, is that it is optional whether or not a Private Folder is stored in the database in which it is created, or in each user's Workspace file (**Desktop.DSK**). If a Private Folder is part of a database, no user other than the one who created the Folder may have access to the Documents it contains. To create Private Folders in a database, a user must have at least Reader access to the database, and the option to store Private Folders within the database must be enabled in the database's Access Control List. If this option is not enabled Shared Folders in a database, you must have at least Designer access.

Folders are created using the **Create, Folder** command on the Notes Client menu, or through a Script or Formula. Using the Create Folder command opens the Create Folder dialog (see Figure 4.99). This dialog box is the same in principle as the Create View dialog (Figure 4.80), examined in the previous section.

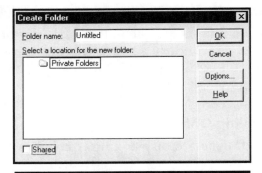

Figure 4.99 The Create Folder dialog box.

When a new Folder is created, its design is automatically based on the design of the default View of the current database. As with Views, you can also base the Folder's design on another existing View, or design the folder from scratch.

Once created, Folders are accessed using the Folders Navigator. Folders can be deleted or removed using the pop-up menu that appears when you right-click on the folder within the Folders Navigator, or using the **Actions, Folder Options** command on the Notes Client menu.

Folder Properties

To edit the design of a Folder, select the Folder in the Folders Navigator and choose **Actions, Folder Options, Design...** from the Notes Client menu. This will open the Design Window, where you can then access the Properties for Folder dialog box. The pages of this dialog are the same as the Properties for View dialog box, examined earlier in this chapter.

Navigators

Defining Navigators

Navigators are similar in principle to maps in an HTML file or hypergraphics in a Hypercard stack or Windows Help file. They give you a means to associate images with actions and information. Several examples of Navigators are available from the Notes Help file (see Figure 4.100 and 4.101).

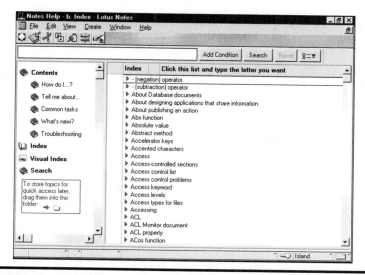

Figure 4.100 Using bitmaps to represent open or closed books helps the user know which View is currently open.

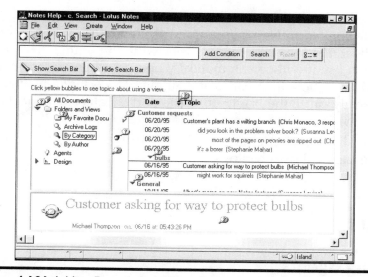

Figure 4.101 Adding Document or View Links to an image creates a powerful interface tool.

Navigators are created using the **Create, Design, Navigator...** command on the Notes Client menu, and they are edited from the Design Heading of the Folders Navigator.

Navigator Properties

A Navigator's properties include its name, an initial View that should be opened whenever the Navigator is opened, and color and sizing options. All of these options are set using the Basics page of the Properties for Navigator dialog box (Figure 4.102).

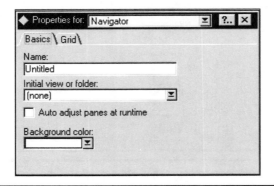

Figure 4.102 The Properties for Navigator dialog box.

The value entered in Name appears in the **View, Show** submenu of the Notes Client. If a View or Folder is selected in the "Initial view or folder" drop-down list, it will be automatically opened whenever the Navigator is loaded. If "Auto adjust panes at runtime" is selected, a Navigator will automatically cause the Navigator Pane of the Database Window to size to the dimensions of the currently loading Navigator.

When placing elements on a Navigator, a grid can be used by adjusting the Grid page settings.

Agents

Defining Agents

Agents are scripts, formulas, or simple actions that perform automatic tasks for the developer or user. Agents can be associated with design elements or can be run from the Actions menu of the Notes Client program. Agents are created using the **Create, Design, Agent...** command on the Notes Client menu. They are edited using the Agents View of the Folders Navigator.

A number of options exist in the Design Pane for an Agent that affect how it runs and what it runs on (Figure 4.103).

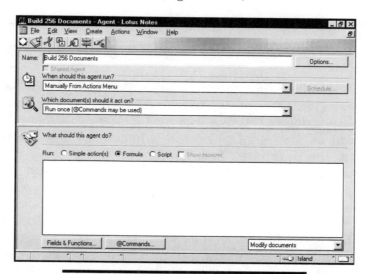

Figure 4.103 The Design Pane for an Agent.

Naming an Agent

The value entered in the Name field is displayed in the Actions Menu and the Agent List. An Agent designed to filter Documents can also be included in the Search Bar list using the Options... button.

Determining when an Agent is Executed

The "When should this agent run?" drop-down list gives you a number of choices for determining when an Agent should execute (see Figure 4.104)

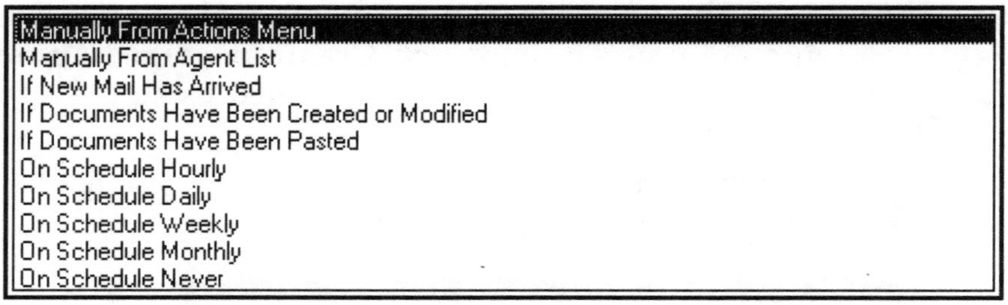

```
Manually From Actions Menu
Manually From Agent List
If New Mail Has Arrived
If Documents Have Been Created or Modified
If Documents Have Been Pasted
On Schedule Hourly
On Schedule Daily
On Schedule Weekly
On Schedule Monthly
On Schedule Never
```

Figure 4.104 Agent run options.

Selecting "Manually from Actions Menu" or "Manually From Agent List" means that an Agent can only be triggered by a user physically choosing the Agent from one of the two locations. Selecting "If New Mail Has Arrived" causes the Agent to execute whenever a new Document is mailed into the database. This is a useful trigger when creating Workflow applications. Selecting "If Documents Have Been Created or Modified" triggers an Agent whenever a new Document is added or an existing Document is edited. Selecting "If Documents Have Been Pasted" triggers the Agent whenever a new Document is pasted into the database. The "On Schedule..." selections allow you to trigger an Agent at a specified interval. When any of these options is selected, clicking the Schedule... button opens the Schedule dialog box (Figure 4.105).

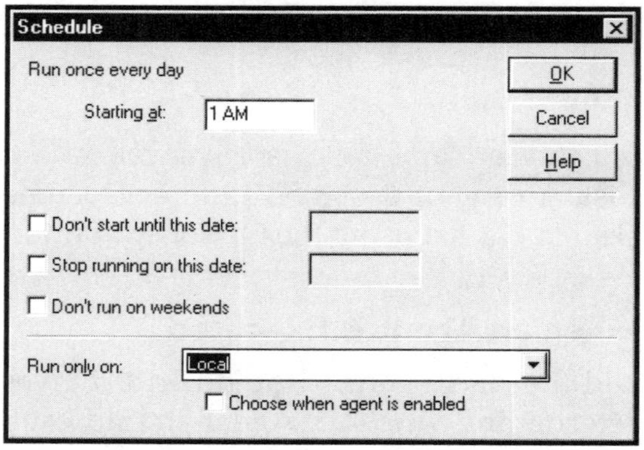

```
Schedule                                         [X]

Run once every day
              Starting at:  [1 AM        ]         [ OK ]

                                                   [ Cancel ]

                                                   [ Help ]

  ☐ Don't start until this date:     [          ]
  ☐ Stop running on this date:       [          ]
  ☐ Don't run on weekends

Run only on:  [Local                           ▼]
              ☐ Choose when agent is enabled
```

Figure 4.105 The Schedule dialog box.

From this dialog, you can trigger the starting time, date or range of dates, and specify what location the Agent should run from.

Specify What Documents an Agent Should Run Against

Depending on the choice made in "When should this agent run?" drop-down list, the "What documents should it act on?" drop-down list will have a combination of the choices illustrated in Figure 4.106.

```
All documents in database
All new and modified documents since last run
All unread documents in view
All documents in view
Selected documents
Run once (@Commands may be used)
```

Figure 4.106 Determining what Documents an Agent should act on when executed.

Suggested Database Design Standards

General

Unless designing an application that will use InterNotes, limit the design environment to 640 x 480 VGA, 16 colors. This is the lowest common denominator for most machines, and will ensure that text, colors, and pictures are consistently displayed across an enterprise.

Forms

1. When naming Forms, use synonyms to create an internal name. Reference the internal name of Forms when creating Formulas or Scripts. Synonyms should be descriptive, but keeping them short allows them to be referred to easily in Formulas and as a component of a field's name (a standard discussed later in this section under the Fields heading).

2. Standardize on one or two Form background colors. Allow developers to select from predefined schemes of colors for labels, text, and other visual elements.

For example:

```
Standard Scheme # 1
Form Background = White
Form Title & Accents Color = Dark Red
Label Color = Dark Blue
Field Color = Black
Title Font = 14 pt Helv Bold
Label Font = 10 pt Helv Bold
Field Font = 10 pt Helv

Standard Scheme # 2
Form Background = White
Form Title & Accents Color = Dark Blue
Label Color = Dark Blue
Field Color = Black
Title Font = 14 pt Helv 14 pt Bold
Label Font = 10 pt Helv Bold
Field Font = 10 pt Helv
```

3. Specify a Default Form. Use a Form that creates a Document (as opposed to a Form that creates Response or Response to Response Documents).

4. Do not set the Store Form in Documents property unless the database will be used in a mail-enabled workflow. When designing Forms that will be stored in a Document, conserve space by using as f

ew graphical elements as possible.

Fields

1. Use a naming convention that allows you to identify the field's type by looking at the name. Here are some prefix suggestions:

tx = Notes Text Field

no = Notes Number Field

dt = Notes Date and Time Field

da = Notes Date and Time Field (Date Only)

ti = Notes Date and Time Field (Time Only)

na = Notes Names Field

re = Notes Reader Names Field

au = Notes Author Names Field

lst = Notes Field that is a List

sh = Shared Field

Another possible convention consideration is the inclusion of the Form's name the field is designed to be a part of if the Form is a single-use field. To reduce confusion and ensure brevity, use the Form's synonym. Using these conventions, a text field designed to contain a user's first name on a contact tracking Form called Contact might be named similar to the following:

```
txContactFirstName
```

A list of text variables designed to hold telephone numbers on the same form might be called:

```
txlstContactTelephones
```

A Shared Field designed to display the current date might be called:

```
dashCurrentDate
```

2. If you are using Readers fields, consider creating an ID with a name that you can include by default in all fields that are set by a Formula or Script. This will allow you access to Documents if you inadvertently program yourself or your users out of a Document.

Labels

1. Select typefaces that translate well across multiple platforms if this type of application deployment is a consideration.

2. Use context-sensitive display options to alter the appearance based on whether a user is editing, reading, or previewing a Document using a Form.

3. Use Hotspots to provide additional information, if needed.

Views and Folders

1. Use synonyms when naming Views for portability.

2. As with Forms, standard color combinations should be employed wherever possible. An example follows:

```
Background Color = White
Categories Font = 10 pt Helv Bold
Categories Color = Dark Blue
Row Font = 8 or 10 pt Helv
Row Color = Black
Unread Documents Color = Red
Totals Color = Dark Blue
Alternate Row Color = Light Yellow/Off White
```

Navigators

Unless designing a database to publish to the Internet via InterNotes, Navigators should use the lowest possible denominator in terms of resolution and color. A full screen Navigator should be no larger than 640 x 480.

Summary

For such a long chapter, a detailed summary would be another chapter in and of itself. Instead, here's the basic progress of the chapter, and what I hope at a minimum you came away with if you're a new Notes developer or an API developer looking at Notes for the first time.

- *Documents* collect fields and objects and are used to store design elements as well as data.

- *Fields* contain objects or information based on their type, and are added to Documents using Forms, Agents, or the Notes Server or Client Software.

- *Forms* organize fields for information gathering and sharing. Fields, labels, and objects are arranged on Forms in paragraphs.

- *Subforms* are components of Forms, designed to make common field groups re-usable.

- *Layout Regions* are components of Forms and Subforms, designed to organize fields using a coordinate system instead of paragraphs.

- *Links, Hotspots, Pop-ups, Buttons,* and *Actions* add automation to Forms, Subforms, Views, Navigators, and Folders.

- *Views* organize Documents. They are similar to a table in that they depend on rows and columns, but their unique treatment of fonts, color, rows, and images makes them more than a standard data table.

- *Columns* are components of Views, designed to return either the value of a field or a formula. Columns can be sorted or categorized.

- *Folders* are Views in which the user defines the Document selection criteria using drag-and-drop selection. Documents stored in multiple Views can be copied or moved to a single Folder.

- *Navigators* organize images into a map to allow the user to find information or execute a process more intuitively. Because Navigators can open Views or other Navigators, or to trigger Agents, Navigators can be used to do nearly anything.

- *Agents* store formulas or scripts to automate tasks for the developer or end user.

Because of the flexibility of these design elements, establishing standards as early as possible benefits both the development staff and the end user.

Developing a Notes Application

Here's where we'll put what we've discussed up to this point into practice. By building a basic contact-tracking application, we'll see first-hand how to design and use Fields, Shared Fields, Forms, Subforms, Computed Subforms, Layout Regions, Views, Folders, LotusScript, and the Formula Language.

Building this application can give you a well-rounded exposure to Notes' capabilities and culpabilities. This will help you decide how far to go with Notes by itself before extending it by using one of the Notes APIs or another tool. (It will also give you a pretty good start on a workgroup contact-tracking system!)

The outline we'll adhere to for this chapter follows:

- Defining our requirements
- Creating the design elements
- Linking the design elements and automating processes
- Reviewing Our finished application

Defining Our Requirements

To begin our application, we need to spend a few minutes discussing our requirements:

- The user should be able to enter and share basic contact information, tracking phone calls, meetings, faxes, and letters over time.

- The user should be able to view basic information about multiple contacts at one time.

- The user should be able to find contacts easily by using the contact's name, company, or location.

- The user should have some control over how contact information is displayed.

- Since we're tracking conversations and correspondence, it is desirable to make entering this information as automatic as possible.

- Finally, the user should also be able to filter shared contacts into a smaller group (to make finding contacts related to him or her easier to find).

- The application needs to run on multiple platforms, because each workgroup uses its own OS (some are all Mac OS, others are OS/2, most are 16- or 32-bit Windows).

- This application should allow different workgroups using different copies of the database to move information between each copy of the database.

- Could the application allow users to work off of the network and remotely as well?

- I suppose there *is* one more item. You see, we're in kind of a hurry to get this application going... could you have a prototype for us to review in, say, two working days?

Addressing our Requirements, One by One

1. An application that allows the user to enter and share basic contact information, tracking phone calls, meetings, letters, and faxes over time.

Requirements for such an application are the following:

- *Basic contact information*—the contact's name, title, company, address, city, state, zip, country, assorted telephone numbers and e-mail addresses, and some general notes.

- *Items to track for phone calls*—the date and time of the call, who placed the call, and some general information about the call's purpose.

- *Items to track for meetings*—all the same information as our phone call, as well as the meeting's attendees and where it was held.

- *Items to track for letters*—who composed the letter when, who the letter is from and to, and the letter's contents.

- *Items to track for faxes*—who composed the fax when, who it's from and to, and the fax's contents.

One contact will have many meetings, letters, faxes, and calls associated with it, so that the idea of using a single large record to hold information isn't as appealing as creating a one-to-many relationship between the call, fax, meeting, and letters records and the main contact record. This is something we can do in Notes fairly easily, but before we begin discussing how Notes will approach solving this problem, let's take a moment to look at it from a more traditional database development perspective.

A relational database developer could approach this problem by creating a collection of objects or tables (depending on the tool), with each object/table representing a subset of the information we've discussed so far (depending on how normalized the developer wants the model to be). When finished, the object/data relationship might look similar to Figure 5.1.

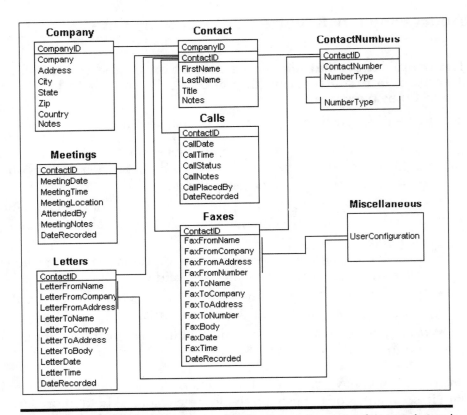

Figure 5.1 Approaching the company and contact information from a relational database developer's perspective.

In this figure, the Company table has a one-to-many relationship with the Contact table (many contacts can exist for a single company). If the address of the company changes, the contacts within that company are automatically updated when the single Company address record is updated. The Contact table has a one-to-many relationship with the ContactNumbers table. The ContactNumbers table uses a small table called NumberType to create a lookup in the ContactNumbers table to identify whether the information being entered is a work, home, secretary, toll-free, cellular, or fax number.

Also in relationship with the Contact table are the Faxes, Letters, Calls, and Meetings tables. These tables contain information specific about their respective type of interaction. Additionally, the Faxes and Letters tables contain information that should be supplied by either data or instructions in a user configuration file (return address and fax number, for example).

We draw out the relational model in Figure 5.1 to help address a comment we sometimes hear when I'm talking about Notes in an IS department. "Notes is not relational." That statement isn't entirely true. Using Notes, you could, in fact, implement the data model we've just drawn out. The resulting application wouldn't be as fast as some of the highly optimized RDBMSs out there, but it would work. Until you needed record locking, that is, or you wanted to have thousands of transactions a minute processed. It might be more appropriate to say, "Notes can't support relational databases on a network the same way that say, DB2, or Paradox, or even dBase does, but it can support relational data models for certain types of applications."

What types of applications? As we mentioned before, there are five broad classes of applications that Notes is well suited for—Broadcast, Discussion, Reference, Tracking, and Workflow/Approval. Typically, Broadcast, Discussion, and References applications don't rely much on relational linking or joins. Tracking and Workflow/Approval applications however, are likely to want information from other tables. In their case, Notes is appropriate where the data does not have to be highly normalized and where the information being tracked or routed is light (a few hundred transactions a day, for example)—contact tracking, for example.

While Response and Response to Response Documents are generally thought of in the context of a discussion application, the potential of using them to create relational tables is obviously there. Leveraging this built-in mechanism allows the records needed to support our contact tracking application to be stored as different Documents within a single database. The only adjustment in our thinking we need to go through is in reducing the amount of normalization between tables in Figure 5.1. Figure 5.2 illustrates our new data model.

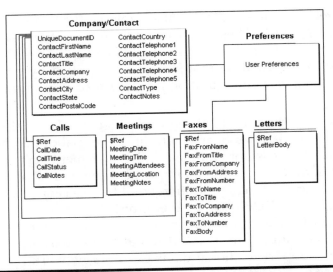

Figure 5.2 Using Notes Documents instead of tables to model the contact information.

In this model, the Contact table and the Company table are combined into a single Document in Notes. The Faxes, Letters, Meetings, and Calls tables are made into Response Documents. The User Preferences will be a Document. The combination of fields in the Contact Document doesn't have to be done. However, doing so simplifies our application considerably and reduces the relationships of the Responses to a single Document.

In addition to the merged fields, notice that the Company/Contact Document also contains a field called UniqueDocumentID. Actually we shouldn't say field in this case...because it's not really a field in the Document, but rather, a visual representation of the Document's Unique ID for our diagram. Every Document created in Notes is given an ID unique to the database it's created in. Since the Unique ID of a Document is an item which can be returned using a developer's LotusScript, the Notes API(s), or the Formula language, it doesn't need to be stored in a separate field.

By contrast, the $Ref field in the Calls, Letters, Meetings, and Faxes Document is an actual field, stored in the Document, and created by Notes whenever a Response Document is generated. It is filled with the

Unique ID of its parent Document, creating a relationship between the two. In essence, the presence of the $Ref field is what differentiates a Response and Response to Response Document from a Main Document in Notes.

NOTE Although our design won't use Response to Response Documents, while I'm on the subject I'll point out that these Documents create a $Ref field based on the Unique ID of the Document or Response Document they were associated with when created. This allows Response to Response Documents to be nested to many levels.

The end result of our changes is now what we could call a relational table that is "less normalized." Is that bad? It depends. Normalization is not the end-all and be-all of database development—it is possible to overnormalize data to the point that getting usable information is an exercise in programming skill and user patience. You only need to look at the booming Data Warehousing industry to see the fruits of overnormalization—data so complex that special applications must be built to condense it prior to reporting on it.

It becomes a matter of using your judgment. For our application, given a workgroup that wants to share information that will be updated lightly, what downgrading the normalization of the contact data costs us (more data must be entered for multiple contacts at a single company, and changing multiple contact addresses becomes more complicated) is more than made up for in the functionality Notes will provide us in meeting the rest of our user's requirements, which follow.

2. The user should be able to view basic information about multiple contacts at one time.

You'd think the user put in this requirement so we could examine Views again, wouldn't you? Since changing our data model allowed us to consolidate all of the basic contact information into a single file, we're going to be able to create a number of Views to display contact, call, meeting, fax, and letter Documents.

3. The user should be able to find contacts easily by using the contact's name, company, or location.

As you'll remember from our survey of Views and Columns, one of a Column's properties is the ability to allow the user to sort information "on the fly." This, combined with categories and other standard View features will make it very easy for any user to find the contact they're looking for.

As an added bonus, the **Edit, Find** command and the Search Bar will make it possible for the user to perform "Query by Example" and other complex searches in a matter of seconds.

4. The user should have some control over how contact information is displayed.

After asking the user for a little more information, what we discovered is that the idea here is to present basic contact information in a variety of ways. Some users prefer to see just the data others want the information to look like a business card. We'll be able to address this issue by using Subforms.

5. It is desirable to make entering this information as automatic as possible.

Aha! Here's where we'll begin to use Formulas and Scripts to make things go faster for the user. I see a lot of Actions in this application's future.

6. The user should also be able to filter shared contacts into a smaller group (to make finding contacts related to him or her easier to find).

Selective replication, the use of Folders, and the ability to create multiple instances of the contact database from a shared template all present possibilities to solve this problem.

7. The application needs to run on multiple platforms

How many user requirements have you seen for data that include this line item? How many times is this the first requirement to get tossed out, in the interest of time? This is not an issue with Notes unless you intend to use OLE, LEL, or Publish and Subscribe, or want to call C code from a Dynamic Link Library (DLL) file.

8. It should allow different workgroups using different copies of the database to move information between each copy of the database.

Would you like to do that programmatically, automatically, through the user, or via mail enabling? LotusScript or the Function Language will do it programmatically. Replication will do it automatically. The Copy-and-paste command will move information through the user. Even mail enabling will do it, allowing you to share information with workgroups that aren't even in the company. It's all built into Notes.

9. Could the application allow users to work off of the network and remotely as well?

Could there be a better question to answer "yes" to? It's a perfect use of Notes to develop an application like this. Replication will allow multiple versions of the workgroup's contact database to keep information in synchronization. That means a laptop/telecommuting-ready application where the user can work off-line any time, anywhere and only connect to get or give updated information.

10. Could you have a prototype for us to review in, say, two working days?

Go back to Figure 5.1. Now, pick your favorite development tool (outside of Notes) and estimate how long it would take to deliver that information to the user's specification.

Assume that the amount of time you've estimated has gone by, and now your application is in use by 20 workgroups in the company. You want to change the data model or a design element. How do you update it all?

Now, come back from that scene and imagine you're about to do the same task in Notes instead.

Creating the Design Elements

Before We Begin

In creating this database, we're going to use a number of means to the end.

In some sections, we're going to ask you to create the design element step by step with us. This is to make this book more useful to new developers or developers experienced with other systems who are looking at the Notes API and Notes for the first time. If you don't have time to do these exercises, consider opening the design element we're discussing in the completed application on the CD and examining it as you read through the section.

In other sections, where it won't affect the new developer's experience but could affect the amount of time an experienced developer would have to spend, we're going to look at the key properties of a design element, and ask that you copy the element from the Contact Database on the enclosed CD and paste it into yours. The completed Contact Database is located in the \NOTES4 folder on the CD.

We'd also like to point out that the order in which we create the design elements may seem a little out of joint to you. Bear in mind, however, that this application had been completed before we started writing the chapter. As such, issues such as dependencies between elements, which element of several would be the best to discuss in terms of robustness or completeness, and our preferences have altered the order somewhat.

Taking Inventory

Based on our requirements, here's the checklist of elements we'll need to create:

- 2 Forms that create Main Documents (Contact and User Preferences)
- 4 Forms that create Response Documents
- Fields on each Form designed to capture necessary information
- 2 Subforms designed to display contact information using two different styles

- 1 Computed Subform
- 3 Layout Regions
- 3 or 4 Standard Views
- 1 Hidden View
- 1 Agent
- Several Actions
- 1 Private Folder

We've already discussed the Contact, User Preferences, Fax, Call, Letter, and Meeting Forms and their fields. The Subforms will be used to display information on the Contact Form based on a value the user selects in the Preferences. The Computed Subform will be the placeholder on the Contact form for these two Subforms.

One of the Layout Regions will be used on a Subform to display contact information in a business card format. The second will be used to group together fields on the Contact Document for editing, and the third will be placed on the User Preferences Form to gather user information.

The Hidden View will be used to store the user's Preferences. To keep users from accidentally deleting preferences or from adding too many preferences, the Agent will be used to take the user to and from the Preferences Document.

The three or four Views will organize the Contacts by First Name, Last Name, Company, and Region. The Private Folder will be used to meet the user's requirement of allowing individuals to filter contacts pertinent to them into a separate location to make these contacts easier to find.

Getting Started

The first step in our journey is to create a new database in which to store our elements using the **File, Database, New...** command. In the New Database dialog (Figure 5.3), select the server where you want the new database to be created (we *always* recommend doing development work on your local drive and then moving your changes to the Server after testing, by the way), the database's Title, and the OS File name you wish to use. You can use an NTF extension if you want this application to be a

Template, or an NSF extension if you want the application to be a standard database.

Before clicking on OK, make sure you've based your new database on the Blank template.

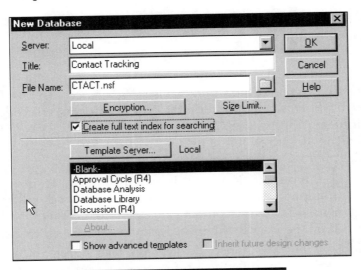

Figure 5.3 The New Database dialog.

The User Preferences Form

Defining the User Preferences Form

The idea behind the User Preferences Form is to allow users to create personal profiles that the tracking application can refer to when displaying information or creating faxes or letters. We'll use LotusScript and the Formula Language to gather this information when it is needed. Figure 5.4 illustrates the completed Form in design mode and Figure 5.5 shows it as it will be seen by the user.

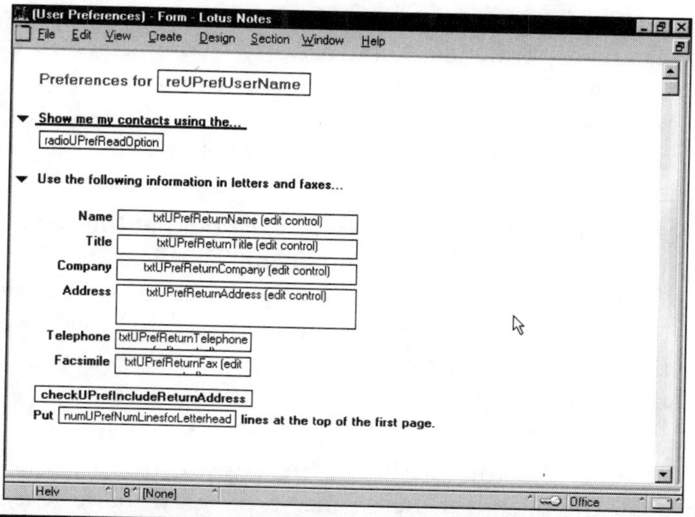

Figure 5.4 The completed User Preferences Form in design mode.

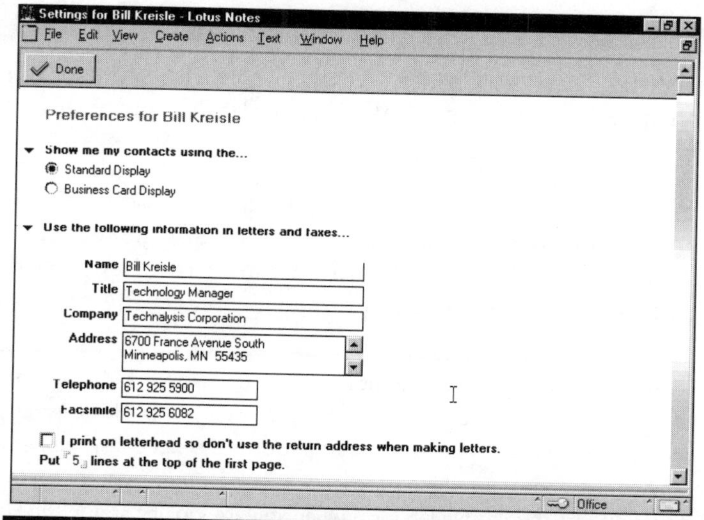

Figure 5.5 The User Preferences Form as seen by the end user.

As you can see in Figure 5.5, the user will have the choice of two different methods to display contact information, as well as fields to enter their personal name, address, telephone, and fax number for use when creating correspondence. There are also two options for the user to choose regarding whether or not they print letters using letterhead stationery. The first option tells our application not to include the return information in letters. The second tells us how many lines to leave at the top of our newly created letters to allow for the letterhead.

If you look at Figure 5.4, you'll also notice a field at the top of the form that makes up part of the "title" of the Form. That is more than a nicety. To allow each user to have a private profile and to make it easy for us to find the profile programmatically, that field is a Reader Names field. This will cause only one Document to appear in the User Preferences View per user when the application is stored on a server.

Finally, looking at Figure 5.5 again, you'll see that there is an Action labeled "Done" at the top of the Form. Again, this may look like a convenience for the user, but there's also a programmatic reason behind its addition to our Form, which we'll examine in the Adding Actions section of this chapter.

Creating the User Preferences Form and Setting its Properties

Start by selecting **Design, Create, Form...** from the Notes Client Menu. Open the Properties for Form dialog, and change the values to match Figure 5.6 by doing the following:

1. Enter `(Preferences)` | `UPref` in the `Form name:` field. The UPref synonym is added to comply with our suggested standard for Form naming (Chapter 4) and to make referring to this Form programmatically and in field names easier on the typing fingers.

NOTE Entering a Form's name in parentheses was the way to hide the Form from the user in Version 3.x. In Version 4.0, this feature still works. However, as you can see on the Basics page, selections exist to perform the same task. Nonetheless, it is a good convention to use the parentheses if for no other reason than to give you an indication that this is a hidden form when you are looking at it in the Forms View.

2. Make sure that the `Form type` is set to Document.

3. De-select `Menu` and `In Search Builder` in the `Include In` section of the page.

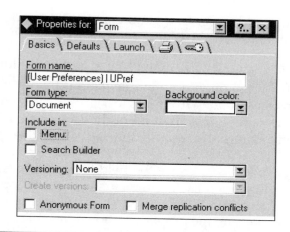

Figure 5.6 The Basic properties for the User Preferences Form.

Because the only time a user should be in the User Preferences Document is when they are setting those preferences, the only other change we will make to the default properties for our Form is on the Defaults page. Select `Automatically enable Edit Mode` in the `On Open` section.

Adding Labels, a Layout Region, and Fields

As noted earlier, the idea behind the User Preferences Document is to create it in such a way that only one Document per user shows up and only the settings a user needs will replicate. To accomplish this, we're going to use a Reader Names field that calculates out to name stored in the User's ID when they create the preferences Document. As such, the first field we're going to add to the User Preferences Form is an additional, hidden, Reader Names field that we will use to store a "Reader Override" value. This allows at least one person, server, or group to have access to the Documents created by each user.

The reason we want to override the other Readers field is simple. Users leave or change names. When they do, the User Preferences

Document they've created in the contact tracking database will no longer be accessible or useful. An override field allows a developer or administrator to clean up unneeded Documents.

When creating hidden fields, a good convention to adopt is to place them at the top or bottom of the Form. There are two reasons for doing this:

1. It gives developers a consistent place to look for hidden fields.
2. Hidden fields are often used in calculations by other visible fields. Since Notes calculates from left to right, top to bottom, placing these fields at the top or bottom of the Document allows them to be used in formulas that require the use of initialized fields.

That said, all that's left is to create the field by selecting Create, Field... from the Notes Client menu while the cursor is at the top of your new Form. This will insert a field called (Untitled). Open the Field's properties, and make sure the properties shown in Table 5.1 are set.

Table 5.1 Properties for the reUPrefReadersOverride field.

Page	Label	Value
Basics	Name	reUPrefReadersOverride
	Type	Readers - Computed
Hide	'Hide paragraph when document is:' section	Select all except 'Hide paragraph if formula is true:'
Font		Set to your design standard for hidden fields

In the Design Pane, set the properties ahown in Table 5.2.

Table 5.2 Assigning code to the reUPrefReadersOverride field.

Label	Vale
Define:	reUPrefReadersOverride (Field)
Event:	Value
Run:	Formula
Formula Window	"LocalDomainServers"

After the field is defined, wrap the cursor to the next line and enter the following text:

```
----- Hidden Fields -----
```

Wrap the cursor to the next line and click on **Text, Text Properties...** from the Notes Client menu. On the Hide page, de-select all boxes except `Previewed for Reading` and `Previewed for Editing`. Enter the label text:

```
Preferences for
```

Add one space beyond the "r" in "for" and create the field shown in Table 5.3.

Table 5.3 shows the Properties for Field dialog settings.

Table 5.3 Properties for the reUPrefUserName field.

Page	Label	Value
Basics	Name	reUPrefUserName
	Type	Readers - Computed

Table 5.4 shows the Design Pane settings.

Table 5.4 Assigning Code to the reUPrefUserName field.

Label	Value
Define:	reUPrefUserName (Field)
Event:	Value
Run:	Formula
Formula Window	@Name([Abbreviate];@UserName)

Select the entire line (label and field) and apply your standard Form title font and color using the **Text** command on the Notes Client menu. Figure 5.7 gives you an idea of how the Form should look so far.

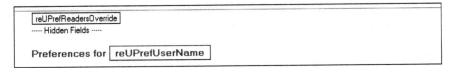

Figure 5.7 How the User Preferences Form should look at this point.

On a line below the field we just created, add the field shown in Table 5.5.

Table 5.5 shows the Properties for Field dialog settings.

Table 5.5 Properties for the radioUPrefReadOption field.

Page	Label	Value
Basics	Name	radioUPrefReadOption
	Type	Keywords - Editable
	Choices	Enter choices (one per line)
	List Window	Standard Display | 1
		Business Card Display | 2
Interface Options	Interface	Radio Button
	Frame	None
	Columns	1
Font		Your standard font/color for fields.

Table 5.6 shows Design Pane settings.

Table 5.6 Assigning code to the radioUPrefReadOption field.

Label	Value
Define:	radioUPrefReadOption (Field)
Event:	Default Value
Run:	Formula
Formula Window	"1"

After the field is created, place the cursor inside the field, and click on **Create, Section, Standard** from the Notes Client menu. This will create an "Untitled Section" on the User Preferences Form. Open the Properties for Section dialog, and enter the text as shown in Table 5.7.

Table 5.7 Section Properties

Page	Label	Value
Title	Title	the Text radio button
	Title Window	Show me contact information using the…
Expand/		
Collapse	Opened for Editing	Auto-collapse section
Font		Your standard font/color for labels.

To be sure that we don't add our next item to the Section we've just created, collapse the Section and place the cursor on the line beneath it. Click on **Create, Layout Region, New Layout Region** from the Notes Client menu. Open the Properties for Layout dialog, and enter the text as shown in Table 5.8.

Table 5.8 Layout Region properties

Page	Label	Value
Basics	Left	1"
	Width	3.5"
	Height	2"
	Show border	Not Selected
	3D style	Not Selected
	Show Grid	Selected
	Snap to Grid	Selected
	Grid Size	0.050"

Figure 5.8 gives you an idea of how the Form should look so far.

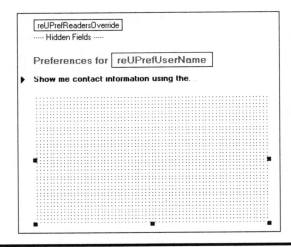

Figure 5.8 How the User Preferences Form should look at this point.

We're going to use the Layout Region we've just created to organize information about the user that the application can refer to when creating letters or faxes. When it's finished, the layout region should look similar to Figure 5.9.

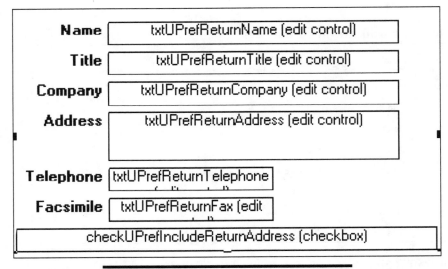

Figure 5.9 The Layout Regions with its fields.

The text labels are created by selecting Design, Layout Region, Text from the Notes Client menu. The fields are created by selecting the Layout Region and then choosing Create, Field... from the Notes Client menu. To ensure that the scripts we enter later will work correctly, please use the same field names used in Figure 5.9 (you don't need to enter the information in the parentheses in each field's name). With the exception of txtUPrefReturnAddress and checkUPrefIncludeReturnAddress, all of the fields will have the properties shown in Table 5.9.

Table 5.9 Properties for most of the text fields on the User Preferences Form's Layout Region.

Page	Label	Value
Basics	Type	Text -- Editable
Font		Your standard font/color for fields on a layout region (may we suggest 8 pt Black Helv).

The txtUPrefReturnAddress field should also have `Multiline` and `ScrollBar` selected on the Display Options page. The checkUPrefInclude-ReturnAddress should use the properties shown in Table 5.10.

Table 5.10 Properties for the checkUPrefIncludeReturnAddress field.

Page	Label	Value
Basics	Type	Keywords - Editable
	Choices	Enter choices (one per line)
	List Window	I print on letterhead so don't use the return address when making letters. | I
Display Options	Interface	Checkbox
	Frame	None
	Columns	I
Font		Your standard font/color for fields on a Layout Region.

After you have created all of the fields on the layout region, place the cursor below the layout region and enter the text:

```
Put
```

After adding another space, insert a new field called numUPref-
NumLinesforLetterhead. Make it an editable number field, with a
default value of 0. One space beyond the new field, add the text:

```
lines at the top of the first page.
```

Finally, select the Layout Region and the line beneath it, and click on,
Create, Section, Standard from the Notes Client menu. Use the same
properties as the previous section we created on this form, except for the
Title window, which should contain `Use the following information in`
`letters and faxes…` Figure 5.10 illustrates how the User Preferences
form should appear at this point.

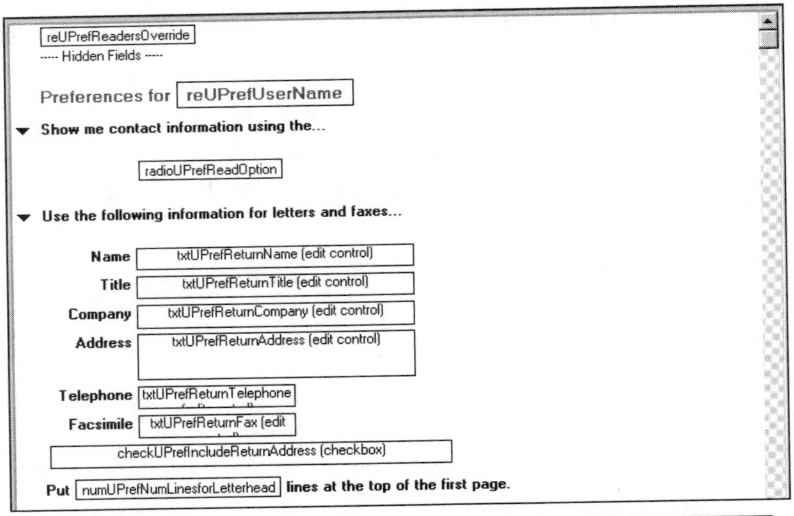

Figure 5.10 The completed User Preferences Form in design mode.

Click on **Design, Test Form…** from the Notes Client menu to view the
Form as it will appear to the end user (Figure 5.11). After you have tested
the Form, close the test window, save the Form, and close the Design
Window.

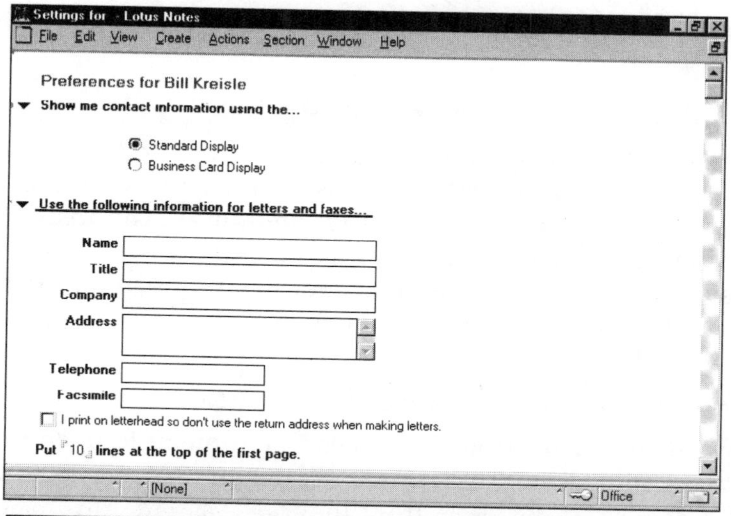

Figure 5.11 The User Preferences Form as seen by the end user.

The User Preferences View

Now that we have a Form that will allow us to create a User Preferences Document, the next step is to create a View that will allow us to filter out this Document so that it is accessible to us programmatically. This will be accomplished by creating a hidden View called User Preferences. I will talk about Views more extensively when we create some of the other Views for this database. For now, please copy the View titled (Preferences) from the sample database that shipped with this book and paste it into your database.

The only item unique to this View that won't be a part of any of the other Views we examine is that, as with the Form, the View's Name is enclosed in parentheses to tell Notes to hide it from the user.

The Set User Preferences Agent

What Is the Set User Preferences Agent?

With a hidden Document and a hidden View in place to store our user's preferences, the question probably arises, "If they're both hidden, how can the user get to them to set or change anything?" The answer to this is the Set User Preferences Agent. This execute-once Agent will be written in LotusScript and designed either to locate and open an existing User Preferences Document, or to create a new one.

Creating the Set User Preferences Agent

Click on **Create, Agent** from the Notes Client menu to open the Design Window. In the Name field, enter `Set User Preferences`. Click on `Manually from Actions Menu` from the `When should this agent run?` drop-down list, and `Run once (@Commands may be used)` from the `Which document(s) should it act on?` drop down list.

In the Design Pane, select Initialize from the Event prompt list, and Script in the Run prompt. Enter the following code between the Sub Initialize and End Sub statements:

```
Dim session As New Notessession
Dim ws As New NotesUIWorkspace
Dim db As NotesDatabase
Dim view As NotesView
Dim doc As NotesDocument
Dim item As NotesItem

Set db = session.CurrentDatabase
Set view = db.GetView("UPref")

On Error Resume Next
Set doc = view.GetFirstDocument
Set item = doc.GetFirstItem("reUPrefUserName")
If item Is Nothing Then
     Set uidoc = ws.ComposeDocument("", "", "UPref")
Else
```

```
        ws.OpenDatabase "","","UPref"
    ws.EditDocument
End If
```

What does this code do? First, it declares and initializes instances of several Notes objects. Next, it sets the NotesDatabase object to point to the currently open database, and sets the NotesView object to the View in the currently open database to "UPref" (the synonym for the View you pasted into the database in the previous section). Next, the script tells the run-time error processing environment not to display errors to the UI, and attempts to set the NotesDocument object to the first Document in the UPref View. After this, the NotesItem object has its properties set to the field rePrefUserName on the first Document in the UPref View.

If this NotesItem has no value after being assigned the field's properties, then no Document was available or the field was not present on the Document. In that case the NotesUIDocument object's ComposeDocument method is called to create a new User Preferences Document. If the NotesItem does have a value, the Hidden View is opened, the Document is selected and the EditDocument method opens the Document to the user's preferences.

Adding an Action to the User Preferences Form

After you've created this Set User Preferences Agent and tested it, you'll notice that once a preferences Document is edited using this Agent, the hidden View we created is still visible to the user. We had to bring the View to the UI to be able to open the User Preferences Document because LotusScript doesn't have a readily available method to open a Document to the UI. This is a livable quirk, but we can make it a little better by adding an Action to the User Preferences form.

To do this, from the Folders Navigator, open the Design header, and select Forms. Double-click on the (User Preferences) Form to open it in the Design Window. Click on **Create**, **Action** from the Notes Client menu.

This will cause the Actions List and the Properties for Action dialog to open. Change the Name of the Action in the Properties for Action dialog from (Untitled) to Done. Select an icon to associate with the properties if you wish, and click on `Include in action bar` from the Basics page.

In the Formula Window, enter:

```
@Command([FileCloseWindow]);
@Command([FileCloseWindow]);
```

This will cause Notes to close the current Document and the View as well (see Figure 5.12). Of course, the user can inadvertently bypass this code by using the **File, Close** command from the Notes Client menu directly, or by pressing the **ESC** key on the Document. However, given the effort required to create the Action, the people it does help are easily worth the work.

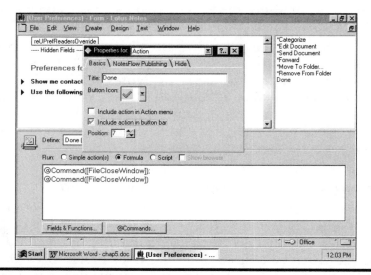

Figure 5.12 Creating the Done Action for the User Preferences Form.

The Contact Record Form

Creating the Contact Record Form

The next Form we're going to create will be designed to hold our primary Contact information. Since it will be very similar to the User

Preferences Form we created in that it will use standard Sections, Layout Regions, Hidden Fields and Actions, we're not going to go over creating the entire Form step by step. Instead, we're going to copy the Contact Record Form from the database on the CD and talk about the details (see Figure 5.13). While you are copying the Contact Record Form, also take time to copy the Business Card and Standard Display Subforms, as we'll examine them here, too.

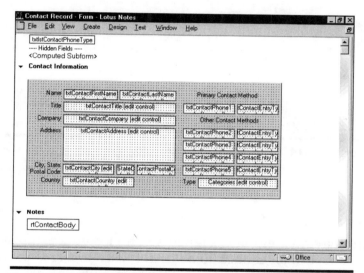

Figure 5.13 The Contact Record Form in the Design Window.

The Hidden Fields on the Contact Record Form

The first thing we'll cover about the design of the Contact Record Form is the purpose of the hidden field at the top of the Form, txtlstContactPhoneType. This field is a computed text field, whose properties are set to allow multiple values. It is used by fields on the Layout Region to populate the drop-down lists for the telephone type as the user enters the number. This consolidates the choices for all five of the txtContactEntryType*x* fields so that making a change later need only be done in one place.

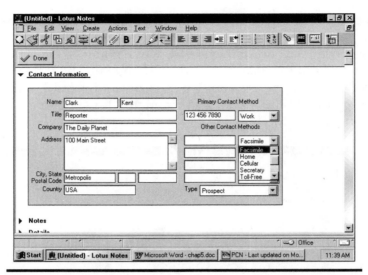

Figure 5.14 The values in these drop down lists are set from the txtContactKeywordsList hidden field.

The Computed Subform

While the Layout Region designed to enter contact information is compact, it isn't small enough to be useful when a user is previewing a Document using the Preview Panes. To help with this problem, we're going to create two Subforms that can be displayed conditionally based on the User's Preferences. Those two subforms are the Standard Display Subform (Figure 5.15) and the Business Card Subform (Figure 5.16), which you pasted into the database earlier.

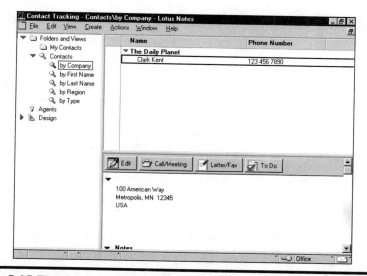

Figure 5.15 The Contact Record opened for reading using the Standard Display Subform.

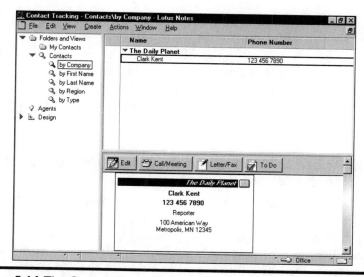

Figure 5.16 The Contact Record opened for reading using the Business Card Subform.

The formula we'll use in the Computed Subform to decide which Subform to display it follows:

```
KeyValue := @Name([Abbreviate];@UserName);
"DispContact" + @Trim(@DbLookup("Notes" : "Nocache" ; "" ; "UPref" ;
KeyValue ; "radioUPrefReadOption"));
```

This formula will use the constant `DispContact` combined with the synonyms we entered earlier in the keywords list of the radoUPrefReadOption evaluate to the string `DispContact1` or `DispContact2` (the synonyms for the two subforms pasted into the database earlier).

Setting the Tab Order of the Contact Record's Layout Region

The next thing to examine on the Contact Record Form is the fields on the Layout Region. Creating and placing these fields is no different than the method we used when we created the Layout Region on the User Preferences Form. However, one item we didn't discuss when we created the User Preferences Layout Region was how to set the tab order of fields on the Layout. There is no provision for this option in the Properties for Field or Layout Region dialogs.

It is done by placing all the fields on the Layout Region, then using the **Edit, Cut** and **Edit, Paste** command on the Notes Client menu to systematically remove and reinsert the fields, one by one. The order in which the fields are cut and pasted onto the Layout becomes the tab order.

Using the Hide/Unhide Page of the Properties for Text Dialog Box to Hide the Layout Region

Since there is a Computed Subform designed to display contact information, the Layout Region we created for entering contacts does not need to be visible when the user is reading a Document created with this form. Clicking on the text above the Layout Region and the Layout Region, then using the Hide/Unhide page of the Properties for Text dialog box incorporates this functionality.

The Call Response Document

Now that we have our two main Forms and Subforms created, the next step is to create the Response Documents that will be associated with the Contact Records. We'll start by creating the first of these Documents, the Call Response Document, together, then by pasting the other Response Documents in from the database on the CD and discussing key elements of them.

Creating the Call Response Document

Click on **Create, Design, Form** from the Notes Client menu to create a new Form in the Design Window. Open the Properties for Form dialog and enter the information shown in Table 5.11

Table 5.11 Properties for the Call Response Form.

Page	Label	Value
Basics	Form name	(Call) | Call
	Form Type	Response
	Menu	Not Selected
	Search Builder	Selected
Defaults	Formulas inherit value from selected document	Selected

NOTE

We selected the Search Builder option to allow users who full-text index this database to use the Call Response Form in a Query by Example search in the Search Builder dialog.

Place the text cursor on the blank form, and enter the text:

```
Placed by
```

followed by a tab. Create a new, editable text field called txtCallPersonCalled. Set the Default Value of the txtCallPersonCalled field in the Design Pane to the following Formula:

```
First:= @If(@Length(txtContactFirstName) > 0; txtContactFirstName +
" "; "");

Last := txtContactLastName;

Company := @If(@Length(Last) > 0 | @Length(First) > 0; ", ";"") +
txtContactCompany;

First + Last + Company
```

This code takes advantage of the `Formulas inherit values from selected document` property of the Call Response Form. It assigns the value of the txtContactFirstName, txtContactLastName, and txtContactCompany fields on the Contact Record to temporary variables. Depending on these values, it also inserts spacing and punctionation. The temporary variables are then strung together and returned to the txtCallPersonCalled field as the default value.

On the next line in the Form, enter the text

```
Call Date
```

followed by a tab. From the Notes Client menu, click on **Create, Design, Shared Field**. This will cause a new Design Pane to open along with the Properties for Shared Field dialog, which you should set to the values shown in Table 5.12.

Table 5.12 The Properties for Shared Field settings for the daSharedResponseDate field.

Page	Label	Value
Basics	Name	daSharedResponseDate
	Type	Time - Editable
	Show	Date

Set the daSharedResponseDate field's Default Value to:

```
@Date(@Today)
```

Close the Design Pane for the Shared Field and save it. If it is not already selected, make sure the Design Window for the Call Response Form is now the active window. Place the cursor after the Call Date label and select **Create, Insert Shared Field...** from the Notes Client menu. Select daSharedResponseDate from the list and click OK.

On the next line of the Call Response Form, enter the label:

```
Call Time
```

followed by a tab. Create a new Shared Field called daSharedResponse-Time with the properties shown in Table 5.13.

Table 5.13 The Properties for Shared Field settings for the daSharedResponseTime field.

Page	Label	Value
Basics	Name	daSharedResponseTime
	Type	Time - Editable
	Show	Time

Set the daSharedResponseTime field's Default Value to:

```
@Time(@Now)
```

See Figure 5.17.

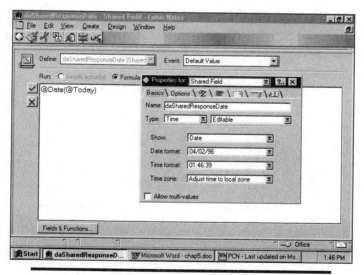

Figure 5.17 Creating the daSharedResponseDate field.

Close the Design Window (Figure 5.17) containing the Shared Field and save changes. Using the **Create, Insert Shared Field…** command, add the daSharedResponseTime field to the end of the Call Time label.

On the next line of the Form, enter the label `Placed By` followed by a tab. Create an editable text field called `txtCallPlacedBy`, and give it a Default Value of:

```
@Name([Abbreviate];@UserName)
```

This formula returns the canonical name of the currently active user ID in an abbreviated form.

Apply the font styles and colors appropriate for your design standards for labels and fields. Select all of the fields currently on the Form and incorporate them into a Standard Section with the title "Details." Figure 5.18 illustrates how the Call Response Form should look so far.

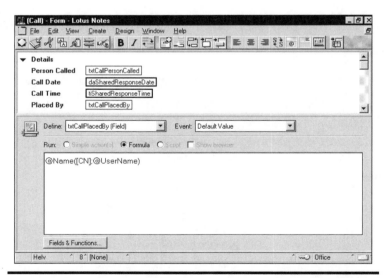

Figure 5.18 How the Call Response Form should look at this point.

Collapse the Details section and add the field shown in Table 5.14 to the Form beneath the collapsed section.

Table 5.14 Properties for the txtlstCallStatus field.

Page	Label	Value
Basics	Name	txtlstCallStatus
	Type	Keywords - Editable
	Choices	Enter choices (one per line)
	List Window	Left Message | 1
		Call Completed | 2
		Will Call Again (no answer or busy) | 3
Display Options	Interface	Radio Buttons
	Frame	None
	Columns	1

On the line beneath the txtlstCallStatus field, add an editable Rich Text field called rtCallBody. Click on the rtCallBody field and collapse it into a Standard Section called Notes. Figure 5.19 shows the completed form in the Design Window.

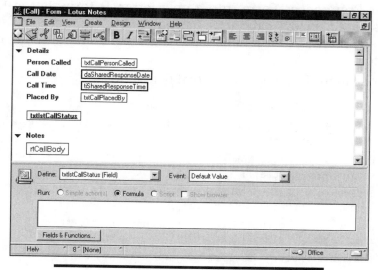

Figure 5.19 The completed Call Response Form.

Close the Design Window for the Call Response Form and save changes.

The Meeting Response Form

The Meeting Response Form is very similar to the Call Response Form. Please copy and paste it from the database on the CD into your database. Notice that it uses the shared fields daSharedResponseDate and daSharedResponseTime.

The Letter Response Form

The Letter Response Form isn't much to look at, field wise, but the formulas behind the fields may be of interest to you, as well as some discussion as to why those formulas are being used. To start our examination, copy the Letter Response Form from the database on the CD and paste it into your database.

The rtLetterReturnAddress Field

Open the Form in the Design Window and place the cursor in the rtLetterReturnAddress field. This field is a hidden Rich Text field, designed to pull the Return Address Information entered by the user in the User Preferences Form into a new letter. It formats the Return Address based on what the user has entered in the User Preferences Form (i.e., no title; title but no company; company but not first and last name, etc.).

The code in the Default Value of that field follows.

```
KeyValue := @Name([Abbreviate];@UserName);

TheName := @DbLookup("Notes": "Nocache" ; "" ; "UPref" ; KeyValue ;
"txtUPrefReturnName");

TheTitle :=@ DbLookup("Notes" : "Nocache" ; "" ; "UPref" ; KeyValue
; "txtUPrefReturnTitle");

TheAddress := @DbLookup("Notes" : "Nocache" ; "" ; "UPref" ;
KeyValue ; "txtUPrefReturnAddress");

TheCompany := @DbLookup("Notes" : "Nocache" ; "" ; "UPref" ;
KeyValue ; "txtUPrefReturnCompany");

@If(@Length(TheName) > 0; TheName + @NewLine; "") +

@If(@Length(TheTitle) > 0; TheTitle + @NewLine; "") +
```

```
@If(@Length(TheCompany) > 0; TheCompany + @NewLine; "") +
@If(@Length(TheAddress) > 0; TheAddress + @NewLine; "")
```

The rtLetterBody Field

Like the rtLetterReturnAddress field, the rtLetterBody field is an editable Rich Text field with a Default Value formula. The formula computes the choices the user made on their User Preferences Document, and uses it to create a basic letter with (or without) a return address, the contact's address, and an opening and closing.

```
KeyValue := @Name([Abbreviate];@UserName);

UseReturn := @DbLookup("Notes" : "Nocache" ; "" ; "UPref" ; KeyValue ;
"checkUPrefIncludeReturnAddress");

NumLines := @DbLookup( "Notes" : "Nocache" ; "" ; "UPref" ; KeyValue ;
"numUPrefNumLinesforLetterhead");

SendingToName := txtContactFirstName + " " + txtContactLastName;

SendingToAddress1 := @If(@Length(@Trim(SendingToName)) > 0;
SendingToName + @NewLine;"");

SendingToAddress2 := SendingToAddress1 + @If(@Length(txtContactTitle) >
0; txtContactTitle + @NewLine; "");

SendingToAddress3 := SendingToAddress2 + @If(@Length(txtContactCompany)
> 0; txtContactCompany + @NewLine; "");

SendingToAddress4 := SendingToAddress3 + @If(@Length(txtContactAddress)
> 0; txtContactAddress + @NewLine; "");

CityState := txtContactCity + @If(@Length(txtContactStateorProvince) >
0; ", "; "") + txtContactStateOrProvince;

CityStateAndZip := @If(@Length(CityState) > 0; CityState + "  "; "") +
txtContactPostalCode + @NewLine;

SendingToAddress5 := SendingToAddress4 + CityStateAndZip +
txtContactCountry + @Repeat(@NewLine; 2);

@If(UseReturn = ""; @Repeat(@NewLine;6) + rtLetterReturnAddress;
@Repeat(@NewLine;NumLines + 1)) + @Text(@Today) + @Repeat(@NewLine; 2)
+ SendingToAddress5 + "Dear " + txtContactFirstName + ":" +
@Repeat(@NewLine;5) + "Sincerely:" + @Repeat(@NewLine;2) +
@DbLookup("Notes":"Nocache";"";"UPref";KeyValue,"txtUPrefReturnName")
```

Figure 5.20 illustrates a letter created using the Letter Response Form.

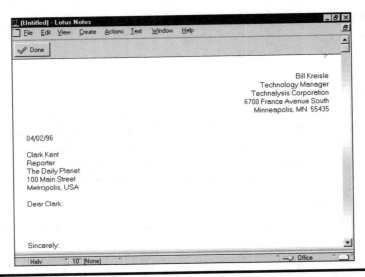

Figure 5.20 A letter composed by inheriting values from the selected document and by looking up values on the User Preferences Form.

This is a very basic approach to creating a letter, granted. But it is a very usable approach if you're going to use this database across multiple platforms or if you have multiple word-processors in use in your workgroup. An alternative approach—creating an OLE object in the Letter Response Document—is also possible, but requires that all users in the workgroup have the same platform and version of the OLE object you insert to ensure consistency.

The Facsimile Response Form

Like the Letter Response Form, the Facsimile Response Form takes advantage of inheriting the selected Document's values combined with accessing the current User Preferences field to create a customized facsimile cover sheet, as illustrated in Figure 5.21.

Add this Form by copying it from the database on the CD and pasting it into your database.

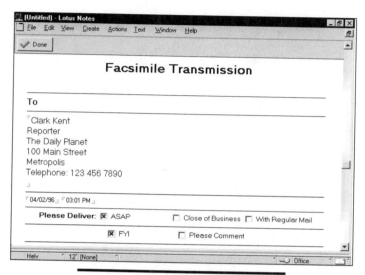

Figure 5.21 A Facsimile Cover Sheet.

The Contacts, by Company View

Now that we have all of the Forms and Subforms created, we can begin to pull them together for the user by using Views. As mentioned earlier, we'll give the user the option to view contacts by first and last name, company, and geography. To see how to create a View, we'll build the Contacts, by Company View together, and paste the other Views in from the database on the CD.

Creating the Contacts, by Company View

Select **Design, Create, View...** on the Notes Client menu. In the Create View dialog, enter `Contacts\by Company | Company` in the `View name` text box, and select the Shared checkbox. Fill the `Select by formula` checkbox also, and enter `SELECT Form != "UPref"` in the Formula window (see Figure 5.22). Click on OK to open the Design Window to a new View.

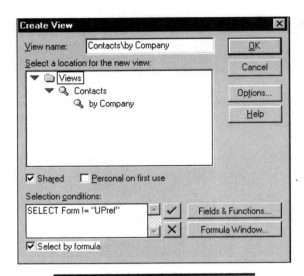

Figure 5.22 The Create View dialog.

Double-click on the first column in the new View to open the Properties for Column dialog. Enter the settings shown in Table 5.15.

Table 5.15 Properties for the first column of the Contacts\by Company View.

Page	Label	Value
Basics	Title	Remove '#' sign and leave this box empty.
	Width	I
	Resizable	Not Selected
	Show twistie when row is expandable	Selected
Sorting	Sort	Ascending
	Type	Categorized

In the Design Pane, select the Field radio button, and `txtContactCompany` from the list that appears when Field is selected.

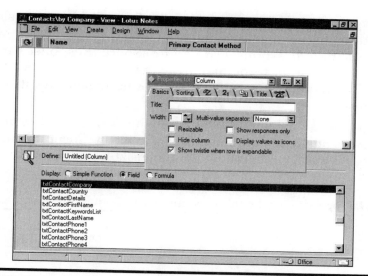

Figure 5.23 Setting properties for the first column in the Contacts\by Company View.

Click once on the column after the first column, and select **Create, Append New Column...** from the Notes Client menu.

Set the properties for the second column to conform to Table 5.16

Table 5.16 Properties for the second column of the Contacts\by Company View.

Page	Label	Value
Basics	Title	leave this box empty.
	Width	1
	Resizable	Not Selected
	Show responses only	Selected

In the Design Pane, select the Formula radio button and entering the following in the Formula window:

```
Form + " -- " + @Text(daSharedResponseDate) + "   " +
@Text(tiSharedResponseTime)
```

This formula takes the value stored in the Form Field (which, since this column deals with responses only, will be Call, Letter, Fax, or Meeting, and the daSharedResponseDate and daSharedResponseTime field converted to text strings. You may recall that these two fields are shared on all of the Response Forms we created—and this is why. It simplifies Views considerably.

Click on the last column of the View in the Design Window and select **Create, Append New Column...** from the Notes Client menu. Set the properties for this third column as shown in Table 5.17.

Table 5.17 Properties for the third column of the Contacts\by Company View.

Page	Label	Value
Basics	Title	Name
	Width	24
	Resizable	Selected
	Show twistie when row is expandable	Selected
Sorting	Sort	Ascending
	Type	Standard

In the Design Pane for this column, click on the Formula radio button, and enter the following in the Formula window:

```
@If(@Length(txtContactFirstName) > 0; txtContactFirstName + " "; "")
+ txtContactLastName
```

Create the fourth and final column with the properties shown in Table 5.18.

Table 5.18 Properties for the fourth column of the Contacts\by Company View.

Page	Label	Value
Basics	Title	Phone Number
	Width	16
	Resizable	Selected

In the Design Pane, use the Fields radio button to set this column to display the contents of the txtContactPhone1 field.

Before closing the new View, open the Properties for View dialog box, and set the properties shown in Table 5.19.

Table 5.19 Properties for the Contacts\by Company View.

Page	Label	Value
Basics	Name	Contacts\by Company
	Alias	Company
Options	Show response documents in hierarchy	Selected
Propeller-Head		Unread Marks Standard-Compute in hierarchy

Adding Some Documents

Now that we have the basic Documents and a View, take a few moments to add two or three Documents to your new database. Having these records will make it easier to follow along with the rest of the design elements we will examine in this chapter.

Other Contact Views

Copy the Contacts\by First Name, Contacts\by Last Name, and Contacts\by Type views from the database on the CD and paste them into your application. The Contacts\by Type view takes advantage of Notes' built-in use of a field called Categories. When you use a keywords field called Categories and make a view where the first column is categorized on that field, you can use the **Actions, Categorize…** command from the Notes Client menu.

The My Contacts Folder

Now that we have the a number of Views that users can share to find information, its time to revisit the user's requirements and take care of the one that asks for a place that users can create individual collections of contacts to make them easier to find. This requirement can be accomplished in Notes using Folders. As we discussed previously,

Folders are similar to Views, with the exception that their selection criteria aren't hard-coded into them. A user or program must add information to a View.

Creating the My Contacts Folder

Select **Create, Design, Folder...** from the Notes Client menu to open the Create Folder dialog. Enter My Contacts in the Folder name field, and click on the Shared checkbox. When you click on Shared, another checkbox called Personal on first use will appear at the bottom of the Create Folder dialog. Click on it, as well.

Click on the Options... button and select Contacts\by Type from the Inherit design from list dialog box. Click OK on both dialogs.

What we just did was create a Folder that becomes private to the user as soon as they drag their first Document into it. In this way, every user will have a My Contacts folder, but each one will only contain information brought in by one user (see Figure 5.24).

Figure 5.24 The My Contacts Folder in the Folders Navigator.

Linking the Design Elements and Automating Processes

Adding Actions

When you started adding Documents to the database, you probably noticed that there were several Actions associated with the Contact Record Form. Because the Response Documents of our application were all created and hidden from the user, they create the link between the Contact Record Document and the Response Documents that will be associated with it. We're using Actions to control the creation of Response Documents to help ensure that responses are associated with the right Documents when they're created.

Open a Document in the Preview Pane or the Document Window and we'll examine each of the available Actions (see Figure 5.25).

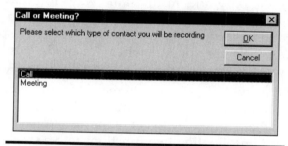

Figure 5.25 Actions on the Contact Record Form.

The Edit Action is there as a convenience to the user. It executes the formula @Command([EditDocument]) when activated. The Action is visible only when a Document is read or previewed.

The Call/Meeting Action is designed to allow users to create either call or meeting records. The formula associated with this action is:

```
which := @Prompt([OKCANCELLIST];"Call or Meeting?";"Please select
which type of contact you will be
recording";"Call";"Call":"Meeting");

@Command([Compose];which)
```

What this code does is display a dialog box with an OK button and a
Cancel button and those two choices to the user (Figure 5.26). If the user
clicks on OK, the choice the user made is used to create a Response
Document. If the user clicks on Cancel, the formula ends before the
@Command([Compose]) line is called.

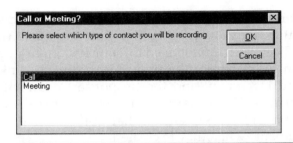

Figure 5.26 Clicking the Call/Meeting Action opens this dialog.

The Letter/Fax Action works in the same way. You may wonder why
two separate types of Responses are consolidated onto a single Action,
rather than creating a separate Action for each type or Response. There is
no hard-and-fast rule we applied when we made this decision—the
primary focus was the conservation of real-estate on the Action bar.

Although Notes will allow you to create any number of Actions to
display on an Action bar, once the number of Actions is greater than the
width of the bar, there is no way to get to the additional Actions. Because
of this limitation, consolidating two functions into a single button allows
more room for other Actions on the bar as the application evolves.

The final Action, To Do, is an example of integrating the information
you are currently working with to another database. In this case, clicking
the To Do action will execute a script that opens a task in the current
mail file and copies information from the current Document into the
newly created Task.

The script for this action follows:

```
Sub Click(Source As Button)
      Dim session As New NotesSession
      Dim ws As New NotesUIWorkspace
      Dim maildb As Notesdatabase
      Dim taskuidoc As NotesUIDocument
```

```
Dim contactuidoc As NotesUIDocument
Dim taskdoc As NotesDocument
Dim contactdoc As NotesDocument
Dim taskbody As Variant
Dim first, last, fullname, title, company, address, city As
Variant
Dim state, zip, tel, typetel As Variant
Dim fulladdr As String

Set contactuidoc = ws.CurrentDocument

Set maildb = session.currentdatabase
maildb.OpenMail
Set taskuidoc = ws.ComposeDocument(maildb.Server,
maildb.FileName, "Task")

Set contactdoc = contactuidoc.Document

first = contactdoc.getitemvalue("txtContactFirstName")
last = contactdoc.getitemvalue("txtContactLastName")
company = contactdoc.getitemvalue("txtContactCompany")
title = contactdoc.getitemvalue("txtContactTitle")
address = contactdoc.getitemvalue("txtContactAddress")
city = contactdoc.getitemvalue("txtContactCity")
state = contactdoc.getitemvalue("txtContactStateOrProvince")
zip = contactdoc.getitemvalue("txtContactPostalCode")
tel = contactdoc.getitemvalue("txtContactPhone1")
typetel = contactdoc.getitemvalue("txtlstContactEntryType1")
fullname = first(0) & " " & last(0)

fulladdr = fullname & Chr$(10) & + title(0) _
& Chr$(10) & company(0) & Chr$(10) _
& address(0) & Chr$(10) & city(0) & _
" " & state(0) & "    " & zip(0) & Chr$(10) _
& tel(0) & "(" & typetel(0) & ")"

taskuidoc.fieldappendtext "Body",fulladdr

End Sub
```

As usual, the first few lines of the script are used to declare instances of Notes objects as well as any variables used in the script. Next, the NotesUIDocument object contactuidoc is set to the current Document in the Workspace (the one where the To Do Action was triggered from). After that, the NotesDatabase object maildb is initialized by giving it the value of the current database. Once initialized, the maildb's OpenMail method is called to change its pointer to the mail database specified in the current Location document of the Private Name and Address Book.

Information from the original contact Document that was used to call the To Do Action is collected into several Variant variables and concatenated into a string along with an ASCII character 10 as a delimiter for each line. Finally, the NotesUIDocument object taskuidoc's FieldAppendText method is called to add the information from the contact Document to the newly created Task (see Figure 5.27).

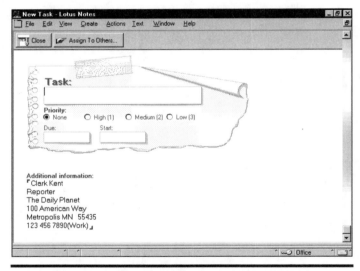

Figure 5.27 A Task Document created using the To Do Action.

At this point, some experienced Notes developers may be wondering why we went through all the hoops we did to get the information from the Contact Document into the Task using the UI, instead of just creating our own Task Form or modifying the Task Form in the mail template. Our answer is that, to reduce the maintenance issues associated with applications that cross multiple databases, using the UI to paste information rather than creating a Form that inherits the information has some appeal. Also, since users with a Lotus Notes Mail license cannot modify the design of their mail database, this allows Tasks created in with the standard or desktop editions of Notes to travel seamlessly between versions.

Reviewing the Finished Application

Let's revisit our design requirements and see how we did. The requirements were:

1. An application that allows the user to enter and share basic contact information, tracking phone calls, meetings, faxes, and letters over time.

   By using the Contact Document, and Response Documents for Calls, Meetings, Letters, and Faxes, we've got this one covered.

2. The user should be able to view basic information about multiple contacts at one time.

   By including name, company, and telephone in each View, basic information for multiple contacts can be seen and used.

3. The user should be able to find contacts easily by using the contact's name, company, or location.

   Views by first name, last name, company, type, and region can all be used. In addition, the region and type Views allow the user to change the sorting order to make contacts easier to locate.

4. The user should have some control over how contact information is displayed.

   Using Subforms and a Computed Subform on the Contact Record Document, the user can view information in either of two methods. These Subforms are selected through the User Preferences Document. Additionally, the use of synonyms on the User Preferences Document and the Subforms makes it easy for you to add additional Subforms to display information if desired.

5. Since we're tracking conversations and correspondence, it is desirable to make entering this information as automatic as possible.

    Using the Response Document's ability to inherit parent information combined with formulas to pull information from the User Preferences Document, the user can create customized letters and faxes automatically.

6. The user should also be able to filter shared contacts into a smaller group (to make finding contacts related to him or her easier to find).

    The My Contacts Folder allows users to group contacts for personal retrieval.

7. It needs to run on multiple platforms, because each workgroup uses its own OS (some are all Mac OS, others are OS/2, most are 16 or 32 bit Windows).

    With the release of Lotus Notes 4.1, client software exists for Windows, Windows NT, Windows 95, Mac O/S, OS/2, and many flavors of UNIX.

8. It should allow different workgroups using different copies of the database to move information between each copy of the database.

    Replication or copy-and-paste can be used to move information with the database as it stands now. With very little work, the database could also mail Contact Documents between different versions of the database.

9. Could the application allow users to work off of the network and remotely as well?

    Replication, replication, replication.

10. One more item. Could you have a prototype for us to review in, say, two working days?

    How long did it take you? A couple of hours? OK, you had a head start, but, honestly, we built this database in about six hours from start to finish.

Where Do We Go From Here?

Now that you have a good idea of what Notes is, and how it can be used, you're ready to do one of several things:

If you're a new Notes Developer, you have a good start towards understanding Notes and its applications. The next step should be the Lotus manuals, and, over time, the second half of this book.

If you're an experienced 3.x developer, you've had a good look at some of the features of 4.x—you should be ready to build some databases! When you need to do more than what 4.x can do, the second half of this book is ready for you.

If you're an API developer, you have a good foundation to refer to when writing API programs, and you're ready to go to the next chapters and find out more about which API is right for the job at hand.

Extending Notes

At this point, you may be saying, "Wow! Notes has a lot of features I can use to create some really cool applications, but wouldn't it be nice if...." If you are, read on! Even if you aren't, you may in the near future. After all, you paid for the whole book, why not read it?

In short, the rest of this book is dedicated to the discussion of how to extend the current capabilities of Notes outside of the Notes application itself. We'll do this by showing you how to access Notes information from C, C++, and Visual Basic using three different development tools: the Notes C API, the Notes HiTest C API, and the Notes HiTest Tools for Visual Basic. It is not intended to be an exhaustive list of all the ways to extend Notes, but it does hit those that are oriented toward solutions that do not use Notes itself as the development tool.

In this chapter, we'll discuss the strengths and weaknesses of each tool (the term *tool* is used loosely here to describe any of the extension methods) and provide possible suggestions on how they can be used. Subsequent chapters will concentrate on particular tools by detailing some of their features and providing examples of how they can be used.

We'll describe the features of each tool within each chapter through the use of example programs. This method not only provides a more concrete way of learning but also provides source code that you can use or modify for your specific needs. The intent is to provide enough information on the usage of each tool to allow you to make intelligent choices on which tool to use, given a certain set of criteria. For this reason, there will not always be an exhaustive analysis of all of the features within each tool, but we'd like to think that those that are discussed will produce the desired effect.

All of the source code for each application described in the following chapters is available on the CD-ROM included with the book. It is organized by the extension method used, the destination platform, and the application name itself. For example, all of the examples created using the Notes C API will be in the directory **NOTESC**, whereas the examples created using the Notes HiTest C API will be under the directory **HITESTC**. Within the **NOTESC** directory, the **WIN16** subdirectory contains applications for use on 16-bit Windows 3.x installations. From here, the **DBVIEWER** subdirectory contains the source code and executables for the database viewer application described in the next chapter. To assist in finding the source code on the CD-ROM, the first time each example is referenced in the book, its full path on the CD-ROM will be provided.

Another thing to note about the following chapters is the set of conventions used. Whenever we discuss a call from one of the API sets, it will be followed by parentheses and bolded as in **NSFSearch()**. The functions we have created internally to a specific application will also be suffixed with parentheses but will not be set in bold. The last thing to mention here is that some of code segments contained herein are taken directly from the applications themselves while others are simply the prototypes for specific APIs. As a rule, the prototypes are provided only if the application's use of the API does not sufficiently expand on the parameters.

Tool Selection: Why So Many?

Before we actually dive into the tools, it is important to understand some of their overall strengths and weaknesses. After all, the first thing you usually do when trying to solve a problem—whether it is building a deck or a computer program—is to determine the best set of tools to use. In addition, you'd probably try to get a high-level understanding of what to expect before you start digging very deep.

A case in point: you probably wouldn't use a hacksaw to cut a piece of plywood; you'd use a table saw. If you didn't have the table saw, the hacksaw would suffice—but it would be a lot more work and the quality of the cut wouldn't be as good. The analogy follows for software development in general and, more specifically, for Notes development tools. Although many of the tools and integration methods described herein can perform many of the same functions, some are better suited for different types of applications.

The following section gives a high-level view of each of the three tools in an effort to make it easier to select the best tool for the application you want to create. After a short description, a list of some strengths, weaknesses, and possible applications of the tool will be provided. The thing to remember is that most of the tools can do many of the same things. For this reason, there may be more than one that will suit your needs. If so, the choice is yours.

Notes C API

There are basically three API sets available for use with Notes. The first—and the oldest—is the native Notes C API. It is probably the most widely used API set today for these reasons. Although the stated goal of the Notes API group is to transition more toward the HiTest C API as the major API set, the standard API set will continue to be supported.

Since its creation, one of the design goals of the Notes C API was to provide a means for external applications to extend Notes in ways not currently available through Notes itself. On the other hand, the Notes C API, or any Notes API for that matter, has never been intended to provide a means of creating an alternative interface to Notes data. In fact, this is expressly prohibited in the latest version of the license agreement.

For the most part, the Notes C API can do just about anything you want to do with Notes data. This includes reading, writing, copying, creating, and deleting anything from Notes databases to fields within documents. The ability to create and manipulate macros (or agents) and formulas is also provided. And, if you wish, you can create forms and views from scratch under program control.

From the other side of the coin, the Notes C API does not allow for the modification of features within the Notes application itself. Nor does it allow for the modification of the Notes desktop or user interface.

NOTE

The one notable exception here is the ability to create an application-defined menu choice available within Notes to allow the user to interact directly with your application. Such an application is called a *menu add-in* application.

Strengths

The Notes C API's greatest strength is the breadth of functionality it provides. It is, by far, the most functionally diverse of all of the API sets. (This is mostly due to the fact that the other API sets are all based on the Notes C API.) There are very few aspects of Notes, other than the user interface limitations described above, that cannot be accessed through the Notes C API.

Strength number two lies in that fact that, because the Notes C API is currently the standard API, it is, at least for now, the first to be available for new platforms and releases. For example, the only API set available for use throughout the development of Notes version 4.0 was the Notes C API.

Another big plus with this API set is that is can be used for cross-platform development. The OS function group allows for a level of abstraction that, if used properly, can make it quite easy to port an application from one platform to another. The HiTest C API was originally developed for use with Windows and OS/2 but is now available on almost all the other Notes platforms. The notable exception is that the version 3.x API is not available on the Macintosh platform. Version 4.0 of the API, however, will be available for the Macintosh.

The last item we'll touch on as a strength is that of the ability of the API to work with Notes data without the need for Notes to be running on the system. (This is actually a feature of all the API sets described in the book.) This is not to say that Notes need not be installed on the system; it must be, as should the DLLs for the API itself (and there are a few). An application created with the Notes C API can run against local and remote Notes databases without the Notes application running. This may not seem like a big deal but it can be a nice feature. An example of this may be a data transfer agent that is hosted on an unmanned server that moves data from a legacy application into Notes at periodic intervals. In this case, there is no need for the Notes application to be running because there is no end user to interact with it.

NOTE

If you do access remote databases through an application, however, a login prompt will be displayed through the API whenever you first attempt to access nonlocal data.

Weaknesses

This API set's greatest strength, its diversity, can also be one of its greatest weaknesses. There are some APIs that have more options than a Mercedes, and setting the options one way versus another can make a big difference, especially in performance.

Another weakness within the API is its structure. As we'll discuss in Chapter 7, the API is defined around what we'll call *loosely defined objects*. In some cases, the Mail object, for example the object structure holds together fairly well. For example, it's pretty easy to know where to go to find an API dealing with a mail function. The Notes Storage Facility APIs, on the other hand, contain a large set of APIs that range from accessing and running a macro to finding database files to comparing fields within a document.

Another weakness, at least in some cases, is that the Notes C API cannot be used to manipulate the user interface. Although this is a design constraint, as discussed earlier, there are certain cases where it would be nice to be able to have a modicum of control over what the user sees and does within the Notes environment.

Macros: even though you can create, delete, and execute macros using this API, it can be a daunting task! If you really want to know how bad it can be, look at the RUNMACRO sample application that comes with the Notes C API set: 1500 lines of code to run a specified macro against a specified database, with a hefty set of restrictions. Suffice it to say, you can do it, but there's an easier way, namely, the Notes HiTest C API.

Last but not least, this API can be unforgiving in certain cases. It is not unusual to meet up with the dreaded "Notes PANIC" dialog box, which shuts down your application and Notes, if it is running. In addition, if you are running Windows 3.x, you usually have to exit Windows and start it up again before you can use any Notes functionality again. (See the OS Functions section in the Notes C API chapter of the book for an example.)

Applications

If you are comfortable with C and/or C++ and you want to really get down and have as much control as possible over your application design and performance, the Notes C API is a good choice. In addition, since the Notes C API currently provides the most diversity of all of the API sets, you may need to use it if you want to do something the other API sets cannot. In reference to the work needed to master it, this API set has been called the *black diamond* of all the API sets, much as black diamond runs in skiing can be the most demanding.

One of the possible uses common to all of the API sets is to create import/export applications. It is fairly easy to read data from Notes and write it into a different form such as a relational database or other file system. Sending data to Notes is just as easy; the only extra step you need to perform is to create a new document if one does not exist.

If your application is doing some heavy-duty mail interaction, you may want to take a good look at what this API has to offer. Even though you could access the mail databases at the database level using any of the API sets, this API set provides more mail-specific APIs and therefore greater low-level control over the mail interface.

The last thing to look at here is that of multiplatform development. If you are planning to do work on more than just Windows and OS/2, the Notes C API is your only choice for now, although this will most likely change in the near future when the HiTest C API becomes the de facto API standard.

HiTest C API

The second API set, the Notes HiTest C API, was originally created by Edge Research, which used to be an independent corporation until it was purchased by Lotus Development Corporation. (For that matter, Lotus Development Corporation was an independent corporation until it was purchased by IBM.) The Notes HiTest C API was—and still is—created on top of the Notes C API, and therefore has no basic functionality that the standard Notes C API does not have. Its main design goals were to reduce the complexity, and increase the robustness, of the native Notes C API.

The complexity reduction basically comes from the fact that the HiTest C API was created based off a set of well-defined objects. Some of these objects exist in the standard API but are not as well defined. Since the object structure is better defined, there tends to be a reduction in code size between the standard API set and the HiTest set. This is mostly due to the smaller number of APIs required to perform the same function. The HiTest documentation states that this reduction has been reported to be as great as 10:1, but it can differ greatly, depending on the application.

From the standpoint of robustness, this API performs more consistency checking than the standard API does. This is possible, again, due to the object structure on which the API is defined. It tends to be much easier to know what a valid state is when the object is well defined.

Strengths

Although we already touched on the biggest strengths of the HiTest C API—complexity, code reduction, and robustness—there are several cases where this can be seen quite clearly. One of these can be found in the process of document selection. In the Notes C API, there are several steps that need to be performed in order to create a list of documents matching a certain set of criteria. In the Notes HiTest C API, the number of steps and their complexity are dramatically reduced.

This comparison is fleshed out further in Chapter 7 within the discussion of the **NSFSearch()** API and within the discussion of the Database object in Chapter 8.

NOTE

Another area where the complexity reduction really stands out is in the realm of macros (or *agents* in HiTest and version 4.0 terminology). This was mentioned as a weakness in the Notes C API section, not because the functionality didn't exist, but because it is so much more difficult when compared to functions available in the HiTest C API.

The HiTest C API has a more flexible error-processing subsystem than does the Notes C API. Although this may not be all that important to some, it can be quite helpful in certain situations. We'll discuss the three available error-handling options in greater detail in Chapter 8.

The last strength we'll mention here is the feature within the HiTest C API to do automatic data conversion and "binding." This feature allows an application to "bind" a local variable of one type to a document field of the same, or different, type. From then on, each time a new document is read, the API automatically loads the application variables with the values from the document and, if necessary, converts them. We'll discuss this further in Chapter 8.

Weaknesses

Mail. What the HiTest C API gains over the standard C API in the macro arena, it loses in the mail arena, at least from a breadth-of-function standpoint. There are currently only two basic mail APIs within this set and, although you can still perform all the mail functions by writing directly to the mail database, it's easier to do it through a set of API calls.

There are still some—but not many—functions available in the Notes C API set that are not available in the HiTest set. There will be, as time goes on, less of a difference among the capabilities but, in certain cases, this can be an issue.

Applications

The HiTest C API is a good choice for any application where low-level control over specific aspects of development are not of major concern. We're not saying that this API set is extremely slow or bloated, just that the encapsulation process over the standard API set creates, by definition, some reduction in granularity.

If you are planning to create an application that works on macros, take a hard look at this API set first. If you find that there are some things you cannot do, you can always go back to using the standard set, but you'll be much further ahead if you can use the HiTest set in this case.

Even with the limitations of the mail interface, there aren't many reasons not to use the HiTest C API set. Because this set will become the de facto API standard, there will probably be more and more people using it as time goes on. Its structure, capabilities, robustness, and future within the realm of Lotus Notes programmability make it a good prospect for just about any C or C++ application. Basically, if you can do everything you want to in the HiTest C API set, use it and don't look back.

HiTest Tools for Visual Basic

The last in the set of APIs we'll discuss is actually a combination of a set of programming tools and an API. The HiTest Tools for Visual Basic is a set of 12 custom controls for use within the Visual Basic development environment. By simply adding the controls to your Visual Basic project, you are provided with a nice set of tools that can be used to access many different pieces of Notes data.

A Basic API is also included in this tool set. It is composed of a set of libraries and DLLs that wrap the APIs available through the HiTest C API. For the most part, all of the APIs available through the HiTest C API are available through the Basic API counterpart.

Strengths

In an attempt to not open a Pandora's box concerning the age-old battle of C versus Basic, suffice it to say that one of the strengths of this tool is that does indeed assist a Visual Basic programmer in accessing Notes information. If you have ever "wrapped" an existing C API for use with Visual Basic, you probably know just how "warped" the results can become (no OS/2 pun intended). In the case of the Visual Tools, the wrapping is done fairly well and the end product is quite easy to use.

The 12 Visual Tools allow you to do some nice things really quickly, especially when compared to using the C API set or the Basic API set directly. They obviously have their limits but, when used in the right way and in the right application, they can make short work of a long project.

Since the Basic API is a wrapper around the HiTest C API, all the strengths and weaknesses discussed under the HiTest C API can be assumed under the Basic API as well.

Weaknesses

One thing we want to mention from the standpoint of weaknesses of this tool is performance. At this level, your application is actually going through several levels of APIs. In addition, the control you have over how each of these levels performs its functions decreases as you go up the ladder. Here again, we're not saying that the HiTest Visual Basic interface is "dog slow." What we are saying is that if you are going to be performing real-time transaction-based processing, you should "find out what the overhead is before you buy the shop."

Applications

If you are going to be creating any user-interface prototypes involving Notes connectivity, the Visual Tools are a good place to start. Even if you are planning to eventually convert to using C, C++, or even designing a Notes form, these tools can be a real time-saver. You'll need to use them a little to understand how they work, but it doesn't take long to make a big impact.

If you are planning on creating an application that integrates to Notes using Visual Basic, this tool set is a must. As for comparing the HiTest Visual Basic interface against the HiTest C interface, it's anybody's guess or preference. We've found that you can do basically the same things with either interface, so the choice is yours.

IDs: Keys to the Kingdom

Just when you thought you were ready to do some coding, something else pops up. In this case, it's a pretty important something, at least to Notes. Its the ubiquitous *Note ID*. As you probably already know, the Note ID is used throughout Notes as a way to uniquely identify a specific instance of a "note" within several different name spaces. It is actually composed of a set of IDs; some atomic entities, and others, composites of these atomic entities. Table 6.1 lists the IDs that compose a Note ID as well as their mnemonics.

Table 6.1 Note ID Components

Component	Mnemonic
Universal Note ID	UNID
Originator ID	OID
Note ID	NID
Global Note ID	GNID
Instance ID	IID
Global Instance ID	GIID

In the next chapter when we talk about ID tables, we'll expand on the description of each of the IDs in Table 6.1. We've introduced them here primarily as a means to an immediate end, to assist us in describing the structure of a Notes database.

Database Structure: What's It All About?

We're just about ready to jump into the code, but not quite. There is one more order of business to attend to and that's to take a look at the Notes database and note structure. Since most of the API sets deal with accessing the data contained within the database itself, it is important to understand, at least at some level, the structure of a Notes database.

There are basically two sets of data in a Notes database. The first set can be thought of as *single-instance* data. This is data that appears only once in the database and is usually accessed using APIs designed specifically for the data. The data in this set is also commonly referred to as the *header information*. The types of information that make up the header information include:

- Database title
- Replication settings
- Access control list
- Replication history
- User activity log

Not all of this header information is available through the APIs (e.g., the replication history and the user activity log). The header information that is available through the API is discussed in Chapter 7 through the development of the DBVIEWER application.

The second set of data is composed of *multiple-instance* data. This is data that can, and usually does, have more than one instance within the database. Most of the data contained in this group, which we'll call the *database body*, is structured in the form of a note. Examples of the data in this set are:

- Icon notes
- Policy notes
- Help notes
- Form notes
- View notes
- Data notes (Documents)
- Filter notes (macros/agents)

The following section takes a closer look at the structure of a note, and Chapter 7 will provide insight on how it can be accessed through the Notes C API.

Note Structure: The Anatomy of a Workhorse

Since many of the pieces of information within a database are stored as "notes," the structure of a note needs to be fairly flexible to allow for the storage of several different kinds of data. As in the database itself, there is a note header and a note body.

The note header basically consists of the following five different pieces of information:

- note ID (NID)
- originator ID (OID)
- last modified time/date
- note class
- privilege mask

Of these, the first three have either been discussed already (e.g., note ID and originator ID) or are fairly obvious (the last modified time/date). The next item, the note class, allows for the determination of the type of information contained within the note. Chapter 7 will talk more about the possible note classes supported and where they can be found. The privilege mask provides the storage for note-specific access rights.

The note body consists of 1 to many "items." Each item has a name, a length, a datatype, and a value. This structure, with the embedded datatype value, allows for quite a bit of flexibility, as does the note structure itself. We'll go into the item structures in more detail in the next chapter, but for now, Table 6.2 lists some of the more common datatypes.

Table 6.2 Note Field Datatypes

Datatype	Description
TYPE_TEXT	Non-NULL terminated text
TYPE_TEXTLIST	List of TYPE_TEXT items
TYPE_NUMBER	64-bit numeric value
TYPE_NUMBER_RANGE	List of TYPE_NUMBER items
TYPE_TIMEDATE	64-bit quadruple word value
TYPE_TIMEDATE_RANGE	List of TIMEDATE items

Table 6.2 Note Field Datatypes (continued)

Datatype	Description
TYPE_COMPOSITE	List of composite data records
TYPE_FORMULA	Database or view formula

Let's Go!

With a bit of understanding of some of the extension methods available and the structure of some of the storage objects in Lotus Notes, it's time to start digging. Over the next three chapters, we'll try to reinforce some of the statements we've made about the advantages and disadvantages of each tool/API set and take a closer look at Notes itself. We'll try to throw in a few tips and techniques along the way too. We certainly hope the applications we develop along the way help as learning tools and seeds for your own applications.

Notes C API

The first method of extending Notes to be addressed is the Notes C API. In this chapter we'll discuss:

- The API set's structure
- The details of some of the major APIs
- How to use the APIs in concert with one another to accomplish specific tasks
- New capabilities in the version 4.0 API
- What it takes to convert a application using the version 3.x set to the version 4.0 set

API Structure: Stuff All Over

As stated in Chapter 6, the Notes C API is structured around a set of loosely defined objects. The routines provided in each group are usually denoted by a specific prefix. Table 7.1 shows most of the major groups and the prefixes associated with them.

Table 7.1 Notes C API Object Prefixes

Operational Type	Prefix
Access Control List	ACL
Add-In Task	AddIn
Compound Text	CompoundText
Conversion	Convert
Distinguished Name	DN
Extension Manager	EM
Events	Event
Full Text Search	FT
ID Tables	ID
Text Lists	List
Log Entry	Log
Mail	Mail
Name and Address Book	NAME
Network Send and Receive	Net
Notes Index Facility(Views)	NIF
Basic Notes Functions	Notes
Notes Storage Facility(Database)	NSF
Operating System-Specific Routines	OS
Statistics Reporting	Stat
Time Manipulation	Time

NOTE

All of the APIs and their parameters are fairly well documented in the Notes API Reference database that comes with the Notes Toolkit. The API User's Guide, which is also included in the Toolkit, contains some good information, along with code samples, on several of the major components of Notes API application design as well.

DBVIEWER: Notes Database Viewer

As discussed in Chapter 6, the technique used to investigate the features of each extension method discussed within the book is through the development of sample applications. The first application we'll develop, the **DBVIEWER**, will serve not only as the basis for discussing some of the major components of the Notes C API, but it can be a nice little tool to have hanging around as well.

The DBVIEWER (\NOTESC\WIN16\DBVIEWER) application provides an overview of the contents of a Notes database, similar to the information found in a Design Synopsis. This is done by using several APIs from some of the different groups listed in Table 7.1. It was created using Microsoft's Visual C++ 1.5 on Windows 3.11 and was compiled for use on Notes Version 4.0. As with most general programs though, there are very few changes that need to be made to convert from a 3.x application to one using the Version 4.0 APIs, and visa versa. In the last section of this chapter, we'll actually discuss what some of the changes are and how to support them. We'll then show you the changes required to convert the DBVIEWER to work under Notes 3.x. After that, a quick recompile using the Notes 3.x API set and we've got a DBVIEWER that works with Notes 3.x as well. This version-independence is not shared by all of the example programs within the book but will be noted, were applicable.

NOTE One of the design features within Notes version 4.0 is that of binary compatibility with version 3.x API applications. This means you will be able to run applications built with the version 3.x API against Notes version 4.0 without changes. If you are planning to create an application that supports both versions, this *binary compatibility* capability allows you to make a single executable application, built against version 3.x, that works for both.

One of the design considerations of the DBVIEWER application was to make the user interface as simple as possible. This was done so as to not obscure the API usage with the complexity that can sometimes be associated with user-interface interactions in Windows. For this reason, you won't see any owner-drawn buttons, tree views, or involved window and control manipulations; we'll leave that for other texts. What you will see are a lot of examples of how to use the APIs, in concert with one another, to create an application that integrates with Notes.

One of the first things you'll see in the DBVIEWER.C file before the entrance of the first Notes C API include file is the DOS and DOSW16 definitions. These definitions are required in order to create the correct base types within the API for your current platform for Notes 3.x and 4.0 respectively. If you want to find the definition appropriate for your platform, look in **GLOBAL.H**.

DBVIEWER starts by using the using the **NSGetServerList()** API to get a list of Notes servers whenever the File...Open menu choice is selected. Once the list is obtained, it is placed into the Servers listbox on the Open Database dialog box. Figure 7.1 shows an example of the Servers listbox when connected to several different servers.

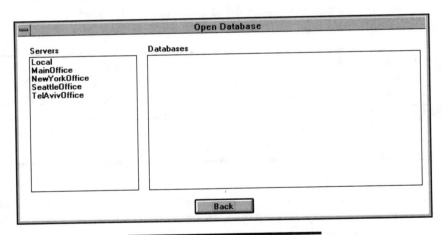

Figure 7.1 DBVIEWER server list.

NSGetServerList() is actually called within the ServerList_Get() function that is called within the WM_INITDIALOG message processing of the Open Database dialog box. It is a fairly simple API that requires the designation of the port to be used to for the search and the address of a memory handle for the resultant list.

If the port name is passed as NULL, as it is in this example, all of the active ports are searched.

```
ServerList_Get(NULL, &hServerList);
    .
    .
    .

BOOL ServerList_Get(CHAR_PTR lpszPort,
                    HANDLE_PTR lphServerList)
{
    STATUS  Status;
    BOOL    fOK = FALSE;

    Status = NSGetServerList(lpszPort, lphServerList);
    if (Status == NOERROR)
    {
        fOK = TRUE;
    }
    return(fOK);
}
```

NOTE

You probably noticed the use of Hungarian notation within the code snippet above. We'll be using it throughout the book as a matter of style only. If you use this type of notation as well, all the better. If you don't, please excuse our intrusion into the personal realm of coding standards but we had to pick something. In any case, we hope you'll want to concentrate more on the semantics than the syntax.

The example above actually shows another of the design considerations we have tried to use throughout the DBVIEWER, which is to create a common set of functions to access each type of "object" used within the application. This was done in an effort to encapsulate functionality and provide you with a means of easily reusing some of the functions. The general function structure for each object is:

- *object*_Get()

- *object_*Destroy()
- *object_*GetCount()
- *object_*GetIndexed()
- *object_*Callback ()

The list returned from the **NSGetServerList()** API, as with most of the lists provided within the realm of this API set, is formatted as a 16-bit value containing the number of strings in the list, followed by an array of 16-bit unsigned values containing the length of each string in the list followed by the list of strings themselves. Table 7.2 shows the structure of a list of three servers named TOM, DICK, and HARRY.

Table 7.2 Notes C API List Structure

Description	Value	Offset	Size (in bytes)
Number of strings	3	0	2
Length of string #1	3	2	2
Length of string #2	4	4	2
Length of string #3	5	6	2
String #1	TOM	8	3
String #2	DICK	11	4
String #3	HARRY	15	5

NOTE   Most of the strings returned by calls in this API set are not NULL-terminated. (They are usually prefixed by a length value.) If your application requires NULL termination, you'll need to do it yourself, after the data is obtained from the API.

Now, if you are asking which of the object groups within Table 7.1 **NSGetServerList()** fits into, the answer is none. Table 7.1 lists the "major" object groups but there are several more ad-hoc groups with one or two APIs that are not in the list. **NSGetServerList()** falls into this category. **NSGetServerList()** is actually in the "Session" object.

NSFSearch: Your Best Friend...Maybe

Upon selecting a server in the server list with a single click, a list of all of the databases on the server is created and displayed in the Databases listbox. This constitutes the first use of the **NSFSearch()** API within the application. Figure 7.2 shows a list of all of the databases available on the local system after the Local server is selected.

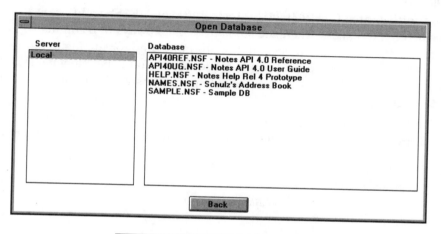

Figure 7.2 DBVIEWER database list.

One of the first things you find when getting into the Notes C API is that enumeration is a search method that is used quite often. Because almost everything in a Notes database is a variation on a theme—the note— enumeration is a nice way to facilitate accessing this kind of information. If your application will do much in the way of searching for specific notes of any type, you will probably use **NSFSearch()**.

The other method that can be used to create a set of documents within a database is by opening what is called a collection on the database. A collection is nothing more than the set of documents defined by a database View. In general, accessing documents using Views is faster than performing ad-hoc searches, especially when using large databases, but this technique is not as flexible. The API routines used to manipulate collections are in the NIF set of routines and will be discussed later in this chapter.

NSFSearch() works on the premise of having you define as many searching criteria as you can on the call and then, through the use of a user-defined callback routine, allowing you to pick and choose among all of the notes that fit the original set of criteria. The callback routine will be called once for every file (or note) that fits the specified criteria. The routine will continue to be called until either all of the notes that fit the search are exhausted, or the callback routine itself returns a nonzero value.

As with Notes C API itself, the strength of **NSFSearch()** can also be considered a weakness. There are so many possible ways of using the API and the associated callback routine, that it can be quite time-consuming to figure out what is going on if you don't know what to expect. In the next few pages, we'll spend some "quality time" looking at the options available when calling **NSFSearch()**.

The following code, taken from the DBVIEWER source, shows how the **NSFSearch()** API was used to get al list of all of the databases on a given server.

```
// use NSFSearch to find all database files
if (Status = NSFSearch(hDir,
                NULLHANDLE,
                NULL,
                // search for summary information on files
                SEARCH_FILETYPE + SEARCH_SUMMARY,
                // recursively search for .NS* files in all
                   subdirs
                FILE_DBANY + FILE_RECURSE,
                NULL,
                // callback routine (called for each file in
                   directory)
                (NSFSEARCHPROC) lpfnCallback,
                // database list handle (passed to callback
                   routine)
                (VOID_PTR) lphDatabaseList,
                NULL))
    {
        fOK = FALSE;
    }
```

This list was actually created using the file-search capabilities of the API, as opposed to the note search capabilities, as denoted by the fourth parameter in the list. By ORing in the SEARCH_FILETYPE search flag, you can have the API search for files. If you want to search for notes instead, don't use the flag, since that is the default search type. The other search flag used here, SEARCH_SUMMARY, instructs the API to return the summary information for each file it finds. If this is not requested, only the SEARCH_MATCH structure(shown below) is given to the callback routine. It basically contains some ID information and the file class.

```
typedef struct
{
    GLOBALINSTANCEID ID;          /* identity of the note within the
                                     file */
    ORIGINATORID OriginatorID;    /* identity of the note in the
                                     universe */
    WORD NoteClass;               /* note class */
    BYTE SERetFlags;              /* match flags */
    BYTE Privileges;              /* note privileges */
    WORD SummaryLength;           /* length of the summary information
                                     */
} SEARCH_MATCH;
```

The summary information, which can be, and usually is, different for class of object, is returned as an ITEM_TABLE. This table encapsulates any number of ITEM structures, the basic blocks of information within a note.

Summary items are those items within a note that can be used in formulas and in searching criteria. They are contained in a special place within the note so that they can be easily and quickly accessed. Most of the item types that are fairly limited in size are usually put into the summary buffer of the note. Items such as rich text fields and attachments are not placed into this area and therefore cannot be specified within formulas and the like. Another type of indexing, full text indexing, is provided for rich text fields, which provides for a level of searching that many of us have come to know and love in Notes. Table 7.3 shows the layout of the ITEM_TABLE structure.

Table 7.3 ITEM_TABLE Structure

Description	Offset	Size (in bytes)
Length of the buffer	0	2
Number of ITEMs	2	2
Array of ITEM structures	4	n*sizeof(ITEM)
ITEM Data	4 + n*sizeof(ITEM)	Depends on item types

Within the ITEM_TABLE, the ITEM structure contains two pieces of information. The first is a 16-bit unsigned value containing the size, in bytes, of the item name. The second in another unsigned 16-bit value containing the size, in byes, of the item data, which includes a datatype (defined as an ITEM_TYPE) and the data based on that datatype.

Now comes the interesting part: the item data, the heart of the summary information. This is the part of the ITEM_TABLE that is truly variant. The classes of data contained here are the item name, its datatype, and the actual item information. Table 7.4 shows the format of the item data contained within a note.

Table 7.4 Item Data Structure

Description	Offset	Size (in bytes)
Item Name	0	length (first value in the ITEM)
Item Datatype	length	2
Item Data	length + 2	Depends on datatype

There are different item types returned for each object type. For example, for files, six items are returned. The descriptive names, item names, and datatypes for each are contained in Table 7.5.

Table 7.5 File Items

Descriptive Name	Item Name	Datatype
Database Name	$TITLE	TYPE_TEXT
Name with Relative Path	$Path	TYPE_TEXT

Table 7.5 File Items (continued)

Descriptive Name	Item Name	Datatype
File Type	$Type	TYPE_TEXT
Last Modified Date	$Modified	TYPE_TIME
Database Size	$Length	TYPE_NUMBER
Database Title	$Info	TYPE_TEXT

NOTE One point to mention here relates to ITEMs of type TYPE_TEXT. Notes, the application, will actually store text values as either TYPE_TEXT or TYPE_TEXT_LIST, whichever it believes is best. Usually, this happens when a text value has more than one line of data but this statement is not a hard and fast rule. The best way to handle this situation is always to provide for extracting text data as both a TYPE_TEXT value and a TYPE_TEXT_LIST value and switch off the provided type.

Now, before we get back to the rest of the parameters in **NSFSearch()**, lets pull all these data structures together by taking a look at some sample data as seen by DBVIEWER. Table 7.7 contains the entire ITEM_TABLE structure assuming that we have only one database file in the list, that being SAMPLE.NSF.

Table 7.6 Example ITEM_TABLE

Description	Value	Offset	Size (in bytes)
Length of the buffer	132	0	2
Number of ITEMs	6	2	2
Item #1 Name Length	6	4	2
Item #1 Data Length	12	6	2
Item #2 Name Length	5	8	2
Item #2 Data Length	12	10	2
Item #3 Name Length	5	12	2
Item #3 Data Length	11	14	2
Item #4 Name Length	9	16	2

Table 7.6 Example ITEM_TABLE (continued)

Description	Value	Offset	Size (in bytes)
Item #4 Data Length	10	18	2
Item #5 Name Length	7	20	2
Item #5 Data Length	10	22	2
Item #6 Name Length	5	24	2
Item #6 Data Length	11	26	2
Item #1 Name	$TITLE	28	6
Item #1 Datatype	1280 (TEXT)	34	2
Item #1 Data	SAMPLE.NSF	36	10
Item #2 Name	$Path	46	5
Item #2 Datatype	1280 (TEXT)	51	2
Item #2 Data	SAMPLE.NSF	53	10
Item #3 Name	$Type	63	5
Item #3 Datatype	1280 (TEXT)	68	2
Item #3 Data	$NOTEFILE	70	9
Item #4 Name	$Modified	79	9
Item #4 Datatype	1024 (TIMEDATE)	88	2
Item #4 Data	07/30/95 11:00:00 AM	90	8
Item #5 Name	$Length	98	7
Item #5 Datatype	768 (NUMBER)	105	2
Item #5 Data	131072	107	8
Item #6 Name	$Info	115	5
Item #6 Datatype	1280	120	2
Item #6 Data	Sample DB	122	9

We're not going to go through the same amount of rigor every time we use **NSFSearch()** within the DBVIEWER, but it is important to understand the basic structure because, as you'll see a little later, it can become more complex when searching for notes.

Let's get back to the parameters for **NSFSearch()**. The first parameter is a handle to a database, or directory, obtained through the use of the **NSFDbOpen()** API.

NOTE The first parameter to the **NSFDbOpen()** call must be a path created with the **OSPathNetConstruct()** API, especially if the path is on a server. The path is created in a Notes-specific format that is pretty easy to decipher—server name + !! + database name—but it's usually just as easy to use the API.

The second parameter, a FORMULAHANDLE, is a handle of a selection formula obtained from using **NSFFormulaCompile()**. Because here we have no selection criteria required to get a list all of the databases, NULLHANDLE is used. The third parameter is only required if the formula in parameter three contains the @ViewTitle function. If such is the case, this title name is then used to satisfy the input for that function.

We have already talked about the fourth parameter, the search flags, and we'll talk more about them later. The item class parameter, number five in the list, provides the means of specifying which search items are to be included in the list. This value contains either FILE_CLASS flags if you are searching for files or NOTE_CLASS flags if you are searching for notes. The values used for the file search in this case are:

- FILE_DBANY—List all .NSF, .NSG, and .NSH files
- FILE_RECURSE—Recursively search through all subdirectories of the parent

Another choice here would have been to use the FILE_DIRS flag and not the FILE_RECURSE flag. This would have provided a list more akin to the Open Database dialog box in Notes that contains files in the current directory, with subdirectory entries as well. In this case, we wanted an all-encompassing list and, since we have the relative path names for each database contained in the $Path item, it seems to suit the purpose. As for the NOTE_CLASS flags, we'll discuss some of them when we do notes searching later on in this chapter.

The sixth parameter is the address of a TIMEDATE structure to be used as another way of limiting the volume of notes, or files, enumerated. If used, only notes that have been updated on or after the time specified will be enumerated. In this case, we want all files, so NULL is used. The seventh parameter is the address of the enumeration callback routine you supply. This is the routine that is called once for each note found by **NSFSearch()**. We'll delve more into the details of callback routines when we perform note searches as well.

NOTE One thing to remember about all callback routines, including those for **NSFSearch()**, is that you will need to make an instance thunk for each when in Windows 3.x (MakeProcInstance(), FreeProcInstance()) and to always export them in your **.DEF** file for all platforms that use that mechanism.

The eighth parameter is a 32-bit value that you can have the search engine pass to the enumeration routine for each note, or file, found. This is most often the address of an allocated space in memory to hold the enumeration information or, as in many cases throughout DBVIEWER , the address of a memory handle that can be reallocated as needed. In the case of the **NSFSearch()** call above, it's just that, a handle to memory space that will contain a DATABASE_LIST structure as defined in DBVIEWER.H.

The last parameter in the list can be the address of a TIMEDATE structure into which the API will place the time and date of the search. This is provided primarily for use as the sixth parameter in subsequent calls to **NSFSearch()**. If NULL is used, this value is not returned. When all is said and done, the friendly part of **NSFSearch()** is that, when used correctly, it can do a lot of things for you. The not so friendly part is the work required to understand all of the options it provides and making it do what you want.

Returning to DBVIEWER, where we have obtained a list of all of the databases on the selected server and displayed them in the Databases list box, selecting a database from the list opens another dialog that is the master controller of interrogating the database, the Display Database dialog box. From here, several types of database information can be viewed. The first two buttons, Header and ACL, provide database header information. You'll probably notice that there is no button for two of the other pieces of header information discussed in Chapter 6, the replication history and user activity log. The reason for this is that the Notes C API does not provide any access to this information. One of the few escapes in functionality in this set but, for the most part, not of major concern.

The Header button displays some general header information as well as the information contained in the first two blocks of the database structure in Figure

6.1, the database title and the replication settings. All of the information within this section is obtained through the Database_*() functions within the DBVIEWER. Figure 7.3 provides an example of the header information obtained from a sample database.

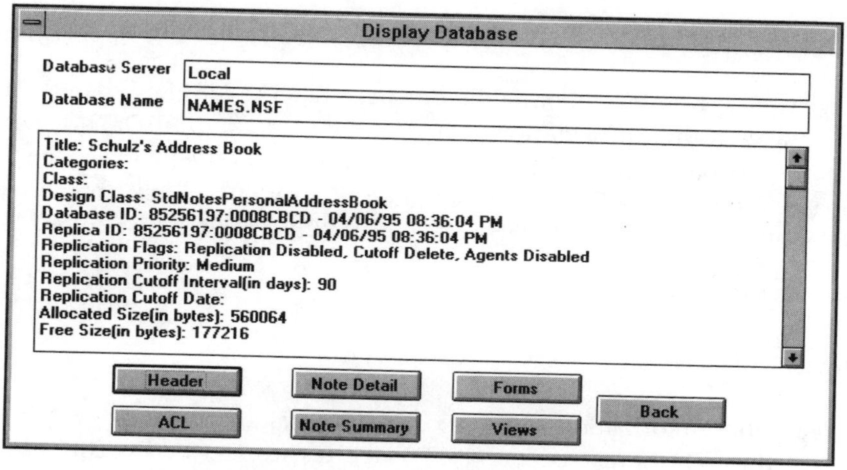

Figure 7.3 DBVIEWER header information.

The first four pieces of information in the list are all obtained through the use of the **NSFDbInfoGet()** API. Given the handle of an open database, a byte string is returned containing the data. Another API, **NSFDbInfoParse()**, can then used to parse out the selected piece of data into a buffer you provide. The example below shows how to access the title of a database using these two APIs.

```
Status = NSFDbInfoGet(hNotesDB, szDBInfo);
if (Status == NOERROR)
{
    NSFDbInfoParse(szDBInfo,
                   INFOPARSE_TITLE,
                   lpszDatabaseTitle,
                   NSF_INFO_SIZE - 1);
    fOK = TRUE;
}
```

The four possible parse flags for **NSFDbInfoParse()** are:

- INFOPARSE_TITLE—Database title
- INFOPARSE_CATEGORIES—Database categories
- INFOPARSE_CLASS—Template name
- INFOPARSE_DESIGN_CLASS—Inherited template name

The next piece of information is the database ID. The **NSFDbIDGet()** API is used to access this information, which is housed as a DBID(TIMEDATE) structure. The only input information required is again the handle of an open database. The database ID is then formatted as a set of two hex double words (DatabaseID.Innards[1] and DatabaseID.Innards[0]) separated by a colon.

```
DBID DatabaseID;

Status = NSFDbIDGet(hNotesDB, &DatabaseID);
```

The replication information is the next block contained in the list and it is all accessed through the use of the **NSFDbReplicaInfoGet()** API. The returned DBREPLICAINFO structure contains several parts: the ID, replication flags, replication cutoff interval, and cutoff date. The following example shows how the replica ID is accessed.

```
DBREPLICAINFO ReplicaInfo;
DBID ReplicaID;

Status = NSFDbReplicaInfoGet(hNotesDB, &ReplicaInfo);
ReplicaID = ReplicaInfo.ID;
```

The replication flags are returned as a set of bit flags containing two different pieces of information. The first set of flags, accessed by ANDing the flags with a special mask, contain a set of boolean flags detailing several different types of information. The sample code below shows how the mask and the boolean flags are used in DBVIEWER.

```
wFlags = ReplicaInfo.Flags & REPLFLG_PRIORITY_INVMASK;
if (wFlags & REPLFLG_DISABLE)
    lstrcat(lpszFlags, "Replication Disabled, ");
```

```
if (wFlags & REPLFLG_IGNORE_DELETES)
    lstrcat(lpszFlags, "Deletes Ignored, ");
if (wFlags & REPLFLG_HIDDEN_DESIGN)
    lstrcat(lpszFlags, "Design Hidden, ");
if (wFlags & REPLFLG_DO_NOT_CATALOG)
    lstrcat(lpszFlags, "Not Cataloged, ");
if (wFlags & REPLFLG_CUTOFF_DELETE)
    lstrcat(lpszFlags, "Cutoff Delete, ");
if (wFlags & REPLFLG_NEVER_REPLICATE)
    lstrcat(lpszFlags, "Never Replicate, ");
if (wFlags & REPLFLG_ABSTRACT)
    lstrcat(lpszFlags, "Truncate Large Documents, ");
if (wFlags & REPLFLG_DO_NOT_BROWSE)
    lstrcat(lpszFlags, "Do Not Browse, ");
if (wFlags & REPLFLG_NO_CHRONOS)
    lstrcat(lpszFlags, "Agents Disabled, ");
```

The second set of information within the replication flags, the replication priority, is a different set of bits that can either be accessed by a combination of flag constants as above, or by using a macro defined within Notes. The macro takes the replication flags and returns a value of 0, 1, or 2 corresponding to low, medium, and high replication priority. The macro usage is shown below.

```
Status = NSFDbReplicaInfoGet(hNotesDB, &ReplicaInfo);
if (Status == NOERROR)
{
    // use Notes-supplicate macro to get priority values from 0 to 2
    // 0 = low priority, 1 = medium priority, 2 = high priority
    *lpwPriority = REPL_GET_PRIORITY(ReplicaInfo.Flags);
    fOK = TRUE;
}
```

The last two pieces of replication information in this section have to deal with replication cutoff information. The first, the cutoff interval, is an unsigned 16-bit value in the DBREPLICAINFO structure and denotes the cutoff interval in days.

The last, the cutoff date, is a TIMEDATE structure containing, you guessed it, the cutoff date.

To complete the header information, the allocated size and amount of free space within the database values are obtained through the use of **NSFDbSpaceUsage()**. Given the handle of an open database, this API returns both of these values as 32-bit unsigned values. The total size of the database is then computed as a sum of these two values.

Access Control Lists:
The "Security" of Notes

Access control lists (ACLs) are an integral part of what makes Notes what it is. Every database has an ACL and, if you create databases from scratch using the **NSFDbCreate()** function, you need to use **ACLCreate()** and the subsequent **NSFDbStoreACL()** to place one into it.

The ACL button within DBVIEWER accesses the ACL for the selected database through the use of the **NSFDbGetACL()** API. From there, we use a friendly enumeration routine, this time having the name **ACLEnumEntries()**. **ACLEnumEntries()** takes three parameters. The first is a handle to an ACL, returned in the **NSFDbGetACL()** call. The second is the address of a callback routine and the third is an optional address to be passed to the callback routine for each enumerated entry in the list. The code fragment below shows how the DBVIEWER sets up to enumerate through the ACLs within a database.

```
BOOL DatabaseACLList_Get(CHAR_PTR lpszFullDatabaseName,
                         HANDLE_PTR lphACLList)

{
    BOOL          fOK = FALSE;
    DBHANDLE      hNotesDB;
    HANDLE        hACL;
    ACL_LIST_PTR  lpACLList;
    FARPROC       lpfnEnumProc;
    STATUS        Status;
```

```
    if (Database_Open(lpszFullDatabaseName, &hNotesDB))
    {
        // get the ACL list handle from the database
        Status = NSFDbReadACL(hNotesDB, &hACL);
        if (Status == NOERROR)
        {
            // initialize the list
            Status = OSMemAlloc(0,
                                sizeof(ACL_LIST) - sizeof(ACL_INFO),
                                lphACLList);
            lpACLList = OSLockObject(*lphACLList);
            if (lpACLList)
            {
                lpACLList->wCount = 0;
                lpACLList->hACL = hACL;
                OSUnlock(*lphACLList);
            }

            lpfnEnumProc = MakeProcInstance((FARPROC)
            DatabaseACLList_Callback,
                                            ghInstance);
            Status = ACLEnumEntries(hACL,
                                    (VOID_PTR) lpfnEnumProc,
                                    (VOID_PTR) lphACLList);
            FreeProcInstance(lpfnEnumProc);
            if (Status == NOERROR)
            {
                fOK = TRUE;
            }
        }
        Database_Close(hNotesDB);
    }
    return(fOK);
}
```

The prototype for the callback routine for **ACLEnumEntries()** looks like this:

```
void far PASCAL DatabaseACLList_Callback(VOID_PTR lpCallbackInfo,
                                         CHAR_PTR lpszName,
                                         WORD wAccessLevel,
                                         ACL_PRIVILEGES_PTR
                                         lpPrivileges,
                                         WORD wAccessFlags);
```

The first parameter is the user-defined address passed in the third parameter in **ACLEnumEntries()**. In our case, this is the handle to our ACL_LIST allocated in the DatabaseACLList_Get() function above. The second parameter is the user name associated with the passed ACL list.

The third parameter, the access level, is one of the seven different possible access levels defined by Notes. Actually, the number of access levels is defined by a constant within the API, ACL_LEVEL_COUNT. The sample code below comes from the DatabaseACLList_Callback() routine in DBVIEWER and shows how the access levels are determined.

```
switch (wAccessLevel)
{
    case ACL_LEVEL_NOACCESS:
        lstrcpy(ACLInfo.szAccessLevel, "No Access");
        break;
    case ACL_LEVEL_DEPOSITOR:
        lstrcpy(ACLInfo.szAccessLevel, "Depositor");
        break;
    case ACL_LEVEL_READER:
        lstrcpy(ACLInfo.szAccessLevel, "Reader");
        break;
    case ACL_LEVEL_AUTHOR:
        lstrcpy(ACLInfo.szAccessLevel, "Author");
        break;
    case ACL_LEVEL_EDITOR:
        lstrcpy(ACLInfo.szAccessLevel, "Editor");
        break;
    case ACL_LEVEL_DESIGNER:
        lstrcpy(ACLInfo.szAccessLevel, "Designer");
```

```
            break;
        case ACL_LEVEL_MANAGER:
            lstrcpy(ACLInfo.szAccessLevel, "Manager");
            break;
        default:
            lstrcpy(ACLInfo.szAccessLevel, "Unknown");
            break;
    }
```

The privileges list, which is the fourth parameter in the callback, is actually a set of ACL_PRIVCOUNT bit flags. The **ACLIsPrivSet()** API is used against this list to determine if the indexed privilege is set. If it is, **ACLGetPrivName()** can then be used to get the user-defined name of the privilege.

```
for (i = 0; i < ACL_PRIVCOUNT; i++)
{
    // if the indexed privilege is set, get the text for it
    if (ACLIsPrivSet(*lpPrivileges, i))
    {
        // get the ACL handle from the passed structure
        hACLList = *((HANDLE_PTR) lpCallbackInfo);
        lpACLList = OSLockObject(hACLList);
        if (lpACLList)
        {
            hACL = lpACLList->hACL;
            OSUnlock(hACLList);
        }
        // get the privilege name
        Status = ACLGetPrivName(hACL,
                                i,

ACLInfo.Privileges[ACLInfo.nPrivilegeCount].szPrivilege);

        // state that we have another privilege to track
        ACLInfo.nPrivilegeCount++;
    }
}
```

NOTE

The privilege names are defined as roles within Notes version 4.0 in the File..Database...Access Control dialog box.

Finally, by ANDing the access flags with the ACL_FLAG_AUTHOR_NOCREATE and ACL_FLAG_DELETE constants, the determination of whether the user cannot create or delete documents, respectively, within the database can be made.

The other ACL APIs involve either the manipulation of entries in the ACL (add, delete, and update) or of the privilege names (get and set). Figure 7.4 shows the access control list information displayed by the DBVIEWER application within a sample database.

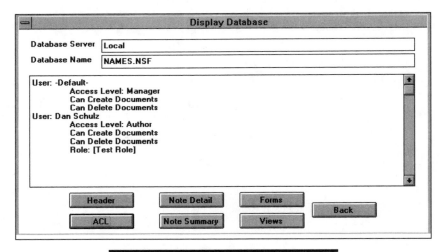

Figure 7.4 DBVIEWER ACL information.

OS Functions: Platform-Independent but Somewhat Unforgiving

Before we get into the "multiple-instance" data within a database, the notes, and how to access them, let's talk a little about some of the auxiliary routines we've been using in some of the sample code above, namely, the OS memory functions.

Throughout the DBVIEWER we commonly use the OS memory functions including **OSMemAlloc()**, **OSMemRealloc()**, **OSMemFree()**, **OSMemGetSize()**, **OSLockObject()**, and **OSUnlock()**. These functions provide a nice way of performing platform-independent memory manipulation. Although they can be used, as in the DBVIEWER, for general memory manipulation, in most cases your application is probably better served using platform-specific memory routines or those provided by the C runtime library.

There is a tangible down side to using the OS memory routines however, in that they can be quite unforgiving when it comes to error conditions. The documentation on these functions includes the disclaimer that, in certain error situations, "a Notes PANIC halt may result." These "PANIC halts" can be so severe that you may need to restart the OS itself.

A case in point: during the development of DBVIEWER on Windows 3.11, a piece of memory was allocated and locked correctly but, before being unlocked, was freed using OSMemFree. Suddenly, PANIC struck! Upon clearing the error and restarting the application through the debugger, the entire system hung and needed to be rebooted. If you're a real glutton for punishment and want to try it yourself, just comment out the `OSUnlock(hHeaderInfo)` from the IDC_HEADER case in the DisplayDatabaseDlgProc() function of DBVIEWER, shown below, and press the Header button on a database.

Remember, unless you really want to see a fatal system crash and burn, you may want to avoid this test.

WARNING

```
// get the header info as a set of strings
if (Database_GetHeaderInfo(szFullDatabaseName, &hHeaderInfo))
{
    lpszHeaderInfo = OSLockObject(hHeaderInfo);
    if (lpszHeaderInfo)
    {
        SendDlgItemMessage(hDialog,
                           IDC_DATA,
                           WM_SETTEXT,
                           0,
                           (LPARAM) lpszHeaderInfo);
```

```
    // REMOVING THE FOLLOWING LINE MAY CAUSE A "PANIC halt"
       OSUnlock(hHeaderInfo);
    }

    Database_DestroyHeaderInfo(&hHeaderInfo);

  }
```

The discussion of the OS memory routines brings up a point that should be mentioned about the Notes C API in general. Since much of the API was designed with an eye on performance, there is very little, if any, validity checking on such things as input parameter values. Passing invalid or incomplete values of this type can cause Notes crashes similar to the scenario described above as well—if you're lucky. The worst-case scenario would be where no crash happens immediately but strange failures occur down the road, where they are much more difficult to track.

We are now at the "heart and soul" of the database, the notes. As stated in Chapter 6, many of the objects that exist in the database that can have multiple instances (e.g., Views, Forms, Documents, etc.) are all stored as notes. Within the general note structure, the note class is the value that determines the type of the note. Moreover, you can use **NSFSearch()** to find just about any combination of notes you want.

The note class is actually passed to the enumeration callback routine in the SEARCH_MATCH structure discussed in the file searching section.

NOTE

The first type of note searching we are going to perform is that of a general search and cataloging of all notes in the database through the use of the Note Summary button. This is done by using the following **NSFSearch()** call.

```
Status = NSFSearch(hNotesDB,
                   NULLHANDLE,
                   NULL,
                   // search all notes providing summary and deleted
      information
                   SEARCH_ALL_VERSIONS | SEARCH_SUMMARY |
      SEARCH_NOTIFYDELETIONS,
                   // enumerate all note types
```

```
NOTE_CLASS_ALL,

NULL,

(NSFSEARCHPROC) lpfnSearchProc,

(VOID_PTR) &NoteList,

NULL);
```

The parameters here should be surprisingly similar to the ones used in the call to **NSFSearch()** to access the list of databases on a server, with the exception of the fourth and fifth. In the fourth parameter, we now use the note-searching capabilities of the API (default operation) as well as requesting that all deleted documents be passed to the callback routine as well.

> Deleted documents remain in the database until they are removed with a compact, or like, function.

NOTE

The fifth parameter now specifies the type of notes to search for. Since, at least in this case, we'll use the callback routine to determine the class the note is in, we'll use the NOTE_CLASS_ALL flag so that all note types are enumerated.

Another point of interest here is the eighth parameter, the address of a NOTE_LIST structure. The reason is that this structure not only contains a counter for every known type of note (or at least those found in NSFNOTE.H) but it also contains the handle to an ID table.

ID Tables: Nice to Have Around

ID tables are not magical; basically they are ordered lists with some built-in compression algorithms. Don't be confused, though; they are not true ordered lists in that there is no guarantee as to the absolute order of entries in the list. This is the primary reason for the existence of the **IDScan()** API, just one of the APIs that support these tables.

Before we get too far down the road of discussing ID tables however, we need to complete our discussion of the Note ID components started in Chapter 6. To aid in describing these ID components, we've included the Notes document information sheets for a specific note within the same database. Figure 7.5 shows the Version 3.x information whereas the Version 4.0 information is shown in Figure 7.6. We'll reference the information in each of these dialogs as we traverse through the set of IDs.

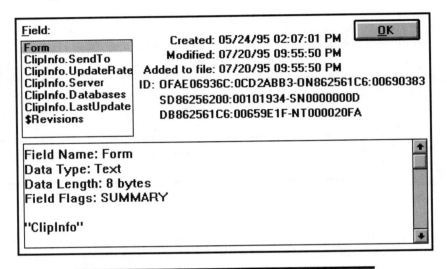

Figure 7.5 Document information: Notes version 3.x.

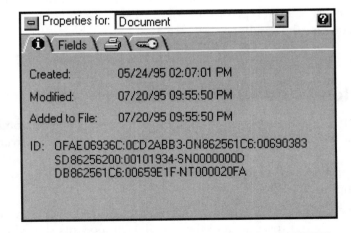

Figure 7.6 Document information: Notes version 4.0.

The first ID we'll talk about is the first part of a note ID you see from the Notes user interface, the universal note ID or UNID. The UNID identifies all notes that came from the same parent, regardless of replication or modification. Therefore, every replica copy and every version of an original note will have the same UNID.

The UNID contains two parts and composes the first line in the document information dialog boxes. The first part, the file ID, is unique among all databases on all servers within the current domain. It is displayed as a pair of eight hexadecimal digits separated by a colon and prefixed with OF(original file). In the above dialog boxes, this potion of the UNID is OFAE06936C:0CD2ABB3. The second part is a time/date stamp that states when the original note was created. This value is displayed in the same manner, prefixed by <u>ON</u>(original note) and is ON862561C6:00690383 in the dialog boxes above.

The originator ID (OID) is composed of a UNID, a sequence number, and a sequence date. This ID changes for each version of the same note but tracks the parent of the note, regardless of replication. That is, an original note, and every direct replica thereof, will have the same OID. If the note is modified, however, the OID will be different for each different version.

The OID sequence number is a double word value that contains, among other things, the version, or sequence number, of the note. The OID sequence date tracks the date and time when the sequence number was augmented. The OID sequence date is prefixed with SD whereas the sequence number has a prefix of SN. Both of these values are seen in the second line of the dialog boxes above (SD86256200:00101934-SN0000000D).

The next ID in Table 6.1 is the NID or note ID (notice there are no quotes here). This note ID is truly that, a simple ID. It is a double word value used to uniquely discriminate among all of the notes in a given database. At a low level, the note ID can be tied back to the absolute position of the note within the database file. Since the note ID contains no database information and is position-dependent, the same copy of a note in different databases will most likely have a different ID. A note ID is usually displayed as a set of eight hexadecimal digits.

A note ID, along with a database time/date stamp, make up a GNID (global note ID). Because of this, a GNID uniquely identifies a note not only within a specific database, but across all databases within a domain. The format of a global note ID is two sets of eight hexadecimal digits, separated by a colon, followed by the eight hexadecimal digits that make up the note ID.

The note ID value is prefixed by the letters NT and, along with the time/date stamp value prefixed by DB, makes up the GNID. The GNID can be found on the third line of the document information dialog boxes above as `DB862561C6:00659E1F-NT000020FA`.

The instance ID (IID) identifies notes at the version level within a given database. To allow for this level of tracking, an IID is composed of a note ID and a modification time/date stamp. Each time the note changes, this modification time/date stamp is changed. It is this process that allows for the maintenance of unread marks within Notes. An instance ID has the same display format as a GNID.

The last of the six IDs within Table 6.1 is the global instance ID, GIID. As with the global note ID, the global instance ID is an instance ID coupled with a database time/date stamp. This allows the GIID to uniquely identify all note versions across all databases. A GIID is usually displayed as a pair of eight-digit hexadecimal numbers, separated by a colon, followed by an IID.

Now let's return to our discussion of the Note Summary button within the DBVIEWER and ID tables. In the callback routine for this function, which is, by the way, the same callback routine used for the Note Detail button we'll discuss in a bit, an ID table is created to hold the IDs of all of the notes that are enumerated. We can track note IDs (NIDs) since we are looking at only one database at a time and note IDs are unique in this domain space (see the "IDs" section in Chapter 6). If we wanted to track notes across several databases, we would need to track global note IDs (GNIDs), which contain both database ID and note ID components. The code sample below shows how the note search callback routine maintains the list of IDs of all of the notes in a database within an ID table.

```
lpInfo = (NOTE_LIST_PTR) lpCallbackInfo;

// if we don't have an ID table yet, create one now
if (lpInfo->hIDTable == NULLHANDLE)
{
    Status = IDCreateTable(sizeof(NOTEID), &(lpInfo->hIDTable));
}
```

```
    // if the note is not currently in the table
    if (!(IDIsPresent(lpInfo->hIDTable, lpSearchInfo->ID.NoteID)))
    {
        // add the note ID to the ID table
        Status = IDInsert(lpInfo->hIDTable,
                          lpSearchInfo->ID.NoteID,
                          &fInsertOK);
        // get the notes' class
        wNoteClass = lpSearchInfo->NoteClass;
        .
        .
        .

    }
```

The first thing we do in the callback routine is to check if an ID table has been created yet and, if not, create one using the **IDCreateTable()** API. The input parameter to this call is the size of the objects to be placed into the ID table, for use in the compression algorithms. The output parameter is a handle to the ID table created. Notice that there is no initial size parameter. The ID table allocates space for values as they are inserted.

The **IDIsPresent()** API is used for every note enumerated to make sure that we don't track multiple copies of the same note. This is needed since there may be times when the search routine will enumerate the same note depending on the activity taking place in the database at the time. If the ID is not found in the ID table, then **IDInsert()** is used to add it.

The two input parameters to **IDInsert()**—the ID table handle and the note ID—are to be expected. The third parameter is the address of a Boolean flag used to determine whether or not the ID was added. The reason for this flag is that if the ID is already present in the table, NOERROR is returned as the status. Therefore, if you are interested in whether or not the note is already in the table, this flag can be tested after the call is made. A NULL can be passed for this parameter if you are not interested in this information. In this case within the DBVIEWER, we pass the flag for completeness but don't check the returned value.

If all we wanted was an ID table with note IDs—that is, if we didn't want to get the individual note type count as well—the **NSFDbGetModifiedNoteTable()**

call could be used to perform the same function, with much less code. By passing the database handle, a note class (same as the fifth parameter to **NSFSearch()**) , a starting TIMEDATE structure, the address of a TIMEDATE structure for the search time or NULL if unwanted, and the address of an ID table, the table can be created with a single call. The example below shows how to duplicate the ID table created in the NoteList_Callback() function using **NSFDbGetModifiedNoteTable()**.

```
// TIMEDATE_WILDCARD searches for all times and dates in this case
TimeConstant(TIMEDATE_WILDCARD, &StartTimeDate);


Status = NSFDbGetModifiedNoteTable(hNotesDB,
                                   NOTE_CLASS_ALL,
                                   StartTimeDate,
                                   NULL,
                                   &IDTable);
```

Once we have the ID table, **IDEntries()** can be used to get the number of entries in the table, as seen in the NoteList_GetCount() function below.

```
DWORD NoteList_GetCount(HANDLE hNoteList)
{
    NOTE_LIST_PTR      lpNoteList;
    DWORD              dwCount = 0;

    if (hNoteList)
    {
        lpNoteList = OSLockObject(hNoteList);
        if (lpNoteList)
        {
            // get the count from the ID table
            dwCount = IDEntries(lpNoteList->hIDTable);
            OSUnlock(hNoteList);
        }
    }
    return(dwCount);
}
```

All we have to do now is access the IDs by index. Unfortunately, there is no API to directly access an indexed entry in the table. Instead, **IDScan()** is used to index through the ID list from the start. The example below, taken from the NoteList_GetIndexed() routine, shows how **IDScan()** can be used to accomplish a "get indexed" function.

The first call to **IDScan()** needs to have the "first call" flag set to TRUE and, in all subsequent calls, it must be FALSE.

NOTE

```
// set the 'first' flag to TRUE for the first ID scan
fFirst = TRUE;

// now lets get the ID
for (i = 0; i <= dwIndex; i++)
{
    // if we get an error getting the indexed ID, report the failure
    if (!(IDScan(lpNoteList->hIDTable, fFirst, lpNoteID)))
    {
        fOK = FALSE;
    }

    // set the 'first' flag to FALSE for all 'next' operations
    fFirst = FALSE;
}
```

Another nice thing about ID tables is that there are several other APIs that take an ID table as an input parameter. **NSFDbDeleteNotes()** deletes all of the notes in an ID table from a given database. **NSFDbStampNotes()** can be used to set a specific item of all notes in a ID table to the same value. And, not to be outdone by notes themselves, there is an enumeration capability for all of the ID values in an ID table provided through the **IDEnumerate()** API.

Finally, cleaning up after an ID table is nothing more than passing the handle of the table to **OSMemFree()**. The thing to remember about ID tables is that they can be used in just about any case where IDs need to be tracked. If performance is a high concern though, and you don't need to use any APIs that require an ID table, you may want to create your own list functions optimized for speed rather than size.

Now that the note search is complete, we now have a count of all of the notes in the databases as well as a count of each individual note type. Figure 7.7 shows the summary information for a database containing several different types of notes.

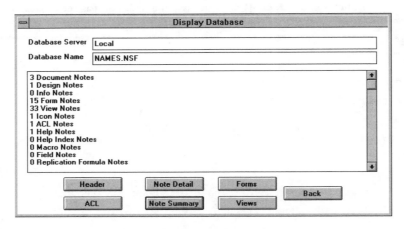

Figure 7.7 DBVIEWER note summary.

Notes Storage Facility(NSF):
Come One, Come All

The largest group of APIs, by far, are those under the Notes Storage Facility(NSF) category. There are functions for dealing with formulas (**NSFCompute*()** and **NSFFormula*()**), databases (**NSFDb*()**), note items (**NSFItem*()**), and notes (**NSFNote*()**), as well as a couple that belong in a category of their own, such as the aforementioned **NSFSearch()**. Much of what is left to be done within the DBVIEWER has to do with either the NSF functions or the NIF functions discussed in the next section.

We are now ready to press the **Note Detail** button within the DBVIEWER. Unlike the rest of the buttons on the Display Database dialog box, the Note

Detail button opens up yet another modal dialog box that is used to display detail information on a note-by-note basis. The Note Detail dialog box, as shown in Figure 7.8, shows several pieces of information for a given note within a database.

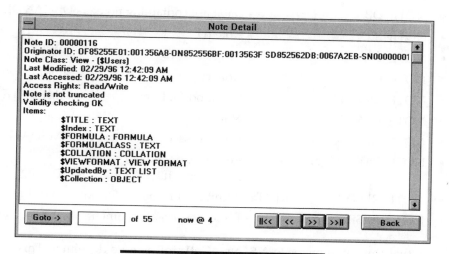

Figure 7.8 DBVIEWER Note Detail.

The first piece of information, the note ID, is easy to access. It's the value we stored in the ID table. It is a 32-bit unsigned value converted to hex. The next six pieces of information, originator ID, note class, last modified time/date, last accessed time/date, access rights, and truncation status are all accessed using the **NSFNoteGetInfo()** call. The prototype for the API is:

```
void far PASCAL NSFNoteGetInfo(NOTEHANDLE hNote,
                               WORD wNoteMemberID,
                               void far *lpValue);
```

NOTE The truncation status is the determination of whether or not the note has been abstracted, or truncated, due to a size limit. This usually occurs when a large note, or one that contains attachments, is replicated with the "Truncate large documents and remove attachments" replication setting enabled.

In a manner similar to the **NSFDbInfoParse()** API described above, the second parameter to this API is a value used to determine the type of information that is desired. These are all NOTE_MEMBER_ID constants defined in NSFNOTE.H. The list of values and resultant datatypes includes:

- _NOTE_DB — Database containing note — DBHANDLE
- _NOTE_ID — Note ID — NOTEID
- _NOTE_OID — Originator ID — OID
- _NOTE_CLASS — Note class — WORD
- _NOTE_MODIFIED — Last modified time — TIMEDATE
- _NOTE_FLAGS — Notes flags — WORD
- _NOTE_ACCESSED — Last accessed time — TIMEDATE
- _NOTE_PARENT_NOTEID — Response document's parent note ID — NOTEID
- _NOTE_RESPONSE_COUNT — Number of response for note — WORD
- _NOTE_RESPONSES — List of response documents — XXXX

Notice that third parameter to **NSFNoteGetInfo()** is a void pointer. This is to allow for passing the address of the appropriate datatype, as described above.

Of the six pieces of information in the list based off the **NSFNoteGetInfo()** call, the access rights and the truncation status do not have direct NOTE_MEMBER_ID flags. Both of these are contained in the _NOTE_FLAGS word and are obtained through ANDing the flags with the NOTE_FLAG_READONLY and the NOTE_FLAG_ABSTRACTED constants, respectively.

The next piece of information, the validity status, is determined using the **NSFNoteCheck()** API. This API probably doesn't get that much use, but it can be useful when trying to find out what is wrong if a note gets corrupted. It basically ramps through all of the items in the note and makes sure the sizes and datatypes are plausible within the context of the current data within the note. The only input to **NSFNoteCheck()** is an open note handle and the returned status can be either NOERROR, ERR_INVALID_ITEMLEN, or ERR_INVALID_ITEMTYPE. The example below, taken from the Note_GetSummaryAsText() routine in the DBVIEWER, shows how this is done.

```
Status = NSFNoteCheck(hNote);
switch (Status)
{
    case NOERROR:
        lstrcat(lpszText, "Validity checking OK");
        break;
    case ERR_INVALID_ITEMLEN:
        lstrcat(lpszText, "Invalid item length found in note");
        break;
    case ERR_INVALID_ITEMTYPE:
        lstrcat(lpszText, "Invalid item type found in note");
        break;
    default:
        lstrcat(lpszText, "Unknown validity check response");
        break;
}
```

The last set of detailed information for each note is the list of items for the note, followed by the actual item type name. As we discussed in Chapter 6, the items are the major component of the composition of a note.

Now, if you were to take an educated guess as to the method used to access the item information for a note, would you guess enumeration? If so, **NSFItemScan()** is the API for you. There are actually several different ways of accessing the information, including parsing through the item table returned to the callback routine from **NSFSearch()**, but all of them are performed through enumeration.

The three parameters to **NSFItemScan()** are all input parameters, an open note handle, the address of an enumeration routine, and an optional, user-defined, 32-bit parameter. The callback routine, on the other hand, is more involved. The prototype for the callback routine used within the DBVIEWER for this API call is:

```
STATUS far PASCAL NoteItem_Callback(WORD wUnused,
                                    WORD wItemFlags,
                                    CHAR_PTR lpItemName,
                                    WORD wItemNameLength,
```

```
VOID_PTR lpItemValue,
DWORD dwItemValueLength,
VOID_PTR lpAppData);
```

The second through sixth parameters here should again look familiar. It is the same information we parsed out of the ITEM_TABLE structure when we were in the **NSFSearch()** callback routine for files. Once again, the item name is not NULL-terminated and the datatype is contained in the first two bytes of the item value. The first parameter in the callback is reserved by Notes for future use.

The last parameter is the familiar user-defined data passed as the third parameter to **NSFItemScan()**. Here, as with almost all other callbacks in the DBVIEWER, we pass the address of a memory handle, this time containing a NOTE_ITEMS structure. This structure has an item count value and another handle containing the name and datatype of each item in the note. When the summary information is to be displayed, a call to the routine Item_GetTypeName() translates the item datatype into a representative string.

We could have gone further with the item interrogation by actually extracting the information for each item. If we would have done so, the best choice probably would have been to use the **NSFItemConvertToText()** API. Given the open note handle, the item name, a buffer for output and its maximum length, and a possible separator character (a semicolon is used, by default, to separate entries in a list), this API converts most of the "text-convertible" item types to a representative character string that is, in this case, NULL-terminated. The return value is the length of the text string created.

```
WORD far PASCAL NSFItemConvertToText(NOTEHANDLE hNote,
                    CHAR_PTR lpszItemName,
                    CHAR_PTR lpOutputText,
                    WORD wMaxOutputTextLength,
                    char cSeparator);
```

For now, we'll forgo this step and discuss item details later when we discuss the WATCHER application. It makes use of the Extension Manager APIs, new to Notes version 4.0.

The "Forms" button within the DBVIEWER uses another variation on the **NSFSearch()** theme to access a list of all of the Forms in the database. In addition, for each Form that is enumerated, we parse out the $TITLE item and the $Fields item to get the form title and number of fields, respectively. The call to **NSFSearch()** used in this instance is shown below. If you want to see at how the items are accessed, look at the FormList_Callback() routine.

```
Status = NSFSearch(hNotesDB,

                   NULLHANDLE,

                   NULL,

                   // search all notes providing summary and deleted
                       information

                   SEARCH_ALL_VERSIONS | SEARCH_SUMMARY |
                   SEARCH_NOTIFYDELETIONS,

                   // enumerate all form notes

                   NOTE_CLASS_FORM,

                   NULL,

                   (NSFSEARCHPROC) lpfnSearchProc,

                   (VOID_PTR) phFormList,

                   NULL);
```

Figure 7.9 shows the summary information for a database containing several forms with several fields in each.

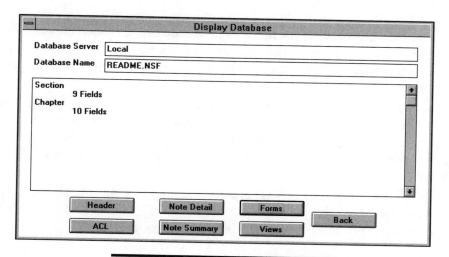

Figure 7.9 DBVIEWER forms summary.

Notes Index Facility(NIF): Performance at a Price

The final piece of functionality in the DBVIEWER is the "Views" button. Here again, we create a list of all of the notes that are of type NOTE_CLASS_VIEW using **NSFSearch()**. Notice that everything here is the same as the call to enumerate the Forms except one, the note class.

```
Status = NSFSearch(hNotesDB,

                NULLHANDLE,

                NULL,

                // search all notes providing summary and deleted
                    information

                SEARCH_ALL_VERSIONS | SEARCH_SUMMARY |
                SEARCH_NOTIFYDELETIONS,

                // enumerate all view notes

                NOTE_CLASS_VIEW,

                NULL,

                (NSFSEARCHPROC) lpfnSearchProc,

                (VOID_PTR) phViewList,

                NULL);
```

The callback routine used for the View list, ViewList_Callback(), extracts the View's $TITLE item, in the same manner we got the title for the Forms above. At this point, we take a quick trip into the realm of NIF (Notes Index Facility) routines.

The NIF APIs center around an object called a *collection*. A collection is simply the list of notes that are either the set of documents contained in a View or a View category. Collections are, from the user interface point of View, created by Notes whenever a View is first opened and updated whenever documents have been added and the View is reopened.

Collections can also be created and/or updated through the Notes C API. The View_GetNoteCount() routine within the DBVIEWER, shown below, is an example of one possible use of collections.

```
DWORD View_GetNoteCount(DBHANDLE hNotesDB,

                NOTEID ViewNoteID)

{
```

```
STATUS              Status;
HCOLLECTION         hCollection;
COLLECTIONPOSITION  CollectionPosition;
HANDLE              hViewNoteIDs;
DWORD               dwCount = 0;
WORD                wSignalFlags;

Status = NOERROR;
if (Status == NOERROR)
{
    Status = NIFOpenCollection(hNotesDB,    // database
                                            // containing view
                        hNotesDB,     // database
                                      // containing data
                        ViewNoteID,   // NOTEID of view
                        // don't update or create
                            collection on open
                        // values of 0 or
                            OPEN_REBUILD_INDEX are
                            COSTLY!!!!
                        OPEN_NOUPDATE |
                        OPEN_DO_NOT_CREATE,
                        NULLHANDLE,
                        &hCollection,
                        NULL,
                        NULL,
                        NULL,         // collapsed list
                        NULL);        // selected list
    if (Status == NOERROR)
    {
        // set the start position to the first in the list
        CollectionPosition.Level = 0;
        CollectionPosition.Tumbler[0] = 0;

        // read the NOTEIDs of all of the notes in the view at
            once
```

```
            // we do this because all we want is the count for this
               function
         Status = NIFReadEntries(hCollection,
                             &CollectionPosition,
                             NAVIGATE_NEXT,
                             1L,              // skip no
                                                 entries
                             NAVIGATE_NEXT,
                             0xFFFFFFFF,       // return all
                                                 at once
                             READ_MASK_NOTEID, // just return
                                                 the NOTEID
                             &hViewNoteIDs,    // buffer
                                                 containing
                                                 returned
                                                 NOTEIDs
                             NULL,             // ignore
                                                 returned
                                                 buffer
                                                 length
                             NULL,             // ignored # of
                                                 entries
                                                 skipped
                             &dwCount,         // number of
                                                 notes
                                                 returned
                             &wSignalFlags);   // signal flags
      if (hViewNoteIDs)
      {
          OSMemFree(hViewNoteIDs);
      }
      NIFCloseCollection(hCollection);
   }
 }
 return(dwCount);
}
```

The first call of any consequence here is the call to access a collection, **NIFOpenCollection()**. A call to this API will automatically perform a partial search of the database for all notes created or modified since the last time the collection was updated by default. If left to do this, by passing a 0 for the fourth parameter, it also updates the collection with entries for the new or modified notes before returning to the caller.

You really need to understand what Notes is doing here before using this API, especially if performance is an issue. If left to the default operation, as described above, this API can take some "quality time" to complete, depending on the note traffic in the database. This is due to the searching that takes place to update the View before it is opened. The trade-offs here are fairly simple:

- If you want the most up-to-date list of notes that belong in the View and you are only planning to make the call to open the collection once or twice within the application, use the OPEN_REBUILD_INDEX flag here. This option discards the current Index and rebuilds the Index from scratch. Just remember, this can be time-consuming, especially from the standpoint of a non-UI application.

- If you want the most up-to-date information but are planning to open the collection several times throughout the life of the application, use the default operation and pass 0 as the value of the fourth parameter. This will simply update the current Index, not start from scratch. In most cases, this option is just as good as, if not better than, OPEN_REBUILD_INDEX in that the Index probably already exists and rebuilding it from scratch is not only unnecessary but can be quite time-consuming.

- If you want the fastest access to the list of notes in the View, generated the last time the View was refreshed, use the OPEN_NOUPDATE | OPEN_DO_NOT_CREATE combination for the open flags, as was done in the example above. This set of flags does not update the collection upon opening and does not create a collection if one does not exist.

Now that we have the handle to all of the notes in the collection, an HCOLLECTION, we can index through the entries in the list using the **NIFReadEntries()** API. This API provides quite a few different options in indexing through the list of Documents in the View. One of the first things to contend with is the COLLECTIONPOSITION structure. This structure contains two pieces of pertinent information, the level, which denotes the level within a category list, and the tumbler, which contains the index into the current level.

The skip flags and skip count, parameters three and four in the call, provide a means of skipping a set of notes before reading begins. The skip flags are actually a NAVIGATE_FLAG value which can be one of 40 to 50 different types. The one we are most interested in here is NAVIGATE_NEXT since we want to start at the top of the list.

Used in combination with the skip flags and the skip count, the collection position can provide a means of starting an Index from nearly anywhere within the collection, provided that you know where you want to go. In the example above, because we want to start at the first note in the collection, we set the level and first tumbler to 0 and state that we want to skip to the first note in the list.

The fifth parameter is again a NAVIGATE_FLAG value used to determine how to position the Index after each note access. Here again, since we want to traverse through every note in the collection, we'll use NAVIGATE_NEXT.

Parameter six tells the API the maximum number of notes to process within the current call to **NIFReadEntries()**. A value of one here would basically allow an indexing scheme where a single note is returned upon each call to the API. In our case, we want the entire list at one time to access the count information, since we are going to discard the list anyway. To do this, use the maximum 32-bit unsigned value (0xFFFFFFFF).

The last input flag tells the API how much information to return for each note in the collection. Some of the possibilities here are the note ID, universal note ID, summary buffer information, sibling and children count. For our purposes, we want the smallest amount of information and the quickest to access possible, so we'll use the note ID(READ_MASK_NOTEID).

Now come the output parameters. The handle of the memory containing the requested data is in parameter eight. Nine holds the length of the returned buffer, NULL if you're not interested, and the number of skipped entries is returned in the tenth parameter. Here again, if you don't want it, don't provide a place to put it.

The next parameter, number eleven, holds the information we are looking for here, the number of notes processed in the read. The last parameter, the signal word, can contain information such as the update status of the collection and/or the fact that more data is yet to be processed. Since we know we may not be up-to-date, due to the use of the OPEN_NOUPDATE

OPEN_DO_NOT_CREATE flag combination, and since we are asking for all the information, we need not check this flag here.

NOTE

When you are through with the memory handle returned in the eighth parameter of **NIFReadEntries()**, it must be freed by the calling routine using the **OSMemFree()** API.

The last thing we do is to close the collection by passing the handle to the **NIFCloseCollection()** API. Figure 7.10 shows an example of the output from the "Views" button within the DBVIEWER.

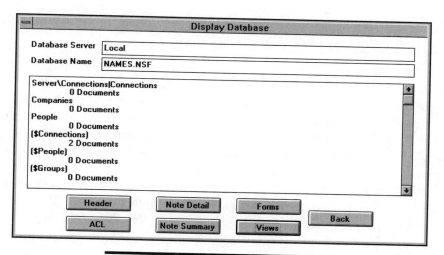

Figure 7.10 DBVIEWER views summary.

There are several other APIs within the Notes Index Facility set we haven't mentioned yet. Other than the **NIFUpdateCollection()** API, which performs an update similar to the default functionality of the **NIFOpenCollection()** operation described above, most of them deal with finding a specific View within a database, or note within a collection, by name, ID, or class. The thing to note here is that, although the API documentation states that these APIs are very efficient, make sure to do some investigation of all alternative methods if performance is an issue within your application. Efficiency does not necessarily mean speed.

DBVIEWER: Where do We Go from Here?

Although the DBVIEWER application provides quite a bit of information on the data contained in a database, one feature that we alluded to earlier is that of being able to drill down on specific items within a note to view the data contained within them. This would be fairly easy to do for item types that can be directly converted to a textual representation, e.g. text, text list, number, time, but can begin to get more complex as you dive into items containing rich text and composite information. And once again, if you want a database viewer that has all of these features, and don't want to build it yourself, get a copy of the Notes Peek application discussed earlier in this chapter. You'll be glad you did!

Mail: Anything You Want, You Got It!

We've already talked about several different sets of the operational groups within the Notes C API but one we haven't touched on yet is the Mail API set. As mentioned in Chapter 6, one of the strengths of the Notes C API is its support of mail functionality. There are about 46 different Mail APIs in this set that do just about everything from A to Z when it comes to mail. This large number of APIs arose because they were originally designed to manipulate mail gateways. If your application works with mail that is not gateway-related, you may want to opt for using the **NSF*()** routines to access mail databases and MAIL.BOX directly. Then again, you may want to dive into these APIs and "do it up right."

To show how some of the mail capabilities can be put to good use, we're going to create an application that takes ccMail import files and converts them into Notes mail messages. The MAILFILE (\NOTESC\WIN16\MAILFILE) application was created under Window 3.11 using Microsoft's Visual C++ 1.5 and was compiled for use on Notes version 4. We've also included a 32-bit version for Windows NT (NOTESC\WIN32\MAILFILE).

NOTE

If you want to compile MAILFILE for use with Notes version 3.x, go right ahead. There are no version-specific changes required.

MAILFILE does not handle all of the keywords that can exist within a ccMail import file. The keywords it does handle are some of the more common ones that you're most likely to see. Although we're not going to include the full ccMail import file definition here, Table 7.7 describes those keywords that are processed and their function.

Table 7.7 ccMail Import File Keywords

Keyword	Description
Message	Begins each new message
From	Message sender
To	Message recipient(s)
cc	Carbon-copy recipient(s)
Subject	Subject of message
Date	Date message was composed
Contents	Begins body of message
File Item	File to be attached to message
Text Item	Text to be included in section of message
Include	File to be included as text into message

The following is an example of a ccMail import file that could be processed by the MAILFILE application.

```
Message:
From: EBUNNY
Date: 12/23/98 11:30 PM CST
To: SCLAUS
Subject: Good Luck Wishes
Contents:
Dear Santa,
Good luck on you full day tomorrow. I am attaching a message
from my Tom Turkey containing his best wishes as well.
File Item: C:\LETTERS\FROMTT\SANTA.MSG
```

In a nutshell, MAILFILE periodically checks a specified set of directories for files with a specified extension. If a file is found, it is assumed to be in ccMail import file format and will be parsed accordingly. Once parsed, the information is then placed into a newly created Notes mail message and processed for transmission.

As you traverse through the code within MAILFILE.C, you'll see the definitions of DOS and DOSW16 as in the DBVIEWER. The ever present **NotesInit()** and **NotesTerm()** calls are also there. You'll also notice the creation of a timer with a time-out value of 60,000 milliseconds or 1 minute. This is what will be used as the basis of our checking interval calculation which, for this reason, can be no less than 1 minute.

The last thing we do before we head off to the main window procedure is to post ourselves a message to initialize the entire process. When the main window procedure receives this application-defined message, WM_INIT_CHECK_FOR_MAIL, the process of determining where to look for the ccMail import files begins. There is no magic here; all we do is get a list of directories, concatenated with semicolons, and a list of extensions, one for each directory, again separated by semicolons. These lists are read from the application .INI file, MAILFILE.INI, using the DIRECTORY and EXTENSION keywords respectively. These lists are then parsed and the fully qualified names of the search paths are created.

The following example shows a MAILFILE.INI file and the search path names that would be generated from it.

```
[MAILFILE]
DIRECTORY=C:\CCMAIL;D:\IMPORT;I:\PROBLEM\RELEASE
EXTENSION=DMP;MSG;PRB


C:\CCMAIL\*.DMP
D:\IMPORT\*.MSG
I:\PROBLEM\RELEASE\*.PRB
```

The checking interval is also obtained from the .INI file using the CHECKINTERVAL keyword and is defaulted to 1 minute.

After we have read in the start-up information, we are ready to perform the first check. To do this, we'll fall through the WM_INIT_CHECK_FOR_MAIL message case right to the WM_TIMER message. The first thing we do here is to make sure we are not re-entering ourselves, which could happen if it takes longer than the defined interval to process all of the mail files. To do this, we just check a global flag(gfCheckingForMail), which is set and cleared before and after we perform the mail processing.

Once we know we are not re-entering our code, we perform a check to see if this is the first time through the code or if the checking interval has elapsed. If either is true, we reset the number of minutes we've been waiting and make a call to check for any mail files.

```
// don't re-enter ourselves
if (!gfCheckingForMail)
{
    // if first time or time to check, do so
    if ((gnMinuteInterval == 0) || (gnMinuteInterval >=
gnCheckInterval))
    {
        gnMinuteInterval = 0;
        gfCheckingForMail = TRUE;
        CheckForMail();
        gfCheckingForMail = FALSE;
    }
    gnMinuteInterval++;
}
```

The CheckForMail() routine is fairly straightforward as well. All we do here is loop through the mail directory paths created above, searching for a file with the specified extension. For each file found, it is parsed into a set of global variables containing mail-specific pieces of information. Although we could describe how all of this is done, what we really want to do is discuss the process performed after the import message file is parsed. Therefore, we'll leave it up to you to go through the parsing logic on your own, and we'll move to the SendMail() routine, which is called after the parsing is complete.

In the SendMail() routine, we are ready to start using the Mail APIs. The first thing to do is to determine the path to the current user's mail file. We'll do this by looking into the NOTES.INI file for the mail server and the mail file name using the **OSGetEnvironmentString()** API. This is done in our GetMailFileInfo() routine.

There are actually several different methods available for finding the user's mail file, including searching the Name and Address book locally or on the current user's mail server. In our case, we'll assume we have a single user on our system and the data within the NOTES.INI file has the data we need.

Once we have the server name and the mail file name, we'll use the **OSPathNetConstruct()** call to create a path to the file. Finally, we get to the first Mail API, **MailOpenMessageFile()**. Given the path we just created to a mail database, this API will return a database handle. In this example, if an error occurs in opening the server mailbox, we'll revert to putting the message into the local mailbox and assume it will be processed later. To do this, we use a NULL for the mailbox file name in the call to **MailOpenMessageFile()**. This feature was added primarily to allow for remote usage and will most likely fail unless the application resides on a mail server, since workstations do not usually have a MAIL.BOX file. The following code is taken directly from the MAILFILE application and provides an example of how these calls are used.

```
// open the message file on the server
OSPathNetConstruct(NULL,
                   szMailServerName,
                   szMailFileName,
                   szMailFilePath);
NSFStatus = MailOpenMessageFile(szMailFilePath, &hMailFile);

// if cannot open mail file, send to local MAIL.BOX
if (ERR(NSFStatus) == ERR_NO_NETBIOS)
{
```

```
    fLocal = TRUE;
    NSFStatus = MailOpenMessageFile(NULL, &hMailFile);
}
```

NOTE

The use of the ERR() macro above provides the ability to mask off the top two bits of an error status that are status flags. This should be done whenever you are performing direct compares of error codes that are nonzero.

Now that we have a mail database open, we're ready to create an empty mail message. This requires the use of the **MailCreateMessage()** API. Again, this is a fairly simple call that takes the database handle as input and provides a note handle on output.

The fun of filling out the mail message now begins. The first order business is to create the list of recipient, "send to," and "copy to" names. These are all stored within the mail note as text lists so we'll use some of the list APIs to help us out. **ListAllocate()** allows for the initial creation of a text list entity.

```
STATUS far PASCAL ListAllocate(WORD num_entries,
                               WORD text_size,
                               BOOL prefix_flag,
                               HANDLE far *list_handle_ptr,
                               void far * far *list_ptr_ptr;
                               WORD far *list_size_ptr);
```

The first two parameters allow for creating the list with an initial number of entries of a given size. In our case, we'll use 0 for both of these values stating that we want the lists to be empty upon creation. We'll talk about how the list is populated in just a minute. The last three parameters are all filled on output and provide the handle to the list, the pointer to the list (locked on output), and the size of the list.

NOTE

Note that **ListAllocate()** automatically locks the list handle upon successful creation of the list and returns the pointer to the list in the fifth parameter. Be sure to unlock the list before manipulating its size or freeing it.

That leaves the third parameter to this call, the prefix flag. This entity instructs the list APIs to either append, or not append, a TYPE_TEXT_LIST datatype designation at the top of the list. The importance of this flag depends on the API you will be using to add the list to a document. In our case, we'll be using a couple of different Mail APIs that require the datatype to be included. One important fact about this flag is that all of the list APIs require it and you must use the same value for this flag on each call to the APIs for a specific list.

Now that we have created the three empty lists, we need to populate them. This is an easy process of parsing the "send to" and "copy to" lists and using the **ListAddEntry()** API to add the names to the appropriate mail list.

```
STATUS far PASCAL ListAddEntry(HANDLE list_handle,
                               BOOL prefix_flag,
                               WORD far *list_size_ptr,
                               WORD entry_number,
                               char far *text_string,
                               WORD text_size);
```

You'll notice from the prototype of **ListAddEntry()** above that the first parameter to the API is the handle to the list we just created using **ListAlocate()**. The previously mentioned prefix flag comes next followed by a pointer to the current list size(updated on output) and the 0-based position in the list that the entry is to take. The final two parameters are the text string to be added to the list and the length of the text string.

We've haven't said too much about the recipients lists yet. The "send to" and "copy to" lists should be fairly self-evident for a mail application but why the need for another list that mirrors the "send to" list? Actually, the recipient list is built by the mailer function within Notes from the other lists. It is then the recipient list that is used by the mail router to deliver the message. In our case, since we are not going through the mailer function, we need to build the recipient list ourselves so that the router can process the message appropriately.

One aspect of the recipient list that needs to be mentioned is that it requires the fully expanded domain path (@DOMAIN) for messages that will be sent beyond the current domain. To accomplish this, MAILFILE uses the **MailLookupAddress()** API call. This API takes an input user name and looks up the fully expanded domain address from the local Name and Address Book and then provides it as output. In general, this call is most useful on mail servers where the Name and Address Book is usually up-to-date. We ignore errors in this case and assume if we do get an error that the user name is valid and in the current domain and that the local Name and Address Book is not current. This may be the case if the MAILFILE application is used on a Notes workstation.

Now that we have the recipient list, we'll use the **MailAddRecipientsItem()** API to add it to the message. Given the handle to the open message, the recipient list handle, and the size of the list, this API adds the list as a TYPE_TEXT_LIST item to the message note. The other lists, "send to" and "copy to," are added to the message using the **MailAddHeaderItemByHandle()** API. A derivative of this API, **MailAddHeaderItem()**, is used to add the rest of the "single text string" information to the message.

NOTE

When using the **MailAddRecipientsItem()** and **MailAddHeaderItemByHandle()** APIs, the ownership of list handles is actually transferred to the message note and should therefore not be freed by the calling routine. The memory for the lists are actually freed once the mail message is closed.

These APIs are quite similar, as you might expect, and are fairly easy to understand. Each takes the handle to an open message note as the first parameter and a MAIL_*_ITEM_NUM constant as the second. This "item code" allows for adding the items without needing to specify the appropriate item names, which is done through the API, given the appropriate constant. All of the available constants here can be found in the MAIL.H include file.

The next two parameters in the APIs either provide the list handle and size or the string handle and size. For the **MailAddHeaderItem()** API, that's all you need. For **MailAddHeaderItemByHandle()**, another optional parameter, the item flag, is available to allow for signing or sealing the list. In our case, we won't use either of these so a value of 0 is used.

The following excerpt from the MAILFILE application shows how the "to" lists are added to the message note as well as some of the other "single text string" items using these APIs.

```
NSFStatus = MailAddRecipientsItem(hMsg,

                            hRecipientsList,

                            wRecipientsSize);
```

```
// The MailAddRecipientsItem and MailAddHeaderItemByHandle
// API attach the list to the message. Therefore, if all
// goes well, we need to make sure we do not deallocate
// the lists on clean-up.
if (NSFStatus == NOERROR)
{
    hRecipientsList = NULLHANDLE;
}


// Add the SendTo and CopyTo items to the message
NSFStatus = MailAddHeaderItemByHandle(hMsg,
                                      MAIL_SENDTO_ITEM_NUM,
                                      hSendToList,
                                      wSendToSize,
                                      0);
if (NSFStatus == NOERROR)
{
    hSendToList = NULLHANDLE;
}


NSFStatus = MailAddHeaderItemByHandle(hMsg,
                                      MAIL_COPYTO_ITEM_NUM,
                                      hCopyToList,
                                      wCopyToSize,
                                      0);
if (NSFStatus == NOERROR)
{
    hCopyToList = NULLHANDLE;
}


// Add the message header information
NSFStatus = MailAddHeaderItem(hMsg,
                              MAIL_FORM_ITEM_NUM,
                              MAIL_MEMO_FORM,
                              (WORD) lstrlen(MAIL_MEMO_FORM));
```

```
NSFStatus = MailAddHeaderItem(hMsg,

                              MAIL_FROM_ITEM_NUM,

                              gszFrom,

                              (WORD) lstrlen(gszFrom));
NSFStatus = MailAddHeaderItem(hMsg,

                              MAIL_SUBJECT_ITEM_NUM,

                              gszSubject,

                              (WORD) lstrlen(gszSubject));
NSFStatus = MailAddHeaderItem(hMsg,

                              MAIL_DELIVERYPRIORITY_ITEM_NUM,

                              gszPriority,

                              (WORD) lstrlen(gszPriority));
NSFStatus = MailAddHeaderItem(hMsg,

                              MAIL_DELIVERYREPORT_ITEM_NUM,

                              szReport,

                              (WORD) lstrlen(szReport));
```

NOTE

Notice that when the form name header item is added above we used another constant containing the form name for a memo note. There are several standard form name available for use in this manner and they, along with the item code names, can be found in STDNAMES.H.

There are two more items that we need to add to the message before we add the body, the composed date, and the posted date. If we are provided a date from the input file, we'll try to convert it using the **ConvertTextToTIMEDATE()** call. If no date was provided or if we get a conversion error, we'll use the current time and date, obtained through using **OSCurrentTIMEDATE()**, as the composed date. The current time and date is always used as the posted date.

The next step is to add the message body. This process can be somewhat involved, depending on the volume and type of information you'll be adding to the message body. In our case, the most we'll be adding is a stream of text, an optional text file, and an optional attachment.

NOTE

Note that this utility does not support multiple include files or attachments, although it would not be very difficult to modify it to do so.

The text stream, obtained from the information following the Contents keyword in the import file, is the first order of business. Since this will most likely be a common part of the message, we've created a routine within the MAILFILE application to add this text to an open message note. Our CreateMessageBody() routine uses three Mail APIs to accomplish this.

The first API, **MailCreateBodyItem()**, allocates an empty body item object, and returns a handle to it as well as its initial size. At this point, this object contains no data and is not attached to the message. The data is added to the message by calling **MailAppendBodyItemLine()**. This API takes the body item handle, the text string, and text length as inputs and returns the new size of the body item on output.

Once the body item has been filled with the text, it is attached to the message through **MailAddBodyItem()**. Passed the open message handle, the body item handle and size, and an optional text translation flag, this API will add the body item to the message with a twist we're not used to seeing. This time the memory handle is not transferred to the message and we must free it ourselves, after the message has been closed.

NOTE

MailCreateBodyItem() should only be used to create body items that are less than 64K bytes in length. If you need to add text to a body that is greater than 64K, **MailAddMessageBodyText()** should be used.

With the body text added to the message, now we need to check for text include files and attachments. Luckily, there are APIs set up to do exactly what we want in each case. If a text file is to be included in the message, that is, a file was specified using the Include keyword in the import file, a simple call to **MailAddMessageBodyText()** will do everything we need. The prototype for this API is:

```
STATUS far PASCAL MailAddMessageBodyText(HANDLE hMessage,
                                char far *ItemName,
                                char far *InputFileName,
                                DWORD  FontID,
                                char far *LineDelim,
                                WORD ParaDelim,
                                char far *TranslateFile);
```

This call has some interesting parameters that provide a good bit of latitude when including text from a file. The first parameter, as might be expected, is the handle to the open message note. The second is the item name to be used, NULL assumes the item named "Body." The third parameter is the fully qualified file name of the text file to be included.

The next four parameters in the **MailAddMessageBodyText()** call all have to deal with preprocessing the text from the file before it is included in the message. The first of the four, the font ID, is a double word value used to define the font to be used for the included text. There are a number of choices here, all of which are detailed in the FONTID.H include file within the toolkit. A value of 0 here uses a Helvetica 10 font. The font used in the MAILFILE application is a Courier 10 font that is defined by the macro FOREIGN_FONT_ID.

The next two parameters specify what character sequences delineate lines and paragraphs within the text file. The line delimiter value is specified as the character string that marks the end of each line. In the text files we're using, the carriage return/newline combination is the delineator ("\r\n"). The paragraph delimiter can be one of five possible values prefixed with PARADELIM_. In our case, a 0 value is used which defaults to PARADELIM_ANYBLANKLINE. This assumes that a new paragraph is to created whenever a blank line is encountered.

The last of the parameters to **MailAddMessageBodyText()** is an optional name of a translation file to be used to translate the text file from its native form to Lotus' MultiByte Character Set (LMBCS). For English, this format is simply an ASCIIZ string. For other languages, this type of translation will need to be performed.

If a file is to be attached to the message, **MailAddMessageAttachment()** is used. Since there is no manipulation of the data within an attached file, this API is much simpler than the previous one. This call takes a handle to the open message and the name of the file to be attached as well as a file name for display.

Our message note is now fully created and augmented and all that is left to do is to send it on its way. There are two possible avenues we can take here, depending on whether we have a connection to the mail server. If we do not have a connection, **MailTransferMessageLocal()** is used to transfer the message to the local MAIL.BOX file. Here again, as with the **MailOpenMessageFile()** API, the call will most likely only work on a mail server due to the presence of a MAIL.BOX file. If the transfer succeeds, the last thing we need to do is to save the message to the user's mail file, using the **NSFNoteUpdate()** API, and the message processing is complete. The excerpt below shows how this processing works within the MAILFILE application.

```
//  if the message is local, transfer message to local MAIL.BOX
if (fLocal)
{
    NSFStatus = MailTransferMessageLocal(hMsg);
    if (NSFStatus == NOERROR)
    {
        NSFStatus = NSFNoteUpdate(hMsg, UPDATE_NOCOMMIT);
        if (NSFStatus == NOERROR)
        {
            // state that the mailing was successful
            fOK = TRUE;
        }
        else
        {
            lstrcpy(lpszErrorMessageString, "Unable to update message
            in local mail file");
        }
    }
    else
    {
        lstrcpy(lpszErrorMessageString, "Unable to transfer message
        to local MAIL.BOX");
    }
}
```

In the usual workstation case, a connection to the mail server would be available and the above code path would not be taken. Instead, we'd send the message to the mail server's MAIL.BOX file. The only difference here is that we have to do some of the processing work ourselves, namely setting up the message note IDs properly.

The first thing to do is use **OSPathNetConstruct()** and **NSFDbOpen()** to create a path to, and open, the mail server's MAIL.BOX file, respectively. Now we have the following task: duplicate the current message note that exists in the user's mail file in the server's MAIL.BOX file with the proper IDs. The IDs we need are the originator ID, the database ID, and the note ID.

From our discussion of IDs in Chapter 6, this makes sense. The originator ID changes for each version of a note, and this is basically a new version of the note, not a replica. The database ID, which is a component of several of the other IDs, is database-specific and must therefore be changed as well. Finally, the note ID must be changed since it is tied positionally to each database.

All of this can happen through the use of four APIs: **NSFNoteGetInfo()**, **NSFNoteSetInfo()**, **NSFNoteUpdate()**, and **NSFDbGenerateOID()**. We used **NSFNoteGetInfo()** earlier in this chapter to read some of the note detail information in the DBVIEWER. **NSFNoteSetInfo()** is the write corollary to this and has the same parameters.

We've mentioned **NSFNoteUpdate()** in passing several times but never really talked about it much. The reason is, there isn't much to it. It is used to save a note back to persistent storage after it has been manipulated in memory. The first parameter to the call is the open note handle and the second is an update options flag word. These update flags can be found in NSFNOTE.H and provide several different types of operations. The operation you'll see most often here is that of UPDATE_NOCOMMIT. This option is basically a lazy write in that it does not force the data to disk immediately but will allow the system to write when it deems best.

The last of the four APIs required to perform the server mail send is **NSFDbGenerateOID()**. You have probably guessed by now that this API returns a note OID being passed a database handle on input. Rather than go through another description of how these calls are used to perform the function at hand, we'll show you the code from the MAILFILE application instead. Sometimes its more fun looking at source code anyway!

```
// save the current IDs for the message
NSFNoteGetInfo(hMsg, _NOTE_OID, &OrigNoteOID);
NSFNoteGetInfo(hMsg, _NOTE_DB, &hOrigDB);
NSFNoteGetInfo(hMsg, _NOTE_ID, &OrigNoteID);

// create a new OID for the server MAIL.BOX file
NSFStatus = NSFDbGenerateOID(hMailBox, &NewNoteOID);
if (NSFStatus == NOERROR)
{
    // set the OID, DBID, and NID for the server's MAIL.BOX
    NSFNoteSetInfo(hMsg, _NOTE_OID, &NewNoteOID);
    NSFNoteSetInfo(hMsg, _NOTE_DB, &hMailBox);
    NSFNoteSetInfo(hMsg, _NOTE_ID, 0);


    // save the message to the server's MAIL.BOX file
    NSFStatus = NSFNoteUpdate(hMsg, UPDATE_NOCOMMIT);
    if (NSFStatus == NOERROR)
    {
        // if all is well, restore the original IDs
        // and update the user's mail file
        NSFNoteSetInfo(hMsg, _NOTE_OID, &OrigNoteOID);
        NSFNoteSetInfo(hMsg, _NOTE_DB, &hOrigDB);
        NSFNoteSetInfo(hMsg, _NOTE_ID, &OrigNoteID);
        NSFStatus = NSFNoteUpdate(hMsg, UPDATE_NOCOMMIT);
    }
    else
    {
        lstrcpy(lpszErrorMessageString, "Unable to update server's
        MAIL.BOX");
    }
}
```

If at this point you are asking, "Why isn't there an API to do this?", you're not alone. The best answer we can come up with is "If it was too easy, anyone could do it."

Well, that's it! How to use the Mail APIs in *n* easy steps (where *n* can be any large number). It's really not all that bad and there is a lot of functionality built in but, like all parts of this API set, if you want to do a lot of things, you'll have to write a little code.

Extension Manager: "Real-Time" Notes

To this point, we haven't really discussed any Notes version 4.0-specific features. Although we'll talk about them in general in the last part of this chapter, we're going to jump the gun a little here and talk about one now, the Extension Manager.

The Extension Manager APIs were created to provide access to some of the agent functionality in Notes version 4.0. The Extension Manager allows you to create a DLL automatically loaded by Notes that provides a real-time hooking callback capability for several different operations within the Notes environment.

The WATCHER (\NOTESC\WIN16\WATCHER) application is a Windows 3.11 DLL that utilizes the Extension Manager capabilities to track when notes are added and subsequently deleted from a database. More specifically, WATCHER was designed to watch the activity through the MAIL.BOX file. Each time a new note is created within the database as, a mail message, the WATCHER will track the note ID, the message source, the message destination, the message subject, and the time the message entered the database. When a note is deleted, i.e., it is sent to the appropriate routing station, the original note is retrieved from the tracking database, using the note ID. From here, the time the note was deleted is saved and the elapsed time, in seconds, between the creation and deletion is computed and saved as well.

NOTE We've also provided the capability to create a WATCHER DLL for Windows NT through the use of a define (#define WATCHER_NT) in the WATCHER source and a different set of make-related files. The NT version of the watcher can be found in the \NOTESC\WIN32\WATCHER directory on the CD-ROM.

The sequence of events that occurs during the normal operation of an Extension Manager DLL are:

- Upon starting, Notes checks if any Extension Manager DLLs are available for loading. (This is done by checking for the EXTMGR_ADDINS keyword in the NOTES.INI file.)

- If such are found, Notes loads the DLL(s) and calls a common entry point within each, MainEntryPoint.

- Within the MainEntryPoint routine of each DLL, calls are made back into Notes, using the Extension Manager functions, to register callback routines to trap whatever events are desired.

- From here on, every time Notes performs a function that is being hooked by any DLL, a call is made to the registered callback routine for the event at the appropriate time.

- At some time in the future, usually when the DLL is unloaded, the DLL unregisters the hooks it created.

Now let's get to the details of how all of this happens by looking at the code within the WATCHER application. The first piece of the puzzle we'll look at is how to assemble the routines in the DLL for proper access by Notes.

A routine named MainEntryPoint must be created within your DLL and exported as ordinal 1. If you do not use ordinal 1, your routine may not be loaded properly on certain platforms, notably Windows 3.x. The WATCHER.DEF file for Windows 3.x is shown below.

```
LIBRARY            WATCHER
EXETYPE          WINDOWS
CODE             PRELOAD MOVEABLE DISCARDABLE
DATA             PRELOAD MOVEABLE SINGLE
HEAPSIZE         4096
EXPORTS
    MainEntryPoint           @1
    NoteUpdated_Callback     @2
    NoteDeleted_Callback     @3
    MailNote_Callback        @4
    WEP                      @5      RESIDENTNAME
```

All callback registrations within the DLL should occur in the MainEntryPoint routine. For the WATCHER application, we are watching two events,

NSFNoteUpdate() and **NSFNoteDelete()**, but we have set up the registration scheme to easily allow for watching any number of events. The example below shows the registration event structure, initialization, and registration calls used within the WATCHER.

```
// global defines, structures, and variables
#define EVENT_COUNT 2        // number of events being watched

// structure for each event being watched
typedef struct
{
    EID                  RegistrationID;        // registration ID
    DWORD                dwRegistrationFlags;   // registration flags
    EMHANDLER            lpfnCallbackProc;      // callback procedure
    WORD                 wRecursionID;          // recursion ID
    HEMREGISTRATION      hRegistration;         // registration handle
    BOOL                 fRegistrationOK;       // registration OK flag
} EVENT_INFO, far * EVENT_INFO_PTR;
    .
    .
    .

// event registration information
EVENT_INFO gEvents[EVENT_COUNT] =
{
    {EM_NSFNOTEUPDATE, EM_REG_AFTER,  NoteUpdated_Callback, 0, NULL,
    FALSE},
    {EM_NSFNOTEDELETE, EM_REG_BEFORE, NoteDeleted_Callback, 0, NULL,
    FALSE}
};
EVENT_INFO gEvents[EVENT_COUNT];
    .
    .
    .

for (i=0; i < EVENT_COUNT; i++)
{
```

```
// get a recursion ID for each event to be processed
Status = EMCreateRecursionID(&(gEvents[i].wRecursionID));
if (Status == NOERROR)
{
    DebugFile_WriteString("Registering Event...");
    Status = EMRegister(gEvents[i].RegistrationID,
                        gEvents[i].dwRegistrationFlags,
                        gEvents[i].lpfnCallbackProc,
                        gEvents[i].wRecursionID,
                        &(gEvents[i].hRegistration));
    if (Status == NOERROR)
    {
        DebugFile_WriteString("Registration Succeeded");
        gEvents[i].fRegistrationOK = TRUE;
    }
    else
    {
        DebugFile_WriteString("Registration Failed");
        gEvents[i].fRegistrationOK = FALSE;
    }
}
}
```

You'll notice we call **EMCreateRecursionID()** before we actually register to watch each event. The call has a single output parameter which is a 16-bit unsigned value that contains a unique recursion ID defined by Notes. This provides a way for Notes to prevent an endless loop within your application. Without this, if your application registered to watch for notes being opened and, within the callback routine, your application opens another note, you would recurse back into you application until you ran out of stack space!

The recursion ID is then used in each subsequent call to **EMRegister()**, the workhorse of the Extension Manager APIs. Of the five parameters within the call to **EMRegister()**, the first four are inputs and the last, the registration handle, is returned on output.

The first parameter is the registration ID. This can be one of any of the over 60 EM_* constants defined within the EXTMGR.H file. Most of these have to deal with actions that occur either to a database, a note, or a collection. Some of the "note events" in the list are:

EM_NSFNOTEOPEN	- Note opened
EM_NSFNOTECLOSE	- Note closed
EM_NSFNOTECREATE	- Note created
EM_NSFNOTEDELETE	- Note deleted
EM_NSFNOTESTAMP	- Note stamped (same item set in several notes)
EM_NSFNOTEOPENBYUNID	- Note opened using universal ID
EM_NSFNOTEREPLICATE	- Note replicated
EM_NSFNOTEOPENEXTENDED	- Note open extended

The second parameter, the registration flags, can be one of two values, EM_REG_BEFORE or EM_REG_AFTER. If you specify EM_REG_BEFORE, Notes calls your callback routine before it calls the internal Notes API to perform the function. This not only allows your DLL to interrogate any of the parameters to the call, or status of the environment, but it also proffers you the ability to have Notes not perform the requested operation. If your callback returns any value other than ERR_EM_CONTINUE, Notes will not call any other registration callbacks for this function nor the actual Notes routine.

NOTE There can be any number of Extension Manager DLLs that are registered for the same event. If more than one callback exists for an event, each callback is made from Notes in the order it was registered.

If EM_REG_AFTER is used for the registration flags, the callback is executed, in order, after the Notes call is completed. In this case, your application has access to the call parameters, as in the EM_REG_BEFORE case, as well as the returned status.

The returned status and call parameters are obtained through the EMRECORD pointer passed to the callback routine. The EMRECORD structure, shown below, contains the registration ID, or EID, and the notification type used in the registration call as the first two elements. The returned status is the third element in the structure. A pointer to the call parameters stack is returned in the fourth element, the VARARG_PTR.

```
typedef struct
{
    EID          EId;                  /* identifier */
    WORD         NotificationType;     /* EM_BEFORE or EM_AFTER */
    STATUS       Status;               /* core error code */
    VARARG_PTR   Ap;                   /* ptr to args */
} EMRECORD;
```

The parameters used within the call can be accessed, in order, using the VARARG_GET macro. This means that if we wish to access the second parameter to the **NSFNoteUpdate()**—the update flags—we need to process the first parameter, the note handle, using VARARG_GET before using the macro to get the update flags. The example below shows how this is done in the NoteUpdated_Callback() routine within WATCHER.C.

```
if (lpEMRecord->Status == NOERROR)
{
    DebugFile_WriteString("Note Updated Callback - Status=OK");
    lpArgs = lpEMRecord->Ap;
    hNote = VARARG_GET(lpArgs, NOTEHANDLE);
    wUpdateFlags = VARARG_GET(lpArgs, WORD);.
    .
    .
    .
}
```

Now, back to **EMRegister()**. The third parameter is the address of the callback routine to be called by Notes when the event occurs. This routine is passed the address of an EMRECORD structure described above. The fourth parameter is the recursion ID we got back from the call to **EMCreateRecursionID()**.

You've probably noticed by now that we've added a debugging capability to the WATCHER DLL that writes information out to a log file based on an INI switch. It's not very high-tech in that it simply writes a file named DEBUG.OUT in the root directory of the C drive. This capability can come in handy, though, during development and especially once the application goes into production and there is no debugger around.

Within WATCHER once again, we have now registered for the **NSFNoteUpdate()** and the **NSFNoteDelete()** events. All that is left within the

MainEntryPoint routine is to return a NOERROR status back to Notes. If we return any other value here, Notes assumes the DLL did not load correctly and displays the error in the status bar.

Now our NoteUpdated_Callback() and NoteDeleted_Callback() routines will be called when any note on the local system is updated or deleted, respectively. And we mean ANY note. For this reason, each time either of the two routines is called, one of the first things done is to determine whether or not the note in question is actually contained in our watched mail box database. If not, the update/delete will be ignored by the WATCHER application.

To get the name of the note's parent database, we first have to get the handle of the database. We can do this by using an API we've used before, **NSFNoteGetInfo()**, with a NOTE_MEMBER_ID of _NOTE_DB. Once we have this, we'll make a call to **NSFDbPathGet()** to get the database name. Given the database handle, this API actually returns the database name in two different formats. The first of these, which is returned in the string pointed to by the second parameter in the call, is called the *canonical name*. This name contains the database name prefixed by the relative path of the database from the Notes data directory. The second name is the *fully qualified name* of the database file, including drive letter if the database is on the local system. If the database is remote, the canonical name and the fully qualified names will be the same.

After the comparison of the newly acquired database name against the name of the watched database, **NSFNoteGetInfo()** is once again used, this time to get the note's ID. As you may remember, we need the note ID to uniquely identify each note in the control database.

The last thing we need to do within the NoteUpdated_Callback() routine is to determine whether this update is due to a note being saved or being deleted. This information is proffered to us through the update flags, which we obtained at the start of the routine. We've already talked about several update flags already but this time we're interested in yet another flag, UPDATE_DELETE. By ANDing this constant with the update flags, we can determine whether or not this specific note update is a delete. If it is, an internal routine named ProcessNoteDelete() is called. If this is a normal save operation, ProcessNoteUpdate() is called.

The second of the two event callbacks, NoteDeleted_Callback(), performs actions similar to the NoteUpdated_Callback() routine: verifying that the note's parent database is the watched database, getting the note's ID, and calling the proper processing routine. The first step is easier in the case of the note delete

processing since the database handle is the first parameter on the call to
NSFNoteDelete(). All that is left to do here is once again call **NSFDbPathGet()**
and compare the paths of the two databases. As for the note ID, its the second
parameter on the call to **NSFNoteDelete()**. Finally, since the only function we're
interested in out of the **NSFNoteDelete()** processing is, surprisingly enough, the
delete function, a call to ProcessNoteDelete() completes the note delete callback
logic. The code below shows the entire NoteDeleted_Callback() routine as taken
from the WATCHER application.

```
STATUS FAR PASCAL _export NoteDeleted_Callback(EMRECORD far *
lpEMRecord)
{
    STATUS      Status = NOERROR;
    DBHANDLE    hNotesDB;
    NOTEID      NoteID;
    char        szCanonicalPathname[MAXPATH], szFullPathname[MAXPATH];
    WORD        wUpdateFlags;
    VARARG_PTR  lpArgs;
    BOOL        fOK;

    DebugFile_Open();
    lpArgs = lpEMRecord->Ap;
    hNotesDB = VARARG_GET(lpArgs, DBHANDLE);
    NoteID = VARARG_GET(lpArgs, NOTEID);
    wUpdateFlags = VARARG_GET(lpArgs, WORD);

    DebugFile_WriteString("Note Deleted Callback");
    Status = NSFDbPathGet(hNotesDB,
                          szCanonicalPathname,
                          szFullPathname);
    if (Status == NOERROR)
    {
        DebugFile_WriteTwoStrings("Parent Database of Note: ",
szCanonicalPathname);

        *if ((lstrcmpi(gszWatchedDatabase, szCanonicalPathname)) ==
0)
        {
```

```
            fOK = ProcessNoteDelete(hNotesDB, NoteID);
        }
    }
    DebugFile_Close();

    // always return continue so the next callback in the chain is
       processed
    return(ERR_EM_CONTINUE);
}
```

NOTE
The usual path taken by Notes to delete the note from the mail box is through the **NSFNoteUpdate()** call using the UPDATE_DELETE update flags. **NSFNoteDelete()** was created in the event that a different path was taken to delete the note from the mail box, e.g., through an API application.

Now let's take a look at how we process a note update in ProcessNoteUpdate(). The first thing we need to do is to determine whether this is the first update of the note, the creation of a new note, or simply the update of an existing one. To do this, we'll open the control database using **NSFDbOpen()** and then check to see if a note with the current ID exists within the control database, using an internal routine called FindMailNote(). If so, we'll ignore the update since we already have all of the information we need from the initial save of the note. If the note is not present, we know we have a new mail note and that we need to process it as such.

NOTE
If at this point you're asking yourself why we didn't use the **NSFNoteCreate()** event as opposed to the update event, the reason is pretty simple. By waiting for the update, we can be sure that most, if not all, of the data within the note has been initialized. If we had have captured the **NSFNoteCreate()** event, none of the mail-specific information such as the source, destination, and subject would have been available to us at that time.

How do we determine whether or not a note exists in a database? Depending on the type of information available on the note, there may be several ways of doing this. In our case, it's back to using **NSFSearch()**, this time with a little different twist. Since we are only searching for a single document note within the database, one with a given note ID, we're going to create a formula to narrow the selection criteria to the scope of a single note.

Formulas are a familiar part of the Notes 3.x operation. They are one of the few ways to perform meaningful operations within the environment. From the standpoint of this API set, **NSFCompute*()** and **NSFFormula*()** are the API classes that manipulate formulas.

The way formulas are used within the FindMailNote() routine in the WATCHER application is fairly simple. First, we'll create the text of a formula that searches for a note with a Form item of "Mail Watcher Info" and a NoteInfo.NoteID item with text of the passed ID. For example, assume we wanted to check for a control note with an ID of 000010A2. The formula string would then look like this:

```
FORM="Mail Watcher Info" & NoteInfo.NoteID = "000010A2"
```

Once the formula string is assembled, the **NSFFormulaCompile()** API is used to compile the formula into its binary form for use in the **NSFSearch()** API. The prototype for **NSFFormulaCompile()** looks quite formidable at first, with its eleven parameters, but it's only the first six that are of usual concern. The last five deal with stating whether or not a compile error occurred and, if so, where in the formula it occurred.

The first two parameters are needed only if the formula is to be used as a column formula in a View. If this is the case, the column name and length are specified here. In all other cases, NULL and 0 are used, respectively. The third and fourth parameters are the formula string and the formula string length. The last two parameters of importance here are outputs from the routine and they are the formula handle, parameter five, and the length of the formula handle, parameter number six.

The code to build the formula string above, as well as the formula compilation and search, is shown below:

```
*lpControlNoteID = 0;

// first of all, convert the note ID to text for use in the formula
DWORDToHexText(MailNoteID, szMailNoteID);
```

```
// now create the formula to find the correct note
lstrcpy(szFormulaText, "FORM=\"Mail Watcher Info\"");
lstrcat(szFormulaText, " & NoteInfo.NoteID=\"");
lstrcat(szFormulaText, szMailNoteID);
lstrcat(szFormulaText, "\"");
DebugFile_WriteString(szFormulaText);

// compile the formula above
Status = NSFFormulaCompile(NULL,
                           0,
                           szFormulaText,
                           lstrlen(szFormulaText),
                           &hFormula,
                           &wFormulaLength,
                           &FormulaCompileError,
                           &wFormulaCompileErrorLine,
                           &wFormulaCompileErrorColumn,
                           &wFormulaCompileErrorOffset,
                           &wFormulaCompileErrorLength);

// if the formula compiled OK, search for the note using the formula
if (Status == NOERROR)
{
    Status = NSFSearch(hNotesDB,
                       hFormula,
                       NULL,
                       0,
                       NOTE_CLASS_DOCUMENT,
                       NULL,
                       (NSFSEARCHPROC) MailNote_Callback,
                       (VOID_PTR) lpControlNoteID,
                       NULL);

    // if no erors occurred in the search and we got an ID, report
success
```

```
    if ((Status == NOERROR) && (*lpControlNoteID != 0))
    {
        fOK = TRUE;
    }
}
return(fOK);
```

Now the call to **NSFSearch()** has one more twist, the specification of the formula handle in parameter two. Since, at least in this case, there should only be one note that fits this criteria, if at all, the callback routine, MailNote_Callback(), simply places the note's ID in the application-defined address passed to it and the job is done.

Of the other **NSFFormula*()** APIs, **NSFFormulaDecompile()**, takes a binary formula and converts it back into its ASCII equivalent. **NSFFormulaGetSize()** returns the size, in bytes, of the binary representation of a formula and **NSFFormulaMerge()** merges one binary formula into another. The last in this group, **NSFFormulaSummaryItem()**, is used in combination with **NSFFormulaMerge()** to build the $FORMULA item of a View note.

The **NSFComputeStart()**, **NSFComputeEvaluate()**, and **NSFComputeStop()** APIs provide for the ability to execute a formula against one or more notes and provide status information based on the result.

If after the search we do not find the IDed note in the control database, we have to create one to contain the set of create-time information. **NSFNoteCreate()** seems to be the logical place to start. Given the handle to the open database, this API returns a handle to an empty note. From here, the note items need to be filled in to flesh out the note itself. We'll use **NSFItemSetText()** to set the Form item to "Mail Watcher Info" and the NoteInfo.NoteID item to the textual representation of the note ID.

The next thing we need to do is to get the source, destination, and subject line from the original mail message and transfer them to the control note. For the source and subject lines, we'll use the same combination of two APIs, **NSFItemGetText()** and **NSFItemSetText()**, with item names of "From" and "Subject," respectively. The following code shows how the mail message source is obtained in this manner.

```
// get source of mail message and store it into the control note
wLength = NSFItemGetText(hNote,
                           "From",
                           szFrom,
                           sizeof(szFrom) - 1);
szFrom[wLength] = '\0';
Status = NSFItemSetText(hNewControlNote,
                           "NoteInfo.From",
                           szFrom,
                           lstrlen(szFrom));
```

NOTE

As you can see from the example above, **NSFItemGetText()** does not return a NULL-terminated string but rather a string and its length. Make sure to always process this string appropriately and to allow for the NULL character in the size parameter passed to **NSFItemGetText()**.

The message destination information is processed a bit differently than the message source and subject. This is needed due to the way Notes stores textual information. If only a single line of text exists within an item, it is usually stored as TYPE_TEXT and is manipulated using the **NSFItemGetText()** and **NSFItemSetText()** APIs. A text field that has multiple pieces/lines of information is stored as a TYPE_TEXT_LIST and is manipulated by a different set of APIs, four of which we'll use in the WATCHER.

The first thing to do therefore is to determine the datatype of the "To" item within the mail note. If it is TYPE_TEXT, we'll use **NSFGetItemText()** and **NSFSetItemText()** as with the previous two items to transfer the information to the control note. If we are processing a text list on the other hand, we need to transfer each of the destinations, one at a time. This is done by first calling **NSFGetTextListEntries()** to get the number of destinations in the list. This API takes the note handle and item name as inputs and returns the number of strings in the list.

Knowing the number of entries in the list, **NSFItemGetTextListEntry()** and **NSFItemAppendTextList()** are used in tandem to get each destination from the mail note and store them into the control note, respectively. Another of the text list APIs, **NSFItemCreateTextList()**, could have been used to create the first destination in the list and then subsequently call **NSFItemAppendTextList()** for the other strings in the list. Since the latter API will, by default, create the list if it does not exist, its not necessary to use **NSFItemCreateTextList()** in this case. The code that performs the transfer of the mail destination(s) among the two notes within the WATCHER application is shown below.

```
// get datatype for destination of mail message
Status = NSFItemInfo(hNote,
                     "SendTo",
                     6,
                     NULL,
                     &wDatatype,
                     &BlockID,
                     &dwItemLength);

// if we only have one destination, process a text type
if (wDatatype == TYPE_TEXT)
{
    wLength = NSFItemGetText(hNote,
                     "SendTo",
                     szTo,
                     sizeof(szTo) - 1);
    szTo[wLength] = '\0';
    Status |= NSFItemSetText(hNewControlNote,
                     "NoteInfo.To",
                     szTo,
                     lstrlen(szTo));
}
// else, process as a text list type
else
{
    // get the number of entries in the list
    wEntries = NSFItemGetTextListEntries(hNote, "SendTo");
    for (i=0; i < wEntries; i++)
    {
        wLength = NSFItemGetTextListEntry(hNote,
                                    "SendTo",
```

```
                                                    i,
                                                    szTo,
                                                    sizeof(szTo) - 1);
            szTo[wLength] = '\0';
            Status |= NSFItemAppendTextList(hNewControlNote,
                                            "NoteInfo.To",
                                            szTo,
                                            lstrlen(szTo),
                                            TRUE);
        }
    }
```

The last item to process within the control note is that of storing the time the note was created. **OSCurrentTIMEDATE()**, an API we used in the MAILFILE application, is used to get the current date and time and another of the item set APIs, **NSFItemSetTime()**, to set the information into the control note.

```
    // store the time the mail note was created
    OSCurrentTIMEDATE(&CurrentTimeDate);
    Status |= NSFItemSetTime(hNewControlNote,
                             "NoteInfo.Created",
                             &CurrentTimeDate);
```

The last thing of importance left to do within ProcessNoteUpdate() is to call **NSFNoteUpdate()** to physically store the note information to disk. With the update completed, we'll close the control note and the mail note on the way out of the routine using **NSFNoteClose()** and we're done.

The ProcessNoteDelete() routine does little more in the way of new API calls than what we've already seen in ProcessNoteUpdate(). The two notable exceptions here would be the calls responsible for calculating the difference between the create and delete timestamps, **TimeDateDifference()**, and the call used to store the resultant difference back into the control note, **NSFItemSetNumber()**. **NSFItemSetNumber()** is simply another in the line of APIs that can be used to get and set values within items. **TimeDateDifference()**, on the other hand, is one of the assorted calls in the "Time" object. These deal with manipulating the Notes TIMEDATE structure in one fashion or another so that your application need not know the low-level content of the structure.

When all is said and done, and your Extension Manager DLL is unloaded, you'll need to use the last of the Extension Manager APIs, **EMDeregister()**, to deregister all the events that were registered. The only parameter to this call is the registration handle returned in the **EMRegister()** call. In the WATCHER, this is done in the Windows Exit Procedure (WEP) routine for the Window 3.x case and in the DLL_PROCESS_DETACH case in LibMain for NT.

WATCHER: Where do We Go from Here?

There are several things that could be done to the functionality within the WATCHER application. One might be to track more information on each mail message (e.g., cc: and bcc: addressees) or to process the message subject as either a text or a text list. In a more general sense, changes could be made to get the item names and datatypes from a table or an INI file, thereby allowing for tracking any type of data within any database. There may be a question as to whether this type of generalization of the WATCHER application would be of any great utility, but it could be done never the less.

That is the end of the discussion of the Extension Manager functionality for Notes version 4.0. We've shown you all three of the APIs in the set but we only registered for two events, note update and note delete. With all of the possible events you can watch, there are a lot of possibilities if you have need of accessing specific types of Notes information in "real-time".

Converting from Version 3.x to Version 4.0: A Day's Work

If you have an existing Notes 3.x API application, it will run under version 4.0 without modification, as we've stated previously. If you wish to convert your application to run natively under version 4.0, the conversion process is usually quite easy.

First of all, it is suggested that you use **NotesInitExtended()** rather than **NotesInit()** starting with version 4.0. **NotesInitExtended()** takes the two command line parameters, argc and argv, as inputs. This allows for passing the Notes executable directory, as argv[0], to the initialization call. Here is how we used the **NotesInitExtended()** API to get the same operation as a call to **NotesInit()**, for the DBVIEWER:

```
#ifdef NOTES_V3
    if (NotesInit())
#else
    if (NotesInitExtended(0, NULL))
#endif
```

The next change you'll probably have to make to your version 3.x application, especially if you are using **NSFSearch()**, is the way in which you access the search match flags. In version 4.0, the MatchesFormula field in the SEARCH_MATCH structure has been replaced by an array of bit flags. The name of the bit flags field is SERetFlags. The code below shows how this change is managed within the DBVIEWER when checking if the enumerated note matches the search criteria:

```
#ifdef NOTES_V3
    if (lpSearchInfo->MatchesFormula == SE_FMATCH)
#else
    if (lpSearchInfo->SERetFlags & SE_FMATCH)
#endif
```

In 3.x versions of the Notes API, the ACL_PRIVILEGES were stored as an array of 10 bytes. In version 4.0, this array has been made part of a structure. If you accessed the ACL privileges using the Notes C API functions and macros in version 3.x, everything will be just fine. If, on the other hand, you accessed these bits directly, your application will need to be modified to reflect this change. The version 3.x and version 4.0 ACL_PRIVILEGES definitions are shown below.

```
For Version 3.x...
    typedef BYTE ACL_PRIVILEGES[10];

For Version 4.0...
    typedef struct {BYTE BitMask[10];} ACL_PRIVILEGES;
```

With the few changes described above completed, compiling and linking with new includes and libraries for version 4.0 should have your application up and running with version 4.0. There are actually a couple more esoteric changes that you may run into but they are quite minor and should be quite easy to deal with if you come across them.

New Capabilities in Version 4.0

To this point, most of the information provided within this chapter exists in Notes version 3.x as well as version 4.0, with the exception of the Extension Manager functionality. As with the Notes application itself, there are several new features within the Notes C API for version 4.0 too.

From the standpoint of major new functionality, the Extension Manager and Notes Flow features are the two most prevalent. Since we've already talked about the Extension Manager, we'll head right on to Notes Flow.

Briefly, Notes Flow provides extensions of the Notes/FX capabilities to an API application. If you are not familiar with Notes/FX, or Notes Field Exchange, it is the feature that allows for the exchange of field data between Notes and several other FX-enabled applications. This is all accomplished through Microsoft's Object Linking and Embedding (OLE) technology. If you are creating an OLE-aware application and want to provide some level of interface among your OLE server and Notes, you may want to talk a look at Notes/FX and Notes Flow.

There are also several new APIs in version 4.0 that did not exist in the version 3.x set. Some of these new functions provide the ability to have more control over mail routing tables. Others deal with providing more control over font attributes and font types. For instance, two more default font macro definitions have been added, DEFAULT_SMALL_FONT_ID and DEFAULT_PPEN_FONT_ID. Several new navigation methods within collections have been provided too as well as a new function to get collection-specific information, **NIFGetCollectionData()**.

At the end of each of the API set chapters, we'll provide a list of suggestions on when and how to best use the specific API set. Since the number of entries in this list varies from set to set, we'll call it our Top *n* list.

Notes C API Top *n*

1. Learn the advantages and disadvantages of using **NSFSearch()** versus collections.

2. If you want to do some neat stuff with mail, this is the API to use.

3. If you want to control or modify Notes dynamically, use the Extension Manager.

4. Export all callback routines and make proc instances in Windows 3.x.

5. Use the "OS" routines predominantly when needed for Notes functionality.

HiTest C API

The second method of extending Notes that we'll explore is the Notes HiTest C API. In many respects, the HiTest C API covers the same ground as does the Notes C API discussed in the previous chapter. Here again, as with the Notes C API, we'll discuss:

- The API set's structure
- The details of some of the major APIs
- How to use the APIs in concert with one another to accomplish a specific task

In addition, we'll talk more about some of the features of the HiTest C API that differentiate it from the Notes C API discussed in Chapter 6.

API Structure

The Notes HiTest C API has a stronger object-oriented structure than does the Notes C API. Although still not organized as true objects, since this is still a C, not a C++ API, there is a more highly defined class hierarchy within this API set. Figure 8.1 shows the "class hierarchy" within the HiTest C API.

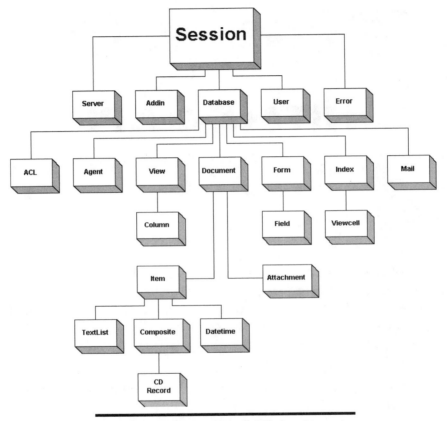

Figure 8.1 Notes HiTest C API class hierarchy.

CLIPSERV: Notes Database Clipper Service

In this chapter, as with Chapter 7, we'll look at the API by developing some applications using it. The Notes Clip Service application, CLIPSERV, provides a means of registering against any number of Notes databases you have access to and having any new note activity within the database mailed to a specific destination. This utility is most useful when used to automatically track changes in several different databases at regular intervals.

NOTE

This same functionality is partially available with some of the built-in functions within Notes version 4.0 with the exception of the multiple database, multiple destinations scenario.

The Windows 16-bit version of CLIPSERV (\HITESTC\WIN16-\CLIPSERV) was created using Microsoft's Visual C++ 1.5 on Windows 3.11 and was compiled for use on Notes Version 3.x. Since the version 4.0 HiTest C API set was not available at the time this book was published, we were not be able to provide a description on the necessary changes required. The thing to remember here, though, is that Notes version 4.0 will allow binary compatibility with applications built using 3.x API sets. Although this does not allow the use of new version 4.0 features, it does provide a backward compatibility that can help during the version transition period.

The 32-bit Windows version of the application (\HITESTC\WIN32-\CLIPSERV) was created using Visual C++ 2.0 on Windows NT, again for use with Notes 3.x. The only difference between the two is the format of the build-processing components. The C source and include files for the application itself are the same for both platforms save for one define, the HiTest operating system definition.

The design of the CLIPSERV applications is as follows: a single Notes database is used as a central controlling mechanism. This database contains a form, ClipInfo, that is used to hold information on each database to be tracked. This information includes the server and name for each database to be tracked, the checking interval (in minutes), and the mail address to receive the new information found within the database. Once this information is gathered for all of the databases to be tracked, a timer is used to periodically check for new activity within each database and send the new information to the specified destination.

One of the first things you'll see in CLIPSERV.C is the definition of HTOS_WIN3 for the 16-bit version. This is one of currently three possible required definitions for the HiTest API. It states that the application will be compiled for use with Windows 3.x as a 16-bit application. HTOS_OS22 would be used to create a 32-bit application for use with OS/2 2.x and HTOS_WINNT to create a 32-bit Windows application. A different dynamic link library is provided for each of the three platforms described. For 16-bit Windows applications, the DLL to be used is W3HTAPI.DLL. Whenever 32-bit Windows functionality is required, the NTHTAPI.DLL is used. The last of the three, OS2HTAPI.DLL, is used for 32-bit OS/2 operation.

Immediately after the definition of operating system type, the HTNOTES.H file is included. This is the major header file for the HiTest API and it holds all of most of the constant and structure definitions for the API set. It also includes another header file, HTFUNCS.H, which contains all of the prototypes for the APIs themselves.

NOTE   The inclusion of GLOBAL.H and NSFERR.H from the Notes C API set that follows the HiTest includes is required to allow for some error checking later on in the application. For now, it is important to note that the Notes C API and the HiTest C API can be used in concert with one another, should the need arise.

Before we start with the APIs, there is another item we should mention from the standpoint of building an application using the HiTest API. The application should be built with a stack of at least 10240 bytes. This is actually the minimum recommended value and should probably be increased if you are doing anything of consequence within your application.

The first HiTest API used within the CLIPSERV application is **HTInit()**. As with its corollary API in the Notes C API, **NotesInit()**, this API must be the first API called when using the HiTest C API set. Conversely, the last API to be used in this set is **HTTerm()**, which corresponds to **NotesTerm()** in the Notes C API. **HTInit()**, in its common form, has a single input parameter, the initialization flags. This flag is 0 in most cases, as is with the CLIPSERV application, unless the application is using both the HiTest C API set and the standard Notes C set together.

If both the Notes C API and the HiTest C API are being used within an application, and if the Notes C API has been initialized before **HTInit()** is called, the initialization flags to **HTInit()** should be set to HTINITF_NO_LNAPI. This notifies the HiTest API that **NotesInit()** has already been processed within the application and should not be executed by the API itself. Subsequently, HTTERMF_NO_LNAPI should be passed as the single parameter to **HTTerm()** in this case as well so that HiTest does not call **NotesTerm()** either.

NOTE If you are using both the standard Notes C API and the HiTest C API within your application, take care to make sure that the initialization and termination sequences for each API set are performed correctly. That is, be sure either to use only the HiTest initialization and termination functions, which themselves call the associated standard API functions, or to perform the standard API initialization and termination outside of **HTInit()** and **HTTerm()** using the NO_LNAPI flags.

At the lowest level, **HTInit()** is actually a macro defined on top of the _HTInit() API. _HTInit() has four parameters, only one of which, the initialization flags, have any meaning at this time; ergo, the macro. The other three parameters, the HiTest version, argc and argv have been added for future use.

The **HTInit()** and **HTTerm()** APIs also provide examples of one of the conventions used within the HiTest APIs, the **HT** prefix. Extending into the conventions a bit more, most APIs within this set have up to four sections within the API name. The first is the **HT** prefix. The second is the class name, which is present in all but the Session object. The third is a verb that describes the action taking place, and the fourth is an optional noun modifier. In addition, the first word in each section is capitalized. For example, one of the APIs in the ACL object shows all four name sections:

```
HTACLGetRole()
```

Error Handling: Have It Your Way

The next HiTest API you'll see is **HTErrorSetBuffer()**. This API allows the application to set up error write-back buffers for use with all API calls. There are actually three methods of error handling supported by HiTest. The first, and simplest, is that of a returned status on most every call. If an error condition has occurred, the returned status will be a nonzero value, something other than HTSUCCESS. From this point, another API, **HTErrorFetch()**, can then be called to get any of three error values: the error status, the error severity, and the error text. This method of first checking for an error and then calling another interrogation API is fairly common among other API sets, including the Notes C API set.

NOTE

When this method of error handling is used, care should be taken to remember that each HiTest API call clears any previous error before it begins. For this reason, remember to trap errors as soon as the call in question has been completed.

The error status values, type HTSTATUS, can be either from the Notes C API or from the HiTest C API, depending on the call used. If the error is generated from the HiTest API, the high-order bit is set within the status value. For convenience, a constant (HTAPI_ERROR) has been defined within HiTest to use as a mask against a status value to determine the origin of the error. The following macro can then be used to determine if the status is a HiTest error or not.

```
#define IS_HITEST_ERROR(x) (x & HTAPI_ERROR ? TRUE : FALSE)
```

The HiTest error values are defined as HTFAIL constants within the HTNOTES.H include file. The error severity values, of type HTERRORSEVERITY, are enumerated in HTNOTES.H as well. Table 8.1 contains the list of severity values for the HiTest C API.

Table 8.1 HiTest Error Severity Values

Severity Name	Description	Value
HTERRSEV_NOERROR	No error occurred	0
HTERRSEV_WARNING	Warning	2
HTERRSEV_NONFATAL	Nonfatal (Normal)	4
HTERRSEV_USAGE	Parameter usage	6
HTERRSEV_FATAL	Fatal	8
HTERRSEV_PROGRAM	Notes internal	10

The call to **HTErrorSetBuffer()** is actually used in another form of error handling supported by this API set. This method still relies on the use of the returned status on API calls but eliminates the call to get the error status. This is accomplished by having HiTest store the error information into application-defined buffers before returning from the API call. Here again, as with **HTErrorFetch()**, you may choose to provide write-back buffers for any of the three error values described above.

The last method of error handling supported by this API set is the most aggressive. In this case, your application provides the address of an error callback function to the HiTest engine itself. The API used to perform this is **HTErrorSetProcedure()**. In this method, whenever an error occurs within any HiTest API, the callback routine is called just before control is returned to the caller. **HTErrorSetProcedure()** has two parameters; the first is the address of the callback routine; the second, which is optional, is a 32-bit application-defined value sent to the callback routine. The callback routine has four input parameters, the fourth of which is this application-defined value. From the prototype of the callback provided below, you can see that the first three parameters are the same three error values discussed within the other two methods.

```
typedef HTSTATUS (HTAPICALLBACKPROC HTERRORPROC)(HTSTATUS code,

HTERRORSEVERITY severity,

char *errmsg,

void *buffer);
```

Although an application can use any or all of the three methods of error handling, one will usually suffice. For the CLIPSERV application, the second method was used. It was chosen over the first method simply to reduce the number of API calls used on error conditions. Conversely, the third method was not chosen because we wanted a single control path without having to check yet another global variable after each API call in order to determine if the processing should proceed. To facilitate this error handling usage, the IsStatusOK routine was created within the CLIPSERV application. This routine is called each time a status is returned from the API set and allows for central control over the way errors are reported. We've also added a little twist here in that an error will be reported to the user within a dialog box if the "ReportErrorsToUser=TRUE" flag is set in the CLIPSERV.INI file.

Now that we have the HiTest API set initialized and the error write-back error buffers in place, the next job we need to perform is to find the database that tells us the information on the databases to watch. This is done by looking for a ControlServer and a ControlDatabase keyword phrase in the CLIPSERV.INI file. As we discussed earlier, this control database is expected to have a specific format and, by default, is assumed to be in a local database called CLIPSERV.NSF.

The format of the database is fairly straightforward. It must contain a form named ClipInfo containing the fields defined in Table 8.2.

Table 8.2 ClipInfo Form Fields

FieldName	Datatype	Description
ClipInfo.SendTo	Names	Name of person(s) to send mail to
ClipInfo.UpdateRate	Number	Number of minutes between database checks
ClipInfo.LastUpdate	Time	Date and time of last database check
ClipInfo.Server	Text	Name of server containing database(s)
ClipInfo.Databases	Text	List of databases to check

Once we know where the control database is, we need to set up a timer for use in determining when to check the watched databases. The timer is set to trigger every minute, allowing us to check for database updates at one-minute intervals.

The last thing we do before "firing-up" the application is to post ourselves a WM_INIT_CLIP_SERVICE message to get the information from the control database. We could have done this in the WinMain() procedure but it seemed to fit better in the main window procedure along with the bulk of the rest of the code. The following code is taken directly from WinMain() within the CLIPSERV application, starting with the call to **HTInit()** and ending with the call to **HTTerm()**.

```
// initialize the Notes HiTest API
if (HTInit(0))
{
    return(0);
}

// set up the error handling buffers
HTErrorSetBuffer(&gHTErrorStatus, &gHTErrorSeverity, gHTErrorText);

// check if errors are to be reported to the user
GetPrivateProfileString("CLIPSERV",
                        "ReportErrorsToUser",
                        "CLIPSERV.NSF",
                        szINIString,
                        sizeof(szINIString),
                        "CLIPSERV.INI");
if ((lstrcmpi(szINIString, "TRUE")) == 0)
{
    gfReportErrorsToUser = TRUE;
}
else
{
    gfReportErrorsToUser = FALSE;
}

// get control database server with clip information (default is
NULL - Local)
GetPrivateProfileString("CLIPSERV",
                        "ControlServer",
                        "",
```

```
                                    gszControlServer,
                                    sizeof(gszControlServer),
                                    "CLIPSERV.INI");

// get control database with clip information (default is
CLIPSERV.NSF)
GetPrivateProfileString("CLIPSERV",
                        "ControlDatabase",
                        "CLIPSERV.NSF",
                        gszControlDatabase,
                        sizeof(gszControlDatabase),
                        "CLIPSERV.INI");

// create a timer to trigger every minute
guiTimerID = SetTimer(ghMainWindow, 1, (WORD) 60000, NULL);

// post ourselves a message to get the control database information
PostMessage(ghMainWindow, WM_INIT_CLIP_SERVICE, 0, 0L);

while (GetMessage(&Message,
                  (HWND) NULL,
                  (WORD) NULL,
                  (WORD) NULL))
{
    TranslateMessage(&Message);
    DispatchMessage(&Message);
}

// destroy our 1 minute timer
KillTimer(ghMainWindow, guiTimerID);

// free all the memory for any clip databases
FreeDatabaseList();

// terminate access to the Notes HiTest API
HTTerm(0);
```

Database Object: A Good Place to Start

At this point, we'll assume we have received our posted WM_INIT_CLIP_SERVICE message within the main window procedure and are ready to get the information for each database to be watched. The first thing we need to do is open the control database. We already have the pertinent information, e.g. database name and server, so all we need to do is call **HTDatabaseOpen()** as shown below.

```
Status = HTDatabaseOpen(gszControlServer,

                        gszControlDatabase,

                        0,

                        &hNotesDB);
```

The inputs to this API are the server name, the database name, and a database open flag word. Of these three, the only one that may raise an eyebrow is the open flag word. In most cases, as in the case here, this flag can be set to 0 and everything will work well. If more functionality is required, one of the following flags can be used.

- HTDBOPENF_PURGE—Purge the database upon opening
- HTDBOPENF_FORCE_FIXUP—Force a database fixup upon opening
- HTDBOPENF_FIXUP_FULL_SCAN—Scan all documents and items
- HTDBOPENF_FIXUP_NO_DELETE—Don't delete bad documents during fixup
- HTDBOPENF_DISCONNECT_ON_ERROR—Close session on error
- HTDBOPENF_NO_ERROR_LOG—Don't log error

The fourth parameter is an output parameter and contains the address of an HTDATABASE. This is a place where, if you're not careful, you'll overlook the fact that this is a function that wraps several Notes C API calls, as well as a chunk of application code, into a single HiTest API call. If you remember from Chapter 7, **NSFDbOpen()** could be called directly when opening a local database but **OSPathNetConstruct()** needed to be called first if the database was on a server. Now, with **HTDatabaseOpen()**, we have one line of code to take the place of several lines.

There are actually 14 different APIs within the Database object. Of these, 7 have direct associates within the Notes C API, as seen in Table 8.3.

Table 8.3 Comparative Database APIs

Notes C API	HiTest C API
HTDatabaseClose	NSFDbClose
HTDatabaseCompact	NSFDbCompact
HTDatabaseCopy	NSFDbCopy
HTDatabaseDelete	NSFDbDelete
HTDatabaseLocateByReplicaid	NSFDbLocateByReplicalD
HTDatabaseOpen	NSFDbOpen

Two other Database object APIs, **HTDatabaseGetProperty()** and **HTDatabaseSetProperty()**, show another way that the HiTest API can reduce the complexity of an application. Rather than creating separate APIs for accessing each type of information within an object, the HiTest API collectively calls all of these pieces of information *object properties* and then creates a single API to access them.

For example, let's say you want to get the ID, class, and title for a database. In the Notes C API, you'd use **NSFDbIDGet()** for the database ID, **NSFDbClassGet()** for the database class, and a combination of **NSFDbInfoGet()** and **NSFDbInfoParse()** for the database title. That's not too bad—four different APIs to get 3 pieces of data—but its not always that easy. To do the same using the HiTest API, you would make three successive calls to the **HTDatabaseGetProperty()** API with three different property constants; HTDATABASE_DBID, HTDATABASE_CLASS, and HTDATABASE_TITLE.

From the prototypes of the two property APIs shown below, you'll notice that the third parameter in each API is a void pointer. This allows for a property-specific data element to be provided with each call. For instance, if you want to get the database title, the third parameter would be the address of a character string to hold the returned title. If, on the other hand, you wanted to get the database replication ID, the address of an HTREPLICAID variable would be used.

```
HTSTATUS HTDatabaseGetProperty(HTDATABASE database,
                               HTDATABASEPROPERTY property,
                               void *value);
HTSTATUS HTDatabaseSetProperty(HTDATABASE database,
                               HTDATABASEPROPERTY property,
                               void *value);
```

Table 8.4 shows the properties that can be get/set for a database(HTDATABASE_) as well as the datatype associated with the property.

Table 8.4 Database Properties

Property	Datatype
CATEGORIES	char[]
CLASS	HTDBCLASS
CREATED	HTDATETIME
DATABASE_FLAGS	HTFLAGS
DATA_LAST_MODIFIED	HTDATETIME
DBID	HTDBID
DBREPL_FLAGS	HTFLAGS
DEFAULT_FORM	HTFORMID
DEFAULT_VIEW	HTVIEWID
DELAY_COMMIT	HTBOOL
DESIGN_LAST_MODIFIED	HTDATETIME
DESIGN_TEMPLATE	char[]
DOCOPEN_DESIGN	HTBOOL
FETCH_DESIGN_FORMULA	HTBOOL
FILEPATH	char[]
FTINDEX_LAST	HTDATETIME
IS_FTINDEXED	HTBOOL
REPLICAID	HTREPLICAID
REPLICA_CUTOFF	HTINT

Table 8.4 Database Properties (continued)

Property	Datatype
REPLICA_PRIORITY	HTREPLICAPRIORITY
SERVER_NAME	char[]
SPACE_FREE	HTINT
SPACE_USED	HTINT
SUMMARY_LIMIT	HTINT
STRICT_BIND	HTBOOL
TEMPLATE_NAME	char[]
TITLE	char[]

The **HTDatabaseCreateFTIndex()** and **HTDatabaseDeleteFTIndex()** calls deal with creating and deleting full text indexes within a database. There are no surprising details about either of these two calls; the parameters provide for the same types of functionality available through the user interface.

The next two database APIs to be discussed, **HTDatabaseList()** and **HTDatabaseListCatalog()**, provide a way to iterate through a list of databases without a callback routine, as needed with **NSFSearch()** in the Notes C API. Within these two APIs you can again see the reduction in code complexity between multiple calls to the same API versus setting up the enumeration callback sequence described in Chapter 7 when using **NSFSearch()**. We'll expand on this when we discuss agent processing later in this chapter. The last database API, **HTDatabaseLocateByTitle()** provides the ability to get a database filename, given the database title. Hopefully you won't need to use this API much as it is an inefficient way to search for a database.

Indexes: Accessing Data with Ease

Now that we have the control database open, the next order of business within CLIPSERV is to get the list of all documents containing clip service information—that is, find all of the documents in the control database created with the ClipInfo form. To do this, we'll create an entity called an *index* within the HiTest API. An index is nothing more than a set of documents within a database. There are actually several different ways to create an index on a database.

- Executing a formula on the database
- Opening a view within the database
- Performing a full text search query on the database
- Executing a selection agent against the database

The method used to create the index in this case is by using a formula. However, the first thing to do is to create an empty Index object on the database. This is done through a call to **HTIndexOpen()**. This requires an input handle to an open database and the address of a variable of type HTINDEX to hold the newly created index on output. The following is an example of how CLIPSERV uses this API.

```
Status = HTIndexOpen(hNotesDB, &ClipInfoIndex);
```

Once we have an index created on the database, we need to get one more piece of information before we actually create the list of documents we need, that being the ClipInfo form ID. To do this, we'll use a Form object API, **HTFormLocateByName()**. Passing the open database handle and the name of the form in question as inputs, the ID of the named form will be returned. If, for any reason, the form cannot be found, HTNULLID will be returned. The code using this call within the CLIPSERV application is shown below.

```
// get the ID of the 'ClipInfo' form for use in the HTIndexSearch API
ClipInfoFormID = HTFormLocateByName(hNotesDB, "ClipInfo");
```

We are now ready to call the **HTIndexSearch()** API, which is used to search the database for the set of documents we need. This API provides the note-searching capabilities of the **NSFSearch()** API within the Notes C API. The first parameter in this API is the database index described above. The next three parameters provide the ability to specify several different pieces of criteria for the search.

The first of these three parameters is optional and contains a formula to be used to restrict the set of documents included in the index. If a formula is used, it is passed to the API in its textual form. This is the usual form for passing formulas within the HiTest API and is another of the notable differences between Notes C API and HiTest C API. In the case of the Notes C API, formulas need to be compiled into their binary form before they are passed to any of the common APIs. In this case, we'll use a value of NULL for the formula text that equates to "SELECT @ALL". We could have created a formula that would select documents based on the form name but the existence of the next parameter makes it a lot easier.

The second parameter of the triad is also optional and contains a form ID. We'll make use of this parameter here since we want all documents in the database built with the ClipInfo form. The last parameter, again optional, is the pointer to an HTDATETIME field or NULL. If the address of an HTDATETIME field is used, only those documents with creation dates on or after the passed date and time will be included in the index. If NULL is used, as is the case below, no selection is performed based on creation date.

```
Status = HTIndexSearch(ClipInfoIndex,
              NULL,
              ClipInfoFormID,
              NULL);
```

NOTE The last parameter in **HTIndexSearch()** performs the same function as the sixth parameter to **NSFSearch()** described in Chapter 7. The difference is that the current date/time is not returned in the **HTIndexSearch()** call as it is in **NSFSearch()**. This is no real problem though since it is really only the current date/time anyway and the **HTDatetimeGetCurrent()** API is always available.

Now that we have an index, let's look at the data. In the Notes C API, we'd open up each document in the list and make subsequent calls to the set of **NSFItemGet*()** APIs to get datatype-specific pieces of data within each document. We could, if we chose to, do the same thing in the HiTest API using a single call, **HTItemFetch()**. In the case of the CLIPSERV application however, we'll use a somewhat different method to arrive at the same information, which will be described in the next section. For now, lets take a closer look at **HTItemFetch()**.

The **HTItemFetch()** API is another good example of how the HiTest C API reduces the complexity of an application compared to the Notes C API. The functionality of several different APIs in the Notes C set is now reduced to a single call in the HiTest set. In addition, as you can see from the prototype of **HTItemFetch()** below, a built-in conversion capability allows having the API perform the datatype conversion as opposed to calling yet another API or doing it on your own.

```
HTSTATUS HTItemFetch(HTDOCUMENT document,    // open document
         char *itemname,        // name of item in document
         HTTYPE *item_type,     // datatype of item
         HTINT *buffer_length,  // length of output buffer
         HTTYPE *buffer_type,   // datatype of output buffer
         void *buffer);         // output buffer
```

A handle to an open document and the name of the item to get the information on are the only two required input parameters to the call. The next parameter is a pointer to the item's datatype which, if set to zero on input, will cause the API to return the datatype on output. The address of the length of the output buffer is next in the list. If NULL, the API assumes that the output buffer is large enough for the requested data. If the address points to a value of 0, the API returns the length of the data on output. If a nonzero value is used, the API will fill text data to that length.

The address of the output buffer type is parameter number five. If the value at this address is zero, the API assumes that no data conversion is required and returns the data in its original data form. If nonzero, the API will attempt to convert the data to requested type. The last parameter is the address of the output buffer for the requested data.

Bindings: Data As You Like It

Although calling **HTItemFetch()** multiple times for each document would work, the HiTest API provides a much better way. Its called *binding*. Basically, this feature allows you to ask the HiTest API to make a connection between a field in a document and a variable within your application. From then on, every time the associated data is read, the HiTest engine will automatically fill the variables with the "bound" data from the data source. This same type of binding is available when accessing data within a specific column in a view, or viewcell, as well.

NOTE

Bound data is read using the **HTIndexLoadDocument()** API, whereas the data is written through **HTIndexUpdateDocument()**.

The API used for binding items in a document is **HTIndexBindItem()** whereas **HTIndexBindViewcell()** is used for binding variables to view columns or viewcells. As you can see from the prototype below, there are nine parameters on the call to **HTIndexBindItem()**.

```
HTSTATUS HTIndexBindItem(HTINDEX index,
                         char *itemname,
                         HTTYPE item_type,
                         HTINT buffer_length,
                         HTTYPE buffer_type,
                         void *buffer,
                         HTINT *actual_length,
                         HTBOOL *null_bool,
                         HTBOOL *update_bool);
```

The first six parameters map to those found on the call to **HTItemFetch()** above with two exceptions. The first is that **HTIndexBindItem()** works on an open index rather than an open document. The second is that the original item type, buffer length, and returned item type are all input-only parameters and are passed as the actual values rather than as pointers.

The last three parameters on this API are all address values and are used when bound data is either read or written. The function of either can be ignored if a NULL value is used. The first of the three is the address of an integer value to contain the actual length of the returned data. When data is read, this value is filled with the actual length of the data. When data is written and this value is nonzero, only the specified length of data is written. If set to 0, HiTest will determine the data length automatically.

The next parameter deals with how items with no corresponding data are handled. If data is read and the specified item does not exist in the data set, a TRUE value is returned here. If the item does exist, this value is set to FALSE. If this value is set to TRUE and a write is performed with an item that contains no data, an empty item is stored. If FALSE is used in this situation, the item is not written to the data repository.

The last of the three is always set to FALSE when reading data. When writing data, set this value to TRUE to have HiTest update this item in the data set. If set to FALSE when writing data, this item will not be changed in the data set.

In the CLIPSERV application, because we have chosen not to use any of the information provided by these last three parameters, a NULL value is used for all. The code below shows how the **HTIndexBindItem()** API is used within CLIPSERV to bind to the SendTo character field, the UpdateRate numeric field, the LastUpdate date/time field, and the server name character field within each document created with the ClipInfo form.

```
// bind the items we want for each document to local variables
Status = HTSUCCESS;
Status |= HTIndexBindItem(ClipInfoIndex,
                "ClipInfo.SendTo",
                0,
                0,
                HTTYPE_TEXT,
                szSendTo,
                NULL,
                NULL,
                NULL);
```

```
Status |= HTIndexBindItem(ClipInfoIndex,
                     "ClipInfo.UpdateRate",
                     0,
                     0,
                     HTTYPE_NUMBER,
                     &dUpdateRate,
                     NULL,
                     NULL,
                     NULL);

Status |= HTIndexBindItem(ClipInfoIndex,
                     "ClipInfo.LastUpdate",
                     0,
                     0,
                     HTTYPE_DATETIME,
                     &LastUpdate,
                     NULL,
                     NULL,
                     NULL);

Status |= HTIndexBindItem(ClipInfoIndex,
                     "ClipInfo.Server",
                     0,
                     0,
                     HTTYPE_TEXT,
                     szServer,
                     NULL,
                     NULL,
                     NULL);
```

Now we're finally ready to look at the data in the index. To do this, we need to navigate through the list of documents. As with many functions within the HiTest API, there are several ways to do so. One way is to use a scheme that accesses documents based on the relative position within the list, much like the Find First, Find Next sequence for finding files on some operating systems. The API used to perform this type of navigation is **HTIndexNavigate()**. Among the parameters on the call to

HTIndexNavigate() are a direction flag and a navigation flag. This API is especially useful if you want to navigate through indexes set on views due to the presence of parent and child relationships, category direction, and navigation flags.

The other type of navigation, and the one used within CLIPSERV, is an absolute addressing method. In this method, a call to **HTIndexGetCount()** finds the number of documents in the index. Subsequent calls to **HTIndexSetPosition()** are used to set an absolute position in the list using a counter. Both of these APIs are quite simple and each requires the specification of an open index on input. Using just this, **HTIndexGetCount()** returns an HTINT value containing the number of entries in the index. **HTIndexSetPosition()** takes another input value, a 1-based position within the index, to perform its function.

Once the position in the index has been set by one method or another, the previously mentioned **HTIndexLoadDocument()** is used to load the bound data for the document at the current position in the index. **HTIndexLoadDocument()**, as with most of the **HTIndex*()** APIs, takes an open index as the first parameter. The second parameter is a flag used to determine how much information is loaded for the specified document. Table 8.5 contains the list of these flags, as well as the kind of data loaded when each is used.

Table 8.5 Document Open Flags

Flag	Description
HTDOCOPENF_SUMMARY_ONLY	Read summary items only
HTDOCOPENF_EXPAND_LIST	Expand all single-value items into lists
HTDOCOPENF_NO_OBJECTS	Do not read attached objects
HTDOCOPENF_ABSTRACT	Only read an abstract of the document

The last parameter on the call is the address of an HTDOCUMENT variable. This is where the resultant data from the read is placed. The excerpt from CLIPSERV below shows that only the summary data for the requested document is loaded since there should not be any other types of data in these documents.

```
Status = HTIndexLoadDocument(ClipInfoIndex,
                             HTDOCOPENF_SUMMARY_ONLY,
                             &Document);
```

NOTE You'll notice that immediately after the call to **HTIndexLoadDocument()**, a special check is made on the returned status to determine if the status is ERR_NOTE_DELETED. This is a Notes C API error code that is passed through the HiTest C API to state that the current note has been deleted and only the deletion stub remains. The need for this constant is why the two Notes C API header files were included in the top of CLIPSERV.C.

At this point, we have a document with summary information at our disposal. We also have our bound variables filled with the appropriate data from the document. However, we still need one more piece of information from the document that we didn't bind to: the list of databases to watch. We chose not to bind to the information because we wanted to show another method of getting data out of a document that is, as is said in HiTest, *unbound*.

Unbound data is basically data within the document that we have to access the old-fashioned way—with a little work. We've already talked about how to do this using the **HTItemFetch()** API but this time we're going to use something a little different. The API is called **HTItemGetPointer()**. The difference between **HTItemGetPointer()** and **HTItemFetch()** deals with who owns the space where the returned data is placed. In **HTItemFetch()**, the calling application must determine the amount of memory required to hold the requested data, allocate it, lock it, request it, then eventually unlock and free it. **HTItemGetPointer()**, on the other hand, manages all of the memory for the data internal to the API itself, including releasing it when the document is closed.

From the prototype for **HTItemGetPointer()** shown below, you can see that the only difference between the parameter lists of these two functions is that the last parameter to **HTItemGetPointer()** is an address to hold the item data pointer.

```
HTSTATUS HTItemGetPointer(HTDOCUMENT document,    // open document
   char *itemname,           // name of item in document
   HTTYPE *item_type,        // datatype of item
   HTINT *buffer_length,     // length of output buffer
   HTTYPE *buffer_type,      // datatype of output buffer
   void **buffer);           // address of output buffer allocated by API
```

NOTE
Since this memory is owned by the HiTest API itself, the data within this buffer should be considered read-only and should not be modified, reallocated, or freed. In addition, care should be taken to make sure the pointer is not used after the document is closed, as it will no longer be valid.

Although we have talked about the great automatic conversion capabilities provided through some of these APIs, we have not as yet used any of them. The sample code taken from the CLIPSERV application below shows a simple example of how easy it is to do so. Even though our conversion is from a possible TEXT type to a TEXT_LIST type, the call would be no different if a more esoteric conversion was required.

```
DatabaseListDatatype = HTTYPE_TEXT_LIST;
Status = HTItemGetPointer(Document,
                     "ClipInfo.Databases",
                     0,
                     &DatabaseListLength,
                     &DatabaseListDatatype,
                     &lpDatabaseList);
```

In this case, all we want to do is to always force the list of databases to be just that, a text list. This is done so that we can always use the same APIs, **HTTextList*()**, to parse the information in the list. The first call in this genre we'll use is **HTTextListGetCount()**. Given the pointer to a text list, returned from our call to **HTItemGetPointer()**, this API will return the number of strings—or in our case, databases—in the list. Once we have the count, we'll index through them using the **HTTestListFetch()**

API. Then, for each database in the list, we'll create another entry in our global database information structure, hDatabaseInfo, and fill it with the data required to check the database and mail a message if an update is found. The information tracked for each database is shown in Table 8.6.

Table 8.6 CLIPSERV Database Information

Description	Datatype
Mail Destination	char[]
Update Rate(in minutes)	WORD
Server Name	char[]
Database Name	char[]
Document ID	HTDOCID
Last Search Time	HTDATETIME

All we have left to do from an initialization standpoint in CLIPSERV is to close the index we created within the control database, using **HTIndexClose(),** and close the database itself with **HTDatabaseClose().**

Initialized! Now that we have an internal list of all of the databases we want to watch, we'll check if any of them have data ready for us right away. After this initial check, the timer we created in WinMain() will notify us at one-minute intervals by sending us a WM_TIMER message. From here, a determination will be made, based off the update rate, on whether to check a specific database for new activity.

The first thing to do when we start to look for new database activity is to look down the list of databases and loop through each one to determine if it is time to check for updates. If so, we'll call an internal routine, ProcessClipDatabase(), to perform the update checks and, if required, mail out the notices. When we're through checking the database, we'll update the ClipInfo.LastUpdate field within the document so that we don't get the same data again (we'll leave that processing for a bit later).

In ProcessClipDatabase(), the first task is to open the indexed database we will be watching by using an API used earlier in the initialization phase, **HTDatabaseOpen().** Then we'll use another API we've used before, **HTIndexOpen()**, to open an empty index on the database.

What we want now is a list of all of the database documents that have been added or modified since the last time we checked the database, or the initial time put into the control database. To do so, we'll use **HTIndexSearch()**, this time using a time/date stamp for the search criterion as opposed to a form ID. For this, HTNULLID is used as the form ID, the third parameter, and the address of the time/date stamp when we last checked the database in parameter four. The call is shown below.

```
Status = HTIndexSearch(NoteIndex,

                NULL,

                HTNULLID,

                &(lpClipDatabaseInfo->LastSearchDateTime));
```

We'll then use **HTDatetimeGetCurrent()** to get the current time and date so that we can track when we last checked the database. After that, we'll use **HTIndexBindItem()** to bind to the form name of each document in the index for use in the subject name of the mail messages. **HTIndexGetCount()**, **HTIndexSetPosition()**, and **HTIndexLoadDocument()** are used again to loop through all of the documents, if any, that have a time/date stamp matching the criterion so that we can mail each document to the appropriate destination.

The mail message to be sent for each newly created/modified document will have, as a subject line, the server, database, and form name for the document. For instance, if a database named UPDATES.NSF was being watched on server SERVER1 and a document was found that was created using the form named UPDATE_FORM, the subject line for the message would be:

```
\\SERVER1\UPDATES.NSF\UPDATE_FORM
```

The goal is now to set up the document in question so that we can use it as the body of the message to be sent. To do so, we need to open the document and then set the STRICT_BIND property within it. This is done to allow the form to be used for interpreting the document when used as the body for the mail message. Of the two API calls made to perform these operations, the first is one we have used before, **HTDocumentOpen()**. The only difference here is that we want to open the document with all information included, rather than in summary. This is done by using a 0 as the document open flags.

The other API used here is **HTDocumentSetProperty()**. The open document, the property type, HTDOCUMENT_STRICT_BIND, and the address of a Boolean value set to TRUE are the parameters used here. The only other properties available to a Document object are the document class, HTDOCUMENT_CLASS, and the universal note ID of the document's parent, HTDOCUMENT_PARENT_UNID.

Mail: As Easy as Can Be

Within the HiTest C API set, there are only two mail APIs, **HTMailCreate()** and **HTMailSend()**. This is a dramatic reduction from the 50+ APIs available for mail in the Notes C API for version 4.0. As mentioned earlier, this variety can be a feature if you want to do very simple mail manipulations, as is the case here, but can be somewhat limiting if you require a lot of flexibility and customization within the mail interface.

The functionality within the **HTMailCreate()** API allows for the creation of a mail message from either an existing note, a HTMEMO structure, or both. The first parameter to the call is a reference to an open database where the document will be created. The second is an optional reference to a document to be used as the source of information for the mail message. In the case of the CLIPSERV application, we'll want to use the document we just opened as the source document. This parameter is required for all mail types except one, a memo. In the case of a memo, all of the data can be supplied within the third parameter, a pointer to an HTMEMO structure shown below.

```
typedef struct
{
    char *send_to;              // Main recipients
    char *copy_to;              // Optional copy recipients
```

```
    char *blind_copy_to;          // Optional blind copy recipients
    char *subject;                // Subject
    char *body_text;              // Use as body only if body_comp is
                                  // HTNULLHANDLE
    HTCOMPOSITE body_comp;        // Use as body, HTNULLHANDLE to use
                                  // ASCII text at body_text instead
    HTMAILPRIORITY priority;      // Delivery priority
    HTMAILREPORT report;          // Delivery report
    HTBOOL return_receipt;        // Whether to request return receipt
} HTMEMO;                         // Simple mail memo structure
```

The HTMEMO structure contains all of the information necessary to complete a simple memo mail message. It can be used alone, or in concert with a source document to create a complete mail message. If both are used, the information in the HTMEMO structure takes precedence over that contained in the source document. This allows for an easy and standard way to know how to override specific pieces of information for use within the message.

NOTE

Since the data in the HTMEMO structure always overrides data within the source document, care should be taken to clear the structure before each use to verify that no unwanted data is used.

Parameter number four in the call to **HTMailCreate()** is the mail type. Table 8.7 shows the possible mail types available within the API.

Table 8.7 HiTest Mail Types

Mail Type	Description
HTMAILTYPE_MEMO	Standard memo
HTMAILTYPE_FORWARD	Standard memo, body is an image of source document
HTMAILTYPE_REPLY	Standard reply, obtains SendTo item from source document
HTMAILTYPE_REPLY_TO_ALL	Standard reply to all, obtains SendTo and CopyTo items from source document.

Each of these types has specific requirements on the source document and on the HTMEMO structure. We've already mentioned that the MEMO type can be created with either of the two or a combination of both. The FORWARD type, the type used in CLIPSERV, is the same as the MEMO type but also requires a source document for the body of the document. The REPLY and REPLY_TO_ALL types both require a source document for the SendTo and SendTo/CopyTo items respectively. They, too, can gather the rest of the information from either or both the source document and HTMEMO structure. The last parameter on the call to **HTMailCreate()** is the address of an HTDOCUMENT. This will hold the newly created document if the call succeeds.

The **HTMailSend()** API is used to send the message document on its way after all of the items within it have been filled out. The two parameters on the call are the open document and a flag used either to state that the message should be saved to the user's mail database or whether the form is to be embedded in the message. We've used the HTMAILF_EMBED_FORM flag here since we cannot assume the form used to create the message will be available to the recipient in the destination database. The constant for the other flag for use here is HTMAILF_SAVE_MAIL.

The code that performs all of the mail initialization and mail transfer steps within the CLIPSERV application is shown below. You'll notice that there are actually two calls to **HTMailSend()**. The second call is used to send the mail message if the current user does not have access to the form used to create the original document. If such is the case, as denoted by a failure status of HTFAIL_FORM_UNAVAIL, the second parameter in this call is set to 0. This will send the message without embedding the form. This should, in most cases, provide enough information to complete the notification process.

```
// clear the HTMEMO structure
// (this is needed so no uninitialized data
//  is used within the mail message)
_fmemset(&MemoInfo, 0, sizeof(HTMEMO));

// set the destination of the message
MemoInfo.send_to = lpClipDatabaseInfo->szSendTo;

// set the subject to \\server\database\form
```

```
    if ((lstrlen(lpClipDatabaseInfo->szServer)) > 0)
    {
        lstrcpy(szSubject, "\\\\");
        lstrcat(szSubject, lpClipDatabaseInfo->szServer);
        lstrcat(szSubject, "\\");
    }
    else
    {
        lstrcpy(szSubject, "");
    }
    lstrcat(szSubject, lpClipDatabaseInfo->szDatabase);
    lstrcat(szSubject, "\\");
    lstrcat(szSubject, szForm);
    MemoInfo.subject = szSubject;

    // create the mail message using the
    // bound document as the message body
    Status = HTMailCreate(hNotesDB,
                        BoundDocument,
                        &MemoInfo,
                        HTMAILTYPE_FORWARD,
                        &MailDocument);
    if (StatusIsOK(Status))
    {
        // send the mail message on its way
        Status = HTMailSend(MailDocument,
                        HTMAILF_EMBED_FORM);

        // if the form isn't available, send without
        if (Status == HTFAIL_FORM_UNAVAIL)
        {
            Status = HTMailSend(MailDocument,
                            0);
        }

        // report any errors on sending
        StatusIsOK(Status);
    }
}
```

The last thing we need to do before we are through with the mail process for the document is to close the bound document using the **HTDocumentClose()** API.

CLIPSERV: Where do We Go from Here?

The first thing usually asked whenever we showed the CLIPSERV application to someone was "Can I have a doc-link to the document rather than the document itself?" The answer to this question is "Yes, but it will take a little work." The work involved here has to do with the use of two new object types within the HiTest API, namely the Composite and CDRecord objects, as well as gathering the extra information necessary to create the doc-link. If you want to get to this level of sophistication, you may want to take a good look at some of the sample applications that ship with the API itself and plan for a little fun.

AGENTRUN: Effortless Agent Processing

As we mentioned in Chapter 6, one of the areas where the HiTest C API excels over the Notes C API is in the area of processing macros, or in the new vernacular, *agents*. We mentioned the Notes C API sample application called RUNMACRO and the 1500 lines of code required to run a macro. What we didn't mention was that there are no actual macro APIs in the Notes C API set. Macro processing within the Notes C API is performed using a combination of NSF, NIF, ID, OS, and several other classes of APIs.

In contrast, the HiTest C API has an Agent object type that contains seven specific APIs. The presence of this object makes agent processing much easier. Even more impressive is the dramatic reduction in the sheer number of calls required to process an agent. To show just how dramatic this is, we'll create an application called AGENTRUN (\HITESTC\WIN16\AGENTRUN) that provides the functionality of the RUNMACRO Notes C sample application plus a whole lot more, in a lot less code. Actually, the code required in the HiTest C API to duplicate the features present in RUNMACRO may approach 20 to 30 lines, at best.

Although it isn't effortless, it will probably appear that way if you have ever used the Notes C API to perform this type of processing.

The rest of AGENTRUN provides a user interface to list the agents available within any Notes database and subsequently display all of the object-specific information for each when selected. As with the DBVIEWER application in Chapter 7, the user-interface used within AGENTRUN is quite simple, a single client window with lots of controls. Again, this was done to allow for more concentration on the functionality of the API set rather than the user-interface code.

As with the CLIPSERV application above, AGENTRUN is provided in both 32-bit and 16-bit Windows versions. The 32-bit version was again created with Visual C++ 2.0 on Windows NT and the 16-bit version using Microsoft's Visual C++ 1.5 on Windows 3.11 and both versions using Notes version 3.x. Again, the only differences within the two projects are in the build processing files. The source and includes are the same.

You'll notice the definition of HTOS_WIN3 (or HTOS_WINNT) again at the top of AGENTRUN.C. As with CLIPSERV. C, this define tells HiTest to set up the include files for use with 16-bit (or 32-bit) Windows. Within WinMain(), **HTInit()** and **HTTerm()** are again used to initialize and terminate HiTest. The only other processing of substance within WinMain() is the creation of the modeless dialog box that will be the main processing window for AGENTRUN.

When the dialog box is created, Windows sends the WM_INITDIALOG message to the AgentDialogProc() procedure. This is where we will gather all of the available servers and display them in a listbox. It is within the message processing for this case that we see more signs of code reduction. If you think back to the DBVIEWER code in Chapter 7, we created the ServerList_Get(), ServerList_GetServer-Count(), ServerList_GetIndexedServer(), and ServerList_Destroy() functions to wrap the Notes C API calls required to get the list of all of the servers available. When all was said and done, this amounted to about 40 lines of code. Now, through the use of the **HTServerList()** API within HiTest, we have reduced the code to a single call!

The call to **HTServerList()** has only two parameters. The first is a list enumeration flag and the second is the address of a string to hold the referenced server name. The set of six enumeration flags common to all of HiTest's object listing APIs is shown in Table 8.8.

Table 8.8 HiTest List Enumeration Flags

Flag	Description
HTLIST_REFRESH	Refresh the list and get the first entry
HTLIST_FIRST	Get the first entry
HTLIST_LAST	Get the last entry
HTLIST_NEXT	Get the next entry
HTLIST_PREVIOUS	Get the previous entry
HTLIST_CURRENT	Get the current entry

Using a combination of HTLIST_REFRESH and HTLIST_NEXT, the only server not enumerated using this API is the Local server. To allow for this omission, AGENTRUN places the Local server in the list first and processes it as a special case further on down the way. The code that creates the list of servers within the "Servers" combo box of AGENTRUN is shown below.

```
// clear the list of servers
SendDlgItemMessage(hDialog,
                IDC_SERVERS,
                CB_RESETCONTENT,
                0,
                0);
SendDlgItemMessage(hDialog,
                IDC_SERVERS,
                CB_ADDSTRING,
                0,
                (LPARAM) (LPSTR) "Local");

Status = HTServerList(HTLIST_FIRST, (LPSTR) szServer);
while (Status == HTSUCCESS)
{
    SendDlgItemMessage(hDialog,
```

```
                     IDC_SERVERS,
                     CB_ADDSTRING,
                     0,
                     (LPARAM) (LPSTR) szServer);
        Status = HTServerList(HTLIST_NEXT, (LPSTR) szServer);
    }
```

Figure 8.2 shows "Servers" listbox filled with several different servers.

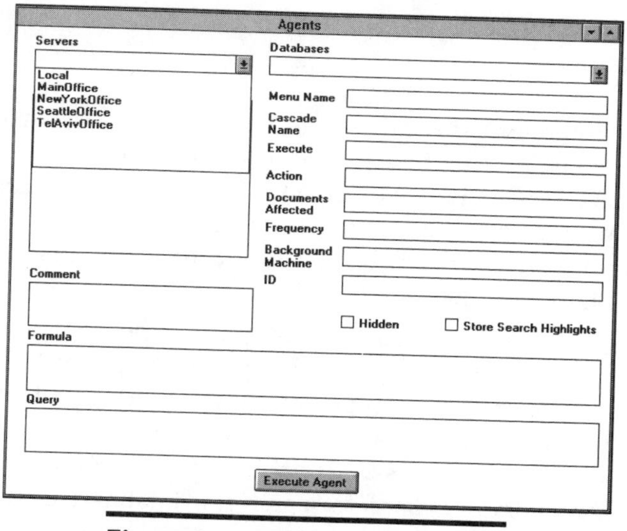

Figure 8.2 AGENTRUN server list.

Once the list of servers is created and the user selects a server from the
list, Windows sends the CBN_SELCHANGE message from the Servers
combo box to the dialog box procedure. The job now is to create a list of
the databases available on the selected server. The difference among the
Notes C API and the HiTest C API in this case is even more striking. The
DatabaseList_*() functions we created in DBVIEWER are a bit more
involved, given the use of the **NSFSearch()** API and the associated
enumeration routines. This time the code reduction comparison among
the two API sets falls in the 100:1 category.

The single HiTest call used in this case is **HTDatabaseList()**. This call
has a few more parameters than does **HTServerList()**, eight in all, but

still provides a single call to enumerate through the entire list of databases. The prototype for the API is shown below.

```
HTSTATUS HTDatabaseList(char *server,        // Input, Optional
                        char *directory,     // Input, Optional
                        HTDBLISTCLASS dblist_class, // Input
                        HTFLAGS dblist_flags,    // Input
                        HTLIST list,             // Input
                        HTBOOL *is_database,     // Output, Optional
                        char *title,             // Output, Optional
                        char *filepath);         // Output, Optional
```

The first parameter in the call is the name of the server on which to perform the search. This is either one of the server names obtained through the **HTServerList()** API or NULL if the list is to come from the local Notes installation. The second parameter is the path to use for the search, relative to the server's Notes data directory. This parameter can be set to NULL to start the search at the data directory itself.

The third parameter is used to specify the type of files to search for. This value can range from searching specifically for databases, directories, and several other types of files, including all file types. The set of HTDBLIST_* constants that can be used here can be found in HTNOTES.H. In the case of the AGENTRUN application, HTDBLIST_DATABASE is used to search for databases only.

The fourth parameter in the list is used to tell the API how to traverse through the directory structure when searching. The possible values here are actually a subset of the FILE_CLASS types available for use in the fifth parameter to **NSFSearch()** when searching for files.

- HTDBLISTF_RECURSIVE—Recurse into subdirectories
- HTDBLISTF_NO_UPDIRS—Do not return the directory entry ".."
- HTDBLISTF_SUBDIRS—Return subdirectories

The fifth parameter is one of the list enumeration flags from Table 8.7 and the sixth is the address of a Boolean value filled on output with TRUE if the current file is a database entry and FALSE if it is a subdirectory specification. The last two parameters are addresses to strings that are filled on output with the database name and the database path, the $TITLE and $Path items, respectively.

NOTE

If you are not interested in knowing whether the returned file is a database or a subdirectory, set the sixth parameter in the call to **HTDatabaseList()** to NULL.

Although most of the processing in AGENTRUN for this message deals with clearing and setting up the format for the strings to be placed into the Databases combo box list, the calls made to **HTDatabaseList()** within it are shown in the coding below. Figure 8.3 then shows the database list resulting from a search of the databases on the local system.

```
Status = HTDatabaseList((LPSTR) gszCurrentServer,
                    NULL,
                    HTDBLIST_DATABASE,
                    HTDBLISTF_RECURSIVE | HTDBLISTF_NO_UPDIRS,
                    HTLIST_REFRESH,
                    NULL,
                    szTitle,
                    szPath);

while (Status == HTSUCCESS)
{
    lstrcpy(szDBName, szPath);
    lstrcat(szDBName, "\\");
    lstrcat(szDBName, szTitle);
    SendDlgItemMessage(hDialog,
                    IDC_DATABASES,
                    CB_ADDSTRING,
                    0,
                    (LPARAM) (LPSTR) szDBName);
Status = HTDatabaseList((LPSTR) gszCurrentServer,
                    NULL,
                    HTDBLIST_DATABASE,
```

```
              HTDBLISTF_RECURSIVE | HTDBLISTF_NO_UPDIRS,
              HTLIST_NEXT,
              NULL,
              szTitle,
              szPath);

    }
```

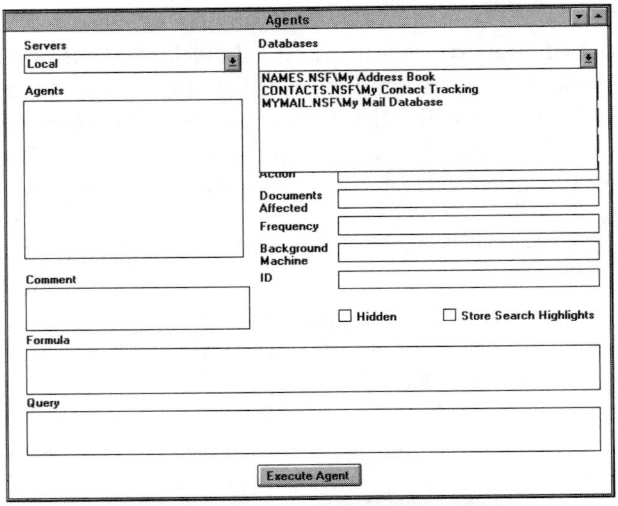

Figure 8.3 AGENTRUN database list.

With the list of databases on the server now created, the user selects one of the databases in the list to request the display of a list of agents within the database. This time the CBN_SELCHANGE message sent from Windows is related to the Databases combo box. This process of enumerating the agents within a database constitutes the first use of the Agent object APIs within AGENTRUN.

As with the processing involved in displaying the server and database lists, most of the code required to create the agents list deals with preparing and formatting data for the user-interface. The essential part of the work done here uses an agent API that performs the same enumeration function as **HTServerList()** and **HTDatabaseList()**. This time the API is named **HTAgentList()**.

The first thing we need to do is open the database that will be the target of the search. The handle to this open database will be used as the first parameter to **HTAgentList()**. We'll do this through the **HTDatabaseOpen()** API, a call we've already discussed. The server name and database name for the call are gathered from the previous selections made in the Servers and Databases combo boxes. When we're through accessing information from the database, we'll use **HTDatabaseClose()** to close it.

With the database open, the call to **HTAgentList()** is quite simple. Given a database and an HTLIST_ traversal constant, the call fills an HTAGENTSUMM structure, passed in the third, and final, parameter. The HTAGENTSUMM structure, shown below, is intended to hold a summary of the information available for an agent.

```
typedef struct
{
    HTAGENTID agentid;                          // Agent ID
    HTBOOL hidden;                              // TRUE if agent is hidden
    char name[HTMAXLEN_DESIGN_NAME];            // Agent name
    char menu_name[HTMAXLEN_MENU_NAME];         // Menu display name
    char cascade_name[HTMAXLEN_MENU_NAME];      // Cascading display name
} HTAGENTSUMM;                                   // Agent summary information
```

NOTE

The name of the structure containing the detailed agent information is HTAGENT and can be obtained through the use of the **HTAgentFetch()** API to be discussed later.

The first entry in the HTAGENTSUMM structure is the agent ID. This ID uniquely identifies all of the agents within a database and is the primary method of addressing agents within the API. The only agent API that uses the agent name as an identifier rather than the ID is **HTAgentLocateByName()**, and it returns an agent ID.

The second entry in the structure is used to determine whether or not the agent is hidden from view within the Notes user interface. Background and mail/paste agents are hidden by default, whereas the other types of agents can optionally be hidden at design time.

The next three entries within the structure all deal with the names available within an agent. These three names are defined through the use of a specific format within the agent name space. The format of the name space is as follows:

```
MENU_NAME\CASCADE_NAME|NAME
```

The first name within the structure, and the last in the above format, is the agent design name. This is the only name of the three that is required for an agent. It is this name that is used when accessing the agent from anywhere other than the user interface, and, if the menu and cascade names are not used, it is used in the user interface as well.

The second and third name entries, the menu and cascade names, are related only to the user interface. The menu name is the name used whenever the list of agents within a database is displayed through the user interface. The cascade name is used to further group a set of macros within the user interface by providing a secondary, cascading name to appear in addition to the menu name. For example, let's assume that we create three macros, all dealing with merging information among different databases. Assuming that the first operates on customers, the second on employees, and the third on vendors, we could set up the cascading menus to provide a grouping effect. The fully qualified names of the three might be:

- Merge\Customers|MergeNumber1
- Merge\Employees|MergeNumber2
- Merge\Vendors|MergeNumber3

Figure 8.4 shows how this cascading menu would look using Notes version 4.0.

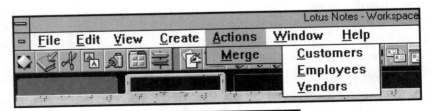

Figure 8.4 Cascading menus.

In the case of the AGENTRUN application, we'll display the agent design name in the listbox. We could have used the actual name used when displayed within the user interface but the logic required to do it is pretty easy and of little value in this case. As for the rest of the information in the summary structure, we are only going to save the agent ID and the hidden flag for each agent we find within the database. We'll save this information in a global handle (ghAgents), using a routine called AddAgentToList() for use later when the user selects a specific agent to view. We won't save the names here since they are given to us again when within the agent detail structure that we'll discuss in just a bit. This processing within AGENTRUN is shown below.

```
Status = HTAgentList(AgentDatabase,
                    HTLIST_REFRESH,
                    &AgentSummary);

while (Status == HTSUCCESS)
{
    // save summary information in local memory
    AddAgentToList(&AgentSummary);

//  add agent name to UI list
    SendDlgItemMessage(hDialog,
                    IDC_AGENTS,
                    LB_ADDSTRING,
                    0,
                    (LPARAM) (LPSTR) &(AgentSummary.name));

//  get the next agent in the list
    Status = HTAgentList(AgentDatabase,
                    HTLIST_NEXT,
                    &AgentSummary);
}
```

All of the agents, if any, within the selected database have now been presented to the user in the Agents listbox. When one is selected, we get an LBN_SELCHANGE message from Windows. (We get the listbox version of this message since the Agents list is a true listbox not a listbox within a combo box.) Now we are ready to get to the heart of the matter, accessing and displaying all of the information we can get on the selected agent. To do this, as noted above, we'll use the **HTAgentFetch()** API.

HTAgentFetch() has three parameters: the handle of an open database, an agent ID, and the address of an HTAGENT structure. To provide for this, we need to once again open the selected database on the selected server using **HTDatabaseOpen()**. Now we need to get the selected agent's ID. This task is quite easy since we stored the IDs of all of the agents before we put them in the list. To do the job of accessing the ID of the selected agent and gathering the agent summary and detail information, we created a routine called GetIndexedAgent().

The first thing done in GetIndexedAgent() is to get the summary information we saved for the selected agent. After saving this information in the passed AGENT_INFO structure, we are ready for the task of getting the agent detail information. Before doing so, however, we need to do one more piece of setup work—set the FETCH_DESIGN_FORMULA property in the database containing the agent. This is required so that the agent's formula can be properly accessed through the **HTAgentFetch()** call. **HTDatabaseSetProperty()** is used to set this property as follows.

```
// this flag must be set to get agent information
HTDatabaseSetProperty(AgentDatabase,
                HTDATABASE_FETCH_DESIGN_FORMULA,
                &fTrue);
```

The components within the HTAGENT, or agent detail, structure, the address of which is passed as the third parameter to **HTAgentFetch()**, are shown below. Notice that the design name, menu name, and cascade name for the agent are contained in this structure as well as in the summary structure discussed above.

```
typedef struct
{
    HTFLAGS agent_flags;          // Agent flags (HTAGENTF_xxx)
    HTAGENTEXECUTE execute;       // Where to execute from
    HTAGENTACTION action;         // Action to take
```

```
    HTAGENTDOCS docs;                        // Documents to apply to
    HTAGENTFREQUENCY background_freq;         // Background agent frequency
    char *comment;                           // Comment
    char *formula;                           // Formula
    char *ftsearch_query;                // Agent full text search query
    char *background_machine;            // Background agent target machine
    char name[HTMAXLEN_DESIGN_NAME];        // Agent name
    char menu_name[HTMAXLEN_MENU_NAME];     // Menu display name
    char cascade_name[HTMAXLEN_MENU_NAME];  // Cascading display name
} HTAGENT;                                   // Agent design information
```

We are now back in the LBN_SELCHANGE message processing after the call to GetIndexedAgent(). We have the agent summary and detail information and are ready to display it to the user. Since much of the work involved in doing this is nothing more than setting strings into edit controls in the dialog box, we'll skip the coding details here. What we will do is discuss each item within the HTAGENT structure as it appears when it is displayed within the dialog box. Figure 8.5 shows the Agents dialog box for a background agent within a sample database for use as a reference for the agent display description to follow.

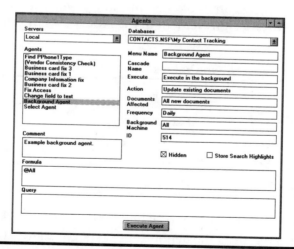

Figure 8.5 AGENTRUN Agents dialog box: background agent.

The first two pieces of information to be processed are the two items from the agent summary structure we saved earlier—the agent ID and the agent's hidden flag. To do this, we'll convert the ID to a hexadecimal string for display in a read-only edit control and the hidden flag will be used to set a check box control.

The agent flags are next in the list. Although called the agent flags, there is only a single flag that is currently defined within the word, HTAGENTF_HIGHLIGHT. This flag is set if the search highlights produced from a full text search query are stored within the documents. This causes the highlights to be displayed whenever the document is opened. A simple ANDing of the flag word and the constant is used to set another check box within the dialog box.

The next four pieces of information put into the dialog box are the second, third, fourth, and fifth items in the HTAGENT structure. These are the only remaining items in the structure that we need to convert to a string before displaying. Because of this conversion requirement, we have created for each item a different routine that takes the item type as input and returns the text string that will represent the type.

The first in this list is the HTAGENTEXECUTE type. The execute type defines where and/or how the agent is initiated. The four possible values here, described in Table 8.9, are fairly self-explanatory and are related directly to a design element in the Notes user interface.

Table 8.9 Agent Execute Type Values

Type	Definition
HTAGENTEXEC_MENU	Execute from menu
HTAGENTEXEC_BACKGROUND	Execute in the background
HTAGENTEXEC_PASTE_MAIL	Execute when document is mailed or pasted
HTAGENTEXEC_EXECUTE_ONCE	Execute once

The conversion routine for this type flag is GetExecuteTypeString().

The next of the four is the action type, HTAGENTACTION. This type has three possible values that again correspond directly to a design element within the user interface. The routine named GetActionTypeString() is used to convert among the values shown in Table 8.10.

Table 8.10 Agent Action Type Values

Type	Definition
HTAGENTACT_UPDATE	Update existing documents
HTAGENTACT_SELECT	Select documents
HTAGENTACT_CREATE	Create new documents

NOTE There is one interdependency within the agent action and execute types. The HTAGENTACT_SELECT action is available only if the agent is executed from the menu, HTAGENTEXECUTE_MENU. This dependency is quite logical in that the other three execute types either do not operate within the scope of a view, background, and mail/paste, or already operate on a view selection, execute once.

The HTAGENTSDOCS type is a bit more involved in that there a six possible values and there are a few more dependencies based on the execute type. This value details the set of documents upon which the agent will be run. GetDocsTypeString() is the routine created to handle the type to string conversion among the types described in Table 8.11.

Table 8.11 Agent Documents Type Values

Type	Definition
HTAGENTDOCS_ALL	Run on all documents in the database
HTAGENTDOCS_UNREAD	Run only on unread documents
HTAGENTDOCS_VIEW	Run on all documents in the current view
HTAGENTDOCS_SELECTED_VIEW	Run on selected documents in current view
HTAGENTDOCS_MAIL	Run on mailed documents
HTAGENTDOCS_NEW	Run on documents created/modified since last run

The interdependencies here are that a background agent cannot run against selected documents within a view, and execute-once agents must always have a HTAGENTDOCS_SELECTED_VIEW documents type. The other dependency is that background and mail/paste agents must always have a documents type of HTAGENTSDOCS_NEW.

Here again, upon looking at these dependencies a little more closely, the logic behind them is pretty clear. The first, background macros not running against selected documents in a view, is required since a background macro is not run in the scope of a view. Since execute-once macros only run against a set of selected documents, the second dependency seems appropriate as well. The last requirement that background and mail/paste agents always run on new documents makes sense too, because you would not want either of these two to run on anything else but new documents.

The last of the four pieces of information in this group is the frequency type and is available only for background agents. The GetFrequencyString() routine was created to process the following four possible values here.

- HTAGENTFREQ_HOURLY
- HTAGENTFREQ_DAILY
- HTAGENTFREQ_WEEKLY
- HTAGENTFREQ_NEVER

The next six items to be displayed in the dialog box are all passed in the HTAGENT structure as string values. The first two, the menu name and the cascade name, have both been discussed already. The comment is the optional string provided within the user interface to be used to further describe the function of the agent.

The next item, the agent formula, contains the information we most likely associate with an agent. It is also the piece of data obtained only if the FETCH_DESIGN_FORMULA property of the source document is set as discussed earlier. The full text-search query string contains the information placed into the search bar within a full text-search query agent. The defined actions for a full-text search query are reported in the formula field described above.

The last item to be displayed is the background machine string. This string contains the name of the system upon which a background agent is run. For all other execute types, this string is not defined.

With that, we've successfully created an application that can be used to browse any agent within any database on any server. The problem is, we still haven't duplicated the operation of the RUNMACRO sample; we haven't actually executed an agent yet. Luckily for us, the HiTest C API has a clever routine called **HTAgentExecute()**.

If you're already thinking ahead here and you're guessing that the parameters to **HTAgentExecute()** are a laundry list of items from the HTAGENT structure, thankfully, you're wrong! Although this API has five parameters, one being an open database containing the agent and two other output parameters, the only two other inputs are the agent ID and an open view index, if required by the agent. The two output parameters are addresses of integer values set to the number of documents scanned and the number of documents affected by the agent, respectively.

So, we know how to open the agent's database, what the agent ID is, and we can easily create two integer values and pass the address of each. All that's left is the view index. To provide for this, the first thing we do when we get the message from Windows that the Execute button has been pressed is to call a routine we've created called GetIndexForAgent().

GetIndexForAgent() is responsible for determining whether or not the current agent requires a view index and, if so, for opening a modal dialog box to allow the user to select among the views within the database. We can determine which agents require a view index through the use of the agent documents type described previously. Of the six possible types, the only two that operate on a view are the HTAGENTDOCS_VIEW and HTAGENTDOCS_SELECTED_VIEW types. For the other four, we can pass an index value of zero to the **HTAgentExecute()** call.

NOTE

Although the HTAGENTDOCS_SELECTED_VIEW documents type should run on a set of selected documents within a view, AGENTRUN will only provide an entire view as input.

If an agent is required, the Database Views dialog box shown in Figure 8.6 is filled with a list of all of the views within the selected database.

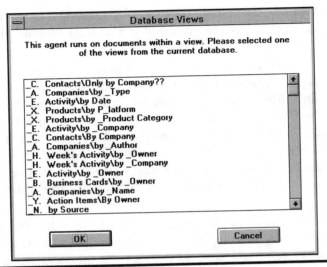

Figure 8.6 AGENTRUN Agents dialog box: view-based agent.

As you can see from the WM_INITDIALOG processing within the ViewsDialogProc() routine, this list requires the use of another of the HiTest object types, the View object.

```
Status = HTViewList(gCurrentDatabase,
                    HTLIST_REFRESH,
                    &ViewSummary);

while (Status == HTSUCCESS)
{
    // if no view name, default to 'Untitled'
    if ((lstrlen(ViewSummary.name)) == 0)
    {
        lstrcpy(ViewSummary.name, "Untitled");
    }

// add view name to UI list
    SendDlgItemMessage(hDialog,
                    IDC_VIEWS,
                    LB_ADDSTRING,
                    0,
                    (LPARAM) (LPSTR) ViewSummary.name);
```

```
Status = HTViewList(gCurrentDatabase,
                    HTLIST_NEXT,
                    &ViewSummary);
}
```

Although there are six APIs within the View object, we need only two of them within the processing for this dialog box, the first of which is **HTViewList()**. As with the call to **HTAgentList()**, **HTViewList()** has three parameters: the reference to an open database, an already familiar list of enumeration flags, and a pointer to an HTVIEWSUMM structure. Something else you'll find familiar about the two calls is that the HTVIEWSUMM structure is identical to the HTAGENTSUMM, other than the fact that we now have a view ID rather than an agent ID.

```
typedef struct
{
    HTVIEWID viewid;                          // View ID
    HTBOOL hidden;                            // TRUE if view is hidden
    char name[HTMAXLEN_DESIGN_NAME];          // View name
    char menu_name[HTMAXLEN_MENU_NAME];       // Menu display name
    char cascade_name[HTMAXLEN_MENU_NAME];    // Cascading display name
} HTVIEWSUMM;                                  // View summary information
```

This time we'll take only the name of the view for display in the listbox and use another View object API, **HTViewLocateByName()** once the user has selected one from the list. We could have saved a list of the view IDs as we did the agent IDs but that would be repetitively redundant.

With the list of views now displayed, the user selects one of the views and then presses the **OK** button. The processing within the IDOK case of the WM_COMMAND message is now to get the name of the selected view within the list and call **HTViewLocateByName()** to get the ID of the selected view. We'll need the view ID so that we can create an index on the view. Remember, we need an index on the view, or the documents defined by the view, not the view itself. The two input parameters to **HTViewLocateByName()** are the database containing the view and the view name.

NOTE

Using any of the **HT*LocateByName()** APIs can be a costly way of performing searches if performance is a key within your application.

An empty index is now created with another call to **HTIndexOpen()**; then the view ID is used to create an index on the view. The API to do this is the call **HTIndexOpenView()**.

```
HTSTATUS HTIndexOpenView(HTINDEX index,
                         HTDATABASE view_database,
                         HTVIEWID viewid,
                         HTFLAGS openview_flags);
```

Of the four, the only parameter on the call to **HTIndexOpenView()** we haven't discussed is the flag word. The flags available here are similar to the flags on the call to **NIFOpenCollection()** that we discussed within the Notes C API set. Here also, care should be taken to understand what you are asking the API to do for you with each flag. Choosing among these flags unwisely can make a very large difference in the performance of your application. Table 8.12 shows the possible values for these flags.

Table 8.12 Agent Execute Type Values

Flag	Definition
HTOPENVIEWF_FORCE_REBUILD	Rebuild of the view on open
HTOPENVIEWF_NO_UPDATE	Do not update the view
HTOPENVIEWF_NO_CREATE	Fail if the view has never been opened
HTOPENVIEWF_FLAT_VIEW	Do not maintain view hierarchy

NOTE

The last view flag should be used only if you want to navigate through a view by absolute index. It is suggested that this mode of operation not be used unless absolutely necessary and should then only be used with small databases due to performance issues.

We are not especially concerned about the performance of AGENTRUN and we want to make sure that the index on the view is as up-to-date as possible. For these reasons, as seen in the call to HTIndexOpenView() below, we used the "force rebuild" open flag.

```
Status = HTIndexOpenView(LocalViewIndex,
                         gCurrentDatabase,
                         ViewID,
                         HTOPENVIEWF_FORCE_REBUILD);
```

Let's run an agent. We now have all of the information we need for the call to **HTAgentExecute()**, including an index to run against, if required. If the agent is executed successfully, a modal dialog box is displayed with the scanned and affected count. If an error occurred, **HTErrorFetch()** is used to get the error corresponding to the **HTAgentExecute()** call and it is subsequently displayed to the user. Also, we need to check if we opened an index for the agent within the call to GetIndexForAgent() and, if so, to close it with a call to **HTIndexClose()**.

AGENTRUN: Where do We Go from Here?

Several things come to mind when looking at possible enhancements to the AGENTRUN application. The first is probably user-interface related and doesn't relate well to the scope of this book. The second enhancement falls into the realm of providing a set of selected documents within a view whenever an agent has the HTAGENTDOCS_-SELECTED_VIEW documents type.

Although we would not want to try to reproduce the Notes user interface here, we could provide a place within the Database Views for the user to enter a selection formula. The formula could then be executed against an index created on one of the available views and the resultant index could then be used as input to the agent. This process would not take too much work in that we have already discussed the API needed to perform the operation, **HTIndexSearch()**. This time, we'd just make use of the formula parameter by passing the string entered by the user.

That's pretty much a wrap for the discussion of the HiTest C API. There's more information that we haven't covered but hopefully we've given you a head start.

Notes HiTest C API Top *n*

1. If you can, use this API set over the Notes C API whenever possible. Your productivity and hours of sleep are sure to be higher.

2. If you are building an application that handles macros (agents) in any way, use this API set over the Notes C API.

3. If possible, make use of some of the more advanced error-handling capabilities provided though this API set. As always, it is better to have too much information when a problem occurs than too little.

4. If you're developing an application that uses a mail interface, make sure the two APIs provided through this API are sufficient before you do much work.

5. Remember, you can use both the Notes C API and the HiTest C API together within an application, all takes is a little work at initialization and termination time.

6. Make use of bound data whenever you can. It is cheap and extremely powerful, especially if you need to do datatype conversions.

HiTest Tools for Visual Basic

The last of the three methods of extending Notes to be discussed are the HiTest Tools for Visual Basic. This method is actually a set of three distinct parts; the HiTest BASIC API, an interoperability layer between the HiTest BASIC API and Visual Basic called the *htGLUE layer*, and a set of 12 Visual Controls, the htVISUAL Controls.

The HiTest BASIC API component for the HiTest Tools is basically the same component that is used by the HiTest C API interface described in Chapter 8, housed in a different set of DLLs. The htGLUE component provides a layer on top of the HiTest C API that allows access to this API from Visual Basic. This component is provided through two **.BAS** files that correlate to the two include files for the HiTest C API. These two files, **HTNOTES.BAS** and **HTFUNC.BAS**, are provided as a part of the default installation on the HiTest Tools for Visual Basic.

The last of the three components, the htVISUAL Controls, are a set of 12 Visual Basic controls (.VBXs) that can be added to the application's Toolbox. These controls can be used like any of the other tools within the Toolbox with one notable exception, "Piped Properties." *Piped properties* are tool properties that can be set by drag-and-drop as opposed to setting them individually at design time or under application control.

Since this extension method is composed of more than just a single component, we're going to break up the discussion into two different parts. The first part will deal exclusively with the Visual Controls and will be centered around an application that uses all 12 controls. Within the second part, we will bring the htVISUAL Controls and the htGLUE layer together to provide a real-life example of how they can be used in concert.

Visual Tools: Drag-and-Drop Heaven

The 12 Visual Tools tie directly either to Notes objects or to Notes control objects. Table 9.1 lists the 12 controls and a short description of their functionality. Each of the controls will be covered in detail within the first sections of this chapter.

Table 9.1 HiTest Visual Controls.

Control	Description
Server Selector	Select among list of servers
Database Selector	Select among list of databases on a server
Database Access	Open a database
Omni Selector	Select among a list of objects (several different objects types)
View Document Selector	Select among Documents displayed as a Notes View
Scroll Document Selector	Select among Documents displayed as a simple list
Document Access Control	Open a Notes Document
Formula	Create a formula for a Document selection
Grid Channel	Display Documents and items in a row-column format
Item Display	Display an item in a Document
Item Edit	Edit an item in a Document
Mail Control	Send Notes mail

There are several features shared by all of the controls that allow them integrate with each other in a tightly bound functional package. The most noticeable of these is the previously mentioned piped properties.

The idea behind piped properties is that the controls, with the exception of the Server Selector, require a certain set of input values in order to function properly. Left to normal practices, these values would usually be provided to the controls either statically at design time through property sheets or dynamically under program control. In the case of the Visual Controls, several, if not all, of the properties required by one control can be provided by another. Piped properties provide a method that allows this association to take place visually, making the task much easier.

The implementation of piped properties is quite simple. Given two Visual Controls —one the source of the properties, the other the destination—right-clicking on the destination control causes the cursor to turn to a disconnected plug-and-socket graphic. Hold down the right-hand mouse button, drag the cursor over the source control, and release the mouse, and the cursor will change to a connected plug and socket, showing that the properties have been piped. A ScreenCam demonstration of this process can be found on the CD in **\HITESTVB\PIPED.EXE.**

Another handy feature of piped properties is that they can be easily interrogated by single-clicking a Visual Control with the right mouse button. This brings up a dialog containing a list of all of the properties within the control that can be set through the piping process and their values.

NOTE

When you are piping properties from one control to another, be sure to release the right-hand mouse button when the crosshairs located on the upper left-hand corner of the cursor are over the destination control. The first thought might be to try to center the cursor over the destination but this move can result in the crosshairs actually being off the control. If this happens, the "Target selection is not an htVISUAL Control" dialog is displayed.

Table 9.2 shows the 12 Visual Controls, the properties that each can have piped to them as inputs, and the properties they can serve to other controls as outputs. This table will be referenced throughout the rest of this chapter whenever the piped properties for a control are discussed.

Table 9.2 Piped properties of Visual Controls.

Control	Inputs	Outputs
Server Selector	—none—	Server Name
Database Selector	Server Name	Full Database Name
Database Access	Server Name, Full Database Name	Database
View Omni Selector	Database	View Name, View ID, Index
Form Omni Selector	Database	Form Name, Form ID
Item Omni Selector	Document	Item Name
Column Omni Selector	View ID	Form Name, Form ID
Agent Omni Selector	Database	Form Name, Form ID
Form Field Omni Selector	Form ID	Field Name
View Document Selector	Database, Index, View ID, View Name	Document ID
Scroll Document Selector	Database, Index	Document ID
Document Access Control	Database, Form Name, Index, Document ID	Document
Formula	Database, Form Name	Index
Grid Channel	Database, Form Name	Index
Item Display	Document, Item Name	—none—
Item Edit	Document, Item Name	Rich Text Composite
Mail Control	Database, Document ID, Composite	—none—

Another way to look at the information in Table 9.2 is through a set of dependency graphs. Figure 9.1 provides a graph showing the controls that can be used as the sources (arrow tail) of all of the properties required by a specific destination (arrow head) control. This graph can be extremely useful when you are just starting to use piped properties in that, given any arrow, if you start with the control at the arrow head and drag it to the control at the arrow tail, a fully defined property association will occur.

Figure 9.2 provides a dependency graph showing those controls that provide only some of the required properties to the destination control. The placement of each control is the same in the two graphs to aid in understanding their relationships.

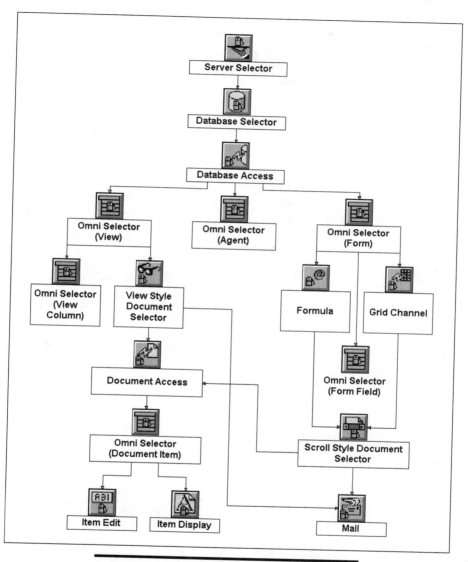

Figure 9.1 Visual Tools dependency graph (full).

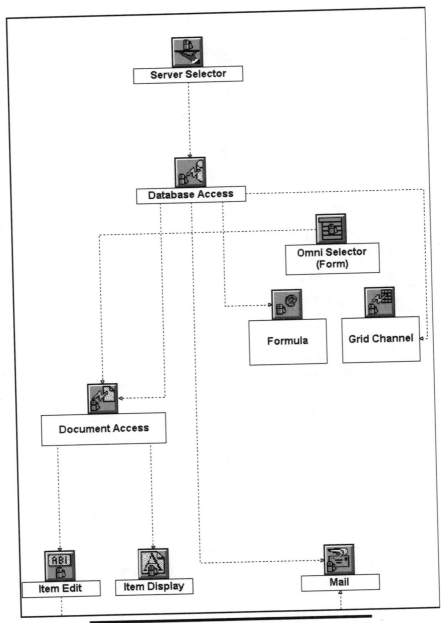

Figure 9.2 Visual Tools dependency graph (partial).

As shown in Table 9.2, each control has a specific set of values that are set when properties are piped to it. Each value has an **Src** suffix indicating that this value is the name of the control that is the source of the value, not the value itself. If the values are to be set directly, the property name does not have the **Src** suffix. For example, when the properties from a Server Selector control are piped to a Database Selector control, the ioServerNameSrc property within the Database Selector is set to the name of the Server Selector control. If, on the other hand, the server name is to be set under program control, the ioServerName property is set to the actual server name.

If both the Src and the non-Src property are set within a control, the Src property always has precedence.

NOTE

This brings up another feature of piped properties that needs to be mentioned—they can be piped from one form to another. This can be seen quite clearly by piping the properties from one control to another and then bringing up the piped properties sheet on the destination control. As mentioned above, by clicking the right-hand mouse button over the control, you can see that the control specified for each property has a form and a control designation. The first sample application we're going to build actually uses this multiform feature. Figure 9.3 shows the property sheet of a Database Selector control after being piped to a Server Selector.

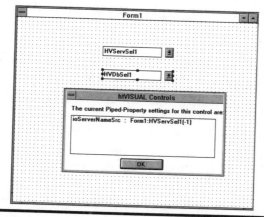

Figure 9.3 Database Selector piped properties sheet.

There is one thing to watch out for when piping properties across forms. When properties are piped from one control to another, the form name used within the property specification is obtained from the LinkTopic property of the form, not from the Name property. This can be especially confusing in a multiple form scenario.

For instance, suppose you are creating the first form in an application, the Name and LinkTopic properties are set to the same value, Form1. If you change the Name property to MyApp and then add another form, now the Name and LinkTopic of the new form are set to Form1. If you now pipe controls between the two forms, there will be an ambiguity as to which form contains the control since the piped properties will contain a form designation of "Form1." This can result in unpredictable behavior from the application and can be difficult to track down.

Event processing is the last point we want to mention concerning the controls as a group. Each control has a set of new methods, events, and properties specific to the HiTest interface. The underlying processing for each control was designed specifically to allow it to work in concert with the other controls in the set to accomplish the designed function. For the most part, when the properties of one control are piped to another, a chaining effect takes place that allows changes in parent controls to be trickled down through the chain of child controls.

Take a simple case of a database control being "linked" to a server control. When the application is first started, the ReReadInputs method for each control is invoked. The server control performs a query of Notes for all available servers within this method, much akin to performing an **HTServerList()**, and adds the list of servers to the control's listbox. In most cases during application start-up, the database control will determine that a server name has not yet been supplied to it—a required input—and will not perform any further processing.

When an element within either of the controls is selected, the "UpdateOutputs" method within the control is called. The UpdateOutputs method on the server control, among other things, will set its ioServerName property to the selected server name and then run its DependentsReRead method. This, in turn, causes all controls linked to the server control, e.g., the database control in this case, to run their ReReadInputs method. This time the database control finds that a server name is indeed available, obtains the server name from the server control's ioServerName property and fills its list with a list of databases on that server. The last thing the database control does, by default, is to reselect any previously selected database in the list. If reselected, the UpdateOutputs method on the database control is run and…, you get the drift!

If left to operate in the default configuration, this "event rippling" works quite well. If, on the other hand, you are planning to do some low-level "event-twiddling," be sure to take the time to read and understand the process-flow information for each control. The documentation that accompanies the HiTest Visual Tools is quite good in this regard.

ALLVIS: Visual Controls Galore

The primary design goal of the application we are about to build, ALLVIS.EXE (\HITESTVB\WIN16\ALLVIS), was to create an application that would use all 12 of the visual controls. For this reason, it may not be the most generally useful of the sample applications within this book but it provides a good look at all the controls and how they can be used. It uses several forms to allow enough display space for all the controls. As each control is discussed, it will be added to the ALLVIS application, culminating in the finished product with the addition of the last control, the Mail control. (ALLVIS was built using Release 2.0 of the Visual Tools and Visual Basic 3.0.)

Server Selector: Nothing to It

The first of the controls we'll discuss is the Server Selector (HSVSEL.VBX). This is the only control within the set that requires no additional input properties to function. Once dragged onto a form, this control manifests itself as a combo dialog box that displays a list of the currently available Notes servers, including a Local server selection. The Server Selector provides the selected server name, as output, to any control using it as the ioServerNameSrc.

NOTE The Server Selector, Database Selector, and Omni Selector controls all allow for three list types through the Style property; dropdown, dropdown list, and simple. The dropdown option, which is the default, provides a list of the available objects as well as an edit box to allow for adding names that do not appear in the list. The dropdown list and simple styles do not have the edit control capability. Within ALLVIS, all of these controls have been set up to use dropdown lists since all are used for display-only purposes.

Actually, the Server Selector does little more than call the **HTServerList()** API, and fill the combo box with the server names. This is exactly what we did during the development of the AGENTRUN application in Chapter 8.

Database Selector: One Input, One Output

The next control in the list is the Database Selector (HDBSEL.VBX). This control is not very complicated: it provides a single output—the database name—and requires only a single input—the server name. From the standpoint of piped properties, the Database Selector can only be used as the database name property source for the Database Access control and can only get the server name from the Server Selector.

As with the Server Selector, the Database Selector is displayed, by default, as a combo box with an edit field. It is filled with the list of databases, or files, on the selected server. The list can be sorted either by database title, by setting the ListByTitle property of the control to TRUE, or by file name, in which case ListByTitle is FALSE. The default sorting type is by database title. Figure 9.4 shows the resultant list of databases available on the Local server after the server name property of the Server Selector has been piped to the Database Selector control.

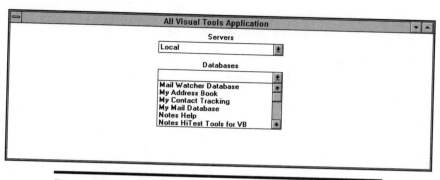

Figure 9.4 Server Selector and Database Selector controls.

Database Access: The First Control Object

As mentioned in the opening part of this chapter, each of the Visual Controls directly relate to either Notes objects, as is the case for the Server and Database Selector, or to a Notes control object. The Database Access control (HDBACC.VBX), is the first of the two control objects contained in the set.

You can think of control objects as nonphysical entities that "control" the state of other objects. For instance, the Database Access control is a checkbox used to determine whether a connection to the database associated with the control is open or closed. Another aspect of control objects is that they have no tangible output to be displayed within the user interface. For instance, the Server and Database Selector controls provide a list of servers and a list of databases, respectively. The Database Access control has no such information for perusal.

By default, the Database Access control is in a checked state and not visible. This provides an open connection to a database whenever the server name and full file name have been provided and the UpdateOutputs method is executed. If you wish to provide the ability for the user to open and close a database connection at their leisure, you would want to set the Visible property of the control to TRUE and probably change the default Caption as well. Figure 9.5 shows the Database Access control as it appears in the ALLVIS application in design mode.

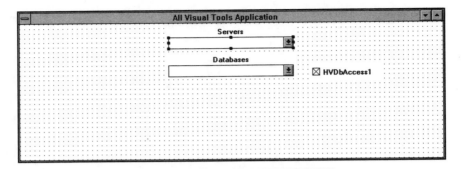

Figure 9.5 Database Access control.

Omni Selector: Six Controls in One

The next control on the list is the Omni Selector (HOSEL.VBX). This control is a combo box that can be configured to list any one of the following Notes objects types:

- Forms
- Form Fields
- Views
- View Columns
- Document Items
- Agents

The object type is stored as the SelectorKind property within the control itself and is set through a modal dialog that appears once the control is placed on a form. Figure 9.6 shows the dialog from which this object type is selected.

The idea behind the design of this control deals with the fact that each of the object types that can be represented in it are single-columned, list-oriented objects. The effort required in accessing the different object types is minimal due to the structure of the HiTest API. If you remember the discussion of the listing API from Chapter 8, you'll notice that each of the objects listed can be obtained through a List API. The only difference among them is the set of parameters required to access each list. Table 9.3 shows the List API that provides access to each object and the parameters required.

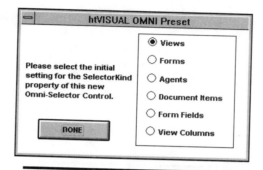

Figure 9.6 Omni Selector Type Dialog.

Table 9.3 Omni Selector List APIs.

Object Type	API	Parameters
Forms	HTFormList()	Database
Form Fields	HTFieldList()	Database, Form ID
Views	HTViewList()	Database
View Columns	HTColumnList()	Database, View ID
Document Items	HTItemList()	Document
Agents	HTAgentList()	Database

One thing you might notice is that not all of the properties piped from one control to another are needed. This is especially true in the Omni Selector control due to the different types of objects that can be supported. Although the extra information has no effect on the outcome, you may want to look more closely at the requirements for each control if you are setting the values under program control. No need to do more than is necessary…at least in a programming environment anyway.

As for ALLVIS, this is the time that we break into multiple forms. What we are going to do is create the forms to follow the dependency graph in Figure 9.1. Therefore, to the main form of ALLVIS(ALLVIS_Main), we'll add a View Omni Selector, an Agent Omni Selector, and a Form Omni Selector. From there we'll create two additional forms, one for the rest of the View side of the graph(ALLVIS_View) and another for the Form side(ALLVIS_Form). Figures 9.7, 9.8, and 9.9 show the list of Notes Views, Agents, and Forms, respectively, within a specific database.

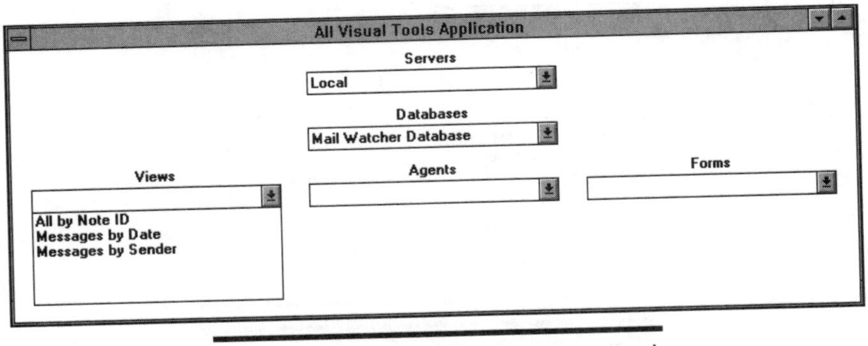

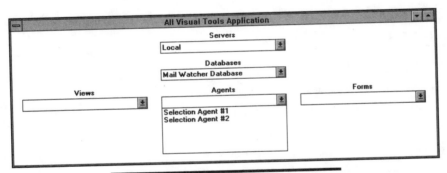

Figure 9.7 View Omni Selector control.

Figure 9.8 Agent Omni Selector control.

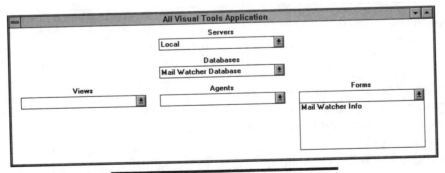

Figure 9.9 Form Omni Selector control.

NOTE The design goal was to make ALLVIS a Visual Control-only application. We've had to modify that a bit since we want to open the auxiliary forms whenever a Notes View or Form is selected from the Omni Selector. To do this, we've added two lines of Visual Basic code. They appear within the HasChanged events of the View and Form Omni Selector controls and are `ALLVIS_View.Show` and `ALLVIS_Form.Show`, respectively.

We'll discuss the other three Omni Selector types, View Column, Form Field, and Document Item, when we come across them as we traverse down the tree in Figure 9.1. For now, let's travel down the View side of the graph where we'll look at five more controls and two of the remaining three Omni Selectors.

View Style Document Selector: Notes Views With a Twist

The HiTest Visual Tools package provides two different controls that deal with displaying lists of Documents in one manner or another. The first one we'll talk about is the View Style Document Selector (HVDSEL.VBX). This control attempts to duplicate a Notes View by fully expanding it and then, for every line of information in the View, adding the text to a listbox. The first "line" in the listbox is a nonscrollable header containing the column names. The subsequent lines either contain things like categories, and totals or Documents. The ability to collapse and expand sections is not currently provided by the control. Figure 9.10 provides an example of how the control looks given a View with several levels of categorization.

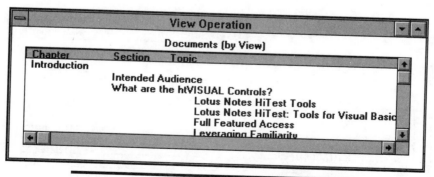

Figure 9.10 View Style Document Selector control.

Two properties within the control that may be of interest, especially from the aspect of performance, are the SizeBeforeVirtualRange and the VirtualRange properties. The SizeBeforeVirtualRange property is used to state how many lines of the expanded View are initially read into the listbox. If the expanded View has more than this number of lines, then the VirtualRange property is used to determine this number. The drawback of setting these values too high on a View with a large set of Documents is: (1) more memory will be used in the process and (2) the response time may suffer substantially. Conversely, if these values are set too low, scrolling through the View will appear "jumpy" due to the frequency of the database hits.

Another property of this control that can be useful from a purely informational standpoint is the DocNumber property. This is a string value that is set to the hierarchical Index of the currently selected Document in the control. The format of this string is a set of level index numbers separated by periods such as 2.14.7 or 1.2.15.12.

Before we go on to the next new control, we'll draw attention to another of the Omni Selectors, the View Column. This control is another combo box that displays the name of each column in the View, the same information that is displayed in the first line of View Style Document Selector. The only difference here is that each column in the View is given an entire line within the list. This can be somewhat confusing at first, since there may be times that the first few lines in the control are blank. This is due to the categorization and/or totaling columns that sometimes appear as the first columns in a View that do not have any titles. If you are going to be giving this list to an end-user, you may want to parse these out of the list first, it may save some support calls. Figure 9.11 shows the View Column Omni Selector in use within the ALLVIS application.

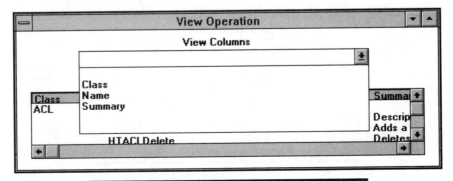

Figure 9.11 View Column Omni Selector control.

Document Access: The Second Control Object

The Document Access control (HDOC.VBX) provides for Documents the same functionality as the Database Access control does for databases, and more. Not only does this control allow for opening and closing a Document through a checkbox metaphor, as does the Database Access control, but it also provides for Create and Delete operations. The three operational types; "Open/Close," "Create," and "Delete" are signaled in the AccessKind property of the control.

In the latter two cases, the control is transformed into a visible push-button control. Another difference here is that there is no output from the control if it is configured for create or delete functionality. The operation is performed and no further information is passed on. Figure 9.12 shows the dialog that appears whenever a new Document Access control is added to a form. This is the dialog that handles the setting of the AccessKind property of the control at design time.

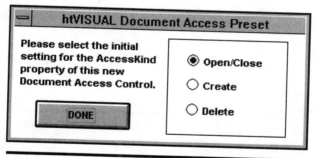

Figure 9.12 Document Access AccessKind dialog box.

From the graph in Figure 9.1, you can see that the Document Access control can gather all of the necessary properties by piping either from a View Style Document Selector or a Scroll Type Document Selector. Within the ALLVIS application, we'll only show Document Access as fed by the View Style Document Selector. In addition, only two of the three operations of this control are used. The Open/Close type has been left hidden and is used as the source of properties for the Document Item Omni Selector discussed below. The Delete operation is also used to allow for deleting a Document off of the Scroll Style Document Selector that will be described within the Form side of the dependency graph.

Traveling further down the graph in Figure 9.1, we are now at the Document Item Omni Selector. You've probably guessed by now that this control provides a combo box which lists the items, by name, within a specific Document. This control does not provide access to the item data however, you'll need one of the next two controls for that. Figure 9.13 shows a list of Document items as might be displayed in the ALLVIS application through the Document Item Omni Selector control.

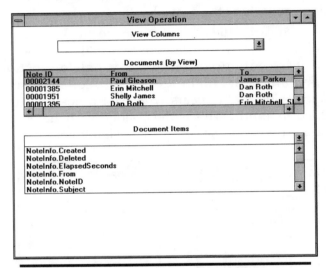

Figure 9.13 Document Item Omni Selector control.

Item Display: Simple but Effective

We are now at the lowest level of interrogation within the realm of the Visual Controls, the item level. There are actually two controls that process items, the Item Display and the Item Edit controls. The first of these two, the Item Display control (HIDISP.VBX), is the simplest and displays item information only in a textual format; things such as file attachments and OLE objects that have no textual representation do not appear within the control. Figure 9.14 shows the output of the Item Display control on a rich text item within a Document.

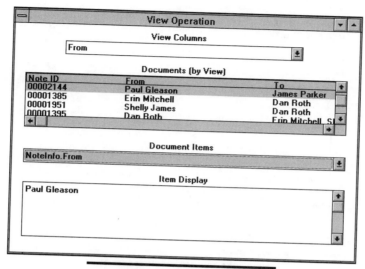

Figure 9.14 Item Display control.

Item Edit: Two Sides to One Story

The Item Edit control (HIEDIT.VBX) is a bit more involved than the Item Display control for basically one reason; the Item Edit control can handle nontextual information as well as textual information. The mode of operation for the control is contained in the PresentAs property of the control, which is set to Text mode by default. However, there are some restrictions on this dual mode of operation.

The first restriction is that the Item Edit Control can be configured to display item information as either text or rich text, but not both at the same time. This means that if you want to display summary-type items as well as rich text items, you will need to create two instances of the Item Edit control with different settings. Figure 9.15 shows the Item Edit control in its two modes of operation as used within the ALLVIS application. You'll notice that only one of the controls is actively displaying information.

```
                    Document Items
NoteInfo.From                                    ±

                      Item Display
Paul Gleason                                     ±




                    Item Edit (OLE)




                    Item Edit (Text)
Paul Gleason (this field is an edit control!)   ±




```

Figure 9.15 Item Edit control.

Although the Text mode of operation is quite simple and involves little more than the Item Display control, note that the data in the control is saved back to the item when the focus is taken from the control and data within it has changed. This does not mean that the item is saved to the Document; that you will need to do yourself or have HiTest prompt you for a save operation whenever the Document is about to be closed. In HiTest API terms, leaving the Item Edit field performs an **HTItemPut()** but not an **HTDocumentSave()**.

NOTE   The other two "lines of code" in the ALLVIS application appear on the "HasChanged" event of the two Item Edit controls. They do nothing more than perform a Document save operation as described above. The code necessary to do this is shown below and will be discussed in more detail later in this chapter.

```
Dim Status As Long
Status = HTDocumentSave(HVItemEdit.ioDocument, 0)
```

The other mode of operation for the Item Edit control is more involved: it uses OLE techniques to successfully complete it mission. The first thing you'll notice as you change the PresentAs property to Rich Text via OLE2 is that the border on the control disappears. What happens is that the control is converted into a special container control into which a Visual Basic OLE control (MSOLE2.VBX) must be placed. The Item Edit control in this case is used merely as a conduit to the OLE control, which performs all the hard work.

Before you add the OLE control, you'll probably want to do two things. The first is to pipe the properties from a Document Item Omni Selector to the Item Edit control. This is due mostly to the fact that the OLE control will, in most cases, totally obscure the underlying HiTest control. For this reason, it is easier just to do it now. The other thing you may want to look at is a property within the Item Edit control, the ConversionFormat. This property determines the type of word processor to be used to "edit" the rich text data. By default, Microsoft Word is used but Ami Pro (or Word 96) and WordPerfect are other options.

Now that the Item Edit control is ready, the OLE control can be put into place. The best thing to do here is to make the OLE control as large as the Item Edit control; this allows you to easily use the bordering and other display attributes of the OLE control. We won't go into the options available on the OLE control. There are a few, and if you are interested, you can always go to the Visual Basic Help system for answers.

Now that the two controls are ready and all of the properties have been correctly set, sending a rich text item to the control will cause several things to occur. First, a new composite handle is created for the item and assigned to the Composite property of the control. Next, the HasChanged event on the control is triggered and then the OLE control is fired up. From here, the OLE control will determine how the rich text field is to be displayed, and ultimately, edited.

One final point before we leave the rich text operation of the Item Edit control: If you have a keen eye on performance, this may not be the control for you. This issue with performance has to do with mostly OLE-related concerns, but you should take care to understand the performance implications before assuming that you have a solution to a real-life problem.

Grid Channel: A View by Any Other Name

With the View side of Figure 9.1 behind us, its time to take a look at the Form branch. Within it, we're going to look at the last four visual controls; Grid Channel, Formula, Scroll Style Document Selector, and Mail. We'll also discuss the last of the six Omni Selector types, Form Field.

The Grid Channel control (HGRIDC.VBX) is probably the most complex of all the visual controls. This is partly due to the fact that it requires, as does the rich-text Item Edit control, an associated Visual Basic control to provide the desired functionality. You can probably guess that the associated control here is the Visual Basic Grid control. And once again, the Grid Channel control simply provides a conduit between the other HiTest BASIC functions within the application and the Grid control itself.

The Grid control functions as a window into a collection of Notes Documents. This is another of the HiTest Visual Controls that function similarly to a Notes View. The display format, by default, has each Document within the collection depicted as a separate row with the item names within the Document being the column headers. This default configuration is the one used in the ALLVIS application. Figure 9.16 shows the Grid control in use within ALLVIS when looking at the WATCHER database we created in Chapter 7.

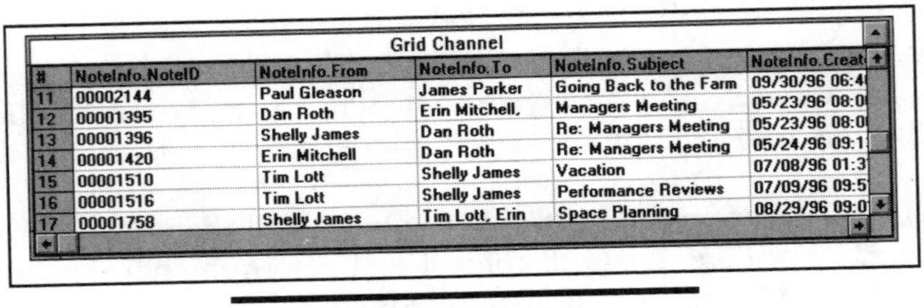

Grid Channel

#	NoteInfo.NoteID	NoteInfo.From	NoteInfo.To	NoteInfo.Subject	NoteInfo.Creat
11	00002144	Paul Gleason	James Parker	Going Back to the Farm	09/30/96 06:4
12	00001395	Dan Roth	Erin Mitchell,	Managers Meeting	05/23/96 08:0
13	00001396	Shelly James	Dan Roth	Re: Managers Meeting	05/23/96 08:0
14	00001420	Erin Mitchell	Dan Roth	Re: Managers Meeting	05/24/96 09:1
15	00001510	Tim Lott	Shelly James	Vacation	07/08/96 01:3
16	00001516	Tim Lott	Shelly James	Performance Reviews	07/09/96 09:5
17	00001758	Shelly James	Tim Lott, Erin	Space Planning	08/29/96 09:0

Figure 9.16 Grid Channel control.

There are several options available within the Grid control that can be used to modify the type and amount of information displayed. The ItemNames property, which is empty by default, can be used to supply an alternative set of columns to be displayed. The format of the ItemNames string is pretty simple. For each column that is to be displayed, add the item name of the field to be displayed on the property line, separating each name by a comma.

NOTE

There is one special case column that can be added to the ItemNames property that provides for displaying the location index similar to the first column on the default display. To do this, simply use the '#' character as the column name.

For example, suppose that instead of displaying all the column information from the WATCHER database we only want to see the Document's location index, who the message is from, who it was sent to, and the subject line. The ItemNames property line in this case would be "#,NoteInfo.From,NoteInfo.To,NoteInfo.Subject".

Another of the options available with this control is the ability to control the range of Documents displayed. Through the use of the DisplayStart and DisplayEnd properties, the range of rows to be displayed within the collection of Documents can be set programatically. The DisplayStart value is used to determine which Document within the collection is to be displayed first within the control. This is a numeric value and is based on the location index within the collection. The DisplayEnd property is used to state the index of the last Document to be displayed.

NOTE

If you set the DisplayEnd property to a value less than the total number of Documents within the collection, the additional Documents will not be sent to the control and therefore will not be displayed within it.

In some cases, limiting the range of Documents displayed within the Grid control by location index alone is not enough, especially when the number of Documents is quite dynamic. To solve this problem, another of the options available within the Grid control, the Formula property, can be used. This formula is just like all others within the HiTest API in that it is text based.

Let's say, for instance, that we wanted to look at the first ten messages sent by Paul Gleason within the WATCHER database. Using DisplayStart and DisplayEnd would obviously not be good enough unless we knew we had a View that selected only those messages sent by Paul Gleason. With the right combination of the DisplayStart, DisplayEnd, and Formula Grid control options however, we can accomplish the task without any special database View requirements.

Figure 9.17 shows the property sheet of the HiTest BASIC Grid control with these properties appropriately set.

Figure 9.18 shows the last of the Omni Selector types, the Form Field type, as it can be seen within the ALLVIS application. This control does little more than provide a list of all of the fields within a Notes Form. It will provide the selected field name to a control on output, but there are currently no visual controls that have an ioFieldNameSrc property. If you want to use the output of this control, you'll need to use it within a control of your own design.

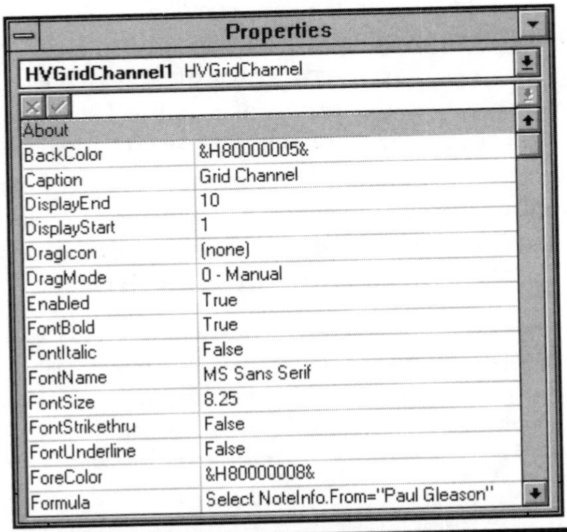

Figure 9.17 HiTest Grid Visual Control with options.

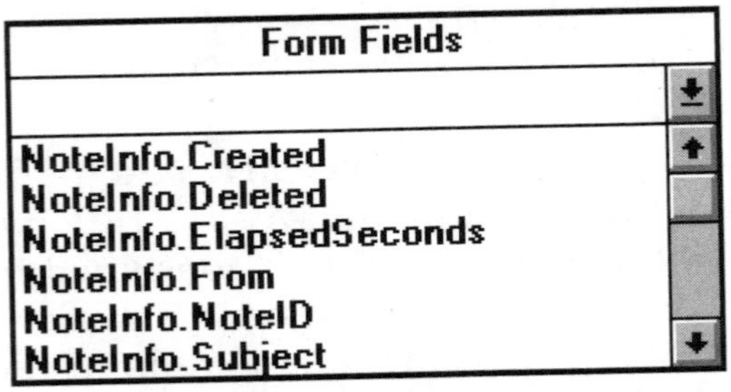

Figure 9.18 Form Field Omni Selector.

Formula: Logic On-the-Fly

The Formula control (HFMLA.VBX), simply put, creates a list of Documents based on the selection criteria defined within the textual formula contained in the control. It takes, as input, a database and an optional Form name. If the Form name is supplied, it is used as an additional selection criteria, along with the formula itself. If it is not supplied, no selection is performed based on the Document's Form. The output of this control, usually destined for a Scroll Style Document Selector, is a HiTest Index object as discussed in Chapter 8.

By default, the Formula control has its Visible property set to "False." This points to the fact that the formula text for the control is usually assumed to be provided programatically, not by the end-user. Within the ALLVIS application, the Visible property has been set to "True" to allow the entry of alternative selection formulas. The default selection formula, Select @All, has been left to provide a default Index to be displayed. Figure 9.19 shows the Formula control as it is used within the ALLVIS application, with the default formula text.

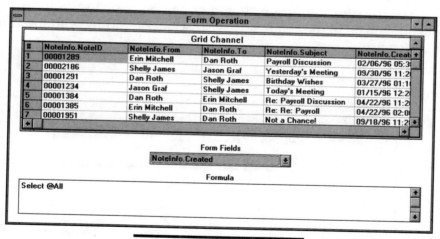

Figure 9.19 Formula Control.

Scroll Style Document Selector: A Scroll Bar that Needs Help

The Scroll Style Document Selector (HSDSEL.VBX) is the second in the set of Document Selectors within this control set but it behaves quite differently from the View Style Document Selector. This control manifests itself as either a horizontal or vertical scroll bar, depending on the value of the Orientation property. It relies on other controls to actually display the information within the selected Document. Within the ALLVIS application, this control passes the selected Document's DocID to a Document Access control as is shown in Figure 9.1. From there, the same pathway is taken as in the case of the View processing above, through a Document Item Omni Selector and then to an Item Display control. There are really very few options available with this control. It just does what it does and that's it.

With the discussion of the Scroll Style Document Selector, we have now completed the Form side of the Visual Controls graph from Figure 9.1. The Mail control, which will be discussed in the next section, is really in its own realm and doesn't belong in either a Notes Form or View classification. Figure 9.20 shows the entire ALLVIS_Form in operation with all of the controls we've discussed, starting with the Grid Channel control.

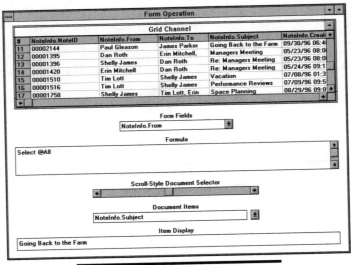

Figure 9.20 ALLVIS_Form Controls.

Mail: More than Meets the Eye

The Mail control (HMAIL.VBX), the last of the 12 visual controls, provides more functionality than one might have expected. Although this control does provide for the ability to mail a Notes Document selected from either of the Document Selector controls, as depicted in Figure 9.1, it also provides the ability to mail an ad-hoc Document with very little input whatsoever. We've chosen to use it in the ALLVIS application in a manner similar to an ad-hoc mailer. For this reason, the control has been placed on the main form, getting its required inputs from the Database control.

The basic operation of the Mail control is as follows: When the ReReadInputs method is triggered, if the database input is a valid database, the control is enabled. Once the button is pressed, one of two things can happen, depending on the value of the AutoMailDialog property. If "True," the mail destination dialog shown in Figure 9.21 is displayed. From here most, if not all, of the mail properties available for use through the HiTest C API are offered.

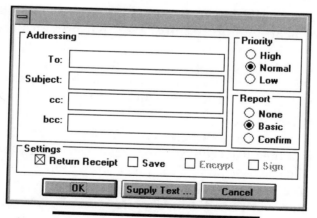

Figure 9.21 Mail Control dialog box.

If the AutoMailDialog property of the Mail control is "False" when the button is pressed, the control assumes that all the required mail properties have already been set into the control and a mail message is sent. Regardless of the value of the AutoMailDialog property, if a Document ID is provided, the Document will be used as the body of the message and any additional body text will be ignored. In this case, the Supply Text... button on the dialog is also disabled. In Figure 9.21, however, the Mail control within the ALLVIS application does not have a Document ID supplied and therefore the Supply Text... button is enabled.

There is another property within the Mail control that cannot by filled by merely piping properties from another control but can be quite useful when it comes to getting the most out of this control. This is the ioComposite property. If this property is set, either programatically or from a rich text Item Edit control, the referenced composite is used as the body of the message. If a composite is supplied, the body text is ignored and the Supply Text... button is disabled, as is the case when a Document ID is provided.

htGLUE: HiTest C API from Visual Basic

Now that we've discussed all of the htVISUAL Controls, we're ready to tackle the second piece of the HiTest Tools for Visual Basic equation, the htGLUE layer. As alluded to in the beginning of this chapter, the htGLUE layer is an interoperability layer that provides access to the HiTest C API we discussed in Chapter 8 from Visual Basic. As with the C API, the htGLUE layer is provided through two files as well, HTNOTES.BAS and HTFUNC.BAS. If you wish to access the HiTest BASIC API from Visual Basic, you will need to add these two files to your Visual Basic project.

The application we have chosen to develop here is one that integrates the use of two of the visual controls, the server selector and the database selector, with the use of several of the functions within the htGLUE layer. The WATCHNFO application (HITESTVB\WIN16\WATCHNFO) makes use of the work we did in Chapter 7 in the Extension Manager section by providing several different ways of looking at the data collected in the **WATCHER.NSF** database. More specifically, it will provide the following five possible graphs of data:

- Average message latency by day of the week

- Average message latency by month

- Message volume by day of the week

- Message volume by month
- Top 10 message senders

In each case the graph type used is a bar graph formatted with a single title line. The body of the graph, from left to right, contains a textual label that is option-specific, the value of the bar on the graph, and the actual bar itself. Figure 9.22 shows the format of the graph as shown when displaying the Top 10 message senders within a WATCHER database.

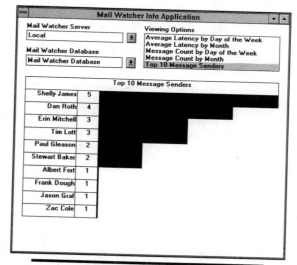

Figure 9.22 WATCHNFO Top 10 display.

As with the ALLVIS application above, WATCHNFO was created using Visual Basic 3.0 and Version 2.0 of the HiTest Tools for Visual Basic.

One of the first things you'll notice about the WATCHNFO application is that the user-interface is functional, but that's about all. Here again, as with many of the applications within this book, the user-interface of WATCHNFO was intentionally left simple so as not to distract from the major focus of the application, the API usage.

The processing within WATCHNFO is as follows: There are several global variables defined within the WATCHNFO.BAS module that hold the currently open database and database Index as well as the current values for the selected option. The number of elements in the values array, gValues, is 12 since that is the largest number of buckets of information for any of the five options, the 12 months of a year. There is another global array that holds the names of the top 10 message senders whenever that option is selected. The labels for the other graphs are constants within the DisplayMonthLabel() and DisplayDayOfWeekLabel() routines. The other items in the WATCHNFO.BAS module are constants for the five option selections and some constants for use in creating the bar graph.

When the form is loaded, the current Index of the current database is cleared and the names of the top 10 message senders are NULLed out within the Form_Load() event processing. On the flip side, the Form_Unload() event processing checks if there is a currently open database and, if so, closes it.

NOTE Any time you use string variables within the realm of the htGLUE interface, make sure they are NULL terminated before use. Within WATCHNFO, at least in most cases, the String() Visual Basic API is used to do this.

As we alluded to earlier, there are two visual controls used within WATCHNFO, the server selector and the database selector. Both of these can be seen in the upper left-hand corner of the WATCHNFO display in Figure 9.22. Even though there are no events trapped on the server selector control, the fact that the database selector is linked to the server selector causes the WatcherDatabase_HasChanged() method to trigger on the database selector control each time a server selection is made. The WatcherDatabase_HasChanged() code below shows how the processing of this event is handled so as to not attempt to open a database when a server is selected with no database name present.

```
' If we have a database selected, open it
If Len(WatcherDatabase.ioFullFileName) Then

.

.

.

End If
```

Since the database selector has been linked to the server selector, each time a server is selected by the user, the database list is filled automatically by the HiTest engine. Once a database is selected, the rest of the code in the WatcherDatabase_HasChanged() method kicks in. This consists of opening the database and checking if the Mail Watcher Info form is contained within it. If so, the list of options is displayed through a call to the RefreshOptionsList() routine within WATCHNFO.FRM. If the Notes Form does not exist within the database, an error message is displayed and the database is closed.

NOTE

Although a database could contain WATCHER notes without having the Mail Watcher Info Form present, we made an assumption here that there would be little value in doing so, at least within the confines of this example.

The WatcherDatabase_HasChanged() processing provides the first look at using the htGLUE layer with our call to the **HTDatabaseOpen()** API. The parameters on this API, as one might expect, are quite similar to those on the corresponding HiTest C API. In most cases, the biggest difference among the same API in C and Visual Basic API is that there are very few definitions for HT types in Visual Basic, except for those that are embodied as structures. For instance, the definition of this API in the C world lists the third parameter as type HTFLAGS, the fourth as an HTDATABASE *, and the return value as an HTSTATUS type. The Visual Basic API definition lists all three of there as generic Long values. This should be of no great concern in that all of the Visual Basic APIs use the same type conversions but it does take some getting used to if you've worked with the HiTest C API very much.

The server name for **HTDatabaseOpen()** is taken from the ioServerName property of the server selector and the database name from the ioFullFileName property of the database selector. From the standpoint of database name spaces, the database selector control also provides two other database name types. One, the ShortFileName property, provides the name of the database file only, without any path information whatsoever. The DatabaseName property contains the display name of the database, or database title, the same one that is displayed in the dropdown list.

We could have used the ioServerName property on the database selector as well but thought we'd break up the monotony a bit and use information from both controls!

NOTE

As you can see from the code sample below, we've extracted the StatusIsOK() routine we developed in Chapter 8 and used it here as well. It's a bit simpler this time in that there is no debugging on/off flag. If the status contains an error code, the error string is obtained through the use of an API we've seen before, **HTErrorFetch()**, and displayed in a message box.

```
Status = HTDatabaseOpen(WatcherServer.ioServerName,
                        WatcherDatabase.ioFullFileName,
                        0,
                        gDatabase)
If (StatusIsOK(Status)) Then
    .
    .
    .

End If

Function StatusIsOK (ErrorStatus As Long) As Integer
    Dim Status As Long
    Dim Severity As Integer
    Dim Message As String

    If (ErrorStatus = HTSUCCESS) Then
        StatusIsOK = 1
    Else
        Message = String(HTMAXLEN_ERROR, 0)
        Status = HTErrorFetch(ErrorStatus, Severity, Message)
        MsgBox (Message)
        StatusIsOK = 0
    End If
End Function
```

Another of the APIs we used in Chapter 8, **HTFormLocateByName()**, is used to check if the appropriate Form is in the database and **HTDatabaseClose()** is used in the error-processing case to close the unwanted database.

```
' Check if the "Mail Watcher Info" form is in the database
FormID = HTFormLocateByName(gDatabase, "Mail Watcher Info")

' If the form is in the database, display the list of options
If (FormID <> 0) Then

    RefreshOptionsList
' If not, report an error and close the current database
Else

    MsgBox ("The database selected is not a WATCHER database")
    Status = HTDatabaseClose(gDatabase, 0)
    gDatabase = 0
End If
```

We now have an open database waiting to be interrogated. The next processing step that will probably occur is the firing of the OptionsList.Click() method. This will happen whenever one of the options in the list is selected by the user. This routine is quite simple in that it only has three lines of code: one to get the index of the selected option; another to call the routine to calculate the values for the chart, CalculateInfoValues(); and the last to call DisplayInfoValues() to display the graph.

CalculateInfoValues() and DisplayInfoValues() are the main controllers for the WATCHNFO application. Given the index of the selected option, each uses a case statement to switch among the five possible options. For the most part, the processing of the first four options is quite similar so we'll usually discuss the common parts for a single option and leave the rest for you to explore on your own. The last option, the list of the top 10 message senders, is unique in many ways and we'll spend a little more time on that one.

The first thing we need to do is create a new Index on the database. As with the C API, **HTIndexOpen()** is used to perform this function and provides an Index on output, given a database on input. Once the Index is open, the case statement is entered wherein each of the first four option types creates a formula string that will create the proper list of Documents within the Index. This is performed in a loop in each case since we are processing notes either by the day of the week the note was deleted, @Weekday, or by the month, @Month. We've also added the requirement that the Document's Form be Mail Watcher Info. With the formula in hand, **HTIndexSearch()** is used to create the list of desired Documents. If all went well to this point, a calculation routine is then called to create the list of values specific to the option, based on the Documents found.

```
Select Case (ListSelection)
    ' Process latency by day of the week
    Case OPTION_LATENCY_BY_DOW
        For i = 1 To 7
            Formula = "SELECT Form=" + Chr$(34) + "Mail Watcher
            Info" + Chr$(34) +
                    " & @Weekday(NoteInfo.Deleted) =" + Str(i)
            Status = HTIndexSearch(gIndex, Formula, 0, EmptyDatetime)
            If (StatusIsOK(Status)) Then
                CalculateLatencyValues (i)
            End If
        Next i
    ' Process latency by month
    Case OPTION_LATENCY_BY_MONTH
        For i = 1 To 12
            Formula = "SELECT Form=" + Chr$(34) + "Mail Watcher
            Info" + Chr$(34) +
                    " & @Month(NoteInfo.Deleted) =" + Str(i)
            Status = HTIndexSearch(gIndex, Formula, 0, EmptyDatetime)
            If (StatusIsOK(Status)) Then
                CalculateLatencyValues (i)
            End If
        Next i
    ' Process message count by day of the week
    Case OPTION_MESSAGES_BY_DOW
        For i = 1 To 7
```

```
        Formula = "SELECT Form=" + Chr$(34) + "Mail Watcher
        Info" + Chr$(34) +

                " & @Weekday(NoteInfo.Deleted) =" + Str(i)
        Status = HTIndexSearch(gIndex, Formula, 0, EmptyDatetime)
        If (StatusIsOK(Status)) Then
            CalculateCountValues (i)
        End If
    Next i
' Process message count by month
Case OPTION_MESSAGES_BY_MONTH
    For i = 1 To 12
        Formula = "SELECT Form=" + Chr$(34) + "Mail Watcher
        Info" + Chr$(34) +

                " & @Month(NoteInfo.Deleted) =" + Str(i)
        Status = HTIndexSearch(gIndex, Formula, 0, EmptyDatetime)
        If (StatusIsOK(Status)) Then
            CalculateCountValues (i)
        End If
    Next i
' Process top 10 message senders
Case OPTION_TOP10_MESSGES_BY_PERSON
    ViewID = HTViewLocateByName(gDatabase, "Messages by Sender")
    If (ViewID) Then
        Status = HTIndexOpenView(gIndex, NULLHANDLE, ViewID,
        HTOPENVIEWF_FLAT_VIEW)
        If (StatusIsOK(Status)) Then
            CalculateViewValues
        End If
    End If
End Select
```

As you can see from the OPTION_TOP10_MESSGES_BY_PERSON case above, if we are going for the top 10 list, we need to open an Index based on a database View. This View is one we've added to the WATCHER database that has the message sender, or NoteInfo.From field, as the first column. We've also set the column to be a category column, which we'll use to our advantage shortly.

There are three auxiliary calculation routines: CalculateLatencyValues(), CalculateCountValues(), and CalculateViewValues(). Of the three, CalculateCountValues() is the least complex. It does nothing more than get the number of Documents in the Index and stores it into the global values array based on the passed array index. **HTIndexGetCount()** is used to access this count, as was done in Chapter 8, and required nothing more than the open Index on input.

CalculateLatencyValues() does a bit more in the way of processing but is still really quite simple. After determining the number of notes in the Index, by using **HTIndexGetCount()**, each Document in the Index is accessed using the **HTIndexNavigate()** API. We touched on **HTIndexNavigate()** in Chapter 8 but never really put it to use. It is used here to do the same function as would a call to **HTIndexSetPosition()**, since this is a flat, Form-based Index and not View-based. The prototype for **HTIndexNavigate()** looks something like this:

```
Function HTIndexNavigate(hgindex as Long,
                    hgdirection As Integer,
                    hgnav_flags As Long,
                    hgdocid As Long,
                    hgindent As Long) As Long
```

Table 9.4 shows the different possibilities available for the second parameter in the call, the navigation style or direction.

Table 9.4 Direction Flags.

Flag	Description
HTNAV_NEXT	Navigate next (depth-first)
HTNAV_END	Navigate to the end
HTNAV_CURRENT	Stay on the current entry
HTNAV_SIBLING	Navigate at the current level
HTNAV_CHILD	Navigate one level down
HTNAV_PARENT	Navigate one level up
HTNAV_MAIN	Navigate at the top level

The last four of these are valid only within the scope of an Index created using a Notes View, a situation that occurs in the top 10 list processing. As you will soon see, we'll get a bit more creative when using this flag in the CalculateViewValues() routine.

NOTE
Within the call to **HTIndexNavigate()** used in the CalculateLatencyValues() routine, the HTNAV_NEXT flag is used to iterate through each note in the Index, one at a time.

The navigation flags, the third parameter on the call to **HTIndexNavigate()**, are a set of quite different operations that can be used to augment the navigation style. Table 9.5 lists the navigation flags.

Table 9.5 Navigation Flags.

Flag	Description
HTNAVF_PEEK	Restore current Index position
HTNAVF_BACKWARD	Go backward (default is forward)
HTNAVF_NO_CATEGORY	Ignore category rows
HTNAVF_NO_TOTAL	Ignore total rows

Here again, the last two flags in the list are valid only if the Index is based on a View. For the uses required in WATCHNFO, we'll always iterate through an Index from the top down without skipping any entries. For this, we'll set the navigation flags parameter to 0.

If the navigation process works, the Document ID of the current Document within the Index is returned in the fourth parameter. In most cases, this Document ID is just that, the ID of the Document within the Index. If, on the other hand, the current row within the Index is not a Document, e.g., it is a total or a category row, the high bit in the Document ID is set, producing an invalid Document ID. If you wish to determine whether the current Document ID is a category, AND it with the HTINDEXDOCID_CATEGORY constant. Also, ANDing it with HTINDEXDOCID_TOTAL will tell you if the row is a total row. If all you want to know is whether the row is a true Document, use the HTINDEXDOCID_SPECIAL_MASK as the AND mask.

The viewcell indent, parameter number five, is valid on output only if the Index is once again based on a View. In the case of a flat Index, this value is always returned as a zero. It takes on a number of different meanings within a View Index, based on the type of the current row. For totals row, the indent is always zero. For categories, it is the cascade indent level as displayed within the Notes user-interface. For Documents, the indent starts at zero for the top-level Document and increases by one for each level of response. The call to **HTIndexNavigate()** used in the CalculateLatencyValues() routine is shown below.

```
' go to the next document in the index
Status = HTIndexNavigate(gIndex, HTNAV_NEXT, 0, DocID, Indent)
```

From here, the indexed Document is opened using **HTDocument-Open()**, the number of seconds that elapsed between the creation and deletion time, the NoteInfo.ElapsedSeconds item, is accessed using **HTItemFetch()**, and the Document is subsequently closed using **HTDocumentClose()**.

```
' open the indexed document
Status = HTDocumentOpen(gDatabase, DocID, 0, Document)
If (StatusIsOK(Status)) Then
    ' Get the latency value from the document
    Status = HTItemFetch(Document,
                        "NoteInfo.ElapsedSeconds",
                        HTTYPE_NUMBER,
                        0,
                        HTTYPE_NUMBER,
                        ElapsedSeconds)

  Rem Don't report error since we may not have a calculated latency yet
    If (Status = HTSUCCESS) Then
        gValues(ArrayPosition) = gValues(ArrayPosition) +
                            ElapsedSeconds
    End If
    Status = HTDocumentClose(Document, 0)
End If
```

The average latency value for the period is then calculated by dividing the sum of all of the elapsed seconds values by the number of Documents.

NOTE

To make things a little easier, we've chosen to calculate latency values to the nearest second. If put into production, you may want to track and format the values as an array of doubles rather than longs.

The last of the three calculation routines, CalculateViewValues(), remains. As the name implies, this routine performs all of its calculations based on a Notes View, or HiTest Index object. The Index used in this case is the one that was opened based on the Messages by Sender View in the CalculateInfoValues() routine. As with the other two calculation routines, **HTIndexGetCount()** is once again used here to get the number of Documents contained in the Index. This value will be used at the end of the routine to determine the number of messages sent by the person designated in the last category in the View.

We are now at a point where we need to do something a little different from what we've seen before. We now have a Index on a database where each of the major categories contains the name of a different person who has been sending mail. What we would like to do is to get each person's name and the total number of messages sent by that person to determine it they are in the top 10 list.

CalculateViewValues() performs this function in a very general manner by making use of one of the View-specific direction flags on the call to **HTIndexNavigate()**. In this case, the HTNAV_SIBLING flag will be used as the second parameter in the call to skip among the top level categories within the Index. When the returned status from the call returns a value other than HTSUCCESS, we'll assume that all of the categories within the Index have been exhausted.

```
' Go to the first category in the index
Status = HTIndexNavigate(gIndex, HTNAV_SIBLING, 0, DocID, Indent)
While (Status = HTSUCCESS)
    .
    .
    .
```

```
' Advance to the next category in the index
    Status = HTIndexNavigate(gIndex, HTNAV_SIBLING, 0, DocID,
Indent)
Wend
```

Each time a new category Document has been found, we need to extract two pieces of information from it. One of the pieces of information will be obtained directly from the category Document itself, using a call we have yet to discuss, **HTViewcellFetch()**. **HTViewcellFetch()** is really nothing more than **HTItemFetch()** performed on a View Document rather than on a database Document. As you can see from the prototypes of the two functions below, the only real difference between the two calls, other than the obvious Document vs. Index reference, is that a column index is used in the call to **HTViewcellFetch()** to identify the source of the information rather than an item name and type.

```
Declare Function HTItemFetch(hgdocument As Long,
                    hgitemname As String,
                    hgitem_type As Integer,
                    hgbuffer_length As Long,
                    hgbuffer_type As Integer,
                    hgbuffer As Any) As Long


Declare Function HTViewcellFetch(hgindex As Long,
                    hgcolumn As Long,
                    hgbuffer_type As Integer,
                    hgbuffer_length As Long,
                    hgbuffer As Any) As Long
```

NOTE At this point you may be asking yourself, "Why didn't they just use item binding as in the CLIPSERV application in Chapter 8?" Unfortunately, the answer here is that item and viewcell binding APIs are just a few of the dozen or so HiTest C APIs that are not supported in the Visual Basic set. Actually, most of the APIs that manipulate addresses of write-back buffers or pointers are not present in the Visual Basic realm due to the problems faced with converting these entities from a C-based platform to Visual Basic.

To get our message sender name from the Index: We know that the sender name is the first column in the View, so the following call to **HTViewcellFetch()** will get us the information we desire.

```
Status = HTViewcellFetch(gIndex, 1, HTTYPE_TEXT, 0, ByVal From)
```

The second piece of information we need is the number of Documents each person has sent or, in other words, the number of Documents contained in each category. Although there are quite a number of ways this could be done, we've decided to take the easy, and most general, road to a solution. This also allows us to use another "undiscovered" Index API, **HTIndexGetPosition()**.

The idea is quite simple, really. For the first category we find, determine the absolute position for the category Document within the Index. For all intents and purposes, it should be 1. From there, each time a new category is found, its position is determined as well. The number of Documents in the previous category is then calculated as the difference of the two positions -1. The only special consideration here is that the ending position of the last category in the list is actually the total number of Documents in the Index, a value we obtained at the top of the routine. The logic behind this processing is shown below.

```
' Get the absolute position of the category in the index
Position = HTIndexGetPosition(gIndex)

' If we aren't on the first category, calculate
' the note count for the previous category and
' check if it is to be added to the top 10 list
If (Position > 1) Then
    NoteCount = Position - LastPosition - 1
    ArrayPosition = CheckForTop10(NoteCount, LastFrom)
End If
LastFrom = From
LastPosition = Position
    .
    .
    .
```

```
' Clean up processing for the last category in the index
NoteCount = DocCount - LastPosition
ArrayPosition = CheckForTop10(NoteCount, LastFrom)
```

Once the number of Documents sent by each person has been determined, the CheckForTop10() routine is called to check if that person is one of the top ten message senders. This routine is nothing more than a very simple bubble sort that stores the sender name and Document count into two global areas for subsequent processing by the display routines. Since there are no HiTest APIs used within the routine, we'll let you breeze through the 12 lines of code on your own, if you so desire.

Everything from here on out within WATCHNFO is Visual Basic-specific. All of the information we need from Notes has already been obtained. We won't go through too much of the display processing within the application other than to give a brief overview of how it was done. So if you're interested, read the next several paragraphs. If not, its on to the HiTest BASIC Tools Top *n* list.

The display processing within WATCHNFO uses the controls on the bottom two-thirds of the form to create the five different bar graphs. The controls on the form consist of a GraphTitle text area and 12 GraphLabel, GraphValue pairs. The GraphLabel field of each pair is set to the textual label for each bar depending on the graph, days of the week, months of the year, or mail sender names. The GraphValue field holds the raw value for each bar graphically depicted within the graph.

Depending on the graph chosen, the appropriate number of label/value pairs are left visible and all others are hidden. For example, only 7 pairs are displayed for day-of-the-week graphs whereas 12 are used for the monthly graphs. The length of each individual bar is calculated by first determining the full range of values to be displayed and then calculating the percentage of that range each bar contains.

HiTest BASIC Tools Top *n*

1. If you're prototyping, use the htVISUAL controls!
2. Just about anything you can do in HiTest C, you can do in VB.

3. If you want to create a quick mailer, use the Mail Control.

4. Remember that the htVISUAL Controls and htGLUE layer can be used together in the same application.

Notes APIs and the Internet

Now that we've discussed each of the three API sets and have created some applications to show how they can be used, it's time to look at the world from a different perspective. Up to this point, the applications we've created were designed with two considerations in mind: First and foremost, the intent was to design the application to show how to use several of the APIs within each set in order to accomplish a specific task. The second consideration was to create the application so that it could be a useful addition to a Notes application toolbox.

Now it's time to break out of the mold of Notes tools and work on something a bit different—the Internet. As we discussed in previous chapters, Notes Version 4.0 has made quite a few strides on the road towards Internet awareness and interoperability with the suite of products collectively called *InterNotes*. One of the tools in this suite, the InterNotes Publisher, provides for the ability to publish the contents of Notes databases for use on the Internet. Publishing, in this case, involves creating HyperText Markup Language (HTML) documents providing facsimiles of Notes Views and Documents that can be navigated in a manner similar to that of the default Notes operation.

Although this publishing capability is quite adequate in most cases, there may be cases where you would like more control over how the information is transferred and formatted for display within the resulting HTML document. In this chapter we're going to create an application that will allow us to do just that—translate Notes Documents into HTML and vice versa—while providing a level of control not currently available with other tools. To do this, we're going to look into one of the operations provided by Internet servers, the Common Gateway Interface or CGI.

The application that we'll be building, NETXFER (\HITESTC\WIN32-\NETXFER), will allow for both reading and writing data to a Notes database. It will operate as a Windows CGI application that is passed, as we'll see, a specific set of command line parameters from the Internet server.

Although the data for the information transfer will come either from Notes or from fields in an Internet form, the information concerning the destination of the data and the specific fields to transfer will be obtained from a Windows INI file, NETXFER.INI. We used an INI file here for one reason, to keep the interface as simple as possible. As with all of the other applications we've built within this book, we put the premium on learning some details on how to use a specific Notes API set, not on learning the Windows interface. We'll talk more about the format of the sections within the NETXFER.INI when we get into the application design section of this chapter.

Before going much further, we need to discuss some of the ground rules. First of all, we're assuming that you have a basic working knowledge of the Internet. This would encompass such things as knowing a bit about the language of the Internet, HTML. NETXFER will not only make use of HTML pages produced outside of the application but will create them internally as well.

The second assumption we're making is that you have already read the chapter in this book on the Notes HiTest C API or at least have a good understanding of the API set itself. This is the API set we'll use to talk to Notes within the NETXFER application. It was chosen over the Notes C API mostly due to ease-of-use issues described in Chapter 6. In addition, this is a great application for using the data conversion capabilities available within item binding.

Finally, if you know about the standard Common Gateway Interface (CGI) conventions, you're all set. Although NETXFER is a Windows CGI application, the general idea is the same. It's the implementation of the way the information is passed that's different. Don't worry if you don't already know a lot about CGI, as we'll discuss the workings of the Windows CGI interface in some detail along the way.

CGI: HTML On-the-Fly

Now, if you're saying, "I thought this section of this book was supposed to discuss the Notes API sets; what are you doing talking about the Internet and Common Gateway Interfaces?", be patient. We'll get to those APIs in a moment. If you are already well versed in the ways of the Internet and the Common Gateway Interface, you may want to skip to the next section. If not, we'll try to take an overview of what it all means and then go on.

The Common Gateway Interface is an architecture that is used by Internet servers to allow access to external, server-based applications from an HTML page on the client. Although there are several different pathways that can be used to allow a client to execute a CGI application on the server, the method we've chosen to support within the NETXFER application is the use of the POST method from an HTML form. If these terms aren't familiar to you, don't worry—we'll walk through them as we describe the design of the NETXFER application.

NOTE If you do want to dive into the internal workings of HTML forms and CGI, you can always do some searching on the Internet. There is a plethora of information out there on these two topics just waiting to be browsed. One such site that describes the Windows CGI 1.1 specification is http://www.city.net/win-httpd/httpddoc/wincgi.htm.

Let's look at the flow of control as it pertains to the execution cycle of a standard CGI application. Figure 10.1 shows six separate steps involved in the process.

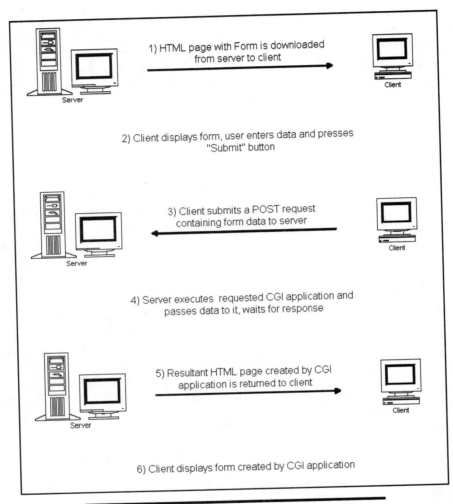

1) HTML page with Form is downloaded from server to client

Server

Client

2) Client displays form, user enters data and presses "Submit" button

3) Client submits a POST request containing form data to server

Server

Client

4) Server executes requested CGI application and passes data to it, waits for response

5) Resultant HTML page created by CGI application is returned to client

Server

Client

6) Client displays form created by CGI application

Figure 10.1 Common Gateway Interface functionality.

First of all, a client requests an HTML page, containing an HTML form, from a server. An HTML form is really nothing more than what its name implies, a means of providing to the user a graphical form that allows data to be input into fields. Figure 10.2 shows an example of an HTML form that allows the user to enter five different pieces of personal information. Table 10.1 shows the information that can be entered and the name of the field within the form where it is stored.

Table 10.1 HTML Form Fields

Information	Field Name
Last Name	LastName
First Name	FirstName
Age	Age
Telephone Number	Telephone
E-mail Address	Email

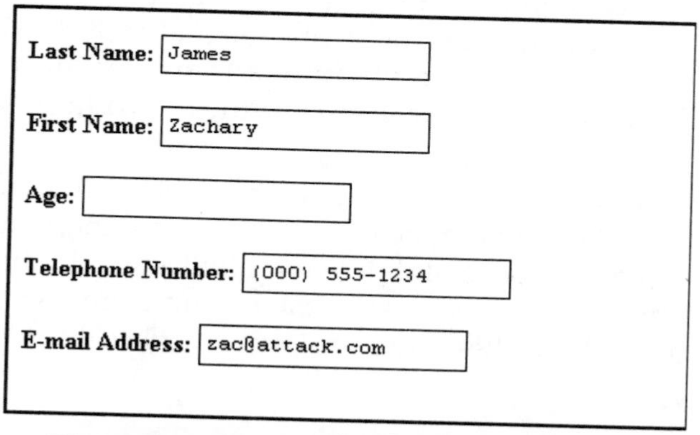

Figure 10.2 Personal Information HTML Form.

The HTML source for this form is shown below.

```
<HEAD>
<TITLE>Personal Information HTML Form</TITLE>
</HEAD>
<BODY>
<FORM>
<B>Last Name: </B> <INPUT TYPE="TEXT" INPUT NAME="LastName"
VALUE="James">
<P>
<B>First Name: </B> <INPUT TYPE="TEXT" INPUT NAME="FirstName"
VALUE="Zachary">
<P>
```

```
<B>Age: </B> <INPUT TYPE="TEXT" INPUT NAME="Age" VALUE="">
<P>
<B>Telephone Number: </B> <INPUT TYPE="TEXT" INPUT NAME="Telephone"
VALUE="(123) 555-1234">
<P>
<B>E-mail Address: </B> <INPUT TYPE="TEXT" INPUT NAME="Email"
VALUE="zac@attack.com">
</FORM>
```

The HTML tag, or element, used to declare the start of a form is, not surprisingly, <FORM> and the </FORM> tag is used to end the form. The <FORM> tag also has modifiers, or attributes, that include METHOD and ACTION. These are the two attributes that provide the setup for enabling CGI functionality. We'll discuss these two in more detail in a moment.

One of the second-level modifiers, or subelements, of the <FORM> element defines a field within the form and an input mechanism for it, the <INPUT> tag. There are several different attributes within the definition of this element but the ones we use in the example are some of the more common. Table 10.2 lists these attributes and describes the role they play.

Table 10.2 INPUT Element Attributes.

Attribute	Description
NAME	The name of the form field
TYPE	The datatype of the field (e.g., TEXT, CHECKBOX, RADIO, IMAGE)
VALUE	The default value of the field
HIDDEN	Do not display the field on the form
SUBMIT	Submit a request to the Internet server

Now that we have an HTML form defined, all we need to do is add the METHOD and ACTION attributes to the <FORM> element to allow the server to execute a CGI application and pass the fields defined in the form to it. The METHOD attribute describes how the server transfers the form data to the server. The two possible values here are GET and POST. The differences among the two are not that important within the context of this discussion but the POST method has fewer limitations. That's the one we'll use within NETXFER.

The ACTION attribute is used to tell the server the location of the CGI application that is to be executed. This location can be specified in several different formats. The two most common formats are either a fully defined Universal Resource Locator (URL) code

```
http://www.whatever.com/wincgi/netxfer.exe
```

or by providing a path that is relative to the server executable.

```
/wincgi/netxfer.exe
```

Any of the possible formats for the CGI application location can be used with no difference in functionality. Many times the choice is made merely by selecting the easiest method for the current situation.

We now have an HTML form with fields and a definition of how and where a CGI application on the server is to be executed. The final step necessary is to provide a method by which the user can submit the request to execute the CGI application to the server. This is done by using one of the <INPUT> attributes mentioned in Table 10.2, the SUBMIT attribute. When this attribute is used, a push-button is displayed on the HTML page. As this button is pressed by the user, the request defined by the form's METHOD and ACTION attributes is sent to the server. The server then takes the request and processes it accordingly. Figure 10.3 shows the Personal Information form with the added tags necessary to send the fields in the form to a CGI application on the server. The HTML source for the form immediately follows the figure.

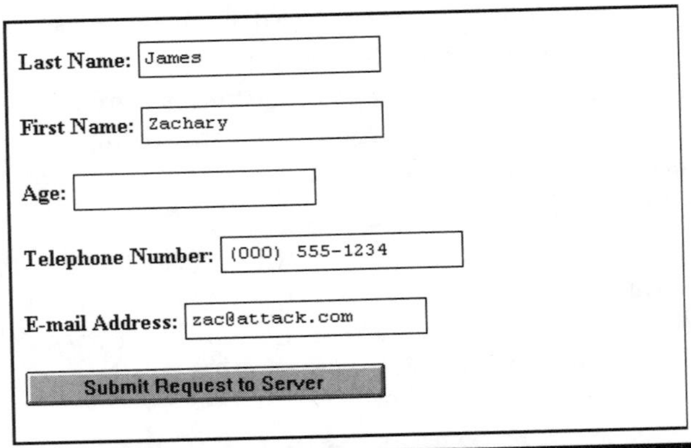

Figure 10.3 Personal Information HTML Form with Submit button.

```
<HEAD>
<TITLE>Personal Information HTML Form</TITLE>
</HEAD>
<BODY>
<FORM METHOD="POST" ACTION="/wincgi/netxfer.exe">
<B>Last Name: </B> <INPUT TYPE="TEXT" INPUT NAME="LastName"
VALUE="James">
<P>
<B>First Name: </B> <INPUT TYPE="TEXT" INPUT NAME="FirstName"
VALUE="Zachary">
<P>
<B>Age: </B> <INPUT TYPE="TEXT" INPUT NAME="Age" VALUE="">
<P>
<B>Telephone Number: </B> <INPUT TYPE="TEXT" INPUT NAME="Telephone"
VALUE="(123) 555-1234">
<P>
<B>E-mail Address: </B> <INPUT TYPE="TEXT" INPUT NAME="Email"
VALUE="zac@attack.com">
<P>
<INPUT TYPE="SUBMIT" VALUE="Submit Request to Server">
</FORM>
```

Windows CGI: How It's Done

We now have a form that can be used to send some information to a CGI application—more specifically, a Windows CGI application—called NETXFER in the WINCGI subdirectory. The question we now have to answer is, "How is the information passed from the server to a Windows CGI application?" Once we know that, we'll create an application that performs three basic steps:

1. parses data passed from the client's form and determines the requested operation

2. performs the appropriate Notes Document read and/or write functions

3. creates an HTML document for the server to return to the client

It's important to mention the components used to create the NETXFER application because of the continuing flux within Internet and HTML and CGI specifications. The Internet server we used for the NETXFER example was the Netscape Communications Server Version 1.12. Because this version of the server was designed using the Windows CGI 1.1 interface specification, this interface will be described below.

At the time this book was written the only available Microsoft Windows platform for this server was Windows NT. This fact simplified the operating system selection. To be totally accurate, we used Windows NT 3.51 Advanced Server. NETXFER was written using Microsoft Visual C++ 2.0 and, as mentioned previously, the HiTest C API.

Let's get back to the Windows CGI information passing mechanism. When the POST method is used to request the execution of a Windows CGI application, the application is invoked with three command line parameters:

1. the CGI data file

2. the CGI content file

3. the CGI output file

The first two files are formatted as Windows INI files with the CGI data file being the one we'll work with exclusively within NETXFER. Not only is the information of the content file fully contained in the data file, but the format of the data is much easier to work with as well.

The CGI content file contains only one type of information, the form field information. The format of the data in the CGI content file format is a single stream of information containing field name/field data pairs, separated by the equals sign (=), and delimited by ampersands (&) with all spaces substituted with the plus (+) sign. For instance, assume a form had three fields named Field1, Field2, and Field3 that contained the information "Data 1", "Data 2", and "Data 3". The CGI content file would therefore contain the following string:

```
Field1=Data+1&Field2=Data+2&Field3=Data+3
```

The CGI data file, on the other hand, contains several sections, three of them dealing with the form field data. The first, the [Form Literal] section, contains the field name/field data pairs in the familiar keyword=value INI file format. The stipulation here is that the field information will be in this section of the file only if the data portion of the field is less than 255 characters. It has no special characters or embedded double quotes (").

If the field in not in the [Form Literal] section due to the restrictions above, and the data in the field is less than 65,535 characters, the information on the field is contained in the [Form External] section. In this case, the format is keyword=filename datasize where:

- keyword field name
- filename fully qualified path and file name of file containing field data
- datasize length of the field data (in bytes)

Finally, if the field contains more than 65,535 characters, the information on the field data is found in the [Form Huge] section. The format of the data in this section is the field name, followed by an equals sign (=) followed by a numeric offset. In this case, all of the field data are contained in the CGI content file and the offset is the byte offset to the start of the field data relative to the start of the CGI content file.

Within NETXFER, we'll only concern ourselves with the Form Literal section and assume all of the field information will fit into that mold.

NOTE

Table 10.3 lists the other sections available within the Windows CGI data file and a description of the type of information they contain. None of the information in these sections is used by NETXFER but we've included them just so you will know where to find more information if needed.

Table 10.3 CGI Data File sections

Attribute	Description
[CGI]	Version, path, and transmission information
[Accept]	List of data types supported by the client system
[System]	Windows-specific information (e.g. content and output file names, etc.)
[Extra Headers]	"Extra" information sent with request
[Form File]	Upload file information

The last of the three files contained in the parameter list on the call to a Windows CGI application is the CGI output file. This is the name of the HTML file to be created by the Windows CGI application that will be subsequently returned to the client for display. The only thing special about this file is that it requires a single-line header that must precede the HTML text. This header line is used to tell the server the type of information contained in the file. For the purposes of the NETXFER application, we'll always return an HTML text file as output. The header line will look as follows:

```
Content-type: text/html
```

Now we've got all the pieces assembled. We've discussed how to generate a request to the Internet server to have it execute a Windows CGI application and the format of the data as it is passed from the server to the Windows CGI application. We have two things left to do: design what we want NETXFER to do, then do it.

NETXFER: The Design

As we stated in the previous section, NETXFER will perform three basic steps: parse data, perform Notes read/write, and create an output HTML document. Let's create a design for the application by looking at each of these steps, one at a time.

In the first step, parsing the data, we'll actually do a bit more than just parse the data sent from the client. As we discussed in the beginning of the chapter, we're going to make use of an INI file for additional setup information. Therefore, we'll need to somehow tie this setup information to the data contained in the client's HTML form. To do this, we'll use the <INPUT> element and one of its attributes discussed in Table 10.2, the HIDDEN attribute. For each form that will be used with the NETXFER application, an invisible field named NETXFERProcess must contain the name of the process to be run. The setup information for this process will then be accessed from the server's NETXFER.INI by using the process name as the INI file section name.

Each process defined in the INI file can have up to seven different types of keywords defined. These keywords are described in Table 10.4.

Table 10.4 Process Keywords.

Keyword	Description
NotesServer	Name of Notes server containing database (NULL if Local)
NotesDatabase	Name of Notes database to transfer data into/out of
NotesForm	Name of Notes Form to be used to store/retrieve data
Destination	Data destination (INTERNET or NOTES)
HTMLTemplate	HTML template file for use when converting Notes Documents to HTML
FieldCount	The number of fields to transfer
Field##	The name of the indexed field within the Notes database (1-based)

To bring this all together, let's say, for instance, that we want to send the personal information we collected in the form in Figure 10.3 to a Notes database. Let's call the process "TransferPersonalInfo" and assume that the pertinent Notes database information is as follows:

Notes Server = MAIN_SERVER

Notes Database = PERSONAL.NSF

Notes Form = Personal Information

This is all of the information we need to complete the HTML form, including the required hidden field.

```
<HEAD>
<TITLE>Personal Information HTML Form</TITLE>
</HEAD>
<BODY>
<FORM METHOD="POST" ACTION="/wincgi/netxfer.exe">
<INPUT TYPE="HIDDEN" INPUT NAME="NETXFERProcess"
VALUE="TransferPersonalInfo">
<B>Last Name: </B> <INPUT TYPE="TEXT" INPUT NAME="LastName"
VALUE="James">
<P>
<B>First Name: </B> <INPUT TYPE="TEXT" INPUT NAME="FirstName"
VALUE="Zachary">
<P>
<B>Age: </B> <INPUT TYPE="TEXT" INPUT NAME="Age" VALUE="">
<P>
<B>Telephone Number: </B> <INPUT TYPE="TEXT" INPUT NAME="Telephone"
VALUE="(123) 555-1234">
<P>
<B>E-mail Address: </B> <INPUT TYPE="TEXT" INPUT NAME="Email"
VALUE="zac@attack.com">
<P>
<INPUT TYPE="SUBMIT" VALUE="Submit Request to Server">
</FORM>
```

The process setup information section in the NETXFER.INI file would look as follows:

```
[TransferPersonalInfo]
NotesServer= MAIN_SERVER
NotesDatabase=PERSONAL.NSF
NotesForm=Personal Information
```

```
Destination=NOTES
FieldCount=5
Field1=LastName
Field2=FirstName
Field3=Age
Field4=Telephone
Field5=Email
```

The second step of the three is that of either storing or retrieving the Notes data for the defined process. The direction of the data flow is based on the `Destination` keyword in the NETXFER.INI file. If set to NOTES, the data is read from the client's HTML form, and a new Notes Document on the defined server and database is created using the named Form as the template. If INTERNET is specified, each of the Documents within the database created with the named Form will be transferred. By default, each Document will be written as a new row in an HTML table. Figure 10.4 provides an example of how an HTML table with several Notes Documents containing personal information might look.

LastName	FirstName	Age	Telephone	Email
James	Zachary	53	(123) 555-4545	ZJ@sportsgalore.com
Loren	Wade	38	(456) 555-2004	Wade@compuhome.com
Street	Xavier	87	(789) 555-1111	XS@sd.com

Figure 10.4 Personal information HTML table.

This brings us to the last of the three processing steps, the creation of the HTML output file. To add a little spice to the NETXFER application, we've added a feature that, although it has little to do with the HiTest C API, makes NETXFER a little more flexible when transferring multiple Documents from Notes. If you wish not to have each Notes Document brought back to the client as a row in a simple table, the "HTMLTemplate" process keyword can be used. The data associated with this keyword is the fully qualified name of an HTML file on the server. This file is assumed to be a fully functional HTML document with two exceptions.

The first exception is that it is expected that the template file contains a set of <NETXFERREPEAT> and </NETXFERREPEAT> tags. These tags are specific to the NETXFER application and are used to define the section in the HTML template file that is repeated for each new Notes Document. Within this repeated section, whenever a field associated with the transfer is to be written to the output file, the field name must be prefixed and suffixed by two percent signs (%%), exception number two. Figure 10.5 shows how the same three Notes Documents in Figure 10.4 are displayed with the following NETXFER repeated section definition.

```
<NETXFERREPEAT>

<HR>

<B>Last Name: </B>%%LastName%%

<BR>

<B>First Name: </B>%%FirstName%%

<BR>

<B>Age: </B>%%Age%%

<BR>

<B>Telephone Number: </B>%%Telephone%%

<BR>

<B>E-mail Address: </B>%%Email%%

<BR>

<HR>

</NETXFERREPEAT>
```

Last Name: James
First Name: Zachary
Age: 53
Telephone Number: (123) 555-4545
E-mail Address: ZJ@sportsgalore.com

Last Name: Loren
First Name: Wade
Age: 38
Telephone Number: (456) 555-2004
E-mail Address: Wade@compuhome.com

Last Name: Street
First Name: Xavier
Age: 87
Telephone Number: (789) 555-1111
E-mail Address: XS@sd.com

Figure 10.5 Personal Information using HTML template.

NETXFER: The Code

Here we are, ready to do some coding. As you may have guessed from the design description, NETXFER is not that large an application from a functionality standpoint. And, with the help of the HiTest C API, it's not that large from a lines-of-code standpoint either. This is, as we've mentioned throughout the second half of this book, one of the biggest advantages of using the HiTest C API over the Notes C API—the sheer reduction in the number of lines of code required to perform a function. The one feature of the HiTest C API that will assist us greatly in this case is item binding. As you'll soon see, it can take a lot of the tedium out of item information access. Enough preaching: Let's write some code.

The first part of NETXFER.C looks very much like all the other source files we've discussed within this book in that the ever-present operating-system-type definition is one of the first definitions you'll see. In this case, `HTOS_WINNT` is used to state that this application will use the 32-bit Windows NT version of the HiTest C API.

The next item of importance within NETXFER is the command line parsing code. Not that it's all that ingenious or revolutionary, but it is a major part of the "parse data" step. The reason we need to do this parsing so early is so we can find out which process we are going to use. Since we expect this to be contained in the `NETXFERProcess` field in the form, we need to determine the name of the Windows CGI data file before we can get it from the [Form Literal] section. Once we have the data file name, we can make a call to the Windows GetPrivateProfileString() API to get the name of the process.

```
// get the process name from the Internet data file [Form Literal]
section

GetPrivateProfileString("Form Literal",

                        "NETXFERProcess",

                        "",

                        gszProcessName,

                        sizeof(gszProcessName),

                        gszInternetDataFile);
```

You'll have noticed that we've added a debugging capability to NETXFER much akin to the one added to the WATCHER application in Chapter 7. Here again, as with the WATCHER, there is really no good way of debugging NETXFER using conventional means. The DebugFile routines were used to provide some level of understanding as to what is going on within the application if error conditions are encountered. The DEBUG() routine was also added to reduce the number of characters we had to type to send out a debug message. We don't think of it as lazy, but as frugal.

The next few lines of code do nothing more than gather the setup information for the process from the NETXFER.INI file. The one thing we will note here is that the field names for the process are read in and placed into a global memory area. This memory is allocated and locked within WinMain() and not released until we exit from the application. We do this since the lifespan of a CGI application should be as short as possible. Within this environment, the server and, more importantly, the client need to wait for the HTML output file to be produced and for the CGI application to exit and return control back to the server. Admittedly, the impact of locking and unlocking a memory area as compared to reading information from a disk file is relatively small but we might as well do the best we can.

The memory area for the field text is allocated and locked in the same manner, again for performance reasons.

NOTE

We have now read in all of the setup information for the defined process and we're ready to transfer some data. This step is initiated by posting the WM_PERFORM_TRANSFER message to the application's main window procedure.

The first thing we do in the WM_PERFORM_TRANSFER message processing is to initialize the HiTest C API using the **HTInit()** call. We set the initialization flags to 0 once again, since we want the HiTest engine to initialize the Notes C API engine for us. The sister function, **HTTerm()**, is also used to terminate the HiTest API when the application exits.

The next API call we need to make is **HTDatabaseOpen()**. Having obtained the server and database name for the process from the NETXFER.INI, we can pass them as the first two parameters in the call. The third parameter, the open word flag, is set to 0 as was done within the CLIPSERV application in Chapter 8. This was done since we don't require any special open functionality, also described in Chapter 8.

After the call to **HTDatabaseOpen()**, you'll notice a call to the StatusIsOK() routine. This is the same routine we've used in several of the previous applications and does nothing more than check if an error has occurred and, if so, uses the **HTErrorGetInfo()** API to get the error text and report it.

HTFormLocateByName() is used to get the ID of the Form involved in the process. The Form ID will be needed whether we retrieve information from, or send information to, Notes. As you'll remember from the discussion of this API in Chapter 8, it's not the speediest way to obtain a Form ID but, unfortunately, it's probably the best way to find the information we need.

Another option here would be to use the **HTFormList()** API. This is similar to the other list APIs we discussed in Chapter 8, with the structure returned in this case being an HTFORMSUMM structure. Table 10.5 shows the contents of the HTFORMSUMM structure, including the

Form name value. Using this API, we could enumerate through all of the Forms in the database, comparing the name contained in the INI file with the name from the HTFORMSUMM structure. Since this is the same basic operation taken by **HTFormLocateByName()**, we might just as well use a single call to accomplish the entire function.

Table 10.5 HTFORMSUMM Structure

Field	Type	Description
formid	HTFORMID	Form ID
hidden	HTBOOL	TRUE if Form is hidden
name	char[HTMAXLEN_DESIGN_NAME]	Form name
menu_name	char[HTMAXLEN_MENU_NAME]	Menu display name
cascade_name	char[HTMAXLEN_MENU_NAME]	Cascading display name

Once we have all of the information that is common to both reading from and writing to Notes, the next step is to open the HTML output file. A call to OpenInternetOutputFile() will do just that. This routine will open the HTML output file, named in the third command line parameter, and write the appropriate header information into it. This header information includes the content type, discussed earlier, as well as the rest of the information dependent on whether we are reading or writing data to Notes. In addition, if we are reading from Notes, the output will depend on whether or not a template file has been specified. If we are writing to Notes, no additional information is written to the file here since all we'll do is report a success or failure once the transfer is complete.

If we are reading information from Notes, and if a template file is not being used, OpenInternetOutputFile() will add a heading title and then create an HTML table that contains the name of each field as a column heading. The HTML that would result when reading a database containing the personal information described above would look something like this:

```
Content-type: text/html

<HTML>
```

```
<HEAD>
<TITLE>HTML page created by NETXFER</TITLE>
</HEAD>
<BODY>
<TABLE BORDER>
<TR>
<TH>LastName</TH><TH>FirstName</TH><TH>Age</TH><TH>Telephone</TH><TH
>Email</TH>
</TR>
```

If a template file is being used, this routine will copy everything from
the template file up to the <NETXFERREPEAT> tag to the output file. It will
then read each subsequent line in the template file up to the
</NETXFERREPEAT> tag and add it to an global array of lines, using the
AddARepeatedLine()   routine.   The   code   for   the
OpenInternetOutputFile() routine is shown below.

```
BOOL OpenInternetOutputFile(void)
{
    BOOL    bOK = FALSE;
    BOOL    bLineFound, bRepeatFound;
    HTINT   i;

    ghOutputFile = File_OpenAsNew(gszInternetOutputFile);
    if (ghOutputFile)
    {
        // write the content type header string to the HTML output file
        File_WriteString(ghOutputFile, "Content-type: text/html");
        File_WriteString(ghOutputFile, "");

        // if we have no template file, use default HTML output
        if ((lstrlen(gszInternetTemplateFile)) == 0)
        {
            File_WriteString(ghOutputFile, "<HTML>");
            File_WriteString(ghOutputFile, "<HEAD>");
            File_WriteString(ghOutputFile, "<TITLE>HTML page created
            by NETXFER</TITLE>");
            File_WriteString(ghOutputFile, "</HEAD>");
```

```
        File_WriteString(ghOutputFile, "<BODY>");

    // if the data is going to the Internet, create a table
       for the data
    if (gDataDestination == TO_INTERNET)
    {
        File_WriteString(ghOutputFile, "<TABLE BORDER>");
        File_WriteString(ghOutputFile, "<TR>");

        // add the header row
        gszTempString[0] = '\0';
        for (i=0; i < gFieldCount; i++)
        {
            lstrcat(gszTempString, "<TH>");
            lstrcat(gszTempString, (LPSTR)
            &(glpaszFieldNames[i]));
            lstrcat(gszTempString, "</TH> ");
        }
        File_WriteString(ghOutputFile, gszTempString);
        File_WriteString(ghOutputFile, "</TR>");
    }
}
else
{

    // go to the repeat section
    bRepeatFound = FALSE;
    ghTemplateFile = File_OpenRead(gszInternetTemplateFile);
    bLineFound = File_ReadString(ghTemplateFile,
    gszTempString);
    if ((lstrcmpi(gszTempString, "<NETXFERREPEAT>")) == 0)
    {
        bRepeatFound = TRUE;
    }
    while (bLineFound && !bRepeatFound)
    {
        File_WriteString(ghOutputFile, gszTempString);
```

```
    bLineFound = File_ReadString(ghTemplateFile,
    gszTempString);
    if ((lstrcmpi(gszTempString, "<NETXFERREPEAT>")) == 0)

    {
        bRepeatFound = TRUE;

    }

}

// find all of the lines in the repeated section
bLineFound = File_ReadString(ghTemplateFile,
gszTempString);
if ((lstrcmpi(gszTempString, "</NETXFERREPEAT>")) == 0)
{
    bRepeatFound = FALSE;

}

while (bLineFound && bRepeatFound)
{
    AddARepeatedLine(gszTempString);
    bLineFound = File_ReadString(ghTemplateFile,
    gszTempString);
    if ((lstrcmpi(gszTempString, "</NETXFERREPEAT>")) == 0)

    {
        bRepeatFound = FALSE;

    }

}

}
    bOK = TRUE;

}
return(bOK);

}
```

If all goes well with opening the HTML output file, the
WM_PERFORM_TRANSFER message processing continues by determining
whether we are reading from, or writing to, Notes. If reading from
Notes, i.e., the data destination is the Internet, we'll need to find all of the
Documents within the database that were created with the named Notes

Form and then transfer the appropriate fields from each Document to the output file. We performed this same operation in the CLIPSERV application through using a combination of the **HTIndexOpen()** and **HTIndexSearch()** APIs. Here again, the only search parameter passed to the **HTIndexSearch()** API is the Form ID that we obtained from **HTFormLocateByName()**.

```
// create a new index on the database
Status = HTIndexOpen(gNotesDB, &Index);
if (StatusIsOK(Status))
{
    // find all of the documents with the named form
    Status = HTIndexSearch(Index,
                    NULL,
                    FormID,
                    NULL);
    ...
    }
}
```

We are now at the point where we'll not only make use of the basic function of item binding but also utilize the automatic data conversion feature. We know that for each Document in the Index, we'll need to access the data contained in each of the fields defined for this process. We also know that we'll need the data in textual form since it will be written directly to the HTML output file, which is text based. As you'll remember from the previous discussion of the **HTIndexBindItem()** API in Chapter 8, it not only allows for automatically loading a program variable with item data each time a Document is read but it allows for automatic conversion of the data as well.

What we've done is simply to loop through all of the fields to be processed and set up to bind the field item to a position in the field text array. This is the same array that was allocated when we read in the fields from the NETXFER.INI file. In addition, as you can see in the fifth parameter in the call shown below, we asked the HiTest engine to convert each field to text before it writes the value to the memory location.

```
for (i=0; i < gFieldCount; i++)
{
    Status = HTIndexBindItem(Index,
                             (LPSTR) &(glpaszFieldNames[i]),
                             0,
                             255,
                             HTTYPE_TEXT,
                             (LPSTR) &(glpaszFieldText[i]),
                             &DataLength,
                             NULL,
                             NULL);

    StatusIsOK(Status);

}
```

Using the same combination of the **HTIndexGetCount()**, **HTIndexSetPosition()**, and **HTIndexLoadDocument()** that we've used before, we can now access each of the Documents within the Index and have the field data automatically set up for writing into the HTML output file. The WriteFieldsToInternetOutputFile() routine is then called to write the field text to the output file in the proper format.

The proper format, in this case, is either a new HTML table row if no template is used or a copy of the repeated section of the template file with the field text replaced, if a template file is used. The formats used for each of these are displayed in Figures 10.4 and 10.5, respectively. When all of the Documents have been exhausted, the Index is closed using **HTIndexClose()** and the HTML output file is then closed using a call to CloseInternetOutputFile(). This routine does little more then terminate the table if no template is used or copies the rest of the template file, after the repeated section, to the output file. The last operation performed is the actual closing of the output file.

Back in the WM_PERFORM_TRANSFER processing, if we are going to write a set of fields from the client form to a Notes Document, the first thing we need to do is create an empty Document in the database based on the named Notes Form. This is all done with one quick call to **HTDocumentCreate()**. This API takes an open database as the first parameter and an optional Form ID as the second. If a Form ID is supplied, strict binding is enforced within the Document once it is created. If not supplied, strict binding is not enforced and the Form is not stored within the Document. If at some point after the Document is created, the Form is to be stored into the Document and strict binding is to be enforced, it can be accomplished through the appropriate calls to **HTDocumentSetProperty()**.

Once the Document is opened, we loop through each of the fields that need to be transferred. First, the field text is obtained from the CGI data file and then it is written into the Document using the **HTItemPut()** API. The prototype of **HTItemPut()** is shown below.

```
HTSTATUS HTItemPut(HTDOCUMENT document,
                   char *itemname,
                   HTTYPE item_type,
                   HTINT buffer_length,
                   HTTYPE buffer_type,
                   void *buffer,
                   HTFLAGS item_flags);
```

The first parameter on the call to **HTItemPut()** is to be expected, a reference to an open Document. The second is the name of the item to be stored. The third is the referenced item's datatype and is required if strict binding is not enabled within the Document. If strict binding is in place, the datatype value can either be provided or left as 0, as was done in the case of NETXFER. The code that handles the transfer of the client's HTML form field information into a Notes Document is shown below.

```
Status = HTDocumentCreate(gNotesDB,
                          FormID,
                          &Document);
if (StatusIsOK(Status))
{
    for (i=0; i < gFieldCount; i++)
    {
        // get field text from the Internet data file [Form Literal]
           section
        GetPrivateProfileString("Form Literal",
```

```
                                (LPSTR) &(glpaszFieldNames[i]),
                                "Not Found",
                                gszTempString,
                                sizeof(gszTempString),
                                gszInternetDataFile);

        // store info into Notes
        Status = HTItemPut(Document,
                          (LPSTR) &(glpaszFieldNames[i]),
                          0,
                          0,
                          HTTYPE_TEXT,
                          gszTempString,
                          0);

        StatusIsOK(Status);
        DEBUG((LPSTR) &(glpaszFieldNames[i]), gszTempString);
    }

    if (Status == HTSUCCESS)
    {
        HTDocumentClose(Document, 0);
        File_WriteString(ghOutputFile, "<H1>Transfer Successful</H1>");
        DEBUG("Transfer to Notes successful", NULL);
    }
    else
    {
        HTDocumentClose(Document, HTDOCWRITEF_DISCARD_CHANGES);
        File_WriteString(ghOutputFile, "<H1>Transfer Failed</H1>");
        DEBUG("Error transferring data to Notes", NULL);
    }
}
else
{
    DEBUG("Error creating new Notes document", NULL);
}
```

And we've finished. This is a neat little application that probably took more time to design than it did to write, largely due to the capabilities of the HiTest C API. For the most part, you'll probably find a similar situation to be true for every application you write using the HiTest C API. Its just that simple.

NETXFER: Where do We Go from Here?

There are a number of ways to extend the capabilities of the NETXFER application. The first might be to allow a formula to be passed as a field within the HTML form. This formula could then be used to create an Index on the database, as opposed to collecting all of the Documents created with a common Form. This would allow more flexibility in determining the set of Documents to be selected while still providing the Form-based selection functionality.

One possible method of accomplishing this would be to add a field named NETXFERFormula to the HTML document containing the formula to be used. This field would then be accessed by NETXFER in a manner similar to the NETXFERProcess field. From here, the only other major change would be to use the passed formula string as the second parameter in the call to **HTIndexSearch()** and to remove the Form ID, the third parameter. Since this would be a flat Index containing only Notes Documents, the rest of the processing within the NETXFER application would not need to be changed.

Another possible way to extend NETXFER might be to allow for the creation of an HTML document based on a given View within a database. This would involve more work than the formula case, in that the resulting Index would be hierarchical as opposed to flat. This means that it would not only contain Notes Documents but also perhaps category and total line entries. In fact, since we've spent more time within the book discussing how to manipulate flat Indexes rather than hierarchical ones, we're going to show you how this additional feature might be implemented in the NETXFER2 (\HITESTC\WIN32\-NETXFER2) application.

NETXFER2: Publishing Views on the Internet

There are two things that need to be decided before we can proceed with the modifications to the original NETXFER application:

- how is the View to be specified?
- what will the output HTML look like?

As for the first question, we've decided to create another keyword in the NETXFER.INI file named NotesView. If the data from a View is to be used to transfer data to the Internet from Notes, the NotesView keyword will contain the name of the View to be used. The use of the NotesView and NotesForm keywords will be mutually exclusive within NETXFER2 and, if both are specified, View will take precedence.

There are obviously different possibilities when it comes to formatting the View information within the HTML output document. We chose a format that minimized the amount of work we had to do with HTML while still providing the information we need. It involves accessing the textual representation of each column within each row in a View and publishing it into a single line of HTML with a fixed pitch font. In addition, if the row within the Index represents a Document, an asterisk(*) will be prepended to the output line. The HTML tags used to accomplish the fixed-pitch font processing are the preformatted text tags, `<PRE>` and `</PRE>`. Figures 10.6 and 10.7 show a simple Notes View and the corresponding HTML output produced by the NETXFER2 application, respectively.

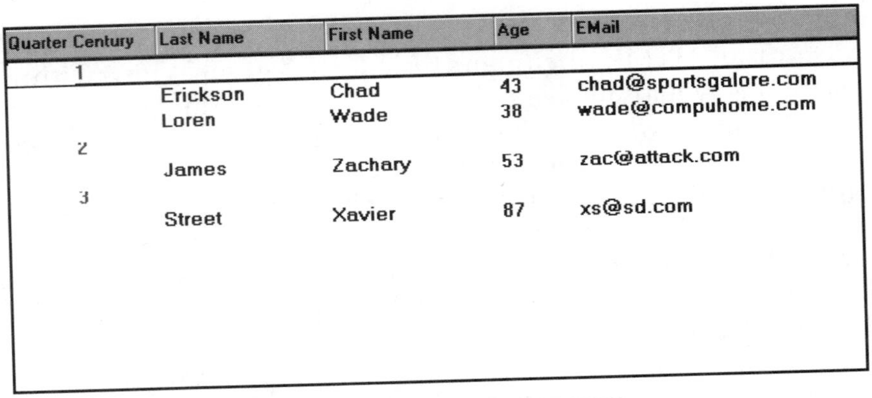

Quarter Century	Last Name	First Name	Age	EMail
1				
	Erickson	Chad	43	chad@sportsgalore.com
	Loren	Wade	38	wade@compuhome.com
2				
	James	Zachary	53	zac@attack.com
3				
	Street	Xavier	87	xs@sd.com

Figure 10.6 Simple Notes View.

```
1
*
            Erickson  Chad       43   chad@sportsgalore.com
*
            Loren     Wade       38   wade@compuhome.com
2
*
            James     Zachary    53   zac@attack.com
3
*
            Street    Xavier     87   xs@sd.com
```

Figure 10.7 Simple Notes View published by NETXFER2.

NETXFER2: Making It Work

The first thing we did to the NETXFER2 application was to add the code to access the View name using the previously mentioned NotesView INI file keyword. All we had to do was add a global variable—gszNotesViewName—to hold the View name and duplicate a section of the Windows GetPrivateProfileString() API code used to access the other variables.

Next was to change the logic in the WM_PERFORM_TRANSFER message processing to allow for either a Form or a View to be used to access the Notes data. The first change on this road was to move the call to **HTFormLocateByName()**. As you'll remember, we made this call early in the code since we needed the Form ID no matter what path we took. With the addition of the View access code, we'll get the appropriate ID, Form or View, at the time it is needed.

As soon as we know that we are planning to send data to the Internet, we'll check to determine whether we want to use a View or a Form to access the information. This is done by checking if the global View name variable has a value. If so, the first thing we need to do is get the ID of the named View using **HTViewLocateByName()**. This API performs the same function as does the **HTFormLocateByName()** but on a different object, a View. The input parameters are similar as well, a reference to an open database and the name of the View. If the View is found in the database, the View ID is returned. If it can't be found or some other error has occurred, HTNULLID is returned. And if you really wanted to, you could use the **HTViewList()** API to provide an alternative way of performing the View search in the same manner as we did with the Forms above. The **HTViewLocateByName()** call used in NETXFER2 is shown below.

```
ViewID = HTViewLocateByName(gNotesDB, gszNotesViewName);

if (ViewID != HTNULLID)

{

...

}

else

{

    DEBUG("Error accessing view in Notes database",
gszNotesViewName);

}
```

At this point, even though we want an Index built on a View rather than a set of Documents, the processing of creating a new Index on the database is still the same, a call to **HTIndexCreate()**. This, however, is where the similarity ends. Since we now want a hierarchical Index based on the output of a View, the **HTIndexOpenView()** API is used.

NOTE

We discussed both of these APIs in Chapter 8; we'll assume you will return there if you need more information on their use.

We now want to step through each line on the View and send that information to a line in the HTML output file. To do this we'll use the same API we used in Chapter 9 to calculate the latency values on the flat Form-based Index, **HTIndexNavigate()**. As you can see from the two code samples below, we've used the same parameter settings in both cases, even though we're using two different languages and Indexes that are dramatically different in content. (Don't you just love well-designed objects!)

```
Chapter 9, WATCHNFO...
Status = HTIndexNavigate(gIndex,
                         HTNAV_NEXT,
                         0,
                         DocID,
                         Indent)

Chapter 10, NETXFER2...
Status = HTIndexNavigate(Index,
                         HTNAV_NEXT,
                         0,
                         &Document,
                         &ViewIndent);
```

From here, as each new line in the Index is obtained, the workhorse of this added functionality—WriteFieldsToInternetOutputFile()—is called until the lines in the Index are exhausted. The changes made to this routine, as well as the other two involved in producing the HTML output file, OpenInternetOutputFile() and CloseInternetOutputFile(), will be the next topic.

The changes required for the open and close routines were really quite minimal. All that needed to be done was to determine whether or not a View was used to send Notes information to the Internet and subsequently add the <PRE> tag before any of the View information was written to the file on open and the </PRE> tag to bracket the preformatted View text on close.

The big news here was the changes required to WriteFieldsToInternet-OutputFile(). The first thing we did was expand the number of parameters used on the call to include the information we needed to access the appropriate information on the View. Parameters two, three, and four are new to this routine and include the Index, the View ID, and the Document ID.

```
void WriteFieldsToInternetOutputFile(int nFields,
                                     HTINDEX Index,
                                     HTVIEWID ViewID,
                                     HTDOCUMENT Document);
```

In general, there were four things we needed to do to create the desired output for each line in the View.

- Prepend an asterisk on the output line if the line is a Notes Document.
- Determine the number of columns in the View.
- Get a textual representation of the data for each column in the View.
- Write the entire set of column information to a single line in the output file.

The determination of whether the current line is a Document as opposed to a category or total row is done using the method described in Chapter 9, by ANDing the Document ID with the `HTINDEXDOCID_SPECIAL_MASK` mask. This mask is defined in HTNOTES.H as 0x80000000, which basically means that valid Document IDs cannot have the high-order bit set. The code that performs this check and prepends the asterisk for Document rows in NETXFER2 is shown below.

```
// if this is an actual document, prefix view line with an
asterisk(*)
if (!(Document & HTINDEXDOCID_SPECIAL_MASK))
{
    lstrcpy(gszTempString, "*");
}
```

As for the second step above, we might not have needed to calculate the number of columns in the View each time this routine is called. We could have done this outside the routine and passed the value in on each call. But the logic was placed here so we could group together the calls made to an as yet undiscovered HiTest object, the *column object*.

The column object is fairly small when it comes to the number of APIs used to support it, three in all, but there is a lot of information that can be gleaned from them. A *column* is distinguished from a viewcell object in that the data for a column object is static within the context of a View. In the Notes vernacular, it is *metadata*. The data for a *viewcell*, on the other hand, changes as each row in the View changes. We require the use of both of these objects to get the information we need.

The first of the column APIs used in NETXFER2 is **HTColumnGet-Count()**. Given a Notes database and View ID on input, this API does nothing more than return the number of columns contained in the View.

```
// get the number of columns in the view
ColumnCount = HTColumnGetCount(gNotesDB, ViewID);
```

Once we know the number of columns in the View, we'll loop through each one and build our output string along the way. The first thing we'll do for each is make a call to **HTColumnFetch()**.

```
Status = HTColumnFetch(gNotesDB, ViewID, i+1, &ColumnInfo);
```

This API has four parameters: a Notes database handle, a View ID, the column index (1-based), and the address of an HTCOLUMN structure. This structure contains quite a few pieces of information, two of which we'll use in NETXFER2; `width_in_eighths`, and `column_flags`.

```
typedef struct
{
    HTINT width_in_eighths;             // column within (in 1/8
                                        characters)

    HTFLAGS column_flags;               // column flags
    HTCOLUMNSORT sort;                  // sorting type
    HTCOLUMNJUSTIFY justify;            // justification info
    HTCOLUMNTOTAL total;                // totalling type
    HTFONTSTYLE font;                   // font info
    HTFORMAT format;                    // format info
    HTTYPE type;                        // datatype
    char *formula;                      // column formula
    char title[HTMAXLEN_COLUMN_TITLE];  // column title
} HTCOLUMN;                             // HiTest column structure
```

The first value in the structure, `width_in_eighths`, is the width of the column in characters times 8. This granularity is needed since this is the step value used when column widths are adjusted by dragging the right-hand header bar from the Notes user-interface.

The column flags are defined as a set of individual bit flags that can be ORed together as the situation warrants.

HTCOLUMNF_HIDDEN	Column is hidden
HTCOLUMNF_RESPONSES_ONLY	Column is a response-only column
HTCOLUMNF_HIDE_DETAIL	Detail is hidden on subtotal columns
HTCOLUMNF_DISPLAY_ICON	Column is displayed as an icon

NETXFER2 uses the column flags to determine if the column is hidden or if it is displayed as an icon. In either case, no information for that column will be transferred to the text-based HTML output file.

```
// don't display anything if the column is hidden or an icon
if (!(ColumnInfo.column_flags & HTCOLUMNF_HIDDEN) &&
    !(ColumnInfo.column_flags & HTCOLUMNF_DISPLAY_ICON))
{
...
}
```

The next check that needs to be made is to determine whether or not there is any information in the column within the current row. For this information, we'll enlist the use of the viewcell object. The API we need to use here is **HTViewcellGetLength()**. Given the reference to an open Index, the column index, and a HiTest datatype on input, the length of the viewcell, when converted to the stated datatype, is returned as a 16-bit value within the fourth parameter.

If the indexed column within the current row is found to have a nonzero textual representation, the second of the two viewcell APIs, **HTViewcellFetch()** is used to get the information. The first two inputs to **HTViewcellFetch()** are that same as those for **HTViewcellGetLength**, an open Index, and a column index. The third parameter is the address of a variable that contains the datatype of the data to be placed into the buffer, provided in parameter five. If set to 0 or NULL, as is the case in NETXFER2, the data will be returned as HTTYPE_TEXT.

The fourth parameter, the address of a buffer length, can be set to NULL if the supplied buffer is known to be large enough to hold the output information. If the value contained in the buffer length variable is 0, the HiTest engine will return the actual length of the data in this location upon return. If set to any other value, the output to the buffer will be truncated if the datatype is HTTYPE_TEXT and the TEXT_TRUNCATE session option is set. The **HTViewcellFetch()** call used in NETXFER2 follows:

```
Status = HTViewcellFetch(Index, i+1, NULL, NULL, szViewcellText);
```

NOTE You may be wondering why we used a call to **HTViewcellGetLength()** rather than just calling **HTViewcellFetch()** for all columns. The answer is that, at least in the 2.2 version of the HiTest C API, calling **HTViewcellFetch()** on a column that has no textual representation can cause some serious problems.

The last piece to the puzzle is to offset the information in each column based on the width of all of the previous columns. This value is tracked in the nColumnWidth variable as each column is processed using the following calculation:

```
nColumnWidth += (ColumnInfo.width_in_eighths / 8);
```

And there it is! A modification to the original NETXFER application that exports a View to an HTML file. The last thing we would probably want to do if NETXFER2 were destined to be an industrial-strength application would be to export each Document within the Index and then add a link to each in the exported View.

Glossary

NOTE

The symbol ★NEW★ indicates a new feature in Notes Release 4.

NOTE

Italicized words in the following entries are defined in this glossary.

About Document

The About Document is usually displayed when you open a *database* for the first time. It contains information supplied by the *database's designer* to help you understand more about the database, such as its purpose and tips on its use. While the About Document generally appears the first time you open a database, the designer may have elected to have the About Document appear every time you open the database or whenever the contents of the About Document have changed.

Access Control List (ACL)

An Access Control List is stored internally in every Notes *database* and allows selective access to a database and its contents. It combines Access *Levels* along with *Access Types* to create a wide combination of possible security levels. Some examples of how the Access Levels and Access Types can be combined to create security include:

- A person who can create new *Documents* in a database but cannot edit them once they have been created
- A person who can create and edit any Document in a database
- A *Notes Server* that can add new Documents and edit existing Documents but cannot delete any

Access Levels

Levels of security in an *Access Control* List. They are combined with Access Types and other options in the Access Control List dialog box to create a security model for a database. The seven Access Levels are:

1. No Access—A person or *Notes Server* in the *ACL* whose access is set to No Access will not be able to open the database containing that ACL.

2. Depositor—A person or *Notes Server* in the *ACL* whose access is set to Depositor will be able to open the *database* containing that ACL, and create new *Documents* in the database. Once the new Document is created and saved, however, the Document's creator will not be able to see the Document, or any other Document in the database.

3. Reader—A person or *Notes Server* in the *ACL* whose access is set to Reader will be able to open the *database* containing that ACL, and read any *Documents* in the database that are not restricted from the user by security features other than the ACL. A person or *Notes Server* with Reader Access in an ACL cannot create new Documents in the database containing that ACL.

4. Author—A person or *Notes Server* in the *ACL* whose access is set to Author will generally be able to create new *Documents* in the

database containing the ACL, as well as edit the Documents he creates after each Document is saved. It is possible, however, that security features other than the ACL may restrict a person or Notes Server with *Author Access* from editing Documents once they have been saved. An Author may also have the privilege of creating Private *Agents* and Private *Folders* in a database.

5. Editor—A person or *Notes Server* in the *ACL* whose access is set to Editor has the same privileges as a person or Notes Server with *Author Access*. In addition, an Editor has the ability to edit his own Documents as well as *Documents* created by other users. An Editor may have the privilege of creating Private *Agents* and Private *Folders* in a database, as well.

6. Designer—A person or *Notes Server* in the *ACL* whose access is set to Editor has the same privileges as a person or Notes Server with Editor Access. In addition, a Designer has the privilege to create new database *Forms, Views, Navigators,* and *Shared* or Private *Folders,* as well as Shared or Private *Agents.*

7. Manager—A person or *Notes Server* in the *ACL* with Manager Access in a database has the same privileges as a user or Notes Server with Designer Access. In addition, a Manager may make changes to the Access Control List of a database or delete the database in its entirety from a Notes Server.

Access Types ★NEW★

Access Types allow *Database Managers* to group members of an *Access Control List* (*ACL*) together for security purposes. Access Types are combined with Access Levels to create granular security.

Examples:

1. A group of persons and a group of servers in the *ACL* may both have Editor Access. However, to prevent deletions from replicating to other instances of a database, the group of servers could be restricted from deleting Documents.

2. Before executing, an *Agent* may check to see if the user executing it is a person or a *Notes Server*. If the Agent's executor is a person, the Agent may display a message saying "This Agent is designed to

be run from a Notes Server. Please contact your Database Manager for assistance."

The six Access Types are:

1. Person
2. Group of Persons
3. Server
4. Group of Servers
5. Group (Persons and Servers)
6. Unspecified

Actions (1)   ★NEW★

Actions represent a condensed programming language new to Release 4.0. Using Actions, common tasks that a user performs can be represented programmatically. What makes Actions distinctive from other methods of programming in Notes Release 4.0 is the Action Builder dialog box, an interactive window designed to allow users extensive control combined with ease of use. One or more Actions can be combined into an *Agent*.

Actions (2)   ★NEW★

A special type of Notes *Agent*. In this context, an Action is an Agent that is specifically designed to be included in an *Action Bar*.

Action Bar   ★NEW★

The Action Bar is a bar across the top of a Notes *View* or *Document* that allows you to execute *Agents* by clicking a button.

Agent

Agents are a combination of *@Functions*, *@Commands*, *LotusScript* Commands, and *Actions*. Agents are designed to automate a process or task in Notes. Prior to Notes Release 4, Agents were referred to as

Macros. Agents are created using the **Create**, **Agent** command on the *Notes Client* menu. Agents can be executed using the **Actions** command on the Notes Client menu, an *Action Bar*, or automatically by a Notes Client or *Notes Server*.

API

The Application Programming Interface is a set of routines provided by an application that allow other applications to access its information under program control rather than through a user-interface.

ASCIIZ String

Also called a NULL-terminated string. A set of characters whose length in determined by the first occurrence of a NULL (decimal 0) in the string.

Attachment

Attachments are files that can be included in a *rich text field* on a *Document*. Attachments can be any file type. For example, you could insert a Microsoft Word Document, an image, or even another Notes *database* as an attachment in a rich text field. Attachments appear as an icon with a text label underneath them that is the file's name.

They are created by choosing **File**, **Attach**… from the *Notes Client* menu while the cursor is in a rich text field on a Document. Once inserted, attachments are activated by double-clicking them and choosing **Launch**, **Detach**, or **View** from the Attachments dialog box.

NOTE When Attachments are added to a Document programmatically (by a program instead of a manual user), they may appear at the bottom of the Document or in an area other than a rich text field.

Button

Buttons are images that can be inserted into a rich text field in a *Document*. When a user clicks it, a small program built specifically for the button, or one or more *Agents* will run. *Document Links*, *View Links*, and

Database Links are special Notes buttons created using the **Edit, Copy As Link** command from the *Notes Client* menu. Instead of running a program, these buttons open a linked *database, View,* or Document on the Notes Client where the link was activated from.

Buttons may also be added programmatically by a *Database Designer* to a *Form* (meaning the button is present whenever a user creates a new Document, or reads an existing Document using a specific Form).

Category

A Category is an element of a Notes *View* or *Folder*. Its purpose is to allow Views and Folders to group *Documents* based on *Fields* that share a common value. For example, in the By Author View of the Teach Yourself... Discussion database, every Document created by a different author is grouped into a different Category.

Collection

A Collection is a the set of *documents* defined or created by a Notes *View* or through the execution of a Notes *Agent*.

Database

A Notes database is a collection of *Documents, Responses,* design elements (*Views, Folders, Forms, Navigators, Agents,* and *Fields*), security features (*ACL*), and administrative information (*Replica ID, Replication* History, and *Selective Replication* information). It is generally stored with an NSF extension, and opened using a *Notes Client* or *Notes Server*.

Database Designer

One or more persons with an *Access Level* of Designer or greater to a Notes *Database*. Database Designers are responsible for the creation of the design elements of a Notes Database (*Forms, Views, Navigators, Action Bars, Agents,* etc.).

Database Link ★NEW★

Database Links are special *buttons* that can be included in a *rich text field* by a user. They are created by selecting a *database* and choosing **Edit**, **Copy As Link**, **Database Link** from the *Notes Client* menu. This moves the Database Link to the clipboard, from which it can be pasted into one or more rich text fields by the user. When a user double-clicks a *Database Link*, the database specified in the link is opened at the Notes Client.

NOTE

Database Links do not override the Access Control List settings (if you create a Database Link and send it to a person via Notes Mail to a user who does not have access to the database, he will not be able to use the link).

Database Manager

One or more persons with an *Access Level* of *Manager* or greater to a Notes *Database*. Database Managers are responsible for the administration of a Notes Database on a *Notes Server* (ensuring that *Replication* is performed successfully, for example). Database Managers also maintain the *Access Control List* of a Notes Database. A database's manager may also be the *Database Designer*.

Database Window ★NEW★

The Database Window combines several subwindows referred to by Lotus as *panes*. It is the primary means of locating and displaying *Documents* in a Notes *Database*, and is opened whenever a user double-clicks an icon on the *Workspace*.

The Panes of the Database Window are called

1. The *Navigator Pane*
2. The *View Pane*
3. The *Preview Pane*

At any time, two of the three panes of the Database Window are optional (they can be turned off by the user, or forced off of the screen by the

Database Designer). The location of the three panes within the Database Window can be controlled by the user via the **View, Arrange Preview** command on the *Notes Client* menu.

DLL

The Dynamic Link Library is a binary executable code module similar to a normal .EXE file that allows applications to link to processes at runtime rather than at compile time. Among the many advantages of using DLLs over static linking are a reduction in code size and the ability to more easily share common code.

Document

A collection of *Fields* and *Labels* arranged for display using a *Form*. Similar in function to a record in a SQL table or DBMS.

A special type of Document called a Response can be included by a *Database Designer* in a database. Response Documents are similar in function to Post-it notes—they contain additional information that is loosely related to a main Document.

Document Link

Document Links are special *buttons* that can be included in a *rich text field* by a user. They are created by selecting a *Document* and choosing **Edit, Copy As Link, Document Link** from the *Notes Client* menu. This moves the Document Link to the clipboard, from which it can be pasted into one or more rich text fields by the user. When a user double-clicks a Document Link, the Document specified by the link is opened at the Notes Client.

NOTE Document Links do not override the Access Control List or other security settings (if you create a Document Link and send it to a person via Notes Mail to a user who does not have access to the database that contains the Document, he will not be able to use the link).

Embedded Objects

Data from other applications can be stored in a Notes *Document* as an embedded object. When activated, embedded objects call the original application that created the embedded data and allow you to update the information. When saved, the updated information is stored in the Notes Document.

This differs from a file *attachment* in that, when activated, file attachments are copies of the data originally stored in the Notes Document. The information in the Document will not be updated unless extra steps are taken by the user.

Fields

Fields are elements of a Notes *Document* designed to hold specific information. Fields are arranged for the user via *Forms*. A user knows what type of information to enter into a Field based on its field type and information contained in the Field's Label. The different types of Fields that Notes supports are:

1. Text—Text fields contain letters, punctuation, space, and numbers that are not used mathematically.

2. Rich Text—Rich text fields allow users to insert pictures, *buttons*, *attachments*, or *embedded objects* as well as use text styles (bold, italics, underlining, different fonts, or color).

3. Keywords—Keyword fields offer predefined text choices that make data entry more convenient and lend consistency to documents. You can generate keywords in several different ways and choose from a variety of display styles.

4. Number—Number fields are used for information that can be used mathematically and can include the characters 0 1 2 3 4 5 6 7 8 9 - + . E e.

5. Time—Time fields contain time and date information and are made up of letters and numbers separated by punctuation.

6. Authors—Authors fields generate a text list of names (user names, group names, and access roles) and are useful for giving people with an *Access Level* of *Author* in the *Access Control List* the right to

edit documents they didn't create without expanding their database Access Level to Editor.

7. Readers—Readers fields allow you to restrict who can read documents created with a form, even if users have Reader (or higher) access in the access control list.

8. Names—Names fields display user or server names as they appear on Notes' IDs and are useful for displaying names when you don't need to assign any type of access rights to documents.

Folders ★NEW★

Folders let you store and manage related documents without putting them into a *Category*, which requires a Categories *Field* in the *Form* used to create the *Document*. Folders are also convenient because you can drag Documents to them.

You can create Private Folders or Shared Folders. No one else can read or delete your Private Folders, while Shared Folders can be accessed by everyone with the ability to read Documents in the database.

To create Private Folders in a database, you must have an *Access Level* of Reader in the Access Control List of the database. To create Shared Folders in a database, you must have an Access Level of Designer.

Form

Forms allow users to create *Documents* that store the *database's* data. A form contains one or more *Fields*. It may also contain *Labels* and graphics to make the form attractive and easy-to-use and buttons that automate tasks or give users extra information. Most databases have several forms, each serving a particular purpose.

Function Language

See *@Functions*.

HiTest

A set of *API* tools originally developed by Edge Research which allows a higher level of access to Notes information than do the native Notes APIs.

Hungarian Notation

A programming technique whereby each variable name is prefixed with a designator that specifies its base type.

InterNotes Web Browser ★NEW★

A component built into every *Notes Client*, the InterNotes Web Browser recognizes *Uniform Resource Locators* in *rich text fields* and uses them to request information from the Internet via a *Notes Server* running the *InterNotes Web Retriever*.

InterNotes Web Retriever ★NEW★

A program that can be run on any Release 4 *Notes Server*, the InterNotes Web Retriever requests information from the Internet and stores it in a Notes *Database*. Retrieval can happen on demand (when requested by a *Notes Client* running the *InterNotes Web Browser*), or automatically by the Notes Server.

Location Document

A Document in your *Notes Client's Personal Name and Address Book*, which contains communication settings you use when you work with Notes in a particular place. For example, you might use a network port at the office to connect to Notes servers on a local area network and use a remote port at home to connect to Notes servers over a modem.

Each of these configurations could be represented by a Location Document that you could make active on the Notes Client when you were at those places.

LotusScript ★NEW★

LotusScript is Lotus' object-oriented basic language. It is designed to allow *Database Designers* access to the greatest possible set of Notes' features programmatically.

Mail Enabling

A feature of a *Notes Server* that allows any *database* to transfer Documents to any other database, similar to the way a person would send information to another person via *Notes Mail*.

Mobile Notes

Mobile Notes is a collection of features in a *Notes Client* designed to allow you to access a *Notes Server* or a network or Notes Servers via a telephone line.

Name and Address Book

This is a file called NAMES.NSF that is stored on every *Notes Client* and Notes Server. The purpose of the Name and Address Book is to allow users and Notes Servers access to the information they need to deliver Notes Mail and to make connections to each other for *Replication* or database access.

At the Notes Client, the Name and Address Book may be referred to as the Personal Name and Address Book. On the Notes Server, the Name and Address Book may be referred to as the Server Name and Address Book.

Navigator ★NEW★

Navigators provide a graphical way for users to find documents or take actions without having to maneuver through views or find menu commands. Notes provides standard navigators called *Folders* that appear in the *Navigator Pane* when you open a *database*. A *Database Designer* can create additional Navigators for an application to perform specific functions, including those with formulas or *LotusScript* programs.

Navigator Pane ★NEW★

An optional component of the *Database Window* designed to display *Navigators*.

Notes Client

A copy of Notes, Notes Desktop, Notes Express, or *Notes Mail* running on a computer.

Notes Mail

Notes Mail allows a *Notes Client* to communicate electronically with other Notes users. Notes Mail requires a Notes Client to have a connection to least one *Notes Server*. If you are not connected to a Notes Server via a network, you can still use Notes Mail by connecting to a Notes Server via modem and telephone line.

A Notes mail message is the same as any Notes *Document*. For example, you can change fonts and colors, add file *attachments* and *OLE* objects, and include *tables*, graphics, *buttons*, and Document, *Database*, or *View* Links. Each Notes user has a database in which to store mail messages.

Notes Server

A copy of the Notes Server software running on a computer. Notes Server software is designed to allow *Notes Clients* to share *databases*, support *Notes Mail*, and facilitate *Workflow*. A Notes Server may also use the *InterNotes Web Retriever* to allow Notes Clients running the *InterNotes Web Browser* access to the Internet via Notes.

Object Linking and Embedding (OLE)

A standard designed to allow applications to store and update data in its native format promoted by Microsoft.

Panes

See *Database Window, Programmer's Pane, Preview Pane, View Pane,* and *Navigator Pane.*

Personal Name and Address Book ★NEW★

See *Name and Address Book.*

Preview Pane ★NEW★

An optional pane of the *Notes Client* that allows you to preview the currently selected *Document* in a *View*. Once a Document is opened, the Preview Pane can allow you to preview a Document's Parent Document or Response, or the contents of Documents linked using *Document Links.*

Private Folders ★NEW★

See *Folders.*

Programmer's Pane ★NEW★

A Pane that is opened in the *Database Window* whenever a user is editing a button or other Notes design element (*View, Form, Field,* etc.). Commonly used by *Database Designers.*

Replica ID

A unique identifier that is a part of every Notes *database*. Databases that share the same Replica ID are called replicas. Only databases that are replicas can exchange information through *Replication.*

To view the Replica ID of a database, select the database on the *Workspace* and choose **File, Database, Properties...** from the *Notes Client* menu. In the Properties for Database dialog box, click on the Information page to see an entry containing the database's Replica ID.

Replication

Notes lets you keep multiple copies of a single database, called replicas, on multiple *Notes Servers* and *Notes Clients*. Replication is the process of exchanging modifications between replicas. Through replication, Notes makes all of the replicas essentially identical over time.

A replica has the same *Replica ID* as the original database.

Replicator

A page on the Notes *Workspace* that allows users to centralize replication tasks.

Rich Text Fields

See *Fields*.

Shared Folders

See *Folders*.

Selective Replication

Notes lets you replicate a subset of documents to a replica so you can limit the size of replicas. Selective Replication can save disk space, reduce the amount of time a *Mobile Notes Client* spends connected to a *Notes Server* and allow you to only work with information in a *database* that is relevant.

Server Connection Document

A *Document* in the *Name and Address Book* that tells a *Notes Client* or a *Notes Server* what telephone number to dial to connect to remote servers or what network protocol to use to reach a Notes Server on a Local Area Network (LAN) or Wide Area Network (WAN).

SmartIcons

SmartIcons are *buttons* that perform an action (for example, italicizing selected text) in Notes when you click them. For many tasks, it's faster to click SmartIcons than it is to pull down menus or recall and type keyboard shortcuts.

Status Bar

A group of clickable areas at the bottom of the *Notes Client* that allow you to quickly perform routine tasks in Notes. A portion of the status bar is dedicated to displaying messages from the Notes Client to the user.

Table

A Notes element that can be inserted into a *rich text field* that allows you to present information in rows and columns. If you are familiar with the concept of *tables* from other database languages (such as SQL), it is important to note that tables in Notes are more like the tables feature in a word processing package than in a database (that is, they contain static information, not dynamic subsets of data).

Using Document

An optional *Document* in a Notes *Database* that is used by the *Database Designer* to provide users with help for using the database's features. It can be opened by selecting a database on the *Workspace* and choosing **Help, Using This Database**... from the *Notes Client* menu.

Uniform Resource Locator (URL)

A string of characters designed to allow World Wide Web browsers to locate documents and files on the Internet.

User ID

A file that uniquely identifies a Notes user. Every Notes user—person or server—has a User ID. Your User ID determines access privileges between your *Notes Client* and *Notes Servers*.

View

Views are lists of *Documents* in a Notes *database*. Views can select, sort, or categorize documents in different ways. Views use the *Fields* stored in each Document to display information, such as who created the Document, when it was created, what the subject is, etc.

A View may show all Documents in a database or only a selection of Documents.

View Link ★NEW★

View Links are special *buttons* that can be included in a *rich text field* by a user. They are created by selecting a *View* and choosing **Edit, Copy As Link, View Link** from the *Notes Client* menu. This moves the View Link to the clipboard, from which it can be pasted into one or more rich text fields by the user. When a user double-clicks a View Link, a *Database Window* with the *View* specified by the link is opened at the Notes Client.

NOTE

View Links do not override the Access Control List or other security settings (if you create a View Link and send it to a person via Notes Mail to a user who does not have access to the database that contains the View, he will not be able to use the link).

View Pane ★NEW★

An area of the *Database Window* dedicated to displaying the contents of the currently selected *View* or *Folder* in a Notes *database*.

Workflow

Any combination of Notes' features that automates processes or tasks. Workflows can be simple, using a single *Action*, or complex, requiring hundreds of lines of code in Lotus *@Function* language or *LotusScript*.

Workspace

The primary interface between the *Notes Client* and the user. The Workspace consists of a number of tabbed pages. Each tabbed page can contain icons for Notes *databases* located on the Notes Client or on one or more *Notes Servers*.

A special Workspace Page called the *Replicator* allows users to centralize replication tasks.

@Commands

Pronounced "at - commands." A subset of *@Functions*.

@Functions

Pronounced "at - functions." A programming language (also called Function Language) that allows *Database Designers* and users to create *Agents* to perform specific tasks. @Functions are more advanced than *Actions*, but not as robust as *LotusScript*. Prior to Notes Release 4, @Functions were the only development language. By supporting @Functions in Release 4, even though the more powerful LotusScript language is available to developers, Lotus helps maintain backwards compatibility with *databases* created using a previous version of Notes.

Installing the Sample Applications

This section describes the details of how to install the sample databases and applications from the book. In some cases, installation is as easy as running the application from the CD or copying it to a specific drive and directory. In other cases, there may be one or more steps involving such things as copying a Windows **.INI** file to the default Windows directory or copying a database to the Notes data directory.

A DDE Popup Calendar Written in Visual Basic 4.0 for 32 bit Windows

This utility can be installed by going to the **\DDE\INSTALL** folder on the CD and running **SETUP.EXE.** This will install the needed **.DLL** and **.OCX** files on your 32-bit Windows PC. It is recommended that you set the install directory in the setup program to your Notes data directory—(C:\NOTES\DATA\), for example.

Source code for this program is located in the \DDE\SOURCE folder on the CD.

Sample Contact Tracking Application in Notes 4

This database is on the CD in the \NOTES4 folder, and is called **MTCONTCT.NSF**. To install this database, copy it from the CD to your Notes data directory—(C:\NOTES\DATA\), for example.

DBVIEWER

The DBVIEWER application(\NOTESC\WIN16\DBVIEWER) on this CD is compiled as a 16-bit application for use with Notes Version 4.0. In addition, since it is a stand-alone executable, there is no install process that needs to be performed. The only requirement is that the directory that holds the Notes executable and the associated support DLLs, is in the current path. Another option is simply to copy the **DBVIEWER.EXE** file to the Notes Version 4.0 directory.

If you wish to have a DBVIEWER application for use with Version 3.x of Notes, refer to the "Converting from Version 3.x to 4.0" section in Chapter 7.

MAILFILE

The MAILFILE application is available on this CD as both a 16-bit and a 32-bit executable. The installation process for this application involves copying three files to specific directories.

- Copy the appropriate **MAILFILE.EXE** to the Notes directory.
- Copy the **MAILFILE.INI** file to the default Windows directory.
- Copy the **MAILFILE.MSG** file to the C:\TEMP directory.

Upon starting the MAILFILE application, it will determine, from the "DIRECTORY=" keyword in the **MAILFILE.INI** file, that the C:\TEMP directory is to be searched. If required, you can change this directory path in the .INI file and place the **MAILFILE.MSG** file within it and the application will function in the same manner. The C:\TEMP directory was used because it is a common path within the Windows environment.

NOTE

Another thing you may wish to do before you start MAILFILE is to change the message recipient name, the text after the To: label, within the **MAILFILE.MSG** file to a mail name within your domain.

WATCHER

The WATCHER dynamic link library is available in both 16-bit (\NOTESC\WIN16\WATCHER) and 32-bit (\NOTESC\WIN32\WATCHER) flavors as well. WATCHER can only be used with Notes Version 4.0 since the Extension Manager functionality is not available in prior versions. It can be installed by performing the following steps.

- Copy the appropriate WATCHER.DLL to the Notes directory .
- Copy the WATCHER.INI file to the default Windows directory.
- Copy the WATCHER.NSF database to the Notes data directory.
- add the following line to the NOTES.INI file.

```
EXTMGR_ADDINS=WATCHER.DLL
```

After restarting Notes, every time a new message is passed into the **MAIL.BOX** database, a new record will be entered into the **WATCHER.NSF** database. In addition, as the message is removed from **MAIL.BOX**, the **WATCHER.NSF** database will be updated with the latency statistics.

CLIPSERV

The CLIPSERV application is available for both 16-bit Windows (\HITESTC\WIN16\CLIPSERV) and 32-bit Windows (\HITESTC\-WIN32\CLIPSERV). CLIPSERV is available for use with both Version 3.x and Version 4.0 of Notes. To install CLIPSERV for use, perform the following steps.

- Copy the appropriate **CLIPSERV.EXE** to the Notes directory.
- Copy the **CLIPSERV.INI** file to the default Windows directory.
- Copy the following to the default Windows directory.

```
W3HTAPI.DLL for Windows 3.x
NTHTAPI.DLL for Windows 95 or Windows NT
```

- Copy the **CLIPSERV.NSF** database to the Notes data directory.

For details on how to set up the CLIPSERV application, see the discussion in Chapter 8.

AGENTRUN

AGENTRUN is available for both 16-bit Windows (\HITESTC\-WIN16\AGENTRUN) and 32-bit Windows (\HITESTC\-WIN32\AGENTRUN). The only requirement is that the directory that holds the Notes executable and the associated support DLLs, is in the current path. Another option is simply to copy the **AGENTRUN.EXE** and the **NTHTAPI.DLL** files to the Notes directory.

If you so choose, you can also copy the **AGENTS.NSF** database to your Notes directory and use it as a sample database for experimentation. This is the same database that is used in the ScreenCam demonstrations of the AGENTRUN application.

ALLVIS

The ALLVIS application is only available in a 16-bit Windows version (\HITESTVB\WIN16\ALLVIS) and you must have Visual Basic Version 3.0 or greater installed on your system. If you already have the HiTest Tools for Visual Basic installed on your system and they are somewhere within your current path, you can run ALLVIS from anywhere.

If you do not have the HiTest Tools for Visual Basic installed, the easiest way to get ALLVIS up and running is by copying all the **.VBX** files and all the **.DLL** files from the ALLVIS directory to your Windows directory. Once this is done, ALLVIS can now be used.

WATCHNFO

Although the WATCHNFO application (\HITESTVB\WIN16\ALLVIS) installation procedure is the same as the ALLVIS application above, copying the **WATCHER.NSF** database to your Notes directory will allow you to use the sample information in the database to test the functions available in WATCHNFO. WATCHNFO is available in a 16-bit Windows version only.

NETXFER

NETXFER (\HITESTC\WIN32\NETXFER) is a 32-bit Windows application that can be used with either Notes Version 3.x or Notes Version 4.0. Since it is a Windows Common Gateway Interface (CGI) application, the installation procedure primarily involves setting up your Internet server properly to allow it to use Windows CGI applications. Once set up, you will need to do is create a **NETXFER.INI** file in your Windows directory that contains the information necessary to perform the required processes. A full discussion of what this entails can be found in Chapter 10.

If you so choose, you can test NETXFER using a set of sample data as provided within the NETXFER directory by performing the following steps.

- Copy the **NETXFER.EXE** to the Notes directory.
- Copy the **NETXFER.NSF** to the Notes data directory.
- Copy the **NETXFER.INI** file to the Windows directory.
- Copy the to **NTHTAPI.DLL** to the Windows directory.
- Copy the **DATA.INI** and **CONTENT.INI** files to the C:\TEMP directory.

From here, use the following command line to have NETXFER export all Documents created with the `Personal Info` form within the **NETXFER.NSF** database to a file named **OUTPUT.HTM** in the C:\TEMP directory.

```
NETXFER C:\TEMP\DATA.INI C:\TEMP\CONTENT.INI C:\TEMP\OUTPUT.HTM
```

NETXFER2

NETXFER2 (\HITESTC\WIN32\NETXFER2) is a 32-bit Windows application, as well. All of the same restrictions described for NETXFER hold true here, as well. If you wish to test NETXFER2 using sample data, use the following steps.

- Copy the **NETXFER2.EXE** to the Notes directory.
- Copy the **NETXFER.NSF** to the Notes data directory.
- Copy the **NETXFER2.INI** file to the Windows directory.
- Copy the to **NTHTAPI.DLL** to the Windows directory.
- Copy the **DATA.INI** and **CONTENT.INI** files to the C:\TEMP directory.

From here, use the following command line to have NETXFER2 export the data within the By Quarter Century View within the **NETXFER.NSF** database to a file named **OUTPUT.HTM** in the C:\TEMP directory.

```
NETXFER2 C:\TEMP\DATA.INI C:\TEMP\CONTENT.INI C:\TEMP\OUTPUT.HTM
```

Index

ccMail, 411
and fields, 230–35
LotusScript, list of, 159–61
Notes function language, list
of, 149–50
process, for CGI, 550
knowledge bases, 33
knowledge, 14–15, 19, 55

L

labels, *249*, 297–98, 315–16
layout regions, 299, 315–16,
320–322
field properties, 246, 319
forms, *218*–222
hiding, 221
tab order, 330
letters, 303, 305
licenses, 66
links, 250–252, 299, 581
ListAllocate(), 415
LN:DI, see Lotus Notes:Document
Imaging
LNHIDE, 174–175
local area network (LAN), 8
local security, 69
LOG.NSF, 76, 78, *79*, 81–82
Lotus 1-2-3, 9, 11–12, 117
Lotus Fax Server, 54
*Lotus Notes Application
Development*, 176
Lotus Notes,
business use of, 28, 36, 45–46
definition of, 13–14

Lotus Notes:Document Imaging,
54
LotusScript, 138, 141, 312
and agents, 26
arguments, 158
example of, 162–63
functions, 158
list of keywords, 159–61
list of operators for, 157–58
overview, 153
subroutines, 158–59
when to use, 161
LotusSphere, 11, 12
LSCONST.LSS, 157

M

Mac OS, 50, 302, 356
and Notes Client, 52, 72
Notes preferences file, 74
mail enabling, *25*, 36, 56, 82,
128–29
developer's perspective,
103–104
person-to-person, 82–94
database-to-database, 94–101
and Notes Mail, 82
person-to-database, 101–102
workflow, 128
MAIL.BOX, 77, 78, *79*, 82–83,
88–92, 94, 99–100, 103, 104, 410
mail/paste agent, 101
MailAddHeaderItemByHandle(),
417–19
MailAddMessageBodyText(),
420–22
MailAddRecipientsItem(), 417–19